School Construction Strategies for Universal Primary Education in Africa

School Construction Strategies for Universal Primary Education in Africa

SHOULD COMMUNITIES BE EMPOWERED TO BUILD THEIR SCHOOLS?

Serge Theunynck

THE WORLD BANK
Washington, DC

Education For All
Fast Track Initiative

© 2009 The International Bank for Reconstruction and Development / The World Bank
1818 H Street, NW
Washington, DC 20433
Telephone 202-473-1000
Internet www.worldbank.org
E-mail feedback@worldbank.org

All rights reserved.

1 2 3 4 12 11 10 09

This volume is a product of the staff of the International Bank for Reconstruction and Development / The World Bank. The findings, interpretations, and conclusions expressed in this volume do not necessarily reflect the views of the Executive Directors of The World Bank or the governments they represent.

The World Bank does not guarantee the accuracy of the data included in this work. The boundaries, colors, denominations, and other information shown on any map in this work do not imply any judgment on the part of The World Bank concerning the legal status of any territory or the endorsement or acceptance of such boundaries.

Rights and Permissions

The material in this publication is copyrighted. Copying and/or transmitting portions or all of this work without permission may be a violation of applicable law. The International Bank for Reconstruction and Development / The World Bank encourages dissemination of its work and will normally grant permission to reproduce portions of the work promptly.

For permission to photocopy or reprint any part of this work, please send a request with complete information to the Copyright Clearance Center Inc., 222 Rosewood Drive, Danvers, MA 01923, USA; telephone: 978-750-8400; fax: 978-750-4470; Internet: www.copyright.com.

All other queries on rights and licenses, including subsidiary rights, should be addressed to the Office of the Publisher, The World Bank, 1818 H Street NW, Washington, DC 20433, USA; fax: 202-522-2422; e-mail: pubrights@worldbank.org.

ISBN: 978-0-8213-7720-8
eISBN: 978-0-8213-7721-5
DOI: 10.1596/978-0-8213-7720-8

Cover photo: Arne Hoel / World Bank

Library of Congress Cataloging-in-Publication Data

School construction strategies for universal primary education in Africa : should communities be empowered to build their schools? / World Bank.
    p. cm.
  Includes bibliographical references.
  ISBN 978-0-8213-7720-8 (paper pack) — ISBN 978-0-8213-7721-5 (e-book)
  1. School buildings—Design and construction—Africa. 2. Education , Primary—Aims and objectives—Africa. 3. Education—Parent participation—Africa. 4. Community organization—Africa. 5. Rural development projects—Africa. I. World Bank.
  LB2319.A4S36 2009
  372.16096

2009018199

Contents

Preface xi
Acknowledgments xiii
Abbreviations xv

CHAPTER 1. THE CHALLENGES OF AFRICA'S PRIMARY SCHOOL INFRASTRUCTURE   1

   The Growth Trend in Primary School Classrooms   1
   The Quality of Primary School Infrastructure   2
   Conclusion   12

CHAPTER 2. SCHOOL LOCATION PLANNING AND CONSTRUCTION NORMS   15

   School Location Planning   15
   School Quality Norms   19
   Inefficiencies of Centralized Planning   24
   Conclusion   25

CHAPTER 3. CLASSROOM CONSTRUCTION TECHNOLOGY   29

   The Classic Classroom   29
   The School Shelter   32
   Local Materials and Appropriate Technology Classrooms   35
   Industrialized Prefabrication   40
   Classroom Prefabrication   42
   The Modern Construction Model   45
   Conclusion   48

CHAPTER 4. TECHNOLOGY FOR SANITATION AND WATER   51

   Sanitation in Schools   51
   Water Supply for Schools   53
   Conclusion   54

CHAPTER 5. PROCUREMENT AND CONTRACT MANAGEMENT 55

Procurement Managed by Central Administration   55
Delegation of Contract Management   66
Decentralization of Contract Management   88
Conclusions   106

CHAPTER 6. SETTING UP COMMUNITY MANAGEMENT 111

Accountability   112
Community Empowerment   116

CHAPTER 7. SCHOOL MAINTENANCE 125

CHAPTER 8. CORRUPTION IN SCHOOL CONSTRUCTION 129

CHAPTER 9. THE DONOR FACTOR 135

CHAPTER 10. FRAMEWORK FOR ACTION 139

What Countries Should Do   142
What Donors Should Do   147
Areas for Further Research   148

APPENDIXES

1. School Infrastructure Matters: The Research Evidence — 151
2. Architectural Design of Primary Schools: Examples of 2- and 3-Classroom Blocks — 156
3. Examples of Appropriate Technology Schools — 159
4. Examples of Latrine Technology — 161
5. A Brief History of Industrialization in the Construction Industry Worldwide — 162
6. Unit Costs of Some Contract Management Agencies in School Construction — 164
7. Implementation Schemes for School Construction Projects Sponsored by NGOs — 166
8. Decentralization of School Construction in Africa: Country Examples — 168
9. The CDD Implementation Process in Benin and Uganda — 172
10. School Construction by Local Government Implementation Arrangements — 173
11. Stakeholder Roles for Primary School Construction in a CDD Approach — 175
12. Toolkits to Harmonize Norms and Standards and Implementation Strategies — 177
13. Illustrations from the Senegal Social Fund Community Handbook — 179

14. Detailed Projections of the Classroom Needs	180
15. Summary of the Various Implementation Schemes	183
16. The Situation of School Construction Programs in Selected African Countries: Who Does What and How	184
17. List of Projects Reviewed	215

REFERENCES   225

INDEX   247

BOXES

- 2.1 School Buildings as a Learning Aid at No Cost   22
- 3.1 School Construction Programs: A Chance for the Informal Sector   31
- 3.2 The Shelter Model in Ghana   35
- 3.3 Three Experiences with Prefabricated Classroom Construction   46
- 5.1 Contracting to NGOs—The Case of Guinea   78
- 5.2 Community Delegation in Mauritania   93
- 6.1 Norms to Be Established by MoEs   114
- 6.2 Essentials for a Community Request   115
- 6.3 Essential Elements of a Financial Agreement   118
- 6.4 Community-based Procurement: Key Features   119
- 6.5 Handbook Essentials   120
- 7.1 Budgeting for School Maintenance in Pakistan   127
- 8.1 Factors That Facilitate and Limit Corruption in School Construction   131
- 8.2 Approach to Limit Corruption at the Community Level: The Senegal Social Fund   132
- 9.1 Characteristics of Sectorwide Approaches   137
- 10.1 Essential Elements of Stocktaking Exercise   143
- 10.2 Technical Audit and Beneficiary Assessment: Key Features   147

TABLES

- 1.1 Growth in Classroom Stock, Needs versus Actual   2
- 1.2 Number and Condition of Primary Classrooms   3
- 1.3 Availability of Latrines and Water   4
- 1.4 Cost of Furniture per Classroom   6
- 1.5 Indicators of Overcrowding   9
- 1.6 School Construction Needs, 2005–2015, for 33 African IDA Countries   12
- 2.1 School Size and Minimum Village Population Required   18
- 2.2 Average Net Classroom Area (m^2) Over Time   21
- 2.3 Office and Storage as Percentage of Classroom Area in 10 Selected Projects   23
- 2.4 Unit Cost of Teacher Housing in Selected Countries   24
- 3.1 Range in Unit Costs of the Classic Classroom Technology in Senegal   33
- 3.2 Unit Cost of Local Material Technology Compared to Informal Sector   38
- 3.3 Comparison of the Cost of Prefabricated Classrooms Compared with the Classic Model   43

4.1 Unit Cost of Latrines in Selected Countries   52
4.2 Cost of Water Supply per School in Selected Countries   54
5.1 Costs of ICB Combined with Community Participation Compared to Other Methods   60
5.2 Evolution of Gross Unit Costs of Classrooms Procured through ICB and NCB   64
5.3 AGETIP Performance at Inception Compared to Previous Administrations   71
5.4 AGETIP Performance Compared to MoE Administration through Other Arrangements   71
5.5 Unit Costs of Classrooms Built by NGOs (3 approaches) Compared with Other Methods   76
5.6 Cost of Classrooms Built by Social Funds Operating as Contract Management Agencies, Compared to Other Agencies   85
5.7 Cost of Classrooms Built by Social Funds with Community Implementation, Compared to Other Agencies   86
5.8 Cost of Classrooms Built by Deconcentrated Branches of Administration Compared with Other Agencies   91
5.9 Cost of Classrooms Built by Communities Compared with Other Management Arrangements   95
5.10 Status of Decentralization of School Construction in Selected Countries   96
5.11 Cost of Classroom Construction Built by Local Government through Different Modalities Compared with Other Agencies   98
5.12 Examples of Gross Unit Costs Obtained in Benin, Ghana, Senegal, and Uganda   100
5.13 Regression Estimates of the Impact of Project- and Country-Specific Variables on the Classroom Construction Cost per Gross m^2 from Various Classroom Construction Projects   102
5.14 Parallel Centralized and Decentralized Projects/Programs During 2000–04 in Selected African Countries   104
5.15 Local Government Expenditure as a Share of GDP and Government Expenditure, 1997–99   104
5.16 Status of Decentralization of School Construction in Selected Countries   105
7.1 The Cost of Maintenance   128
10.1 School Construction Needs, 2005–15, for 33 African IDA Countries   140
10.2 Financing Needs for EFA in 2015 in 33 African Countries   141
10.3 Estimated Annual Cost of Maintenance of the Programs to Be Built in the 33 African Countries During 2005–15   142
10.4 A Stock-taking Exercise on Who Does What and How in Primary School Construction: Example with Ghana   145
A12.1 Norms and Standards   177
A12.2 Toolkit for Donor Harmonization in Implementation Strategies   178

FIGURES

1.1 Typical School Furniture in African Classrooms   5
1.2 Gross Enrollment Rates and Distance to School in Chad, Guinea, Mali, and Niger   7

1.3 Cross-Country Comparison of Randomness in the Allocation of Classrooms across Primary Schools   1   1
1.4 Primary Gross Enrollment Ratios in Ethiopia, Urban and Rural   11
2.1 Economies of Scale in Primary Education: Expenditure per Student as a Function of School Enrollment   17
2.2 Distribution of Villages and Schools in Eastern Chad (Mongo subprefecture)   18
2.3 Standard Classroom in Senegal in the 1990s   20
2.4 Minimum Area per Student   2   0
3.1 The Most Common Classic Classroom Type   30
3.2 The School Shelter Model: The Example of Niger   34
3.3 The Earth-built Literacy Center in Chical Built by the NGO Development Workshop in 1980   36
3.4 A Typical Local Materials Classroom: Niger IDA-financed Education II Project   36
3.5 Technologies Used in United States Home Construction, by Region, 2001   41
3.6 Prefabricated Classroom in Madagascar—The Steel Structure   42
3.7 Scheme of the Industrialized Prefabrication of Classrooms in Madagascar   44
3.8 The European Union Fund Model   47
3.9 A Simple and Modest Classroom: The Mauritanian Model   48
4.1 The Dry Pit Latrine: An Example from Mali   52
4.2 Handicap-Friendly Latrine: The Example of Uganda   52
5.1 Centralized Bulk Procurement Process   57
5.2 Scheme of Combining Bulk Procurement of Imported Materials with Community Participation   59
5.3 Scheme of Combining Bulk Procurement of Imported Materials with Microenterprises: The Example of Niger (1987–2001)   63
5.4 Centralized National Competitive Bidding   64
5.5 Cost per Gross m^2 of Classroom Works Procured by Administration through ICB and NCB   65
5.6 Management of School Construction by a Contract Management Agency   69
5.7 Cost per Gross m^2 of Classroom Works Procured by Administration through ICB and NCB, and by CMAs through NCB   72
5.8 Scheme of School Construction Implemented by NGOs   74
5.9 Cost per Gross m^2 of Classroom Works Procured by Administration, CMAs, and NGOs   75
5.10 Social Fund Operating as a Contract Management Agency for Communities   8   1
5.11 Social Funds Operating as a Financer of Communities to Implement Their Project   82
5.12 Cost per Gross m^2 of Classrooms Procured by Administration (ICD and NCB), CMAs, NGOs, and Social Funds When They Act as CMAs   84
5.13 Deconcentration of Implementation Responsibilities to Lower Levels of Administration   89
5.14 Cost per Gross m^2 of Classrooms Procured by Administration (ICB and NCB), CMAs, NGOs, SF (as CMAs), and MoE Decentralized Offices   90
5.15 Delegation by Ministry of Education to Communities   92

5.16 Devolution of School Construction to Local Governments 97
5.17 Cost per Gross m² of Classrooms Procured by Administration (ICB-NCB), CMAs, NGOs, SFs (as CMAs) and MoE Decentralized, and Local Governments 97
5.18 Cost per Gross m² of Classrooms Procured by Administrative CMAs, NGOs, SFs (as CMAs), Local MoEs Decentralized, Local Governments, and Communities 101
5.19 Simultaneous IDA-funded Projects Financing School Construction with Different Approaches in Senegal. 2005 106
6.1 The CDD Scheme for School Construction 112
6.2 School Construction in a CDD Approach: Main Responsibilities of the Four Actors 113
6.3 Senegal Social Fund Handbook Illustration for Training Communities in Establishing a Community Development Committee 119
6.4 Deconcentrated Planning, Community Empowerment, and Financing through Fiduciary Agency 122
10.1 Total Classroom Construction Needs for 33 African IDA Countries 140
A3.1 The Koranic School of Malika, Senegal 1978: Sand-Cement Vault Technology 159
A3.2 Rosso (Mauritania) 1979: School Built with Earth and Vault Technology by the NGO ADAUA 159
A3.3 Diaguily School, Mauritania, 1988: Sand-Cement Vault Technology by UNESCO 159
A3.4 Earth-built School in Niger (1986–87) by MoE with World Bank Assistance 159
A3.5 Primary Schools with Stabilized Earth Bricks, Senegal, 1984 160
A3.6 Typical Implementation Scheme for International NGOs Using Local Materials Construction 160
A10.1 Devolution to Local Governments that Directly Implement School Construction 173
A10.2 Delegation to Local Government and Subsequent Delegation to CMAs 174
A10.3 Devolution to Local Governments and Subsequent Delegation to Local Communities 174
A14.1 Additional Classrooms Needed for 33 African IDA Countries 180
A14.2 Need for Replacement of Temporary Classrooms for 33 African IDA Countries 181
A14.3 Need for Replacement of Overaged Classrooms for 33 African IDA Countries 181
A14.4 Total Classroom Construction Needs for 33 African IDA Countries 182

Preface

According to 2005 estimates from the United Nations Education, Scientific and Cultural Organization (UNESCO), an estimated 45 million children do not attend primary school in Sub-Saharan Africa. Yet over the past decade, African countries have made significant progress in expanding access to primary education, and particularly since the year 2000. This progress was buoyed by a higher level of political will and better education policies within countries, and through a variety of commitments, made between donors and country recipients, that promise to increase aid for primary education and improve its effectiveness. These agreements include, for example, the Education for All (EFA) goals adopted in 1990 and again in 2000, the Millennium Development Goals (MDGs) adopted in 2000, the Monterrey Consensus of 2002, and the Rome and Paris Declarations on Alignment and Harmonization agreed to in 2003 and 2005, respectively.

In 2002, developing countries, donors, and other development partners also created a global partnership, the Education For All–Fast Track Initiative (EFA-FTI) to specifically translate these international commitments into action on the ground in support of the EFA and Millennium Development goals of complete, quality, primary education for all children. As a result of these efforts, the World Bank's 2006 Global Monitoring Report concludes that since 2000, the number of countries that have either achieved, or are on track to achieve, universal primary completion increased significantly, and that faster rates of progress are observed in countries that have joined the EFA-FTI.

These achievements, however, have placed great stress on school infrastructure, which is limited, is of poor quality, and is not growing fast enough. School infrastructure is a non-negligible cost for achieving the EFA goals and MDGs for primary education. Infrastructure comprises a large share of aid to primary education and of the cost of providing quality primary education more generally to all children. Actualized infrastructure costs are estimated, in this study, at $32 dollars per student and per year, compared to an average recurrent unit cost of $60 (see chapter 9 for a more thorough elaboration of this cost). Yet little information is available on infrastructure requirements to achieve these goals, nor how to achieve them more cost-effectively.

The provision of education infrastructure involves six main elements: the school planning and resource allocation norms and processes, the construction technology applied, the management of the construction process, donor behavior, corruption, and maintenance. These elements impact on results in one or more ways: on the ability to scale up infrastructure provision and/or on the cost and quality of the infrastructure.

This book examines the scope of the infrastructure challenge in Sub-Saharan Africa and the constraints to scaling up at an affordable cost. It assesses the experiences of African countries with school planning, school facility designs, construction technologies, and construction management over the past thirty years, and draws lessons on promising approaches to enable African countries to scale up the facilities required to achieve the EFA goals and MDGs of complete quality primary education for all children at the lowest marginal cost.

The book is organized along the following lines. Chapter 1 reviews the nature and scope of the primary school infrastructure challenges. Chapter 2 reviews the experience of African countries with school planning and resource allocation norms and how they have affected the volume, functionality, and distribution of primary school facilities. Chapters 3, 4, and 5 examine the impact of construction technology and approaches to construction management on the cost of school infrastructure and the ability to scale up. Chapter 6 delves more deeply into how to set up one of the most cost-effective approaches to school provision—the community-based approach. Chapter 7 looks at maintenance issues. Chapter 8 deals with corruption and chapter 9 with donors. Chapter 10 provides an estimate of the infrastructure cost of the EFA challenge and recommendation for countries and donors to improve the efficiency of the resources spent for school construction.

Data for a large part of the analysis in this book were collected on about 250 individual projects in 30 different countries, 23 of which are in Sub-Saharan Africa, and 7 in Latin America, East Asia or South Asia. Most of the data are from the past 10 years, but the database also includes cost data from as far back as the 1980s. Forty-five percent of the projects were financed by the World Bank, about 10 percent by governments, and the rest by other development partners. Unit cost information was mainly collected from World Bank project documents and consultant studies on school construction financed by the World Bank or other donor agencies and were adjusted to 2006 prices.

Acknowledgments

This book would not have come into being without the interest and support of three persons in the World Bank: first, *Robert Prouty*, who in 2002 gave me the opportunity to write a working paper entitled "School Construction in Developing Countries: What Do We Know?" Some years later, *Birger Fredriksen* encouraged me to encapsulate my thoughts through a piece of analytical work on school construction strategies in Africa. These thoughts became the manuscript of this book. The work was completed thanks to the kind, close, and efficient supervision from *Jee-Peng Tan*, who provided me support, advice, and encouragement.

The initial drafts benefited from the inputs of *Paud Murphy, Sverrir Sigurdsson*, and *Michael Wilson*. The economic analysis, which gives robustness to the conclusions of the study, was carried out by *Kirsten Majgaard*.

The ideas presented in this study took shape over the years through my direct experience and work in African countries while I was on the staff of a nongovernmental organization and United Nations agencies, and while I was a freelance consultant and researcher. After I joined the World Bank, the ideas were further shaped through my involvement in numerous World Bank-financed operations in education and community-driven development (CDD) in African and Asian countries. I owe an immense intellectual debt to the experts in the education sector and elsewhere with whom I have had the pleasure and privilege to work. In the World Bank, I am deeply indebted to *Rosemary Bellew, Robert Prouty, Alassance Diawara, Mourad Ezzine*, and *Sajitha Bashir*. Among my counterparts in African countries, I wish to acknowlege such experts as *Khardiata Lo Ndiaye, Boubacar Ndiaye, Abdel Wedoud Kamil, Nebghouha Mint Mohamed Vall, Frank Tigri, Abderrahim Ould Ahmed Salem, Hamoud Ould Cheikhna*, and *Ismail Ba*, to cite a few. I also learned from the work of others including *Carel Halfman, Douglas Lehman, Henk Meijerink, Lawrence Dowdall, Merten Treffers, Leo Sinke, Daniel Dupety*, and *Souleyman Zerbo*. Last but not least, I am also intellectually obligated to the many experts and nonexperts at the grassroots level: community leaders, villagers, farmers, masons, and others who taught me a great deal about the practical realities and complexities of development challenges on the ground. They all deserve my deepest gratitude.

Editing with clarity the ideas expressed in this book was a challenge. It was so because the topic of this book cuts across several sectors, among them education, construction, technology, procurement, CDD, and decentralization. *Rosemary Bellew* carried out invaluable editing improvements, clarifying the storyline, deleting nonessential text, and correcting my "Frenglish." I also benefitted from the editorial support of *Bruce Ross-Larson* and *Sean A. Tate*. Efficient logistical support was provided by *Mohamed Diaw* and *Amy Ba*.

Peer reviewers of the study included *Adriaan Verspoor, Bernard Abeillé, David Warren, Giacomina de Regt, Mourad Ezzine, Meskerem Mulatu, Robert Prouty*, and *Sundaram Krishnakumar*. The review meetings were chaired by *Yaw Ansu*.

To all of the above, I express my deepest and sincere appreciation.

Serge Theunynck
April 1st 2009

Abbreviations

ABUTIP	Agence Burundaise des Travaux d'Intérêt Public
ACA	Agence Cooperation et Aménagement
ADAUA	Association pour le Développement d'une Architecture et d'un Urbanisme Africains
AfDB	African Development Bank
AFVP	Association Francaise des Volontaires du Progrès
AFDS	Association du Fonds de Développement Social
AGDS	Agence de Gestion de la Dimension Sociale du Developpement
AGECABO	Agência Cabo-Verdiana de Promoção do Emprego e do Desenvolvimento Local/Cabo Verdean Agency for Public Works
AGEFIB	Agence de Financement des Initiatives de Base
AGETIP	Agence d'Exécution des Travaux d'Intérêt Public
AGETIPA	Agence d'Exécution des Travaux d'Intérêt Public (Madagascar)
AMDU	Mozambican Association for Urban Development
AMEXTIPE	Agences Mauritanienne d'Exécution des Travaux d'Intérêt Public pour l'Emploi
ATETIP	Agence Tchadienne d'Execution de Travaux d'Interet Public
BAD	Banque Africaine de Développement
BADEA	Banque Arabe pour le Développement Economique en Afrique
BCI	Budget Consolidé d'Investissement
BEPS	Basic Education and Policy Support
BESIP	Basic Education Sector Investment Program
BESSIP	Basic Education Sub-sector Investment Program
BID	Banque Islamique de Développement
CBO	community-based organizations
CDC	Community Development Committee
CDD	community-driven development
CMA	contract management agency

CRESED II	Second Education Sector Development Project
DANIDA	Danish International Development Agency
DCES	Direction des Constructions et des Equipements Scolaires
DFID UK	Department for International Development
EDI	Economic Development Institute
Edu-II	Second Education Project
Edu-III	Third Education Project
Edu-V	Fifth Education Project
EFA	Education for All
EFA-FTI	Education for All–Fast Track Initiative
ESCP	Education Sector Consolidation Project
ESP	Education Sector Project
ESSIP	Education Sector Strategic Investment Plan
ESSP	Education Sector Strategic Plan
EU	European Union
FA	financing agreement
FDA	French Development Agency (FAD)
FCFA	Franc Communauté Financière Africaine
FID	Fonds d'Intervention pour le Développement
FID-EPT	Fonds d'Investissement pour le Développement—Education pour Tous
FINNIDA	Finnish International Development Agency
GEAI	Groupement d'Etudes pour une Architecture Industrialisée
GMT	grassroots management training
GRIP	Grassroots Initiative Project
GRZ	Government of the Republic of Zambia
HIPC	heavily indebted poor country
HRDP	Human Resources Development Project
ICB	international competitive bidding
IDA	International Development Association
IDB	International Development Bank
ILO	International Labor Organization
JICA	Japan International Cooperation Agency
KfW	Kreditanstalt für Wiederaufbau (German government–owned development bank)
LCB	local competitive bidding
LG	local government
LGDP	Local Government Development Project
LICUS	low-income country under stress
MASAF	Malawi Social Action Fund

MDG	Millennium Development Goals
MINED	Ministère de l'Education
MoE	Ministry of Education
MoRD	Ministry of Rural Development
MPP	Micro-project Program
MPU	Micro-project Unit
MPW	Ministry of Public Works
NCB	national competitive bidding
NGO	nongovernmental organization
NIGETIPE	Agence Nigerienne d'Exécution des Travaux d'Intérêt Public
NRIP	National Rural Investment Project
NUSAF	Northern Uganda Social Action Fund
OECD	Organisation for Economic Co-operation and Development
OPEC	Organization of Petroleum Exporting Countries
OPEP	Organisation des Pays Exportateurs de Pétrole
OPSUP	OPEC Primary School Upgrading Project
OSEO	Œuvre Suisse d'Entraide Ouvrière
PAC	Projet d'Appui aux Communes
PADEB	Basic Education Project
PAOEB	Projet d'Appui à l'Organisation de l'Enseignement de Base
PASE	Projet d'Appui au Secteur de l'Education
PCPEP	Projet de Construction de Prototypes d'Ecoles Primaires
PCPEPMRG	Porjet de Construction de Prototypes d'Ecoles Primaires en Milieu Rural de Guinée
PCU	Project Coordination Unit
PDRH	Projet de Développement des Ressources Humaines
PEDP	Primary Education Development Project
PEQT	Projet Education de Qualite pour Tous
PFDS	Projet de Fonds de Développement Social
PIU	Project Implementation Unit
PMC	Project Management Committee
PNDSE	Programme National de Développement du Secteur Education
PNUD	Programme des Nations Unies pour le Développement
PROMEF	Projet de Consolidation et de Modernisation de l'Education et la Formation
PPTE	Pays Pauvres Très Endettés
PUSE	Programme d'Urgence pour le Secteur de l'Education
PWECP	Public Works and Employment Creation Project
QUIPS	Quality and Improvement in Primary Schools
SESP	Second Education Sector Project

SF	social fund
SFG	School Facility Grant
SHRDP	Second Human Resource Development Project
SRP	Social Recovery Program
SSDP	Social Sector Development Project
SWAPs	sector-wide approaches
TESP	Third Education Sector Project
UNCDF	United Nations Capital Development Fund
UNESCO	United Nations Educational, Scientific, and Cultural Organization
USAID	United States Agency for International Development
VCSP	Village Community Support Project
ZAMSIF	Zambia Social Investment Fund
ZEPIU	Zambia Education Project Implementation Unit

CHAPTER 1

The Challenges of Africa's Primary School Infrastructure

Primary school infrastructure in Africa has not been growing fast enough to accommodate all school-age children, and a large share of the existing stock is unsafe and unsuitable for learning. At the same time, resources are often inefficiently and inequitably allocated, allowing greater access for some populations than for others. If these trends continue, the primary school infrastructure needed to provide quality education for all children by 2015 will be grossly inadequate in volume, quality, functionality, and distribution. These problems are due not only to insufficient resources but also to inefficient planning norms and practices, unsuitable construction technology, and inefficient construction management processes.

THE GROWTH TREND IN PRIMARY SCHOOL CLASSROOMS

Table 1.1 shows some estimates of the average annual increase in the classroom stock for 10 African countries in recent years, compared with the annual growth in the classroom stock required to accommodate all school-age children by 2015 with 40 students per classroom.[1] If we extrapolate the pace of actual classroom construction during the late 1990s and early 2000s into the future, on average, the classroom stock is growing only half as fast (56 percent) as necessary. According to this measure, in Burkina Faso, Burundi, Chad, and Rwanda the current increase in the classroom stock is less than 40 percent of the requisite volume. Only Guinea, Madagascar, and Mauritania are experiencing an increase in their classroom stock that is consistent with the Education for All (EFA) objective. Most of the school construction programs submitted by African countries to access EFA-Fast Track Initiative (EFA-FTI) funds propose to multiply the construction rhythm by a factor ranging between two to four.[2]

These are estimates of the stock only, however, not of the total number of classrooms that need to be constructed by 2015 to reach the capacity required—which can be significantly higher, depending on the quality of the existing buildings, which are generally poor in Africa.

Table 1.1   Growth in Classroom Stock, Needs versus Actual

Country	Annual growth in classroom stock needed 2005–15 (gap assessment)	Growth in classroom stock per year (actual)	Growth period	Actual vs. need (%)
Burkina Faso	4,194	1,577	1997–2003	38
Burundi	2,119	792	1999–2003	37
Chad	2,944	1,059	1996–99	36
Congo	960	593	1996–2001	62
Guinea	1,598	1,485	1996–99	93
Madagascar	2,848	2,770	1999–2004	97
Malawi	2,261	1,214	2000–05	54
Mauritania	445	519	1996–99	117
Rwanda	1,854	688	2000–03	37
Uganda	4,988	2,786	1993–2003	56
Average	2,421	1,348		56

Source: Author's projections for 2005–15. The data on classroom stock growth are from statistical yearbooks of the ministries of education (Burundi, Malawi), from Group 5 2005, or from World Bank project documents. The gap assessment refers to Burns et al. (2003).

THE QUALITY OF PRIMARY SCHOOL INFRASTRUCTURE

A large number of primary schools throughout Africa fail to provide a healthful and conducive learning environment for children. The quality of the primary school facilities, that is the package of facilities offered, their durability and functionality, is often abysmal. Many schools in Sub-Saharan Africa consist of classrooms only, and temporary structures form a large share of the classroom infrastructure. There is no potable water. There are no working sanitary facilities, nor any other school facility, such as an office or storage space for learning materials. Further, school furniture is often broken or lacking entirely. Research suggests that these conditions have a significant negative impact on whether children attend and complete primary school and whether teachers show up for work. (Refer to Annex 1 for a review of the research literature.)

TEMPORARY STRUCTURES

Temporary structures represent a large share of classrooms in Africa. Many of these classrooms were built by communities themselves. Table 1.2 shows that across the 15 countries for which data are available, 28 percent of classrooms are temporary or substandard, reaching as high as 63 percent in Chad, where most classrooms are made of plant materials, such as millet stalks (secco) that require rebuilding every year. For the most part, temporary classrooms, like those in Guinea, are built of earth walls that erode easily, topped with a wooden roofing structure prone to

Table 1.2 Number and Condition of Primary Classrooms

Country	Number of classrooms in 2005 (actual or estimated)	Percent of classrooms listed as temporary, built from nonpermanent materials, needing rehabilitation, or in poor condition
Benin	26,681	31
Burkina Faso	21,590	4
Chad	18,970	63
Congo	7,850	31
Ghana	62,110	12
Guinea	21,630	20
Madagascar	44,480	11
Malawi	36,700	21
Mauritania	10,160	28
Mozambique	45,880	46
Niger	26,220	47
Rwanda	30,420	44
Senegal	24,140	8
Uganda	113,920	38
Zambia	31,100	16
Average		28

Source: Statistical yearbooks, Group 5, and World Bank project documents.
Note: Number of classrooms in Benin, Madagascar, and Malawi are actual; others are projections based on most recent data available. Number of substandard classrooms is taken from most recent data.

termite attacks. Community-built classrooms are also small, typically limited in space to a maximum of 20 to 30 students.[3] Windows must necessarily be small also. A larger classroom space would require a foundation, a wall structure made of modern materials, such as cement, and a roof structure made of squared wood or steel, which is often beyond the means of poor communities.

These facilities have significant drawbacks that jeopardize the achievement of quality primary education for all. First, they are maintenance-intensive. Because of the limited durability of the materials used, the classrooms require regular rebuilding. Second, they are unhealthy for humans because they provide an insufficient minimum of space, ventilation, and light. Third, the classrooms cannot be used in the rain, which reduces the instructional and learning time children receive and, consequently, their level of achievement. For example, a review of the World Bank's assistance to education in Ghana concluded that improvements in the availability and quality of school infrastructure had resulted in higher primary school enrollment and increases in English and math achievement. These achievement gains were primarily due to the greater amount of instructional and learning time children received because more schools were able to function normally when it rained (World Bank 2004d). In another study, Glewwe and Jacoby (1994) estimate the

Table 1.3 Availability of Latrines and Water

Country	Schools with latrines (%)	Schools with water (%)	Year
Burkina Faso	55	38	2004
Chad	33	60	2003
Ghana	54	44	2004
Senegal	36	33	2000
Uganda	100	50	2004
Zambia	50	52	2002
Average	55	46	

Source: Group 5 and World Bank project documents.

gains in learning achievement in Ghanaian middle schools due to repairing leaking roofs at 2.0 standard deviations in reading and 2.2 in math. In Mauritania, students attending classes in concrete buildings had statistically better scores in the end-of-primary exam than their peers learning in mud-built classrooms or under a tent (World Bank 2001d).

WATER AND SANITATION

Table 1.3 shows the availability of latrines and potable water supply in six African countries. On average, only about half of all schools in these countries have latrines and water supply. Uganda is a notable exception where all schools reportedly have sanitary facilities.[4] Further, where latrines exist, they are often insufficient in number and out of service due to inadequate understanding among users about how they function, and lack of maintenance and up-keep. In Zambia, for instance, only half of the available toilet facilities are currently functioning (Group 5 2006e).

The backlog of water and sanitary facilities is rising every year because countries still, today, do not consider them an integral and necessary part of a school facility and, therefore, do not plan for them. For example, in Senegal, where only 39 percent of schools have sanitation facilities and only 33 percent have access to potable water, between 2000 and 2004, the government's school construction program built 6,600 classrooms but only 800 latrines, covering only 22 percent of the new sanitation needs (World Bank 2000d, Dupety 2005a). Only in recent years have a few countries begun to incorporate water and sanitation as an essential component of school infrastructure. For example, Mauritania began to include water and sanitation as an essential part of primary school facilities in 2001. Chad did the same in 2002, and Guinea began to include these facilities in all new schools since 1989, while planning to retrofit the 4,300 schools without them over a 10-year period (World Bank 1995b, 2001c, 2001f, 2003b).

The absence of these facilities poses not only a health hazard for the children, but also results in lower school attendance and higher teacher absenteeism. Numerous studies have found that the availability of potable water and sanitary facilities increased school enrollment and completion levels.[5] For example, in Ethiopia, Chaudhury, Christiaensen, and Asadullah (2006) found that the availability of water in the nearest school increased the probability of boys' school attendance by 15 percent, and the availability of latrines increased their attendance by 7 percent. In Pakistan, the construction of separate latrines for girls significantly increased their enrollment in primary schools (World Bank 2004o). In India, a UNICEF assessment estimated that the provision of potable water and sanitary facilities would increase girls' enrollments from 47 to 66 percent in the targeted schools (Sey et al. 2003). Further, studies on teacher absenteeism in Bangladesh, Ecuador, India, Indonesia, Peru, and Uganda found that teacher absenteeism was higher in schools with worse infrastructure. In particular, lack of toilets was correlated with high rates of teacher absenteeism, which ranged between 11 and 27 percent. (Chaudhury, Hammer, et al. 2006).

SCHOOL FURNITURE

Furniture in most African schools is designed more for preventing theft or community use than for pedagogical purposes.

The most common type of classroom furniture in African primary schools is the traditional one-piece, two- or three-seater desk and bench model built of solid wood or of a combination of wood and tubular steel. The latter is common in the Sahel, where wood is a scarce commodity. Figure 1.1 shows a typical example of the desk-bench made of solid wood. Because the desks and the benches are heavy, sturdy, and joined together, they are resistant to vandalism and can accommodate more students in the given space. Malawi and Mozambique have introduced furniture made of concrete, a more extreme model that is virtually impervious to vandalism or theft. Mauritania requires that the desk-bench be anchored in the concrete floor. However, the design and immobility of the furniture is poorly suited to modern classroom teaching strategies, such as group work and multigrade teaching.

At the other end of the spectrum is furniture that is lightweight, flexible, and easily moved within the classroom. This consists of tables accommodating one or several students with individual chairs. The furniture is made of tubular steel, wood, plywood, or plastic. Although the light weight of the furniture makes it easily vulnerable to abuse when moved

Figure 1.1 Typical School Furniture in African Classrooms

Source: Unesco 1990a.

Table 1.4 Cost of Furniture per Classroom

Country	Average unit cost[a]	Year
Burkina Faso	1,833	2004
Gambia, The	1,623	1993
Ghana	1,250	2001–03
Madagascar	1,600	2004
Malawi	1,659	2006
Mauritania	2,015	2002
Mozambique	1,986	1999–2005
Senegal	1,572	2000–04
Uganda	1,110	2004
Zambia	1,400	2004
Average	1,605	

Source: Group 5, Dupety, Theunynck.
Note: Unit costs include the cost of furniture for a staff room.
a. Per classroom in selected projects (US$)

around in the classroom and its similarity to domestic furniture makes it more vulnerable to theft, it is more suitable to modern pedagogical practices and for multigrade teaching.

African schools often lack an adequate supply of furniture. Shortage of seats amounts to 14 percent in Burkina Faso (2002/03), 24 percent in Ghana, 33 percent in Lesotho (Group 5 2006a and 2006b, World Bank 2005a). In Malawi, only 35 percent of sixth grade pupils had a desk to sit at in 2000 and a mere 29 percent had writing places (World Bank 2004e). However, furniture seems to play a role in students' learning: Tan, Lane, and Coustere (1997) found that lack of adequate furniture in the first grades in the Philippines was associated with a drop of −0.32 standard deviation in math and −0.29 standard deviation in reading. The absence of furniture is not always explained by the cost. Table 1.4 shows the cost of furniture per classroom in 10 African countries. The cost of furnishing one classroom averages about US$1,600, ranging from US$1,110 in Uganda to US$2,200 in Mauritania where all materials are imported, i.e., 20 percent and almost 50 percent of classroom unit cost,[6] respectively. New school construction programs sometimes neglect to include furniture even when financed by foreign donors.[7] Moreover, no African country has yet put in place a furniture replacement policy.

DISTANCE TO SCHOOL

Distance to school remains a problem for many children. Recent enrollment surges in several African countries have increased the stress on the slower-growing infrastructure. Several indicators of this stress are large classes and an increasing use of double and triple shifts, which shorten the effective instructional time that each child receives.

The evidence is overwhelming and unambiguous. Schools must be located as close as possible to children's homes, preferably within the village. The closer the school is to home, the more likely parents are to send their children to school and to do so at the appropriate age. Research shows that "the single most important determinant of primary school enrollment is the proximity of a school to primary-age children" (Lockeed and Verspoor 1991). Long distances have a sizeable impact on enrollment (Filmer 2004). Long distances to school not only increase the opportunity cost of attending school, but also tax the stamina of children and can place them in vulnerable situations. Further, studies in Pakistan, Côte d'Ivoire, and Ghana find that distance poses a particularly acute barrier for girls to attend school (Kane 2004, World Bank 2005m). In Ghana, Zambia, and Lesotho, grueling distances to school also caused parents to defer schooling until their children were older, which increased the probability of dropping out (Lavy 1993, Kane 2004, World Bank 2005a). In Chad, Guinea, and Niger school enrollment drops precipitously when children are expected to attend school in a village other than their own, even if that village is nearby (Lehman et al. 2004). In Senegal, the distance to school is inversely related to the probability to be in school (World Bank 2008a). Similarly, in Pakistan, many families in villages without schools refuse to send their girls to a school outside the community (World Bank 2005m).

Evidence from African countries suggests that enrollment and retention decline significantly beyond a distance of even 1 to 2 kilometers, or a 30-minute walk, particularly for younger children. Figure 1.2 shows that in Chad, Guinea, Mali, and Niger, enrollment rates are 50 percent lower for boys and girls when the nearest school is between 1 and 2 kilometers from home. These results are confirmed by numerous other studies, although the size of the impact may vary across countries.[8] In Mali, the enrollment rate is almost 30 percentage points higher for children who live less than 30 minutes from school, compared with children who live more than 45 minutes away (World Bank 2006d). In Côte d'Ivoire, a distance longer than 2 kilometers has a strong negative impact on enrollment. In Burundi, the difference is 10 percentage points for the two groups. When the satellite school model is often used, this approach generates high dropout rates.[9] For example, a 2003 study in Chad found that enrollment dropped off steeply in satellite villages that were expected to send their children to consolidator schools: 80 percent of enrolled children came from the 8 percent of the villages that had the schools and the remaining 20 percent from the 92 percent satellite villages (Lehman 2004). Similar results were observed in Burkina Faso, where the satellite school model promoted in the mid-1990s with UNICEF support was abandoned in the mid-2000s, when each satellite was allowed to become a small complete school (Bagayoko 2005). Retention also declines significantly with distance beyond 2 kilometers, or a 30-minute walk. In rural Benin, primary school children who walk more than 30 minutes drop out 1.8 times more than those who cover shorter distances (World Bank 2008b). There is also a wealth of evidence of the relation between distance to school and enrollment and retention in such Asian countries as India and Indonesia (Foster and Rosenzweig 1996, Duflo 2001). Data from Mauritania show that distance

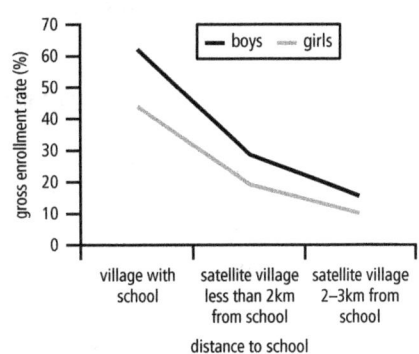

Figure 1.2 Gross Enrollment Rates and Distance to School in Chad, Guinea, Mali, and Niger

Source: Lehman et al., 2004.

also affects performance. Students living less than 1 kilometer (km) from their school perform statistically better than those who walk farther (World Bank 2001d).

All these elements advocate for a habitation-to-school distance well below 2 km or a 30-minute walk, which is significantly lower than the norm used in most African countries for planning purposes, which can be as high as 5 km. Despite the evidence, in many countries children have to walk long distances to get to school. In Mali, 30 percent of rural children walk more than 45 minutes (World Bank 2006d).[10] In Malawi, 34 percent of the children travel more than 2 km (World Bank 2004e). In Uganda, only 54 percent of households were within 2 km from a primary school in 2005 (Okidi and Guloba 2006). In Ethiopia, 61 percent of the rural pupils walk more than 2 km and 33 percent more than 5, in 2000 (World Bank 2005f). In Rwanda, more than 53 percent of the pupils live more than 30 minutes from a school; this percentage is 56 percent in Côte d'Ivoire (World Bank 2003c and 2005s). In Uganda, a country with a high enrollment rate but a low completion rate, 57 percent of families live at a distance of 2 or more kilometers from a primary school and 22 percent live 4 or more kilometers away (Group 5 2006d). In Lesotho, 69 percent of children who have never been to school live more than 30 minutes from a school (World Bank 2005a cited by Lewis and Lockheed). In Ghana, building a school in a community located at more than 1 hour's walking distance from the nearest school will increase enrollment in that community by 5 percent (OED 2004).

Distance is a particularly important constraint for physically disabled children. Physical disabilities that impair mobility constitute one of the most common disabilities among African children. The prevalence of mobility disability is estimated at 3 percent in the 6–14 age group in Rwanda, and at 1.2 percent in Benin, where 66 percent of the school-age children living with a handicap are not enrolled in schools (Christian Blind Mission and International Center for Eye Health 2006). The situation is even worse for girls, whose enrollment rate is three times lower than for handicapped boys (Jadin 2004). It is painfully obvious that mobility-impaired children must have easy access to school. The further the school, the more arduous and impossible the journey becomes.

OVERCROWDING AND MULTIPLE SHIFTS

Many classrooms are overcrowded. Table 1.5 shows the ratio of pupils to classrooms in 14 countries for which recent data are available. On average, across this group of countries, each primary school classroom accommodates 63 students, generally within one shift. The lowest average class sizes are found in Niger (38:1) and Ghana (40:1), whereas classrooms in Malawi and Uganda may pack in more than 100 and 86 children, respectively. Within country, the variation is likely to be equally wide, with some schools more overcrowded than others.

Table 1.5 Indicators of Overcrowding

Country	Ratio teachers to classrooms	Ratio pupils to classrooms	Ratio pupils to teachers
Burkina Faso	0.9	49	52
Chad	1.1	70	66
Congo	1.1	74	65
Ghana	1.2	37	31
Guinea	1	47	45
Madagascar	1.2	63	52
Malawi	1.2	86	72
Mauritania	1.1	44	41
Mozambique	1.1	73	67
Niger	0.9	38	42
Rwanda	1	60	60
Senegal	1.1	53	49
Uganda	2.1	112	53
Zambia	1.7	72	43
Average	1.2	63	53

Source: Pupil and classroom data are from School Census data, Group 5 2005, or from World Bank project documents. Pupil teacher ratios are from UNESCO 2005.
Note: Data are for the most recent year available (between 1999 and 2005).

To address the problem of overcrowding when resources are limited, economists and planners often advise the use of multiple shifts, whereby different cohorts of students attend school during different hours of the day, so as to more fully use the existing infrastructure, rather than investing in new schools or expanding existing ones. The cost savings can be significant. In Ethiopia, for instance, 44 percent of the government's schools operate in two shifts (World Bank 2004o). In Burundi, as many as 61 percent of public primary school students used double shifts in 2003–04 (World Bank 2006c). In Rwanda, the use of double shifts is practiced in the first two grades of primary school, which represents the difference between the need for 730 new classrooms per year and three times as many if the use of double-shifts is phased out (Pichvai 2004a).

The savings, however, need to be balanced against the potential negative consequences of using double shifts. Studies of student achievement cast some doubt on the educational effectiveness of this strategy. In an analysis of learning outcomes across 21 African countries, using double shifts is shown to have a strong negative impact on student achievement due to the reduced number of hours double-shift students spend in school relative to their single-shift peers. This result appears in countries such as Madagascar, which operates each shift with separate teachers, as well as in Senegal, where one teacher teaches both shifts (Michaelowa and Wechtler 2006). The difference in learning time between single- and double-shift students can be enormous, such as in the case of Burundi, where single-shift students receive twice as many instructional hours as their double-shift peers (World Bank 2006c).

Numerous other studies show that students in classes with high student to teacher ratios, up to a threshold of 60 students per class perform just as well as students in smaller classes. However, beyond 60 students per class, learning outcomes deteriorate (Mingat 2003). However, the physical space obviously sets an upper limit on class size. Most schools in Africa today have been built to accommodate a maximum of 40–45 students. It would not be responsible policy advice to suggest cramming up to 60 students into an already minimal space designed for only 45, or 20, in many cases. The space in the typical African classroom is already at a bare minimum, generally only the minimum space required for proper ventilation and aisles to allow for entry and exit. Thus, if all children are to be accommodated in a single shift, more classrooms are needed. How many more depends on the number of students the classrooms are expected to accommodate, while ensuring maximum student-to-teacher ratios and minimum norms of public health and safety. If more schools need to be built, it is necessary to build them in the most cost-efficient manner without compromising learning outcomes.

INEFFICIENT RESOURCE ALLOCATIONS

The problems of poor infrastructure are often exacerbated by an inefficient and inequitable distribution of construction resources. Throughout Africa, it is not uncommon to encounter schools with empty classrooms coexisting with unmet needs nearby. For example, in Guinea where the primary gross enrollment ratio is only 81 percent, as many as 16 percent of the 15,600 classrooms available were recorded as unused in 2000 (World Bank 2001c). In Madagascar the number of unused classrooms declined sharply from 20 percent in 2000 but remains at 7 percent of the 50,000 classrooms in 2005 (MENRS 2007).

Indeed, throughout Sub-Saharan Africa, the geographical distribution of schools seems to bear little relationship to the distribution of the students. Rather, the distribution appears to be quite random. In Burkina Faso, the enrollment observed in six-classroom schools ranges from 30 to 880 pupils, clearly inefficient on both tails of the distribution. Figure 1.3 compares the proportion of the variation in the number of classrooms not accounted for by enrollments in six African countries. Of the six countries, Malawi has the highest randomness in the distribution of classrooms. More than 70 percent of the variation in the number of classrooms in Malawian schools cannot be explained by school enrollment. In most of the other countries, around 40 percent of the variation is not related to enrollment but to other factors.

Figure 1.3 Cross-Country Comparison of Randomness in the Allocation of Classrooms across Primary Schools

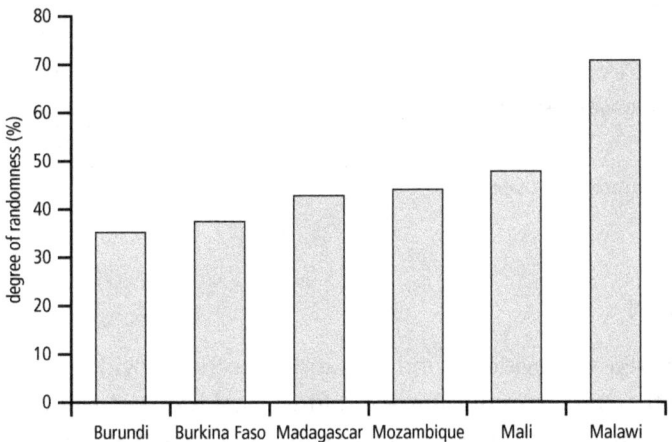

Source: Analysis of school census data from Burundi (2003–04), Burkina Faso (2003), Madagascar (2004–05), Mozambique (2003), Mali (2004–05), and Malawi (2004).
Note: The degree of randomness is calculated as 1 minus the R-square from the linear regression relating the number of classrooms to the number of pupils, with schools as the unit of observation.

In countries where overall coverage is low, such as in Ethiopia, urban children are much more likely to have access to school than their rural peers as shown in Figure 1.4. Urban areas are better served, partly due to resource allocation decisions that have traditionally favored urban areas. They have also been aided by the presence of a private (construction) sector, and greater wealth, which allows households to step in where government fails. In Guinea, for instance, half of the classrooms constructed between 1997 and 2000 were built in the capital, Conakry, thanks to a dynamic private sector construction industry and private financing, which accounted for the majority of classrooms constructed (World Bank 2001c). In the absence of the private sector, conditions would have deteriorated. Likewise, during times of rapid urbanization and in the absence of a dynamic private sector, service in urban areas may deteriorate, as occurred in Mauritania during the 1990: the proportion of classrooms declined from 13.3 percent to 12.6 percent of total classrooms while the population increased from 20 percent to 24 percent.

Figure 1.4 Primary Gross Enrollment Ratios in Ethiopia, Urban and Rural

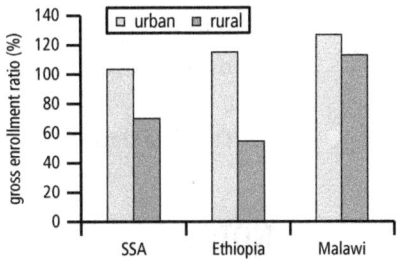

Source: World Bank 2005f.
Note: Sub-Saharan Africa (SSA) and Ethiopia are based on 2000 data (grades 1–6), and Malawi on 2002 data (grades 1–8).

Table 1.6 School Construction Needs, 2005–2015, for 33 African IDA Countries

	Increases classroom stock	Annual construction need 2005–15	%
Construction of additional classrooms	Yes	117,000	60
Replacement of temporary/substandard classrooms	No	48,000	25
Replacement of overaged classrooms	No	30,000	15
Total		195,000	100

Source: Author's calculation (see chapter 10).

CONCLUSION

The available research evidence and operational reality provide sufficient evidence to conclude that a basic minimum—and functional level—of school infrastructure must be a necessary component of any credible strategy that aims to achieve the Millenium Development Goal of complete, quality, primary education for all children. Primary school infrastructure should satisfy the basic requirements of accessibility, durability, functionality, safety, and public health.

Today, across Sub-Saharan Africa, the number of primary schools is not growing fast enough nor are they of acceptable quality. In order to accommodate all primary school-age children in safe environments, we estimated that the 33 IDA-eligible countries in Sub-Saharan Africa will need to construct an estimated 2 million classrooms with related facilities, such as water and sanitation, by 2015 (table 1.6). To put this into perspective, this is more than double the 1.9 million classrooms available in 2005, and about 2.6 times the average pace over the past 10 years.[11] This estimate includes classrooms needed to accommodate all out-of-school children (1.2 million), and to replace substandard facilities built with nondurable materials (0.5 million), as well as buildings that deteriorate with age (0.3 million) as their life span generally does not exceed 30 to 40 years.[12] Since school expansion started after African countries became independent, the classroom stock has been gradually aging. By 2015, classrooms built before 1975 will need to be replaced. For Sub-Saharan Africa, this represents at least 30,000 classrooms per year, bringing the total number of classrooms to be built to 195,000 per year.

This is a daunting challenge but not insurmountable.

NOTES

1. The annual growth in the classroom stock needed between 2005 and 2015 is estimated by comparing the classroom stock needed in 2015 to achieve the goal of complete primary education for all children, using estimates by Bruns et al. (2003), with the

estimated stock of classrooms that would exist in 2015 if the past years' rate of growth in classroom stocks were extrapolated into the future. A class size of 40:1, by 2015, is also used in the simulations by Bruns et al.

2. Country Leadership and Implementation for Results, in the EFA-FTI Partnership, Tunis, December 3–6, 2007.

3. Because of the roofing technology and material limitation. When roofs are supported by bush tree trunks, the maximum distance between walls is not more than 3 meters

4. The number of sanitary facilities is not the only exceptional feature In Uganda, their quality is also exceptional because all sanitation blocks include one handicap-friendly box.

5. See also Mason 1994, Glewwe and Jacoby 1996, Lloyd et al. 2003.

6. In 1995, given the high cost of furniture compared with buildings, the Mauritanian Government decided to exclude furniture and therefore was able to build 50 percent more classrooms with the same amount of resources Such a radical tradeoff was maintained during 5 years. It was culturally acceptable because in the Saharan tradition, furniture is limited to rugs and mattresses. However, since 2000, the government has reversed its position and furniture is systematically included in the school construction package.

7. Such as the Third OPEP-financed project in Senegal during the period 2000–04 (Dupety 2005a).

8. Country Status Reports: World Bank 2004h, 2005s, 2006c, 2006d.

9. The satellite model combines lower primary education through satellite-schools in small villages with upper primary in a consolidated school located in a larger village that is strategically situated to attract upper primary students to one centrally located village.

10. In Mali, the average household distance to the nearest primary school was 6.6 kilometers in 1995–96 (DHS Mali).

11. The speed of new classroom construction in SSA is assessed in recent years based on data for 10 countries (for each country we have collected data for at least 3 years within the period 1996–2005). Extrapolating from the 10 countries to the group of 33 low-income SSA countries, we roughly estimate that about 75,000 classrooms are built each year in the 33 countries.

12. The estimate assumes a student per classroom ratio of 45. Based on the data in Annex 1, we assumed (more conservatively) that 25 percent of the classroom stock in the 33 countries is made of temporary/nondurable materials and will need to be replaced within the next 10 years.

CHAPTER 2

School Location Planning and Construction Norms

The poor condition of the primary school infrastructure in Africa, the slow pace of scaling-up provision, and the instances of inefficient resource allocations are partly attributable to a lack of proper planning and of clear and appropriate infrastructure norms and resource allocation criteria. Experience with school location planning in Africa suggests a widespread absence of planning norms, and when norms do exist, they are often inappropriate or not applied. Centralized planning processes compound these inefficiencies, as do donors who introduce their own norms and specifications irrespective of the country's standards and experience.

SCHOOL LOCATION PLANNING

School location planning was originally developed as a way to allocate scarce resources according to common technical criteria, or norms Also known as school mapping, it became popular in Africa in the late 1960s. School mapping was largely based on a process initiated in France in 1963 to aid in the implementation of a major reform in secondary education—the introduction of the college, or middle school. School mapping was rolled out in many countries with the assistance of donors and other international agencies.

As a result of the work on school mapping, many countries have developed some norms to guide the allocation of infrastructure resources while endeavoring to achieve more equitable access. School mapping norms are generally of three types—norms relating to *accessibility and efficiency*, those relating to the *quality of the facility*, and those related to the *construction technology*.

- *Accessibility and efficiency norms* include guidance and criteria to apply to determine whether to establish a new school or expand an existing one, and where. Typically, school planners divide up the country into school catchment areas by applying norms regarding the minimum population required to establish an economically viable school and a maximum distance that children should be

expected to travel from home to school. The school size required depends on the population in the catchment area. Increasingly, when determining size and space requirements, countries also factor in school management methods to maximize the use of space through double shifts or multigrade teaching.
- *School quality* norms concern norms about space and auxiliary facilities that are required to attract and keep children in school in a positive and healthy learning environment at an economical cost. They include norms related to adjunct facilities, such as water and sanitation, offices, and storage, as well as the functionality of each building, including accommodation for handicapped students.
- *School construction technology* relates to the materials, engineering, and workmanship that are needed for building functional and durable facilities. This is discussed in the next section.

Experience in school planning throughout the Africa region suggests that the distance norms applied are too high, particularly in mountainous areas where the terrain makes for a more arduous journey, and the school size norm is generally too large. The result is schools that are still too far from home and the coexistence of unused facilities in some locations with oversubscribed schools in others.

DISTANCE NORMS

The distance norm is the maximum distance children are expected to travel to school; it defines the school catchment area. Combined with a norm of minimum population in the catchment area to establish a school, the distance norm is at the heart of school mapping. The distance norm, adopted in the 1970s and commonly applied, is to locate schools within a radius of 3 kilometers (km) from home, in line with the recommendations of the International Institute for Education Planning (IIEP) in Paris and the World Bank (Gould 1978). Some countries with low density, such as Chad, have larger distance norms that use a 5-km norm to reach the normed threshold of population in the catchment area (Lehman et al., 2004). However, research and experience clearly show that parents consider a distance of 3 km too far for young children to walk. Reducing that distance necessarily implies the need for more and smaller schools, rather than fewer and larger schools, for as distance decreases the population in the catchment area falls. Multigrade teaching, then, must be an integral part of the school planning strategy to ensure the efficient utilization of facilities, although this has proven difficult to achieve.

Countries exhibit a common tendency to plan for larger schools rather than smaller schools, on the assumption that larger schools yield economies of scale, thereby lowering per student operating costs. Across African countries, a standard school is generally built of one or several blocks, each containing two or three classrooms. Resources are allocated by classroom block, using the application of some minimum norms using a one-grade, one-classroom model of about 40–45 children per classroom. In Ethiopia, for example, the smallest primary school is a four-classroom model with one teacher for each grade (1–4). In West Africa, the six-classroom model where each of the six grades of primary schooling can be taught in a separate classroom, is the most common model.

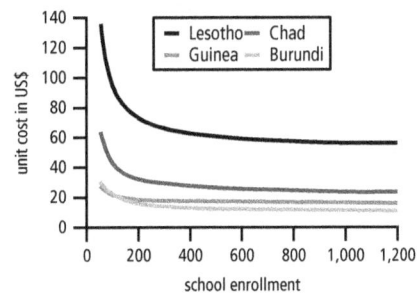

Figure 2.1 Economies of Scale in Primary Education: Expenditure per Student as a Function of School Enrollment

Source: World Bank 2005a, 2005l.

However, given the population density in many African countries, the average school model for rural areas needs to be the smallest that is economically feasible, rather than the largest. Figure 2.1 illustrates the results of an analysis of economies of scale across four African countries. Economies of scale mean that larger schools have lower unit costs, on average, than smaller schools: larger schools can better use the teachers and other resources provided, as there are more students to share in the fixed costs of running schools. In this sample, when schools enroll at least 200 students, or 33 students per grade in a typical six-grade, single-class school, the marginal cost of enrolling an additional child is at a minimum. In other words, although the marginal cost of adding one more student to a school is higher in small schools, larger schools have no significant marginal cost advantage over schools with 200 students. Therefore, for this sample of countries, the optimal minimum size of a primary school of 200 students represents the size beyond which the opportunity cost of students having to travel longer distances to a larger school may far outweigh any gains in lower operating costs per student. For capital costs, economies of scale do not apply for classrooms which are—or should be—proportional to enrollment. For latrine investment, economies of scale are nullified for latrines when the school enrolls at least 100 students since the recommended norm is two boxes for 100 students, allowing separate use of girls and boys (UNESCO 1986). The only economy of scale would come from the water supply, for which the unit cost would be the same regardless of school size.

If we apply the 200-student optimal size across Sub-Saharan countries, taking into account that primary school-age children represent an average of 16.9 percent of the population, an optimal school needs a catchment area with a minimum of about 1,200 inhabitants, as shown in Table 2.1. A six-classroom school needs a population of 1,400 inhabitants in the catchment area. A substantial proportion of villages falls under this threshold. In Senegal, for example, 96 percent of villages fall under this threshold, and more than half have fewer than 200 inhabitants. The average village in Madagascar has a population of 320 and requires one to two

Table 2.1 School Size and Minimum Village Population Required

Number of classrooms in a school	Number of pupils in the school	Ratio of school-age population (6–12)	Population of a village adequately served by the school
1	40	16.9	237
2	80	16.9	473
3	120	16.9	710
4	160	16.9	947
5	200	16.9	1,183
6	240	16.9	1,420

Source: Author's calculations.

classrooms.[1] In Mauritania, the population of the average village in the three eastern regions is 1 02 (Lehman et al. 2 004). Population is scattered in villages and hamlets, often more than 3 km apart. Figure 2.2 displa ys the geographical distribution of villages in eastern Chad in 2 004, showing that most villages are farther than 3 km from schools. In these circumstances the goal of providing all students with a place in school requires countries to plan for much smaller schools, organized in multigrade classes, or b y other methods, such as alternativ e year intakes.

Figure 2.2 Distribution of Villages and Schools in Eastern Chad (Mongo subprefecture)

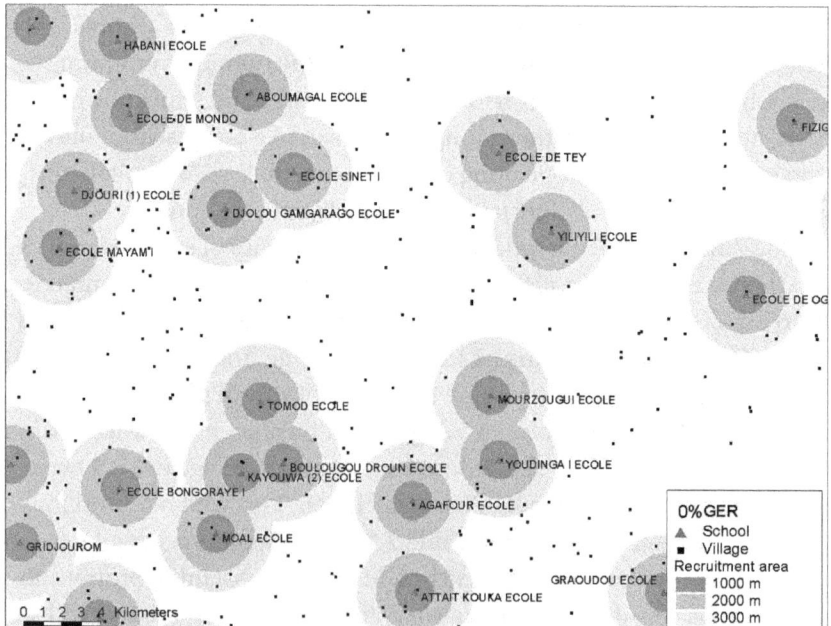

Source: Lehman et al. 2004.
Note: Points are villages. Dark circles are 1-km radius from existing schools, lighter circles are within a 2-km radius.

In areas where the distance between villages is large, the provision of schools would logically be on a one-per-village basis to keep the school close to the homes (Gould 1978).

Table 2.1 shows the possible efficient school according to village population, based on a norm of 40 pupils per classroom and using multigrade teaching. A one-classroom school providing six grades may effectively address the education needs of very small villages with a population below 240. In villages with populations between 240 and 475, a two-classroom school, with each classroom accommodating three grade levels, would cover the village needs. In villages of 475 to 710 inhabitants, a three-classroom school, with each classroom accommodating two grade levels, can be used. Finally, in villages between 710 and 950 inhabitants, a four-classroom school is necessary, with at least two classrooms functioning in multigrade.

Some countries have adopted such small-school models as part of their school-provision strategy, although this is rare to find in Africa, where countries have been reluctant to adopt multigrade teaching. Yet, multigrade teaching is not a new invention. It has been, and remains, a common strategy in developed countries to provide basic education more efficiently in rural areas where the population is widely dispersed. Further, considerable research evidence demonstrates multigrade teaching to be at least as effective as, and often more effective than, single-grade teaching in terms of learning outcomes. India, for example, adopted a policy of providing schools within a maximum of 1 km from home. To achieve this, it was necessary to have a strategy to provide quality education in small schools, schools that may have only one classroom.[2] In 1999, the government of Rajasthan recognized that the majority of the schools to be built were in remote areas with populations under 200, or 30 primary school-age children (World Bank 2001h). The government decided to revise the state norm of two-classroom schools and adopt a cost-effective, one-room building specifically designed to accommodate multigrade teaching while being easily expanded to two rooms if the enrollment so required. This experience demonstrates that school buildings can be flexibly designed to convert a one-classroom school into a two-classroom school as demand or population increases.

SCHOOL QUALITY NORMS

Few countries have school quality norms, and therefore a shared concept of a primary school. Although most countries have norms regarding how large a classroom should be, most have no norms for the provision of offices and storage spaces, libraries, or meeting and staff rooms. When such additional facilities exist, there are no rules regarding their composition and size. In the absence of such norms, most African countries have a plethora of construction projects, usually donor-financed, each following its own space norms and mix of facilities, depending on the financier. These decisions are most often donor-driven.

CLASSROOM SIZE

Many primary school classrooms in Africa are too small for the number of students they end up accommodating, partly because the norms applied regarding classroom space are too low. The norm for classroom size results from the combination of two other norms: (a) the number of students per classroom and (b) the unit space per student.

- Regarding the first norm, the World Bank has long recommended 45 students (Gould 1978), but most classrooms built in recent years were constructed by Ministries of Education to accommodate 40–60 students in desk-benches lined in rows, each seating at least two students as illustrated in the Senegal example in figure 2.3. Despite the evidence that class size does not have an impact on student learning when it is less than 60 students (Mingat 2003), a student-teacher ratio of 40:1 is currently used by the World Bank for Education for All (EFA) estimates because this ratio is observed in the highest-performing countries. (Mingat, Rakotomala, and Tan 2002).

Figure 2.3 Standard Classroom in Senegal in the 1990s

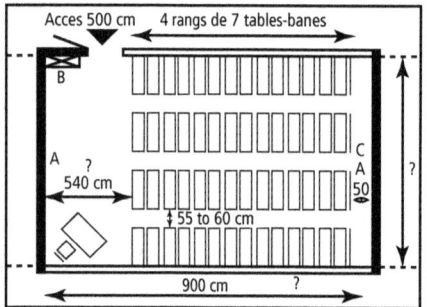

Source: DECS 1997.
Note: Used area: 56.95 m²; maximum capacity: 60 students.

Figure 2.4 Minimum Area per Student

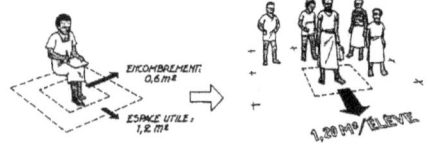

Source: World Bank 1993b.

- The second norm is related to the space needed by students and teacher to move in the classroom to perform learning/teaching activities. In the 1980s, the most common area norm was 1.0 m² per student (UNESCO 1986) still used by countries such as Senegal in the 1990s (figure 2.3). However, the unit space allocated by African countries increased to 1.2 m² per student, as recommended by IIEP and the World Bank as shown in figure 2.4 (Beynon 1998, World Bank 1993b). This norm is, however, the basic minimum. It provides only the space necessary for air flow, people flow, and rapid exit in case of emergency.[3] It provides for no other space, such as materials storage or a library corner, the latter having a proven impact on students' achievements.[4] It is not enough to manage multigrade learning, in which students need to work in independent groups while the teacher and his or her student-assistants circulate between groups. These requirements call for a norm of 1.4 m² per student.

Table 2.2 Average Net Classroom Area (m²) Over Time

	Average until 1986	Average 1986–90	Average 1991–95	Average 1996–2000	Average 2001–06
Burkina Faso					56.0
Burundi					72.3
Chad			63.0	58.5	
Ethiopia					40.5
Gambia, The				50.9	
Ghana	40.0	58.5		55.5	52.0
Guinea		48.0	48.0	50.5	56.0
Madagascar				54.2	50.0
Malawi					77.0
Mali				63.0	
Mauritania			49.5	49.5	51.5
Mozambique			62.1	56.2	56.6
Niger		60.9			56.0
Rwanda					48.0
Senegal	59.2	59.2	59.2	57.4	60.9
Uganda				48.2	
Zambia		54.6	54.0	53.0	52.0
Average	49.6	56.2	56.0	54.3	56.1

Source: Data collected from about 100 projects.

For classrooms built in recent years, the average size of the typical classroom is between 48–56 m². Table 2.2 shows the actual range of classroom sizes found among 17 African countries. In the majority of countries (11), the average classroom size falls precisely in this range, suggesting the application of the same space norms. The exceptions are Ethiopia, which has much smaller classrooms, and Burundi and Malawi, which have significantly larger classrooms. However, if many among these countries (Chad, Burundi, Madagascar, Mozambique, Rwanda, and Uganda) build classrooms to theoretically accommodate 45 students, in practice, they actually accommodate many more.

If the pedagogic value of the school facility and the efficient use of multigrade classrooms drive the norm, rather than minimal air and security considerations exclusively, this would result in larger classrooms than the current standard.

AUXILIARY PURPOSE-BUILT FACILITIES

In countries that have planned for office and storage space, most have made provision for one office and one storeroom for every three classrooms. This is a reasonable norm. The concept is often to take the opportunity of building a two- or

BOX 2.1   SCHOOL BUILDINGS AS A LEARNING AID AT NO COST

Building as a Learning Aid (Bâlâ) is an Indian initiative based on the idea that the physical environment provided by the school buildings can be used as a resource in the teaching/learning process, and can contribute toward pupils' learning and teachers' pedagogy. The Bâlâ approach makes use of any physical element of the building, which is turned into teaching/learning material at no additional cost. The image on the right shows an example of the use of doors for learning geometry. Window grills can be used to show fractions. Building repairs and maintenance can be creative teaching/learning exercises. The Bâlâ initiative includes nearly

150 design ideas that use elements of classrooms, corridors, and the outdoors to address the school curriculum (mathematics, science, language, creative expression, energy, and the environment). There is widespread dissemination and acceptance of these ideas in India. They also may be of great benefit in African schools.

Source: Vaipeyi 2005.

three-classroom block to include additional space between two of the classrooms, or at the end of the building. Plans of these classroom-blocks can be seen in Appendix 2. Such additional space is low cost, since one-quarter or one-half of its walls are already paid for as classroom walls. Table 2.3, which is built on a sample of 12 projects financed by 17 different donors in nine countries, shows that the ratio of additional space necessary to accommodate these two additional rooms averages only about 20 percent of the classroom area when using this strategy.

Practices vary greatly both within and across African countries in the inclusion of other purpose-built facilities, such as libraries, laboratories, home economics rooms, canteens, boarding facilities, and sometimes housing for teachers. When considering these facilities, one must rigorously assess the costs and benefits, as well as the decision rules that would guide resource allocations for these facilities. Such facilities have high direct costs and significant opportunity costs since the resources required may be better spent on higher-priority items, such as classrooms, latrines, or a potable water supply. In Ethiopia, for example, a country with only 32 percent of rural children enrolled in primary school in 2000, many primary schools are endowed with libraries and laboratories (World Bank 2005f).

Table 2.3 Office and Storage as Percentage of Classroom Area in 10 Selected Projects

	Net area per classroom m²	Gross area per classroom m²	Expanded gross area per classroom					Difference between extended gross and gross (%)	Project name	Financers
			Classrooms	Office	Store	Other	m²			
Burkina Faso	63.8	70.4	3	1	1		86.2	123	Panier commune	Canada, the Netherlands, IDA
Gambia, The	54.9	59.4	3	1	1		75.3	127	Primary Education Project	IDA
Ghana	55.5	60.2	3	1	1		73.3	122	Future in Our Hands	Sweden
	66.2	71.1	2	1	1		82.2	116	Microproject Program	EU
Guinea	48.7	53.0	1	1	0		57.8	109	Primary School Project in Medium and Low Guinea	KfW
	56.0	60.6	1	1	0		69.9	115	Primary schools in forest region	PlanGuinea
Mozambique	55.3	61.4	2	1	1	1	90.7	148	Education Sector Program, Rural Primary School Project	IDA, IDB
Niger	60.9	65.7	3	1	1		72.6	111	PADEB	IDA
Senegal	57.0	63.4	2	1	1		74.5	117	PEQT	World Bank, AfDB
Uganda	48.2	54.0	1	1	0		66.6	123	School Facility Grant	FDID, United Kingdom, the Netherlands
Zambia	47.2	52.9	3	0	1		64.2	121	Social Recovery Fund	World Bank
	52.4	58.3	3	4	2		73.9	127	BESSIP	Danida, DFID, Finland, Ireland, the Netherlands, Norway, GRZ
Average 1	55.5	60.9					73.9	122	12 projects, 17 donors	
Average 2	55.5	60.9					72.4	119	Same as above without Mozambique	

Source: Plans of the facilities provided by Group 5 and collected by Theunynck.
Note: For a complete list of acronyms, see p. xv.

Table 2.4 Unit Cost of Teacher Housing in Selected Countries

Country	Unit cost of teacher housing (US$)	Year
Burkina Faso	13,125	2004
Gambia, The	18,039	1997
Ghana	9,667	2001–03
Malawi	12,643	2006
Mozambique	10,534	1999–2005
Uganda	8,388	2004
Zambia	17,650	2004
Average 7 countries	12,191	

Source: Group 5; ST.

However, a recent review concluded that neither type of facility was used for its intended purpose. Worse yet, due to their purpose-specific design, neither could be easily used as a general purpose classroom and, therefore, both types remained unused (Theisen 2002).

Teacher housing is a somewhat different issue but equally important because it is often advocated as a strategy to attract teachers to teach in rural areas and to reduce high rates of absenteeism due to travel to and from school. Sometimes this is a necessity in remote areas due to a lack of housing and of a housing market. At other times, teacher housing is viewed as an additional incentive. However, teacher housing is costly. Table 2.4 shows that the average cost of teacher housing in select African countries ranges between US$10,000 to US$18,000, or between the cost of one to two classrooms in those countries. Although several countries have experimented with providing teacher housing in rural areas, to our knowledge, none of the programs have been evaluated. In light of the cost and absence of research demonstrating its cost effectiveness, teacher housing should not be considered as a necessary part of a standard minimum school infrastructure package Each country must determine whether building houses for teachers is the most cost-effective strategy to attract and retain teachers in remote areas and reduce absenteeism. It should then set strict criteria and decision rules regarding the allocation of these resources.

INEFFICIENCIES OF CENTRALIZED PLANNING

Through at least the 1980s, and still in many countries today, school location planning remains centralized at the level of the Ministry of Education (MoE) or its branch offices. Under this model, the process of school planning and the decisions made follow a top-down, centrally managed, and often supply-driven approach. Based on norms regarding distance, space, and minimum and maximum acceptable class sizes, the MoE determines whether a school should be built and where, often with inadequate consultation with communities themselves.

This centralized process matches the centralized nature of government in many African countries, and is convenient for donors, who generally transfer their financing for school infrastructure through projects with the MoE rather than through the government budget, as well. However, experience shows that this approach has resulted in numerous inefficiencies. First, it often results in inappropriate decisions on school size and location that compromise the achievement of the EFA and Millennium Development Goals for education because MoEs tend to apply norms mechanically, to treat school mapping as a desk exercise, to use poor and outdated information, to fail to consult with communities, and to use staff that are often insufficiently qualified—generally, former teachers with only short-term training in education planning. A further weakness of centralized school planning is its lack of transparency. Decision criteria are not well known outside the MoE, and allocation decisions can be more easily influenced by political intentions rather than relative need. As a result of these flaws, it should not be surprising to find schools that are inappropriately located, sometimes in the middle of nowhere, schools that are under- or oversized, and some populations that are better served than others.

CONCLUSION

The experience with school planning demonstrates that, in order to reach all children and efficiently utilize resources, countries must move away from large school models in rural areas in favor of a network of smaller multigrade schools that are located in each village. When the school-age population in the village falls under 20, however, other methods of providing access to education for these children—without construction—should be considered, such as distance education or correspondence.

To make this switch from planning for larger schools equidistant from communities to smaller schools close to home requires that countries change current planning and resource allocation norms and practices relating to distance and school size. The distance norm must be reduced to under 2 km at a maximum, the number of classrooms should be determined on the actual population size in each village, and the classroom size should allocate at least 1.4 m^2 per student to accommodate a resource corner and the management of multiple grades within the same classroom. Because one standard model will not suit all circumstances, MoEs should provide guidelines and a menu of models depending on the population size, rather than rigidly applying the same norms across all communities. Furniture models require similar flexibility.

Community and local government input into the development of these norms and their direct involvement in school location decisions must become common practice.

Countries must also adopt minimum infrastructure requirements regarding the mix of facilities and land requirements that constitute a productive, healthy, and safe learning environment for children. Whereas it may be debatable whether this minimum school facility package should include offices, enclosures, and other adjunct facilities, it should include sanitary facilities, the availability of potable water, and furniture as an integral part of the school design while providing guidelines for the allocation of resources for these other facilities. Addressing the need for water and sanitation will require the MoE to provide a menu of simple and economic water supply systems and latrines adapted to the different local conditions, and ensuring not only the provision of these facilities in new schools but also retrofitting all existing schools that lack them.

These norms, once established, should be used by all infrastructure projects, whether they are financed by the government or by development partners. Sadly, this is not the case today. There is little evidence that governments and donors are harmonizing their approaches. Senegal provides an illustrative example where the MoE adopted a sector strategy in 2000 that was endorsed by the local donor community. Nevertheless, donors continue to finance different menus of facilities IDA, for example, finances a package of facilities that includes classrooms, office and storage, a four-hole latrine, and a well. Multisectoral programs managed by local governments or communities finance latrines, a water supply, and sometimes fencing. On the other hand, the government of Senegal, the African Development Fund and OPEC, which together represent 60 percent of the total number of classrooms built during 2000–04, do not finance any nonclassroom facility (Dupety 2005a). Guinea, The Gambia, and Uganda provide useful counterexamples, but unfortunately they are not the norm. In Guinea, for example, a standard facility package was promoted by UNESCO in 1990 and subsequently followed by all donors. The package includes a three-classroom bloc, an office, a storage area, a block of five latrines, and a well. Similar approaches were adopted in The Gambia and Uganda.

CHILDREN WITH SPECIAL NEEDS

In addition to distance barriers, school facility location and design often hinder the accessibility of school to children with physical disabilities who cannot climb stairs or access classrooms with their wheelchairs. In some countries, children of school age living with mobility disability is estimated at 3 percent (Christian Blind Mission and International Center for Eye Health 2006). Zambia, one of the few countries to track the information on pupils with disabilities, records that 1 percent of enrolled students have physical disabilities (Group 5 2006e). Yet solutions are simple and not costly when built into the school planning process and school design itself. Appropriate solutions include paying careful attention to the topography of the school site to provide accessible routes, minimizing stairs by avoiding multiple school levels, and providing wider door openings and building ramps. Including these aspects in the planning and design of schools is far less costly than retrofitting existing schools (Lynch 1994, Baquer and Sharma 2005, Steinfeld 2005).

The latrine design should allow students with physical disabilities to use them. Almost no countries have specific disabled-friendly architectural designs for latrines; Uganda is an exception. The cost of making one latrine per school accessible and usable to physically disabled children involves a larger internal area and door, with handles on inner walls. The cost with these additions is low compared with the overall cost of a latrine-block.

NOTES

1. This is in line with the current distribution of schools, which shows that half of the schools had one or two classrooms in 2006 and 71 percent had three classrooms or fewer (MENRS 2007).

2. Another interesting example is the United States where the Single Teacher Schools (STC) accounted for 63 percent of the schools in 1930 and 47 percent in 1950. The STC model gradually disappeared by the end of the century with the expansion of the school bus system, which made it possible to enroll most primary students in larger schools.

3. The minimum norm of 1.0 m^2 is a mandatory security requirement in public places, such as theaters, where the public is seated in rows facing the screen or the stage (Neufert 2006).

4. In OECD countries, the existence of library materials in schools explains 2.5 percent of the variation in mathematics performance, whereas the quality of infrastructure explains only 1 percent of the variation, according to the Program for International Student Assessment-PISA (Knapp et al.).

CHAPTER 3

Classroom Construction Technology

Whereas the planning and decision norms largely affect the efficiency and effectiveness of school infrastructure inv estments, the school construction technology employed influences the cost, durability, and ability to scale up construction to the level required. By school construction technology, we mean the materials, engineering, and w orkmanship that are needed for building functional and durable facilities.

The vast experience of African countries over the past 30 years with various forms of school construction technology rev eals tw o main patterns . First, "inno vative" technologies that w ere intended to lo wer the cost of school infrastructure and increase the v olume ha ve done neither . Y et, these technologies are continually resurrected at various times, mainly by donors, with the same results Second, the use of the very same technology results in a wide range of costs depending on the implementation arrangements.

This section review s the experience with construction technology in Sub-Saharan Africa and the lessons learned; the next section review s the efficiency of the implementation arrangements when using the same technology.

Countries have built classrooms with fiv e main types of technologies that w e shall call (1) the *classic classroom,* (2) the *shelter model,* (3) the *local materials and appropriate technology classroom,* (4) the *prefabricated classroom,* and (5) the *modern construction model.*

THE CLASSIC CLASSROOM

The classic classroom accounts for the v ast majority of toda y's stock of long-lasting classrooms in Africa. This very popular architectural model has been used, with slight adaptations, in almost all school construction programs implemented by governments, communities, contract management agencies, and development partners. Among 228 construction projects in our sample carried out over the past 30 years, 91 percent involved construction of the classic classroom.

Figure 3.1 The Most Common Classic Classroom Type

- **Floor**: in concrete (100% of the projects)
- **Walls**: in block masonry (100%) broken down in load-bearing walls (60%) or non-load-bearing walls with concrete columns (40%)
- **Ring-beam** in concrete (66% of the projects)
- **Roofs**: generally in corrugated metal sheets (80% of the projects) on steel trusses (45%) or wooden trusses (35%)

An example from The Gambia

Source: Synergy 1997a.

Figure 3.1 pro vides an illustration of the classic model from the Gambia. A dditional examples from other countries are in Appendix 2. The review of about 100 projects shows that, typically, the floor is made of concrete with a smooth top screed. W alls are made of cement-block masonry or fired-bricks , and are either load-bearing (60 percent of projects) or nonload-bearing with concrete columns (40 percent of projects). A concrete ring-beam is essential for structural stability and wind and earthquake resistance although only an estimated 66 percent of the projects review ed have them. R oofs are generally (80 percent) made of modern materials , typically corrugated metal or asbestos-cement sheets , placed on steel or w ooden trusses. The remaining 2 0 percent used concrete slabs on concrete beams. Window spaces, suitable to any climate and lighting need, can be easily accommodated without technical constraints

The advantages of the classic classroom are several. First, the technology applied in the classic classroom is similar to that applied b y small- and medium-size contractors in the formal and informal sector in the country when building lo w-cost housing. Since the housing industry represents about 80 percent of the construction industry in all countries, and a large share of housing is built b y craftsmen in the informal sector, most local contractors and craftsmen are familiar with modern building materials and technology, such as cement blocks and corrugated iron roofing sheets.[1]

Second, b y applying technologies that are broadly used in the country b y small- and medium-size contractors and the informal sector, countries have been able to significantly scale up classroom construction when the model is combined with an efficient procurement and contract management process.

Third, because they are built from modern and "classic" technology, the solidity and durability of classic classrooms can easily comply with n ational or international technical norms—ev en in earthquake-vulnerable countries—and the compliance of their design and construction process with these norms can be checked by external controllers.

Fourth, the externalities of using the classic model are significant both in terms of growing the local construction industry and in impro ving standards and skills more generally in the industry. The school building can provide a model for other buildings, particularly houses for lo w- and moderate-income people, by demonstrating the effectiv eness of a few inexpensiv e technical impro vements, such as a solid foundation and concrete ring-beam, which are also desirable in homes. Further, as small contractors of the informal sector become increasingly familiar with these technologies, they are in a better position to promote them and advise their clients accordingly (see box 3.1).

Fifth, the classic classroom is a more politically and socially accepted model, one to which countries return once external promoters of alternative technologies have gone. This is because parents prefer buildings similar to the type of housing that they themselves would build if they had resources sufficient to finance a more durable house than one built of local materials.

BOX 3.1 SCHOOL CONSTRUCTION PROGRAMS: A CHANCE FOR THE INFORMAL SECTOR

The explosion of the informal sector in Africa during the recent past is a structural situation that has an impact on the future. The micro- and small enterprises will remain the backbone of most of developing countries. The informal economy provides the bulk of the nonagricultural jobs: 87 percent in Ghana; 85 percent in Cameroon; and from 67 to 78 percent in Benin, Burkina Faso, Côte d'Ivoire, Mali, Niger, Senegal, and Togo. Within the informal sector, the construction subsector is quite active in developing countries—as the craftsmen-construction industry is in developed countries. In Senegal, the informal sector provides 80 percent of the total employment in the construction sector, which occupies 15 percent of the total manufacturing labor (2004). The informal construction sector is highly linked to the formal construction sector; the former providing to the latter the bulk of its supply in materials and business through subcontracts.

Every year in Africa, about 65,000 classrooms are built by governments and communities, providing about US$600 million of business opportunities for the construction sector. In most countries the informal sector is currently building more than half of these schools but without norms and standards. Through Ministry of Education (MoE) construction programs, AGETIPs, and Social Fund projects, several countries have successfully opened the school construction business to the informal sector (such as Senegal, Niger, Mali, Mauritania, and Uganda) and therefore have moved to mass production in line with EFA objectives. While AGETIPs have opened the business to the group of small- and medium-sized enterprises, social funds, and some MoEs (such as Mauritania) have widened it to craftsmen and microenterprises. According to this study, EFA calls for 200,000 classrooms a year to close the classroom gap and to replace substandard and overage classrooms. This represents between US$1.35 billion and US1.85 billion of construction business opportunities, without counting the business of building toilets, water supplies, and other school facilities. This represents between US$200 million to US$250 million per year of salary volume.* Only massive involvement of the informal sector would allow countries to face such a challenge. In addition, in most African countries the formal construction sector is already overstressed, with increasing opportunities for large contracts resulting from the recent economic upturn. Such countries therefore have a tendency to subcontract school construction to smaller contractors of the informal sector who execute the works.

Compared with all other buildings, a classroom is the simplest type of building to erect. Building normed classrooms is the best opportunity for small-scale informal contractors to learn the minimum technical specification to make a building durable. School construction programs are irreplaceable opportunities to improve the skills of the informal construction sector, if they are given the opportunity to compete for local small contracts and receive adequate site supervision. Last but not the least, the informal construction sector offers local job opportunities to postprimary or postjunior secondary graduates.

Source: Charmes 2001; DIAL 2007; Haan 2001; ILO 2002a; Johanson and Adams 2004; Kante 2002.
Note: *On the basis of about 15–16 percent of construction costs for salaries (AGETIP 2004; Faso Baara 2006a).

However, the increasing use of the classic technology did not translate into a uniform cost of construction. Unit costs vary widely within a country, even when the architectural design and technology are the same. Table 3.1 shows an example from Senegal, where a large array of government and donor-funded projects, using a similar architectural design and technology, achieved costs ranging from a low of US$6,700 to a high of US$48,000, more than seven times as expensive. This situation obtains in other countries as well. This suggests that the architectural design and technology are only one determinant of the cost of classroom construction. The other determinants lie elsewhere, such as in the procurement and management arrangements.

THE SCHOOL SHELTER

The shelter model can be an efficient way to drive down the costs of classroom construction. There are, however, a number of challenges associated with this model, and so far none of the experiments have ultimately taken root.

Table 3.1 Range in Unit Costs of the Classic Classroom Technology in Senegal

	General project data			Technology		Implementation/procurement arrangements				Unit costs			
Project name	Usual project acronym	Years	Number of class-rooms	Gross area m²	Materials	Funding agency	Executing agency	Procurement agency	Procurement method	Per classroom US$	US$ per m²	Index	Source
Primary Education Development Project	PEDP	1987–94		61.50		IDA	MoE	MPW	ICB	13,200	215	2.0	a
School Construction Project III	OPEP-III	2000–04	125	67.34		OPEP	MoE	MoE/DCES	NCB	9,118	135	1.3	b
School Construction Project	BID	2000–04	500	67.34		IDB	MoE	PCU	ICB	17,811	264	2.5	b
School Construction Project IV	JICA-IV	2000–04	323	65.34	cement	JICA/Japan	JICA	JICA/Japan	In Japan	47,764	731	7.0	c
Education For All Project -1	EFA-1	2000–04	1,000	63.38	block	IDA	MoE	AGETIP	NCB	9,190	145	1.4	d
National Rural Infrastructure Project	NRIP	2000–04	67	63.38	walls, corrugated iron roof	IDA	MoRD	Local gov	LCB	8,493	134	1.3	d
Education Supply Improvement Project	PAOES	2000–04	345	65.17		DFA/France	AGETIP	AGETIP	NCB	12,575	193	1.8	b
Communal Support Project	PAC	2000–04	15	63.38		IDA	Local gov	AGETIP	NCB	8,992	142	1.4	b
Social Development Fund Project	PFDS	2001–04	115	63.38		IDA	AFDS	Communities	LCB	6,655	105	1	d
Government School Construction Program	BCI	2000–04	4,134	67.34		Gov/BCI	MoE	MoE/DCES	NCB	8,392	125	1.2	b

Source: (a) World Bank 1995g; (b) Dupety 2005; (c) World Bank 2000d; (d) Diouf 2006.
Note: For a complete list of acronyms, see p. xv.

Figure 3.2 The School Shelter Model: The Example of Niger

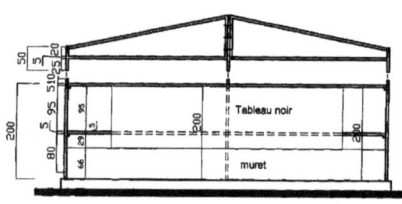

Source: Zerbo 2008.

The shelter is typically composed of a concrete foundation and floor. Concrete piles support a modern material roof with girder support. Often the roof is made of corrugated iron sheets supported by steel trusses, although there are variations on this model across countries. In Niger, for example, the shelters are supported by a 50 mm gauge steel-tube structure supporting a thatched roof (see figure 3.2). The structure is generally built by a contractor, whereas the walls are expected to be built by communities using various local materials.

The shelter model can be a useful strategy within a particular context, notably during emergency situations where a large number of classrooms are needed rapidly at low cost. Since the structure is made of modern materials, it is safe and durable, having a life span of about 25 to 30 years. In addition, shelters are significantly less costly than fully complete classrooms. In Ghana, for example, between 1980–96, more than 16,500 pavilion-classrooms were built at a low average cost of less than US$60/m², compared with US$154/m² for the classic classroom (Group 5 2006b). This approach contributed significantly to the dramatic increase in primary school enrollment and completion rates (World Bank, OED 2004). Malawi tested the shelter approach in 1995 to cope with the million additional children who flooded primary schools after the 1994 decision for free primary education (IEG 2006b). The Ministry of Education (MOE) planned to build 1,600 classrooms[2] with the objective to cut costs by half from US$4,000 for classrooms previously built by the PIU. (World Bank 1995d). Since 2003, Niger is currently building shelter-classrooms at a cost of US$62 per m², less than half the cost of US$147 per m² for the classic model (World Bank 2003g). This approach is currently promoted in Burundi by UNICEF.

Yet, despite the simplicity, adaptability, durability, and low cost of the shelter model, most countries that have used the approach have abandoned this model in favor of the classic model for several reasons.[3] First, community completion of the classrooms has tended to be negligible, so many classrooms remain in a state of permanent noncompletion. Second, the shelter model tends to be accepted by communities and governments only when the conditions are dire, such as following a natural disaster, or in the poorest of countries with a large share of out-of-school children, such as Niger. Otherwise, from a social perspective, the shelter model often represents second-class status and offers little visible evidence of a more hopeful future. Malawi abandoned the approach for an additional reason: only half of the shelters were erected by project's end, due to procurement issues related to importing the structures through ICB. Niger decided in 2007 to drop the shelter approach in favor of the classic classroom.

BOX 3.2 THE SHELTER MODEL IN GHANA

School enrollment in Ghana was about 1.3 million children in the early 1980s and the status of facilities was very low. In 1986 the government embarked on an ambitious reform program to boost enrollment and adopted the shelter approach to build a large number of classrooms quickly. The IDA-financed projects (Education Sector Adjustment Credits), followed by the Primary School Development Project, spend 30 to 67 percent of their resources in school building.

A total of 16,500 shelters were built between 1986 and 1996, an average of 1,650 per year. This was possible because of the very low unit cost of the shelters built at US$/m² 60, only 40 percent of the cost of a classic classroom. This was, indeed, a highly cost-effective way to invest in facilities. The program is estimated to account for a 4 percent increase in enrollment by reducing distance to school, and to dramatically increasing the number of hours of instruction by reducing the number of classrooms not used under rain, from more than half to less than one-third.

Despite a huge remaining backlog of classes without classrooms (still 19,000 in 1995–96 out of a total stock of 70,000), the government decided in 1993 to abandon the shelter model in favor of the classic model, which was financed under the subsequent program (BESIP).

Source: OED 2004, Group 5 2006b.

LOCAL MATERIALS AND APPROPRIATE TECHNOLOGY CLASSROOMS

The 1960s through the early 1980s was a period of increasing interest and experimentation in "appropriate technologies." The concept of appropriate technology was derived from Gandi's ideas and action on self-reliance. In the world of development, the concept first appeared around 1957 with the establishment of the Canadian Brace Research Institute, which was set up to develop appropriate technology concepts and applications. The movement picked up steam after 1965 with the creation of the Intermediate Technology Development Group, established by the economist Ernst Schumacher, to explore alternative technologies in agriculture, construction, water, and energy.[4] This movement was fueled by the series of oil crises and oil price hikes in the 1970s and early 1980s, which gave impetus to the search for substitutes for oil-based materials, such as cement. Further, several influential economists of the time began warning of the limits to the growth of industrialization and its negative effects on the environment (Meadows et al. 1972, Schumacher 1980). For the prophets and gurus, it was urgent to find new oil-free technologies and put humans at the center of production, rather than machines. Joining the movement, the development community enthusiastically supported the search for more appropriate technologies across all sectors with the blessing of the United Nations, which proposed to support "another development" (Hammarskjöld 1975).[5]

In the construction sector, appropriate technology largely translated into the use of local materials for construction, mainly through methods to improve the stability and durability of earth as a construction material. This approach was significantly influenced by a popular publication, *Architecture for the Poor* (1969), written by the prominent Egyptian architect Hassan Fathy. Application of this approach started in Latin America with soil-cement technology and later spread to Africa during the 1980s. Engineers and researchers went to work on developing appropriate technologies, such as press-compression and oil- or cement-stabilization. In the process, the technology of compressed earth, originally invented in the 18th century by François Cointereaux, was rediscovered.[6] Other techniques to save wood, a diminishing resource in many African countries, promoted forgotten traditional architectural forms, such as Nubian vaults and domed-earth roofing. Figures 3.3 and 3.4 show examples of this technology in school facilities.

Figure 3.3 The Earth-built Literacy Center in Chical Built by the NGO Development Workshop in 1980

Source: Development Workshop.

Figure 3.4 A Typical Local Materials Classroom: Niger IDA-financed Education II Project

Source: Photo Christian Rey, cited in Theunynck 1994.

With their past history of earth construction, African countries were highly receptive to this movement. Development agencies showed keen interest and provided generous support to test earth-based and plaster (gypsum) construction designs for schools in Africa. Throughout the 1970s and 1980s, African countries implemented hundreds of experiments supported by a large range of donors including most bilateral donors, the World Bank, the African Development Bank, the EU and UN Agencies particularly UNESCO, which financed a large number of school prototypes through its regional offices in Senegal (Bureau Regional pour l'Education et le Développement en Afrique, BREDA) and Sudan.[7] One of its best-known experiments is the training school of Nianning in Senegal, which was widely considered a masterpiece of sand-cement-vault technology and received the 1978 Aga Khan Award for Islamic Architecture. In 1984, a French university opened a master's degree program in earth-based architecture with the support of CRATerre, a specialized research institution established in 1979. (Refer to Appendix 3 for other prototypes, such as the Koranic school of Malika in Dakar, which also received an Aga Khan Award, and the BREDA prototype of Diaguily in Mauritania.)

These hundreds of appropriate technology experiments were implemented by African governments mainly through cooperation with international NGOs such as the British Development Workshop, the Swiss Association pour le Développement d'une Architecture et d'un Urbanisme Africains, the French Association Française des Volontaires du Progrès, the Groupe de Recherche et d'Etudes Technologiques, and CRATerre, operating under Memorandums of Agreement with concerned governments.[8] As contractors, their obligations included providing materials and tools, hiring labor, and training and supervising the workers.

Following three decades of investment in experimentation, from 1970–2000, the results failed to confirm the expected benefits in three main areas. The buildings constructed in local materials, such as improved earth or gypsum-plaster, or with vaulted or dome technology, proved more expensive and less durable than those built by the formal or informal sector with modern technologies (Wyss 2005). The cost of walls built with compressed soil-cement blocks was 30 to 100 percent higher per square meter than walls built with classic cement blocks (CRATerre 1989, Theunynck 1994, Wyss 2005). Waterproofing vaulted and domed roofs proved extremely difficult and costly. For example, the Institut Panafricain pour le Développement, which built such buildings with financing from the Swiss cooperation had a 38 percent cost overrun because, after construction, the vaults and domes needed to be waterproofed with a paxalumin cover. Even so, the building remained beset by roof leaks (Theunynck 1994). The durability of the buildings was also very limited; many lasted less than 10 years before crumbling.[9] Such weak resistance in normal conditions leads to strong recommendations to avoid such types of technologies in earthquake-vulnerable regions.

A 1993 study comparing the direct costs of construction by the informal sector with projects promoting improved local materials concluded that, on average, the informal sector outperformed the local materials projects. Evaluation of recent experiences of earth-vaulted rooms conducted in 2002–05 in Burkina Faso provides similar conclusions (Wyss 2006b).[10]

Table 3.2 shows the typical range of unit costs associated with local materials technology pilots compared with the classic classroom. In three pilots, costs of the local materials and classic classroom were comparable. In all other cases, however, the local material classrooms were on average more than twice the cost of the classic classroom constructed by the formal and informal sectors, using modern technology based on cement-walling and modern roofing. Further, the transfer of the appropriate technology from promoters to users required costly technical assistance from international agencies, NGOs, and consulting firms for the training of

Table 3.2 Unit Cost of Local Material Technology Compared to Informal Sector

Country	Project/prototype	Year	Donor/implementer	Type of technology	Durability	Cost per m² (current US$)	Source	Cost per m² of classic construction by informal sector	Source
Senegal	Training Center in Nianning	1977	UNESCO	Sand-cement walls and vaults	Good	56	a		h
	School of Derkle in Dakar	1983	EU	Plaster/gypsum walls and vault	Collapsed in 1988	131	b	48	
	Coranic School of Malika	1979	Daara Association (NGO)	Sand-cement walls and vaults	Good	132	c	(in 1980)	
	Third Education Project	1983	World Bank/firm	Sand-cement walls and vaults	n.a.	117	d		
Mauritania	Low-cost housing project in Rosso	1980	ADAUA (NGO)	Stabilized-earth bricks walls and vault	Dilapidated	70	e	44	f
	Primary school in Diaguily	1988	UNESCO	Sand-cement walls and vaults	Good	98	f	(in 1982)	
Mali	Primary schools	1982–87	AFVP (NGO)	Stabilized-earth bricks walls roofs in corrugated iron	n.a.	31–51	g	55	h
	Low-cost housing project in Banconi	1982	France/ACA	Stabilized-earth bricks walls roofs in corrugated iron	n.a.	52	h	(in 1982)	
	Training Center Gabriel Cisse in Segou	1987	Church/Climats-Altech (Private firm + NGO)	Stabilized-earth bricks walls and vault	n.a.	115	i		
Niger	Literacy Center in Chical	1980	PNUD/Development Workshop (NGO)	Earth-bricks walls and vaults	n.a.	322	j	130	k
	Education III	1986	World Bank/MoE	Stabilized-earth bricks walls and vault	n.a.	160	k	75	

Source: (a) Dellicour et al., 1978 (11,500 Fcfa); (b) Theunynck 1994, p. 719; (c) Abdullac 1979, p. 37; (d) World Bank 2000d, Annex 12 (2,883,876 Fcfa), net area 55.6 m², gross area (less buttresses) 63.36 m²; (e) Theunynck 1994, p. 807; (f) UNESCO 1988, pp. 6–7; (g) Schools of Kalabankoro, Kambila, Kalifabougou—data from Derisbourg and AETA 1987; (h) ACA 1982, p. 58; (i) Houben and Guillard 1989, pp. 69–87; (j) DMN 1980, p. 7.
n.a. Not applicable.
Note: For a complete list of acronyms, see p. xv.

contractors, and skilled and unskilled construction workers. When these costs are taken into account the real price difference is much higher.

The use of local materials also failed to reduce cement consumption. A study comparing seven local materials projects shows that, even stabilized with only 4 to 6 percent of cement, earth bricks consume an average of about 100 kg of cement per cubic meter of stabilized compressed earth, slightly higher than the 95 kg of cement per cubic meter of cement hollow bricks (Theunynck 1994). Other studies indicate that walls made of earth-stabilized blocks require between 10 percent and 30 percent more cement than cement-block walls (Wyss 2005).

Further, the approach was difficult to scale up because it did not correspond to local know-how. The technology required a high level of skill among workers and local contractors, which was difficult to achieve, even on a small scale and with costly international assistance. Scaling up this model would not be feasible. For this reason, none of the school construction projects piloted in Burkina Faso, Niger, or Senegal with IDA financing provided convincing evidence to scale up the approach (World Bank 1995a; World Bank 1996d; World Bank 2004o).[11] A 1993 World Bank review of the experience of Sahelian countries concludes: "This research very quickly reached its limits, running into difficulties in transferring the know-how both to the formal and informal construction sectors" (Abeille and Lantran 1993).

Lastly, the classroom design was less appropriate for learning that those constructed by the modern sector. Due to the limited durability of stabilized earth or sand, walls were thick (or reinforced with numerous buttresses) and windows narrow. On one hand, this design generated improved climatic comfort in dry countries, particularly when roofs were vaulted which created important air-volume. On the other hand, the construction severely limited natural lighting making the classrooms too dark.

For all these reasons, local materials technology was never adopted by governments, communities, or local contractors. In all cases, the method failed to survive once the donor assistance ended. These lessons had already been learned as early as the late 1970s in Latin America, which experimented earlier than African countries. In 1978 the Brazilian government tested soil-cement technology for the construction of school buildings, financed by the World Bank. However, because the experimental program did not yield replicable results, the government decided to return to more traditional, modern methods (World Bank 1989a). By the end of the 1980s, construction in local materials had largely been abandoned in African countries and elsewhere, although periodically it continues to be resurrected.

The local materials appropriate technology approach not only failed for school construction, but also in low-cost housing.[12] And it applied to a range of materials and technologies, such as raw earth, fired bricks, stabilized earth, laterite cut blocks, gypsum-plaster, and bagged sand (Wyss 2004).[13] In very few countries, such as Mali where several large public buildings were erected using earth, such as the Bamako museum, few local contractors learned and tested the technology. Local materials research or implementation is now confined to architectural heritage and well-financed construction projects, such as hotels and restaurants. The huge volume of lessons learned from experience shows that one should not entertain any illusions about the capacity of local materials and appropriate technology to scale up low-cost school construction. Nevertheless, the concept is regularly revived: between 1997 and 2005 not less than three guides for earth construction were published.[14] It will probably regain support with the 2007 hike in oil price.

INDUSTRIALIZED PREFABRICATION

Prefabrication means that large portions of buildings, such as walls and roofs, are factory produced off-site, delivered, and assembled on-site. Compared with more traditional labor-intensive, on-site construction, prefabrication requires a larger capital investment to import building segments or to construct a plant to produce them. This higher cost is intended to be more than offset by savings in labor and mass production.

International experience with prefabrication dates to the 19th century. In the United States, prefabrication was introduced in the early 1800s to mass-produce affordable housing for the middle classes. Business boomed during the main gold rushes (1829–55) when thousands of buildings were shipped to mushrooming towns. At the turn of the 20th century, mass merchandisers, such as Sears and Roebuck, sold thousands of houses through catalogues These shops closed during the Great Depression of the 1930s, and prefabrication on a mass scale died out in the United States (Richman 1994). Ironically, at the same time that prefabrication died out in the United States, it became popular in Europe, where architects in France, Germany, Sweden, and Great Britain experimented with the application of principles of automobile manufacturing to mass-produce low-cost housing and improve its quality. The movement started in Germany in the 1930s with the Bauhaus, founded in 1919 by Walter Gropius and closed in 1933 by Mies Van der Rohe, and expanded after World War II with the reconstruction challenge.[15]

History has shown that, despite these numerous attempts, the construction sector is the unique production sector where industrialized mass-production has not taken root. In every country, even in the most industrialized, small construction projects are still generally built by small- and medium-size contractors at competitive prices compared to prefabricated buildings. As a result, the construction industry as a whole has remained labor intensive, composed of small- and medium-size contractors or enterprises (Cassimatis 1969, Barthélemy 1986). In France, for example, where the construction industry amounted to €72 billion in 2006, nearly 50 percent of the 342,000 enterprises registered in 2004 were

Figure 3.5 Technologies Used in United States Home Construction, by Region, 2001

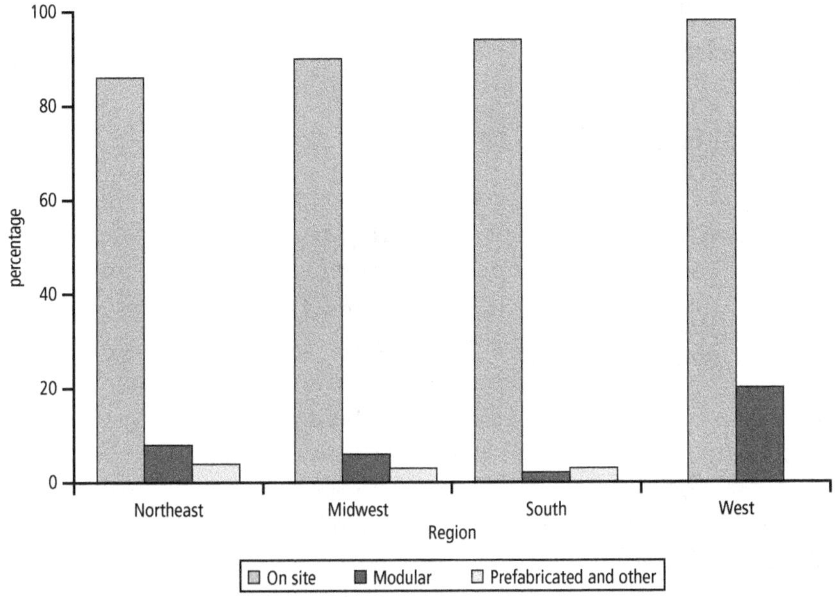

[Bar chart showing percentages of On site, Modular, and Prefabricated and other construction by Region (Northeast, Midwest, South, West). On-site construction dominates in all regions at approximately 85-98%.]

Source: SCHL 2003.

family-owned with no employees, and 40 percent had fewer than 9 employees. They account for more than 60 percent of the construction sector's production (INSEE 2004, Batiactu 2007).[16] Data on the construction sector show that in Japan, small and medium-sized builders represented 99 percent of the 565,000 construction firms in 1996 (Sugi 1998). In the United States, there are about 2 million construction firms and their number has not changed since the 1970s. Most are one-person firms (Finkel 1997). Figure 3.5 shows that, in the United States, in 2001, less than 2 percent of the new houses were prefabricated, and only about 4 percent were built with prefabricated modular elements (refer to Appendix 4 for a brief history of industrialization in the construction industry worldwide).

The industrialization failure is due to three main factors. First, studies show that economies of scale are few in prefabricated buildings, particularly when the infrastructure is small and widely dispersed (Carassus 1987, Finkel 1997, Koskela and Vrijboeuf 2001). The exception is in situations where a large number of multistory buildings are constructed on the same site and labor is in short supply (Kin 2004).[17] This is clearly not the case with primary schools in Africa. Second, a 2001 ILO report concluded that prefabrication may be appropriate in economies where labor is expensive and there is full employment. However, in countries with low wages, surplus labor and high unemployment, such methods make little economic sense. Finally, the large number, and flexibility, of small- and medium-size enterprises has allowed them to adapt and remain highly competitive with large industrialized builders.

CLASSROOM PREFABRICATION

Decisions to opt for prefabrication are often based on misplaced notions among decision makers about the cost effectiveness and quality of prefabrication, compared with labor-intensive construction methods.

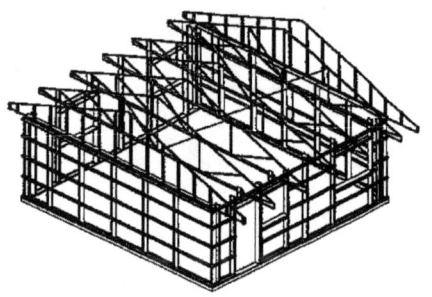

Figure 3.6 Prefabricated Classroom in Madagascar—The Steel Structure

Source: FID 2004b.

Mass production of classrooms through prefabrication is an attractive concept because of the predictable, and yearly repetitive, large numbers of identical rooms to be built. Prefabrication of classrooms was introduced in several countries during the 1970s, and continues to resurface periodically. Figure 3.6 shows an example of a prefabricated classroom in Madagascar.

Wherever prefabricated classrooms have been introduced, the approach was justified on the assumption that since classroom and school designs can be standardized, and technical specifications clearly established, prefabrication of classrooms could multiply supply more rapidly and at lower cost compared with labor-intensive methods. Yet when we examine the history of attempts at prefabricated classrooms, the results are extremely poor in terms of cost and delivery.

Table 3.3 summarizes the experience of five countries with prefabricated classrooms compared with the classic model. In all cases, the cost per m^2 was higher than the cost of the classic classroom constructed by small- and medium-size enterprises in the country. In the six countries, the cost of prefabrication ranged between 1.3 and 3 times higher than the classic classroom. Costs were consistently and substantially higher than originally estimated by between 1.2 and 1.4 times. Further, in all cases, delivery fell short of agreements both in terms of numbers of classrooms and agreed time frame. In Pakistan, only 5 percent of the classrooms contracted were delivered. In Madagascar, only 45 percent were delivered, and that with a 3-year delay.

Several factors explain these results:

- First, procuring suppliers for prefabricated classrooms requires international competitive bidding, since enterprises with the capacity to prefabricate buildings are generally found in developed countries. However, competition is

Table 3.3 Comparison of the Cost of Prefabricated Classrooms Compared with the Classic Model

	Classic Model (comparator)				Prefabrication of classrooms							
				Cost per classroom (current US$)			Cost per classroom in US$			%/ classic model	Number of classrooms		
Country	Years	Technology	Procurement method		Technology	Procurement method	Expected	Contracted	Actual		Contracted	Delivered	Source
Pakistan	1985–86		ICB	4,500	Lightweight wall panels	ICB	3,500	5,020	7,000	156		<5% of contract	a
Philippines	1994–05		LCB by MPW	10,000	Full prefab steel classroom	ICB	9,200		10,000	100		<75%	b
Ethiopia	2001–02	Cement block walls, corrugated iron roof	ICB	9,000	Precast wall panels	ICB			14,000	156		100%	c
Madagascar	2004–06		ICB by donors (average)	11,400	Modular prefab elements	ICB for materials NCB for work	10,000	9,500	11,400	100	1,400	45% three years later	d
			NCB-LCB by FID (average)	8,500						134			
Mozambique	2000–02		ICB	8,900	Full prefab classroom	ICB			26,500	298	375	100%	e

Source: (a) World Bank 1987b, pp. 15, 75, 113; World Bank 1995f, p.130; (b) Theunynck 1995; World Bank 1996c; (c) Theisen 2002; (d) MENRS 2007; (e) Group 5 2006c, pp. 19–20.
Note: For a complete list of acronyms, see p. xv.

44 • School Construction Strategies for Universal Primary Education in Africa

limited because few firms specialize in prefabrication. This limited competition drives up the cost and largely explains the significant difference in the cost originally estimated and the actual cost of production.

- Second, when the construction involves a large number of small buildings dispersed throughout the country, as is the case for primary schools, the cost of importing and transporting building segments to construction sites is much higher than that of transporting construction materials such as cement, lumber, tiles, or roofing sheets for on-site construction. Transport costs are amplified by the absence of usable roads. Indeed, transportation of building segments to many rural and remote areas is simply infeasible.
- Third, when industrialized classroom producers are foreign firms, they have little representation in the country and need to subcontract the on-site assembly work to local firms. Coordination between timely shipment to the country of industrialized items, transport to the sites, and timely operation of subcontracted national firms is problematic. The complexity and length of the implementation scheme are illustrated in figure 3.7.

Figure 3.7 Scheme of the Industrialized Prefabrication of Classrooms in Madagascar

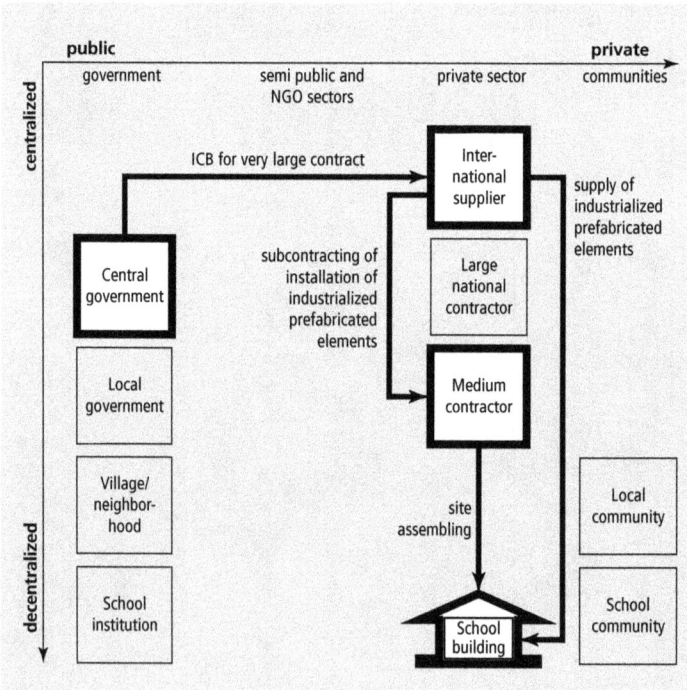

Source: Author's figure.

- Fourth, on-site assembly requires few but highly skilled, product-specific workers that are generally unavailable in the country (World Bank 1995f). This requires importation of these skills to train the few local workers required. However, even when training is provided, the transfer of skills and competencies to undertake this highly sophisticated work is difficult to achieve, given the current skill level in many African countries.
- Fifth, the durability of prefabricated classrooms is low and maintenance is complicated because industrialized panels are light structures that are highly vulnerable to shocks, and impossible to repair with the materials and technical capacity available. They cannot accommodate subsequent improvements, such as new electrical wiring because the installation will damage the infrastructure. Further, they do not facilitate instructional use because nothing can be nailed to the walls.
- Finally, the main cost savings associated with prefabrication is the savings in the cost of labor, which, ironically, is in abundant supply in Africa. Indeed, prefabrication does little to provide employment and to strengthen the local construction industry. In the absence of prefabrication, the local small- and medium-size enterprises and workers in the informal sector would be contracted to build the schools, thereby generating employment in rural areas and helping to improve the standards and quality of the local construction industry. Substituting prefabrication for local development can generate frustration in the communities since the investment has no impact on local employment, as shown in the case of the Philippines. Box 3.3 illustrates these problems in school construction in three countries that were early adopters of prefabrication for school construction, and one country currently attempting it.

The experience with prefabricated classrooms clearly points to the conclusion that prefabrication is not a viable solution to the challenge of scaling up the provision of primary school infrastructure in Africa. Despite the multiple attempts across both developed and developing countries, prefabrication has never succeeded in providing a solution to mass production of buildings and classrooms. The construction sector is the only sector that has stubbornly refused industrialization. Examples of prototypes of industrially prefabricated buildings are now of increasing interest for antiques dealers and collectors.[18]

THE MODERN CONSTRUCTION MODEL

During the 1970s and 1980s, modern technology for construction, suiting the technical capacity of the (often foreign) modern sector of construction, was promoted by European countries. For example, the European Union Fund promoted a model with a uniquely designed roof, consisting of welded metal frames, on the

BOX 3.3 THREE EXPERIENCES WITH PREFABRICATED CLASSROOM CONSTRUCTION

Pakistan and the Philippines were among the early adopters of prefabricated classroom construction technology. Madagascar is an example of a current attempt to replicate this failed model.

Pakistan. In the mid-1980s, the government of Pakistan adopted prefabrication to significantly increase the number of primary school classrooms, improve the quality of construction, and lower the average cost per classroom by at least 20 percent (from US$4,500 to less than US$3,500). The construction of 6,000 classrooms in three provinces—Baluchistan, North West Frontier Province, and Sindh—were put out for international competitive bidding to produce all-weather lightweight panels to be assembled on site. Only one bid from a local firm for 3,000 classrooms in Baluchistan and NWFP was considered responsive, but the firm was unable to carry out more than 5 percent of the contract for several predictable reasons. First, the main contractor lacked the necessary industrial experience and capital. Second, the transportation of prefabricated classrooms through the existing low standard routes and paths proved to be an insurmountable barrier. Third, the prefabricated classrooms called for precision in the preparation of the foundation and installation of the anchor bolts that local contractors could not achieve. To remedy this problem, the bidding process excluded local village contractors from the bidding process. This exclusion resulted in local resentment and on-site labor problems. In the face of all these issues, the contractor eventually defaulted and the cost per classroom ended up being at least double the cost initially estimated.

The Philippines. During the early 1990s, the Philippines constructed about 10,000 classrooms a year. Around 1995, the government opted to prefabricate 26,300 classrooms as a result of a recent ban on logging, as well as objectives to lower the cost of construction from US$10,000 to US$9,200 per classroom and simplify management by reducing the number of construction contracts it would have to manage. Firms in Manila prefabricated the steel buildings and delivered them to the sites where they were assembled in about two weeks. Although assembly time was rapid, any cost savings was eliminated by the actual cost of site preparation by local governments. Further, due to poor road and land conditions, more than 25 percent of the classrooms could not be transported to, or assembled on, the site. Finally, the sophisticated technology generated frustration in the communities because the investment had no impact on local employment and required unavailable high-tech technology for maintenance. The Philippines subsequently abandoned prefabrication in favor of conventional classroom construction technology.

Madagascar. In 2004, Madagascar opted to prefabricate classrooms in order to increase the gross primary school enrollment rate from 80 to 88 percent in the 2005–06 school year. The MoE selected a Contract Management Agency, the Fonds d'Intervention pour le Développement (FID), to manage the process on its behalf. The agency launched a limited international bidding process for the prefabrication of 1,400 classrooms among 10 international firms from five continents. Only three submitted proposals. The contract was awarded to a U.S. firm that subcontracted assembly work to domestic medium-size contractors. The contract provided for the full completion of works in 5.5 months (4 months for industrial production and shipment, and 1.5 months for on-site assembly) compared with 12 months for classrooms constructed by local contractors. The program was also expected to generate a 20 percent cost saving over the prevailing price of per classroom achieved by local contractors. After 3 years of implementation, less than half the classrooms had been delivered at a (pretax) cost of US$11,400. This was not lower than traditional classroom construction classrooms financed by donors through ICB, but more than one-third higher than the average of classrooms built by the FID under NCB through the CMA and community approaches, and 15 percent higher than the expected costs.

Sources: Pakistan: World Bank 1987b; World Bank 1995f. Philippines: Theunynck 1995; World Bank 1996e. Madagascar: Group 5 2005; MENRS 2007, Theunynck 2006.

top of which bowed iron sheets were soldered (see figure 3.8). The sophistication of the roof technology required technical capacity only available from large contractors in the modern construction sector. The roofing was almost twice the cost of a concrete roof executed by small- and medium-size enterprises, and four times the cost of a roof in corrugated metal sheets (Theunynck 1994). Overall, this model

Figure 3.8   The European Union Fund Model

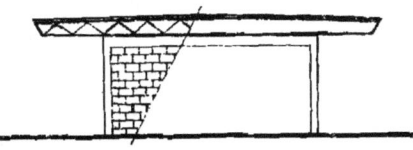

Source: European Union.

reached unit costs as high a US$500 per m^2 (UNESCO 1984). Although it had been built by the hundreds in every African country, countries abandoned this donor-driven model when the donor financing was discontinued.

CONCLUSION

No more testing is needed. The most "appropriate" technology for school construction is that which has the greatest potential of mass production at low cost on the local market, using small- and medium-size enterprises in the formal and informal sectors. This also means simple designs using technologies familiar to the local construction industry and generally means modern techniques—cement blocks for walls, corrugated-iron roofs, and reinforced concrete structure.

Figure 3.9 A Simple and Modest Classroom: The Mauritanian Model

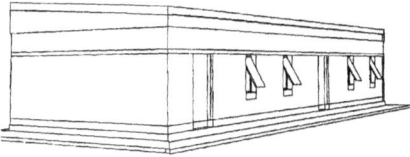

Source: PDEF Mauritania.

Figure 3.9 shows an example of such a design in Mauritania. The design has a life span of 25 years and is easily implemented by small-scale local contractors from the formal or informal sectors. This is probably the most modest model among all African classic models.[19] Since the mid-1980s, many countries in Africa have followed this approach and adopted the classic model. In Burkina Faso, Senegal, Niger, and Mali, reductions of construction costs by 30–50 percent were therefore made possible (Abeillé and Lantran 1993). In terms of technology, this route seems the most promising: it is consistent with historical construction trends, by which the informal sector moves fairly quickly, and it generally leads to lower costs.

Sadly, much of this has mostly remained donor driven. Nevertheless, through the large array of past and current projects financed by donors and governments, all African countries have now acquired enough experience in classroom design to easily move toward a standard set of classroom models to be applied by all projects, regardless of origin of funds. Indeed, they know by their own experience or that of others, what does not work: local materials and too-sophisticated modern technologies, including industrialized prefabrication. They may know that the approach of the shelter technology may be a solution, but not for the long term. They can also learn from their own experience that the simple modern technology of the "classic model" allows them to scale up school construction programs at affordable costs. Indeed, through the current extensive development of the informal construction sector, capital requirements, logistics, and skills exist in every country to scale up construction of the classic model, albeit at different levels of quality and cost. Success depends on strong cooperation with the local industry and the right choice of technology. It also depends on the willingness of governments with their supportive donors to take stock of lessons learned and to move toward a harmonized model. The Fast Track Initiative supports this movement under the Paris Declaration on harmonization.

NOTES

1. For example, in a 1992 survey in Burkina Faso, Yars (1999) finds that 71 percent of houses were built by craftsmen in the informal sector.
2. The shelter was called "shell" because of the shell-type steel structure test-piloted by UNICEF.
3. Ghana abandoned in 1996, Malawi in 2000, and Niger in 2007.
4. The Intermediate Technology Development Group is an international NGO founded in 1966 and registered in the U.K. that works in Latin America, Southern Africa, and South Asia. In 2006, it had 16,000 regular supporters specialized in helping people use technology for solutions to poverty.
5. In 1975, the UN Secretary General proposed "Another Development," and the UN supported the establishment of several centers for the research and promotion of appropriate technologies in Africa, such as the Center for Adapted Technologies in Mali. European universities and a large number of donors also provided support.
6. The technology of compressed earth bricks was first applied by François Cointereau in the 18th century, using a wine press. The appropriate technology efforts also renewed interest in the CINVA-RAM press invented in 1952 by Paul Ramirez, at the Centro Interamericano de Vivienda y Planeamiento in Bogota, Colombia.
7. For example, the World Bank financed 30 pilot schools with the technical support of CRATerre in Burkina Faso, two prototypes made of earth-bricks with vaulted roofs in Niger, and Nianning-type schools in Senegal (World Bank 1979b, 1985c, 1986).
8. CRATerre is a French research laboratory created in 1979 the School of Architecture of Grenoble (France) providing training and technical assistance in earth-built construction.
9. Several examples of this include the houses built in local materials by ADAUA in 1983 in Fada N'Gourma; in Burkina Faso the *Centre de Formation de Monitrices Rurales* in Kamboincé; housing *Cité An II*, a housing project built in 1986 in the same country; an EU-financed prototype of a classroom built with dehydrated gypsum in the school of Derkle (Dakar, Senegal) built in 1983, which collapsed in 1988; and low-cost housing also built with dehydrated gypsum by the NGO ADAUA in 1980 in Nouakchott (Mauritania), which had all collapsed and been replaced with classic construction by 1990 (Theunynck 1994).
10. The recent experience conducted in Burkina Faso in 2002-05 by the NGO "La Voute Nubienne," with technical support of CRA Terre and French government financing, shows that 100 percent of earth-roofed rooms built by the NGO are not competitive compared with corrugated-iron roofed rooms built by the informal sector in rural areas (Wyss 2006b).
11. In Niger, the Primary Education Development Project abandoned the local material approach after two prototypes (1986–87) and shifted to simple techniques mastered by local builders (World Bank 1996d). Burkina Faso abandoned it after 10 school prototypes (in Yagma, Noongandé, Zoetgomdé, Songa, and Loumbila) built in 1990–91, and only half completed at the end of the Primary Education Development Project (World Bank 1995a). They are dilapidated at present (Wyss 2005a). In Chad, earth school prototypes were built in the 1980s by NGOs with support of the Swiss cooperation, but also to no avail (Oumarou 1993, World Bank 2003b).

12. An international forum held in Berlin in 1987 on low-cost housing and local development concluded that appropriate technology for construction never broke into the construction market (Habitat Forum Berlin 1987).

13. Fired bricks also have environmental drawbacks when they are fired with wood, as in Rwanda. In exceptional situations, such as in highlands of Madagascar, handcrafted fired bricks are an efficient low-cost material used on a large scale by the both formal and informal construction sectors. In this country the firing energy is provided by rice-husk, a no-value by-product of rice production with no environmental drawback.

14. See Norton 1997; Gurney 2004; Wolfskill et al. 2005.

15. In France, the Groupement d'Etudes pour une Architecture Industrialisée, GEAI, was founded in 1945, led by the French architect Le Corbusier and engineers Marcel Lods and Jean Prouvé, who adapted the methods of car and airplane construction to house construction. In Great Britain, there was a major push to construction industrialization through the Large Panel System–LPS (DTI 2001a).

16. The sector of small construction enterprises showed strong vitality by a 5 percent yearly business increase (FCGA 2007).

17. Hong Kong is the example of successful industrialization.

18. A prototype of an industrially prefabricated modular house—the "Tropical House"—designed in 1951 by the engineer Jean Prouvé for tropical countries, shipped to and built in Brazzaville (Congo), has been recently rediscovered by an antiques dealer. Recognized as a master piece of modern industrialized architecture, it was reassembled in New York City in 2007 and sold by Christie's auction at US$5 million. Another prototype of the same Tropical House is exhibited on the terrace of the Centre Pompidou, Paris. *The Herald Tribune*, May 20 and June 7, 2007.

19. This model has been built since 1990 through World Bank–financed projects: Education III and V, and PNDSE. However, this model is not friendly to the physically disabled, and should be adjusted to provide larger spaces and ramps for exit and entry in the case of wheelchairs. It costs very little to incorporate such adjustments into new construction of classrooms and latrines (Social Fund Senegal).

CHAPTER 4

Technology for Sanitation and Water

SANITATION IN SCHOOLS

Three basic types of installations exist to neutralize human waste in schools. Two are waterborne: the centrally operated wastewater treatment system and the septic tank system. The third type is dry. The centrally operated waterborne system is typically associated with urban settlements where the cost of connections and maintenance is low. The septic tank is recommended in towns where central systems are unavailable. The septic tank is composed of a sealed tank in which bacteria associated with human waste are rendered harmless through fermentation. The remaining effluent is drained away into the porous soil of septic fields called soakaways. Investment costs are high, but maintenance is low. Both systems require plentiful running water to function well.

Most of the school sanitation systems are of the third type: the dry-pit latrine, which is also the most maintenance intensive. Many dry-pit latrine designs have been field-tested in Africa because most sites are far from running water access. Figure 4.1 shows one example of dry-pit latrines that have been widely tested and proven efficient in diverse country contexts. Other examples are provided in Appendix 5. One of the better-known dry-pit latrine models is the Ventilated Improved Pit (VIP) latrine. The VIP has functioned well under controlled field tests, but has typically failed for lack of maintenance when implemented on a large scale. VIP latrines have two chambers that must alternate in use. While one chamber collects human waste, the other must be inactive for about a year to allow the waste to ferment and desiccate into a dry hazard-free substance that can be safely removed. Rainwater must be prevented from entering the fallow chamber. VIP latrines also include a natural ventilation shaft from the collection chambers that helps reduce offensive odors. An insect screen at the top of the ventilation shaft prevents flying insects from spreading fecal matter. The insect screen must remain unbroken and unclogged. VIP latrines work well only when regularly maintained.

Figure 4.1 The Dry Pit Latrine: An Example from Mali

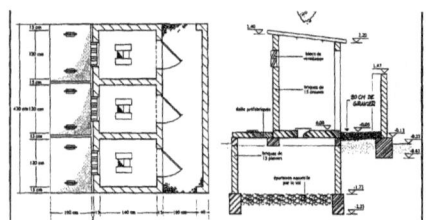

Source: World Bank 1993b.

Figure 4.2 Handicap-Friendly Latrine: The Example of Uganda

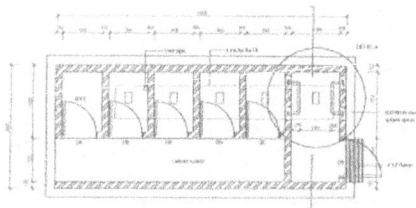

Source: Group 5 2006d.

Figure 4.2 shows the Uganda model of a handicap-friendly latrine-block with one larger unit accessible by a ramp to accommodate a wheelchair, and handles on both lateral walls that handicapped children can grip. This type of architectural arrangement is very rare in African countries, but needs to be disseminated in order to render schools handicap inclusive, a condition for achieving Education for All.

Guinea provides an example of the difficulty in properly using and maintaining dry-pit latrines. Starting in 1995, with financing from the World Bank, the government of Guinea adopted a model of one block of five VIP latrines for three classrooms. However, the model was not understood by the users. By 2003 the latrines were unusable. None of the 1,200 latrine blocks had ever been emptied, and in each individual stall, both holes were open and both pits used simultaneously rather than alternately (Dupety 2003).

Latrines are not very costly. Table 4.1 shows the unit costs of latrines per classroom across eight African countries. The cost per latrine averages about US$2,000 across this group of countries, ranging

Table 4.1 Unit Cost of Latrines in Selected Countries

Country	Latrine cost per school or classroom-block in selected projects (US$)	Number of classrooms per school or block	Latrine unit cost per classroom in selected projects (US$)	Year
Burkina Faso	9,600	3	3,200	2004
Ghana	6,000	6	1,000	2001–03
Madagascar	7,600	5	1,520	2004
Malawi	1,172	1	1,172	2006
Mauritania	1,858	2	929	2002
Mozambique	1,980	7	283	1999–05
Senegal	998	1	998	2004
Uganda	8,360	7	1,194	2004
Zambia	4,050	3	1,350	2004
Average	4,624	4	1,294	

Sources: Group 5 2006a–d; author.

between US$1,000 in Senegal and Uganda to more than US$3,000 in Mauritania and Burkina Faso. In comparative terms, the cost of one latrine averages 23 percent of the cost of one classroom, ranging between 11 percent in Madagascar to 34 percent in Mauritania, where sandy soils make the construction of underground pits technically difficult. Nevertheless, latrines are a necessity, and such countries as Uganda have shown that when strong government commitment and reasonable unit costs are present, finances can be mobilized to provide all primary schools with latrines. In Uganda, about 120,000 latrine stalls were operational in 2002, more than 35,000 of them having been built within the past 5 years (Group5 2006d). Nevertheless, the remaining and stubbornly unresolved problem is maintenance.

WATER SUPPLY FOR SCHOOLS

There are five basic types of technology for potable water provision: rainwater tanks, a well, borehole, a water stream, or a pipe connection to a communal water supply. Rainwater tanks collect and store rainwater runoff from classroom roofs, and are therefore appropriate in regions with difficult access to underground aquifers and enough rain to fill the tank for the school year. Rainwater tanks are often used in such African countries as Rwanda and Madagascar also because this is the less expensive means of supplying water; however, this advantage may be offset by health risks when regular maintenance is not carried out to keep water clean over time. Water wells have been used in schools with a shallow underground aquifer, as in The Gambia, for example. A well is an excavation dug down to access the underground aquifer to withdraw water by hand or with a pump, supplying water at a low cost. However, sound planning and careful maintenance are required to prevent contamination of the water well and the underground aquifer. When the groundwater is too deep for a well, a borehole, equipped with a pipe and a pump, often manually operated, needs to be drilled toward the groundwater. Boreholes are significantly more sanitary than open wells because the water source itself is protected from contamination by its depth. However, they are found in very few schools because the machinery and techniques to drill them are costly and their maintenance requires technology skills that are far beyond users' capacity, making this technology hardly affordable by MoEs' investment and recurrent budgets.

Most wells do not function as intended (Dupety 2003). In the sample of nine countries shown in table 4.2, unit cost ranges from less than US$1,800 in Senegal to almost US$19,000 in Madagascar. The average cost in this sample is about US$8,000. The main reasons for such a wide range are probably the geological constraints of accessing water in rural areas, the type of water supply, the type of pump and tank if any, and the implementation arrangements to contract the works. For example, in The Gambia, the successful system of school water supply is a modern

Table 4.2 Cost of Water Supply per School in Selected Countries

Country	Cost of water per school (US$)	Year
Burkina Faso	11,000	2004
Gambia, The	10,471	1993
Ghana	8,571	2001–03
Madagascar	18,750	2004
Malawi	4,975	2006
Mozambique	4,900	1999–05
Senegal	1,840	2002–04
Uganda	2,000	2004
Zambia	9,000	2004
Average	7,945	

Source: Group 5 and ST.

well that serves both the school and the village. The water supply is designed to be accessible from both sides, well-protected against the risk of water stagnation, and equipped with a side system of cattle troughs. Its high cost is not explained by geological characteristics—in this riverbed country, water is easily accessible—but by the high standard of the multipurpose supply combined with the delegation of works to the ministry.

CONCLUSION

Ministries of Education (MoEs) have limited knowledge of water and sanitation technology. They are not always aware of technical recommendations provided by the national strategies for water and sanitation that are implemented under the responsibility of other ministries. When resources are limited, they too often prioritize access to education, that is, classroom construction, to the detriment of water and sanitation; and donors have too often followed suit. African schools are therefore very far from being adequately equipped. Providing adequate water and sanitation services to all new schools and retrofitting all existing ones—necessary to achieve EFA—require that MoEs not only include water and sanitation in the minimum infrastructure package for primary schools but also provide adequate resources for them. They must also link up with sector ministries in charge of water and sanitation to choose the most adequate and affordable technology, possibly share costs, receive professional technical advice during implementation, and train school staff and the community in proper maintenance. Donors should not finance any school construction programs that do not reduce the water and sanitation deficiencies.

CHAPTER 5

Procurement and Contract Management

Services required to build schools involve the supply of materials and skilled workers, site supervision to ensure technical quality, and management of the contracts with the suppliers. Often, in large programs, a sample-based technical audit is also performed by an independent contractor as a further control on the quality of construction. Several types of approaches have been used to secure these services for the construction of primary schools. These approaches involve different procurement and management arrangements, each having an impact on costs, delivery time, and ability to scale up and reach rural and remote areas.

This section reviews the strengths and weaknesses of procurement and management approaches to securing construction services used over the past 30 years. On the procurement side, we review the experience with centralized international and national competitive bidding, and price quotations. On the management side, we review the experience with management by public administrations, contract management agencies (CMAs), NGOs, social funds (SFs), and communities. We first describe these approaches and the rationale for their introduction and then analyze their performance in terms of delivery and comparative cost. Only costs of schools built to last at least 25 years are considered in this chapter, excluding technologies using local materials, either traditional or "appropriate." The issue of differences of quality of construction is not addressed in depth in the present study because there are not enough data to discuss it. However, when technical audits are available, they provide relevant data on the quality of built facilities.

PROCUREMENT MANAGED BY CENTRAL ADMINISTRATION

THE FIRST MODEL: CENTRALIZED MANAGEMENT WITH PROCUREMENT THROUGH INTERNATIONAL COMPETITIVE BIDDING (ICB)

Centralized management by the MoE or Ministry of Public Works is an approach that most, if not all, countries have traditionally used, whereby the central ministry office allocates the resources for school construction, procures the works, evaluates and awards the contracts through the National Tender Board, pays the contractors, and supervises the construction work.

One of the earliest approaches to procuring construction services used centralized management combined with international bulk procurement for the full delivery of classrooms, including the provision of materials, labor, and site supervision. Centralized bulk procurement for the full delivery of classrooms involves packaging a large number of individual school sites into one or a few large bidding packages, which are then put out for ICB. Management of the packaging and process is usually done by the central Ministry of Education or of Public Works.

Following the independence of many African countries in the 1960s, ICB was nearly the sole procurement approach used for donor-financed school construction programs. Most primary school infrastructure financed by the IDA, AfDB, and EEC, among others, continued to use this approach through the 1980s. At the time, donors deemed this approach appropriate to the context. New government administrations were just developing and management capacity was weak. African administrations were highly centralized. In most African countries, following independence, the construction industry was highly concentrated in the hands of a few foreign contractors (eventually with a local basis), which resulted in high prices and increased potential for corruption. National contractors were few, and small- and medium-size enterprises were even fewer. In addition, centralized bulk procurement was considered specifically attractive for school construction because classroom needs are large. Thus, the ICB approach seemed to match the context. It aimed to address capacity weaknesses of national administrations, lower the cost of construction, and contain corruption in several ways. First, bulk packaging was seen as more compatible with weak procurement capacity of government agencies as it required fewer contracts for the procuring agency to manage. Fewer and larger contracts were also more compatible with limited donor response capacity. Second, reliance on large contractors with strong financial and technical capacity was seen as a way to compensate for weak technical monitoring and contract management capacity of government agencies. Third, the increased competition among private enterprises was expected to result in competitive prices. Finally, the use of the donor's ICB procedures was seen as a way to safeguard against corruption since donors reviewed the procurement process and gave their nonobjections at various stages.

Figure 5.1 illustrates the actors and steps involved in a typical ICB process. Usually, large firms, whether foreign or national, subdivided the contract into smaller lots and subcontracted the works to smaller local enterprises, which were unable to gain access to public procurement due to the high turnover and investment capital requirements. Thus, the large firms operated as contract management agencies securing local contractors and supervising their work. However, such subcontracting was generally an informal practice, often illegal, thus limiting quality control

Figure 5.1 Centralized Bulk Procurement Process

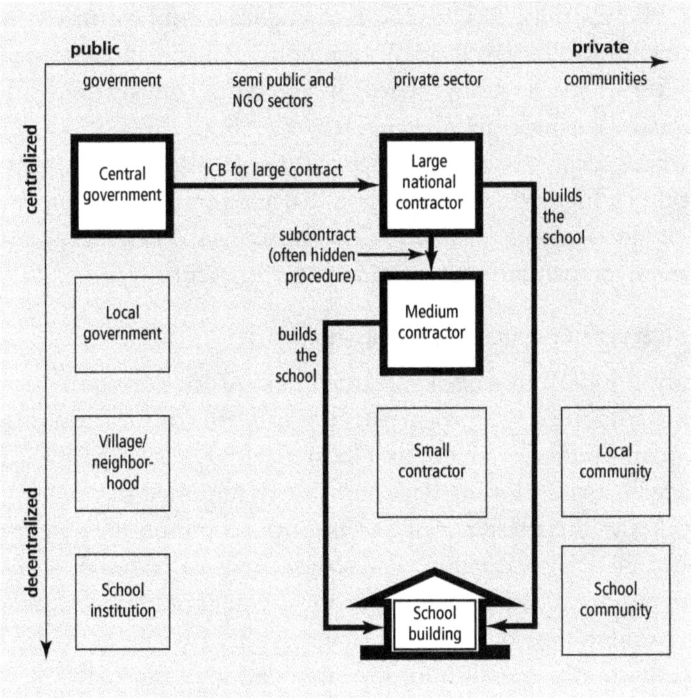

Source: Author's figure.

by the contracting administration. This development also provided lessons learned for the future creation of CMAs.

By the end of the 1980s, ICB procurement for the delivery of primary classrooms showed clear limitations in its effectiveness to meet the scale of the needs required at a competitive price. Construction costs were high, averaging between US$15,000 and US$30,000 per classroom in 1980 prices.[1] The high costs result from several factors. First, architectural design was sophisticated and followed the aforementioned *modern construction model*. Second, international competition was limited because primary classrooms are small works dispersed throughout the country, which attracted the interest of few large firms. However, at the country level, most enterprises were unable to meet the bidding requirements. Third, as a result, the few interested and qualified contractors often formed cartels in order to fulfill the technical requirements, and divided up the public construction market among themselves, thereby driving up prices. Fourth, procurement procedures were lengthy and cumbersome, resulting in prolonged delays, which further drove up costs. Finally, local construction industries were developing and becoming increasingly competitive with international suppliers.

Based on this experience, in the beginning of the 1990s, the IDA and EEC abandoned the use of ICB procurement for primary school construction, whereas the AfDB and OPEC continued in the 2000s to finance school construction programs through ICB with similar results in, for example, Ghana and Zambia (Group 5 2006b and 2006e).[2] As a whole, the review found that, on average across countries and time, classrooms procured through ICB cost about US$480 per m^2 in 2006 prices. However, such very high average cost masks some differences over time. Prices were much higher in the past when ICB and foreign contractors were the norm, and are lower—but still very high—nowadays, when it is an exceptional method used in a much more competitive environment.

Variation 1: ICB with Community Participation

Another early approach to school construction in Africa, common during the 1970s–1990s, combined ICB procurement of modern construction materials with community contributions of labor and local materials. These programs were centrally managed by MoEs for the bulk purchase of imported materials, and often implemented with the assistance of NGOs for the community-based aspects.

This approach was expected to yield cost savings on materials and labor. Savings on materials would come from ICB procurement of imported materials that individual communities could not procure cost effectively. Savings would also come from community contributions in labor and local materials, such as sand, gravel, and water, to construct the building. Technical assistance was also provided to communities to help them organize and implement their part. In addition to the cost savings, common arguments presented for community contributions are that they reduce overall project costs and promote community empowerment and ownership, which results in a greater willingness to maintain the building and ultimately leads to sustainability (World Bank 2002c, Wilson 2006).

This approach proved inefficient, although saving costs compared with previous full ICB, but no cost advantage compared to full national competitive bidding (NCB), and was generally abandoned at the end of the 1980s. However, community contributions continued to be incorporated into school construction programs.

Figure 5.2 illustrates the implementation path and points to one of the main problems with the approach—the difficulty of synchronizing the delivery of inputs coming through two separate channels. Similar to the experience with prefabrication, it proved nearly impossible to coordinate the delivery of materials with the availability of community labor. On the government side, bulk procurement of imported materials resulted in long delays. Materials were delivered at unexpected times, and at times when community labor was unavailable. From the community side, the counterpart materials were also not always mobilized when they were needed, often owing to the community's financial constraints. In Zambia, time

Figure 5.2 Scheme of Combining Bulk Procurement of Imported Materials with Community Participation

[Figure: Diagram showing relationships between public/private and centralized/decentralized actors. Public side includes government (Central government MoE, Local government, Village/neighborhood, School institution) and semi public and NGO sectors. Private side includes private sector (International supplier, Large national contractor, Medium contractor, Small contractor) and communities (Local community, School community). Arrows show: ICB supply of imported materials from Central government to International supplier; mobilizes schools; supply imported materials; provides support; provides support to supervision; provides labor; mobilizes the school community; all connecting to the School building.]

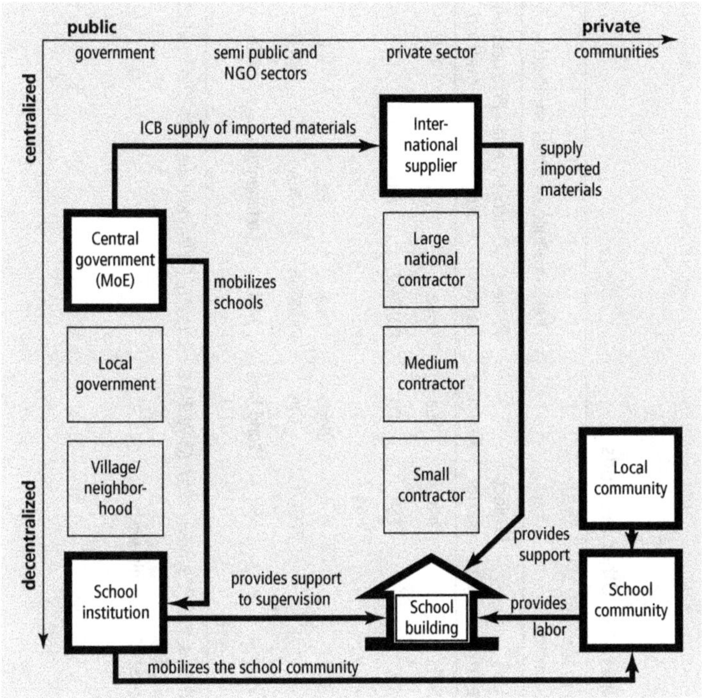

Source: Author's figure.

completion was not less than 2 years and often 4 years (Group 5 2000a). In Burkina Faso, work sites faced major disruptions, leading the government to put an end to the approach after 13 years of implementation (1985–98) and to turn the work to the contract management agency Faso Baara (World Bank 1991a and 1999a).[3] In the Gambia (1990–99), coordination of community labor with the delivery of imported materials resulted in 2- to 3-year delays. In Senegal, the approach was also experimented with during 12 years (1987–99) and was found extremely time-consuming, compared to the NCB approach (World Bank 1995g).

Unit costs proved lower than when works were fully procured through ICB, but substantially superior to those obtained by procuring the full package of materials and works from local enterprises through national or local competitive bidding (table 5.1). Bangladesh, Burkina Faso, Senegal, The Gambia, and Zambia provide examples. In Zambia, under a 1993 OPEC-financed project, the unit cost of class-rooms, including 25 percent community participation, was one-third higher than

Table 5.1. Costs of ICB Combined with Community Participation Compared to Other Methods

		Performance of bulk procurement of imported materials combined with community participation for works						Performance of other methods					
Country	Years	Project name	Financer	Project agency	Procurement agency	US$ per m²	Source	Project name	Financer	Project agency	Procurement agency	Procurement method	US$ per m²	Source
Burkina Faso	1985–94	Education III	IDA	PIU/MoE	PIU	50%	a	n.a.	n.a.	n.a.	n.a.	ICB	100%	a
Gambia, The	1993–95	ESP phase 1	IDA	PIU/MoE	PIU	152	b	ESP Phase 2	IDA	PIU/MoE	PIU	NCB	110	b
Senegal	1993–99	SHRDP	ESCP	PIU/MoE	PIU	316	c	n.a. PEDP-1	donors IDA	n.a. PIU/MoE	PIU CMA	ICB NCB	494 233	d c
Zambia	1993	OPSUP	OPEC	ZEPIU	OPEP-ZEPIU	215	e	SRP	World Bank/EU	MPU	Communities	LCB	161	f

Source: (a) World Bank 1991a, 1995a; (b) Education Sector Project (Synergy 1997, World Bank 1999c); Synergy 1997; (c) World Bank 1995g; (d) World Bank 1993e; (e) World Bank 1995 OPEC Primary School Upgrading Program (Group 5 2000) ; (f) Social Recovery Project/ZAMSIF (Group 5 2000).
Notes: Unit costs are adjusted to 2006 prices using the U.S. GDP deflator. For a complete list of acronyms, see p. xv.
n.a. Not applicable.

the unit cost achieved by a parallel community-based project that procured the works inclusive of labor and materials for the same quality of classroom (Group 5 2000s). In The Gambia, construction costs were 38 percent higher than those achieved by the MoE using NCB procedures.[4] In Senegal, the approach initially resulted in lowering costs from previous full ICB by 36 percent, although it was found 36 percent more costly compared with NCB approach without counting the cost of extensive technical assistance (World Bank 1995g and 1993e).

The Question of Community Participation

No country has, in practice, a standard rate of community cost recovery. Rather, community contribution rates are generally project specific. They vary widely across donor and type of project; that is, whether the project is an education project, a social fund, or an urban, rural, or local development project. Across projects, rates of community contributions for classroom construction generally range between 0 and 25 percent. At the high end, an example is the community school construction program in Mauritania, which requires a 25 percent community contribution, and which built 3,000 classrooms in 15 years. The successful European Union–financed microproject programs generally require a 15 percent contribution. Many social fund programs use a 5 percent community contribution share.

Although these are all successful examples of communities contributing their share, the lack of a common and applied policy results in some communities having to contribute more than others, generally the rural communities. An illustrative example is Chad, where parent associations were expected to contribute 10 percent of the construction cost under an IDA-financed project. In fact, contributions were not required when the construction was managed by a contract management agency (AGETIP), while it was between 5 and 10 percent when the construction program was managed by NGOs (Lecysyn 1997). Mauritania is a similar case of double rules for urban and rural communities.[5] Further, community participation policies propose contributions for health, water supply, electricity, and agricultural extension services, without consideration of the aggregate impact on the poor.

Parent and community contributions are rarely recognized or captured in public accounts. Ironically, despite their significant help to complement the government's budget, the contributors are rarely given any recognition. For example, in Benin, communities were not handed the keys to their schools until they had met their cash contributions to construction costs in full. Although receipts were kept at the Ministry of Finance, there was no attempt to publicize and thus encourage and reward their participation (World Bank 2000 ICR). Even rarer is any systematic attempt to capture these contributions in public accounts.

Experience has also shown that community financial or in-kind contributions do not necessarily generate the commitment, nor capacity, to maintain the building.

Examples of this include Guinea and Niger (Dupety 2003, World Bank 1996d, ADE 2006). Further, financial or in-kind contributions are not an indicator of community empowerment. Rather, empowerment is achieved when communities can manage the construction themselves.

Variation 2: ICB Combined with Microenterprises

An approach close to the previous one, also experimented with during the 1980s–1990s, combined ICB procurement of modern construction materials (as in the previous approach) with procurement of labor from small local microenterprises or masons selected through local competitive bidding (LCB).

This approach was also expected to generate cost savings for reasons similar to the previous approach as regards the procurement through ICB of imported materials that may not be easily available in the local market. Savings on labor would also come from the use of local enterprises whose prices for labor are not comparable to these of large foreign or domestic enterprises. This approach was expected to yield cost savings on local labor without involving the same volume of technical assistance required when community has to perform all labor activities, although communities were nevertheless often invited to provide local materials. Another objective was to support the development of the local construction industry by providing business opportunities to small local firms that may be further easily contracted for maintenance works.

This approach also proved inefficient. Although it produced cost savings compared with previous full ICB, it proved too difficult to implement and was generally abandoned at the end of the 1990s. Figure 5.3 illustrates the implementation path, and shows the complexity of the scheme resulting from the multiplicity of delivery channels that proved impossible to synchronize.

Niger is a good example of this approach. In 1987, the government decided to abandon the unsuccessful previous ICB approach for school construction, and shift to the aforementioned combined approach.[6] The PCU managed ICB procurement of nonlocal materials, contracted local masons for the works, and mobilized communities for local materials. In 1995, units costs were half that of previous ICB (Oumarou 1993, World Bank 1996d).[7] The approach was continued during the subsequent education project until 2001, but with poor results—delays, below-standard quality, resulting in early deterioration, high risk of misuse of imported materials, inability to mobilize community participation—and was therefore abandoned (World Bank 1994, 2002e, 2003g). The Asia region had a similar experience. For instance, in 1980, Bangladesh combined local labor contracts with large materials contracts procured through ICB. After paralyzing delays, Bangladesh rapidly shifted to contracts inclusive of labor and materials (World Bank 1980, 1990b).

Figure 5.3 Scheme of Combining Bulk Procurement of Imported Materials with Microenterprises: The Example of Niger (1987–2001)

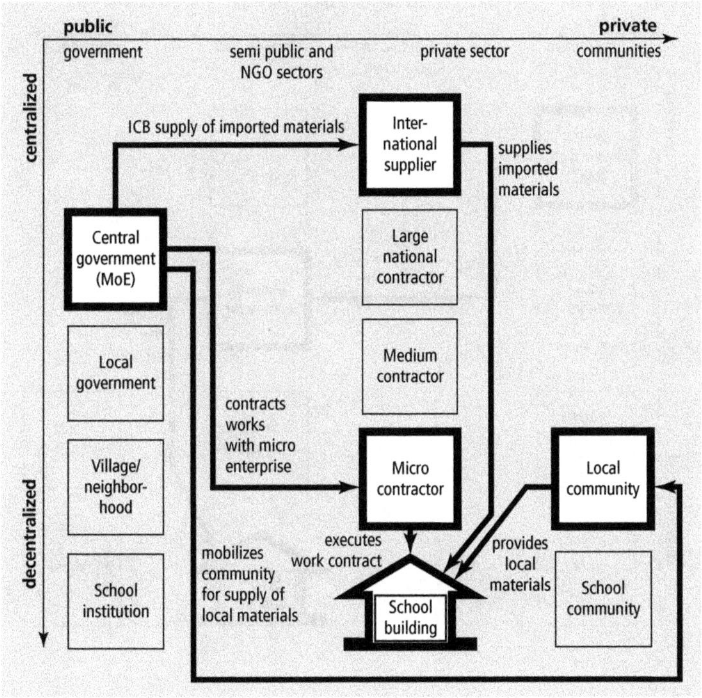

Source: Author's figure.

THE BIG SHIFT: CENTRALIZED MANAGEMENT WITH PROCUREMENT BY NATIONAL COMPETITIVE BIDDING

Following years of unsatisfactory experience with centralized ICB procurement—and various attempts to keep ICB through combined approaches—it became increasingly apparent for African countries, that if they were to meet the infrastructure required to provide all children with quality primary education, particularly in rural and remote areas, other strategies were needed.

To achieve larger scale and contain costs, ways had to be found to grow small- and medium-size contractors in the country by opening up opportunities, and increasing both available capacity and competition over time. The approach, therefore, would need to procure services more compatible with what national enterprises in the formal and informal sector could deliver. That meant less sophisticated technology and smaller bid packages and procurement of construction services through NCB processes. This approach became common in the

Figure 5.4 Centralized National Competitive Bidding

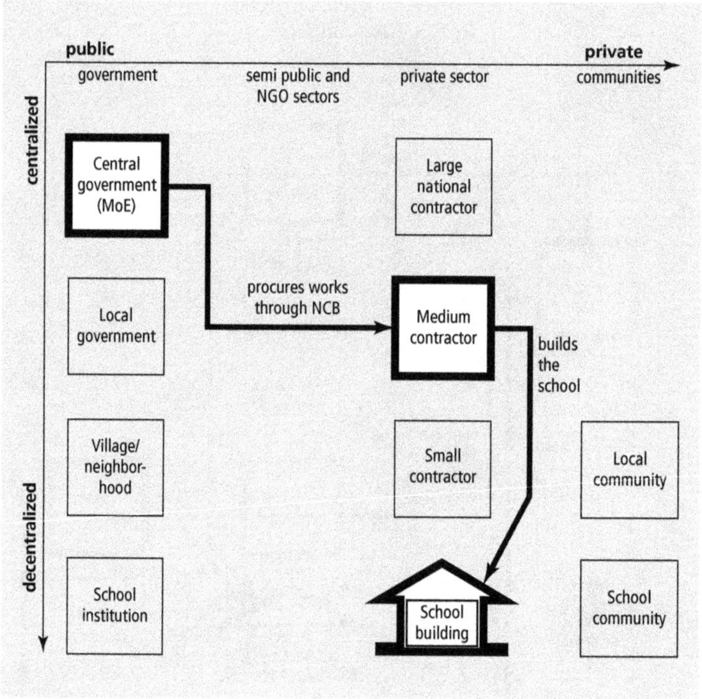

Source: Author's figure.

1990s. Figure 5.4 illustrates the process. The only differences between the ICB and NCB process are national rather than international publicity of the invitation to bid, and lower technical qualification requirements that would allow smaller enterprises to compete.

The switch in procurement methods from centralized ICB to centralized NCB, along with the decrease in technology sophistication, resulted in significant cost savings. Table 5.2 shows average costs across projects managed by central administrations through ICB and NCB of the 193 projects of SSA countries reviewed in the study. First, across time, the average cost per gross m^2 of classrooms procured through ICB decreased sharply. Costs were as high as US$1,150 per m^2 in the 1970s when classrooms were generally built in modern technology by foreign contractors. They fell to an average of US$269 per m^2 in the last decade, presumably because of the combined effect of an increased reluctance of

Table 5.2 Evolution of Gross Unit Costs of Classrooms Procured through ICB and NCB

Decades	Average gross unit costs		
	ICB (US$/m²)	NCB (US$/m²)	Difference (%)
1970s	1,150		
1980s	466		
1990s	333	182	45
2000s	269	189	30

Source: Averages from list of prices in Appendix 15 in 2006 prices.

foreign firms to bid in countries where large local firms are more competitive, and of the impact of increased competition in the developing construction industry, facilitated by the shift from modern technology to the less sophisticated classic classroom technology. Second, since the inception of NCB procurement for classrooms in the 1990s, average costs of classrooms procured under NCB are comparatively lower, between US$180 and US$190 per m^2, representing 30 percent cost savings in the last decade, presumably because medium-size local firms are more competitive than the large ones.

In all countries, the shift from centralized ICB to NCB procurement translated into cost savings of similar magnitude. For example, in 1998, when Senegal allocated about US$2 million of its own budget annually for school construction, the Ministry of Education's Department of School Construction procured the buildings through NCB and achieved a unit cost of US$8,130 per classroom (US$9,600 in 2006 prices), compared with an average of US$18,000 in 1982 (US$32,500 in 2006 prices) under ICB procurement (World Bank 2000d). Unit costs per m^2 resulting from ICBs in the 1980s were 2.5 times these from NCBs in the 1990s in current prices, thus more than three times in constant prices.

As a result of this cost advantage, by the early 1990s, countries and all major donor agencies shifted from large procurement packages and ICB processes to smaller bidding packages and NCB. Among donors, willingness to shift from ICB to NCB has been gradual and some donors still continue to recommend ICB, although not in all countries they support. Figure 5.5 illustrates that during the past two decades for which we have data for both procurement methods, classrooms built through ICBs remains 70 percent more costly than these built through NCBs. For comparison purposes, we will use in the following sections the average unit costs resulting from ICBs conducted only during the past two decades, for which we also have unit costs from other procurement methods.

One notable exception is that the Japan International Cooperation Agency (JICA), which does not finance NCBs, continues to manage procurement in Japan and limits competition to Japanese firms at very high cost. Japanese-funded schools are usually in urban areas and follow project-specific technical

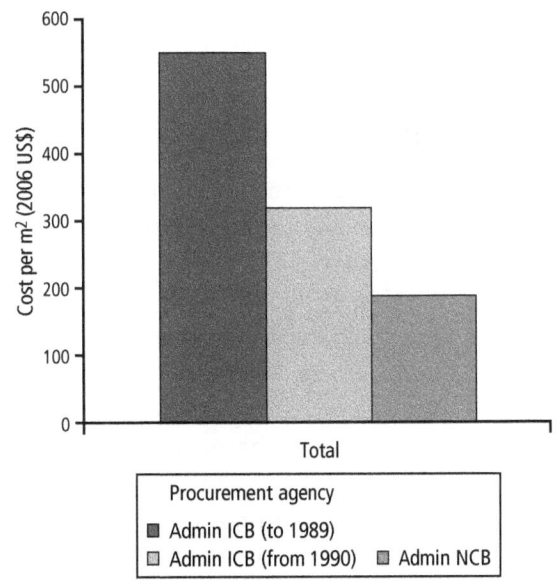

Figure 5.5 Cost per Gross m^2 of Classroom Works Procured by Administration through ICB and NCB

Source: List of projects in SSA countries in Appendix 18.

specifications. Procurement of works is bid in Japan to Japanese contractors which, in turn subcontract to national contractors. Works supervision is generally done by Japanese consultants. As a consequence, unit cost is generally much higher than those of other projects. For example, in Zambia, JICA unit costs were 4.5 times that of ZAMSIF (Group 5 2006e). Because this arrangement is unique, JICA-financed projects are not included in the present comparative cost-analysis.

Although far less costly, centralized NCB procurement has shown several limitations. The approach has failed to deliver the quantity required and long delays are the rule rather than the exception, mainly due to weak contract management capacity. For example, in Senegal, NCB procured construction programs have shown long delivery delays (Dupety 2005a, World Bank 2001h). In Madagascar, less than 5 percent of the 2,028 classrooms planned to be built by the administration in 2004 through NCB were actually built by 2006 (MENRS 2007). In Rwanda, centrally managed projects using NCB have been slow in producing results, constructing only 240 classrooms per year between 2002–05 (Pichvai 2004).[8]

DELEGATION OF CONTRACT MANAGEMENT

Along with smaller procurement packages and multiple suppliers comes a need for greater management capacity to effectively manage the larger contract volume. To address this issue, many countries adopted a variety of strategies, sometimes simultaneously, to draw on all available capacity in the country. These strategies include delegating contract management to agencies, such as CMAs, NGOs, and social funds, and decentralizing contract management to local MoE offices, to local governments, and to communities.

DELEGATION OF CONTRACT MANAGEMENT TO AGENCIES

We use the term "agencies" to mean nonprofit organizations that are created to manage and implement public sector programs, but that work outside the government and have no vertical hierarchical relationship with a line ministry (Laking 2006). Agencies of this nature were developed to manage public programs for which the government lacked capacity and efficiency, owing to cumbersome procurement and financial management procedures, a lack of skilled staff within the civil service, political interference in technical issues, corruption, or lack of accountability mechanisms in public service delivery. Agencies are characterized by their independent management and flexibility in management and procurement procedures.

In western countries, such agencies date back to the 16th century in Sweden, the 19th century in Germany, and more recently, the 20th century in the United

Kingdom and the Netherlands. A good example of such an agency in the United States is the New York Port Authority, which built the network of bridges and tunnels that link Manhattan to New Jersey—a task that exceeded the capacity of the state or local government to manage.

In developing countries, three types of agencies have been introduced since the 1980s: CMAs, social fund agencies, and independent service authorities, the latter being established in fragile states where governments are ineffective in spending revenues to deliver services.

Contract Management Agencies

We define CMAs as agencies specifically established to manage procurement and contracts for the construction of social infrastructure, such as public schools, health facilities, and markets. In francophone Africa, CMAs are commonly known as *Agences d'Exécution des Travaux d'Intérêt Public* (AGETIP), or Executing Agencies for Construction in the Public Interest. The World Bank was a chief proponent of CMAs and supported their establishment in many countries throughout Africa.

AGETIPs were established to achieve several objectives. An overriding objective was to demonstrate that a private sector approach to the construction of public infrastructure was more efficient than management by government. Thus, AGETIPs were established to test procedures for the delegation of construction management from the public to a quasi-private sector. A second objective for the establishment of CMAs was to alleviate poverty by providing temporary employment for unskilled labor. To achieve this, the operating procedures of CMAs typically specify that at least 20 percent of total construction costs must be allocated to labor. Finally, CMAs were also expected to demonstrate the feasibility of labor-intensive construction practices promoted by ILO, and increase the number and capacity of small- and medium-size contractors throughout the country by allowing them to compete for small public works contracts, and by providing timely professional supervision and quick payment for work completed. (Wade 2004; Diou et al. 2007.)

The first AGETIP was founded in 1989 in Senegal, followed by 19 others in 16 countries. All are linked through a professional network.[9] Although largely financed by public funds, the agencies have nonprofit status, are managed independently of government, and have an independent board that oversees their operations and governance. They also use simpler and more flexible procurement and disbursement procedures than those applied in the public sector, and recruit staff from the private sector at a competitive salary. Accountability is safeguarded through independent technical and financial audits. AGETIPs were established to operate initially in urban areas and demonstrate success before expanding to serve rural areas.

In a review of agencies in Organisation for Economic Co-operation and Development (OECD) countries, Laking (2006) concludes that agencies have improved the credibility and efficiency of public sector performance without lowering the overall quality of public governance. He notes, however, that the OECD experience also shows the difficulty of insulating agencies from the surrounding environment and government institutions. Laking concludes that when the overall environment and public institutions are nonperforming and when corruption and patronage are pervasive, it is unlikely that agencies will be immune to such contagions. A common cycle is discernible. Initially, agencies are successful and outperform government institutions, delivering on time and at lower cost and thereby providing a role model for other institutions. However, because agencies are not isolated from the environment, they eventually adopt behaviors similar to those found in the public sector and vice versa.

The experience of AGETIP in Africa is quite similar. Experience suggests that agencies have permanently changed the rules of the game for the better in the domestic construction industry. They have broken the monopoly of large contractors by opening up the market of public contracts to previously excluded small- and medium-size enterprises, which therefore proliferated, thereby increasing competition and lowering construction costs.[10] Most people agree that AGETIPs have played a key role in the birth of the construction industry (Frigenti and Harth 1998, Diou et al. 2007). They have helped countries to fill the contract management capacity gap. They have also promoted minimum standards to raise the quality of construction executed by domestic contractors. On this basis, some countries have recently issued laws to regulate the delegation of public works to CMAs.[11] Administrations, in turn, have recognized the interest of some innovations promoted by CMAs and often adopted them, such as the outsourcing of work supervision to independent architectural/engineering firms (Cape Verde).

CMAs in School Construction

The construction of schools benefited from the overall improvements in the national construction sector in African countries. Scattered small contracts, procured through NCB or the comparison of three quotations, became the norm for the procurement of school construction, and independent supervision by private architectural and engineering firms became the norm for quality assurance. Ministries of Education in at least six countries have delegated the management of substantial primary school construction programs to AGETIPs with the support of donors, principally the World Bank, the AfDB, the Agence de Fonds de Développement, and Kreditanstalt für Wiederaufbau.[12] In Mauritania, the Ministry of Education delegated the management of lower-secondary school construction in larger towns to AMEXTIPE, while it scaled up a successful community-based approach for the construction of primary schools. Figure 5.6 illustrates the CMA approach applied to school construction.

Figure 5.6 Management of School Construction by a Contract Management Agency

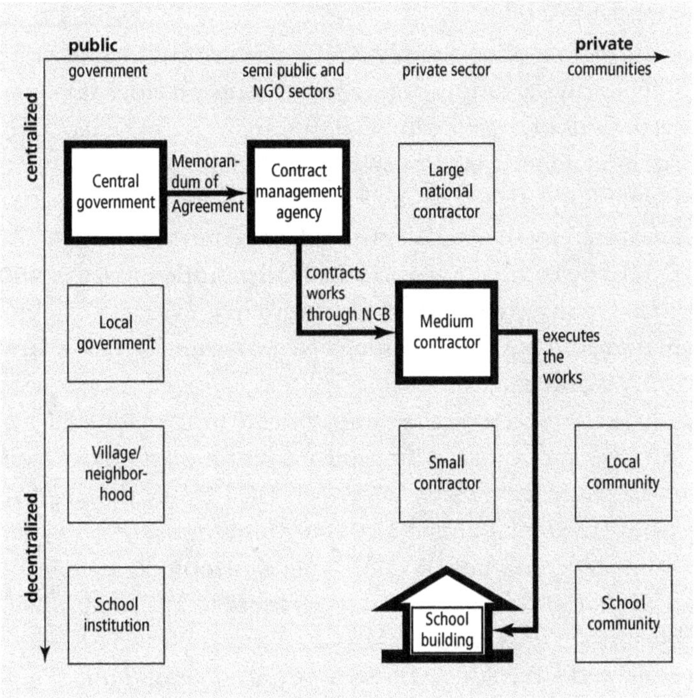

Source: Author's figure.

Experience with CMAs in school construction has been highly positive, although not uniformly so within all countries. The experience shows that the AGETIPs have filled an important capacity gap and substantially helped to expand the school infrastructure network in Burkina Faso, Cape Verde, and Senegal. In Burkina Faso, although the initial experience with Faso Baara in 1995 was not very satisfactory in terms of cost, delays, and fund management, as Faso Baara gained experience and procedures were adjusted, Faso Baara successfully built 37 percent of the 3,650 classrooms constructed in Burkina Faso during 2001–2005, and the MoE continues to use its services today (World Bank 1999a, Group 5 2006a). In Senegal, the first country to use AGETIP for school construction, AGETIP built 27 percent of a total 7,950 new classrooms constructed throughout the country by different agencies between 2000–04 (Dupety 2005a).[13] In Cape Verde, the MoE turned the entire school construction program implemented by the Ministry of Public Works to AGECABO, which dramatically increased the pace of works. In The Gambia, GAMWORKS was not initially expected to be cheaper than the previous MoE-managed approach but was used to tap into additional capacity to scale up the national school construction program (World Bank 1998a). In fact, GAMWORKS built 72 percent of the thousands of classrooms built in 1999–05 (World Bank 2005k).

Table 5.3 shows four examples of AGETIPs, which, at their inception, consistent with Laking analysis, outperformed by far the previous implementation arrangements for school construction that they replaced. In Senegal, from 1994 to 1998, AGETIP built about 2,000 classrooms on behalf of the Ministry of Education and brought unit costs down by half—from between US$13,200 per classroom when procured by the MoE using NCB procedures, to $6,700 (World Bank 2000d). By 2001, the cost per classroom had fallen further to US$6,400. In Cape Verde, AGECABO reduced costs by 25 percent from previous classroom construction program managed by MoE through NCB (Theunynck 2005, Siri and Goovaerts 2002, World Bank 1999b).

However, AGETIPs also have their limitations. The cost advantage of AGETIPs may not always be, or remain, competitive over time with other management options within a particular country. Between 1994–1998, the Chadian AGETIP was contracted by the MoE to build 150 classrooms under an IDA-financed project with an estimated budget of US$8,250 per classroom. It completed the work in 1996 for US$11,150 per classroom, an overrun of 35 percent, which triggered the discontinuation of its services midway through the project (World Bank 2003b). In Mali, under the Education Sector Consolidation Project, a parallel approach using a large NGO as an umbrella organization working with a group of smaller NGOs delivered classrooms at US$108/m^2 lower than the US$133/m^2 achieved by AGETIPE-Mali in 1989–96 (World Bank 1996b). Table 5.4 shows a sample of six projects managed by AGETIPs in six counties where these agencies have been operating for several years; in this sample, they achieve unit costs that are higher than these achieved by the Ministry of Education through other agencies using NCB.

Samples in table 5.3 and 5.4 show mixed results. Figure 5.7 shows that, on average, classroom construction projects managed by the administration and by CMAs through the NCB procurement achieve comparable unit costs of US$180–190 per m^2 (in 2006 prices).[14] This result supports Laking's last conclusion: over time, CMAs and the public sector eventually adopt similar behaviors leading to similar results. Actually, central administrations and CMAs tend to apply the same procedures, tend to target the same contractors through the same level of publicity for the invitation to bid and similar approaches to package the works to be proposed for bid, and obtain the same unit costs.[15] The difference between administrations' and CMAs' performances is not, indeed, in the unit cost; it is in the ability to deliver large programs and to deliver them on time, as evidenced by the experience in Senegal, The Gambia, Cape Verde, for example.

Table 5.3 AGETIP Performance at Inception Compared to Previous Administrations

	Performance of the AGETIP-type agency						Performance of previous administration				
Country	Agency name[a]	Project ID[a]	Year of start	US$/ classroom	Source	Agency name	Project ID[a]	Year of implementation	US$/classroom	Source	Difference (%)
Chad	ATETIP	BEP	1993	11,150	a	State	ERP	1988–94	18,000	b	−38
Cape Verde	AGECABO	SSDP	2002	13,460	c	MoE	PROMEF	2000–02	18,000	d	−25
Mali	AGETIP Mali	ESCP	1989	8,000	e	Donors	n.a.	mid 1980s	19,600	f	−59
Senegal	AGETIP	SHRDP	1992	6,700	g	MoE/MPW	PEDP	1987–94	18,000	h	−63
Average				9,650					18,400		−46

Sources: (a) Basic Education Project (World Bank 1993a); (b) Education Rehabilitation Project (World Bank 1993a); (c) Social Sector Development Project (Theunynck 2005a); (d) Education and Training Consolidation and Modernization Project (Theunynck 2005, World Bank 1999b); (e) Education Sector Consolidation Project (World Bank 1996b); (f) World Bank 1989c; (g) Second Human Resource Development Project (PDRH2) (World Bank 2000d); (h) Primary Education Development Project (World Bank 1993e).
Note: n.a. Not applicable. For a complete list of acronyms, see p. xv.

Table 5.4 AGETIP Performance Compared to MoE Administration through Other Arrangements

	Performance of the AGETIP-type agency					Performance of other agencies					
Country	Agency name	Project ID	Year of implementation	US$/m²	Source	Agency name	Project ID	Year of implementation	US$/m²	Source	Difference (%)
Burkina Faso	Faso Baara	PTTE and PAOEB	2000–04	150–153	1	MoE (provincial offices)	Panier commun	2002–04	108	1	140
Burundi	ABUTIP	PWECT	1996–07	169–182	2	MoE (PIU)	FDA	2005	106	3	166
Cape Verde	AGECABO	SSDP	2001	308	4	MoE	n.a.	2004	265	4	116
Madagascar	AGETIPA	AfDB Project	2004–06	301	5	MoE (PIU)	BAD-BADEA	2005–06	223–248	5	128
Niger	NIGETIPE	AfDB Project	2005	175	6	MoE (PIU)	FKfW	2005	160	6	109
Senegal	AGETIP	EFA-1	2000–04	152	7	MoE (PIU)	BCI	2000–05	131	7	111
							OPEC	2000–05	142	8	
Average											128

Sources: (1) Group 5 2006a; (2) World Bank 2007b; (3) Dupety 2006; (4) Theunynck 2005a; (5) MENRS 2007a; (6) Zerbo 2008; (7) Diouf 2006; (8) Dupety 2005a.
Note: Unit costs are adjusted to 2006 prices using the U.S. GDP deflator. For a complete list of acronyms, see p. xv.
n.a. Not applicable.

Figure 5.7 Cost per Gross m² of Classroom Works Procured by Administration through ICB and NCB, and by CMAs through NCB

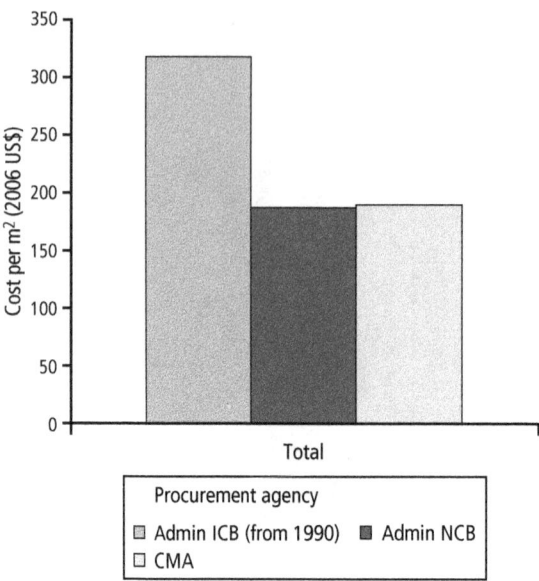

Source: List of projects in SSA countries in Appendix 18.
Note: Unit costs are adjusted to 2006 prices.

Other limitations of CMAs are the following:

- Many CMAs have not expanded their capacity sufficiently to cover the rural areas and thus continue to operate mainly in urban, or easily accessible, areas (Diou et al. 2007). Unless CMAs are able to scale up cost-effectively to address the needs of rural areas, it is unlikely that they will be in a position to contribute significantly to meeting the primary school infrastructure needs in rural areas.
- In order to contain management costs, AGETIPs often resort to increasing bid packages, thereby reducing the number of contracts to manage. However, larger bid packages result in the selection of contractors on the basis of their capital and turnover, too large to be interested in working in remote sites. For example, in Senegal, the package proposed for bids was generally composed of 20 classrooms, whereas a bid package of this size effectively limits competition to medium and large contractors and excludes the small contractor and the informal sector. As a result, contractors tend to deliver on the schools located near main roads and neglect remote sites.
- AGETIPs have not been able to maintain their cost advantage over time. This may be because CMAs are successful role models and other institutions adopt similar practices, as initially intended, the need for the CMA is no longer apparent. In Cape Verde, for example, because of the success of AGECABO in lowering costs, the MoE adopted AGECABO's procedures and achieved similar results. The approach was later adopted by local governments as well.
- AGETIPs were set up as a solution to the lack of capacity of governments; however, they also appear as part of the perpetuation of low public governance problem because the countries in which they operate neglect to improve the performance of the administration. One of the reasons may be that the mandate to build governments' capacity was given to agencies.[16] In Senegal, the 2006 Public Expenditure Review notes that the mushrooming of 15 agencies following the AGETIP model has removed responsibilities of concerned ministries, which are bypassed by almost all decision-making processes (World Bank 2006b).

The use of CMAs, such as AGETIPs, is a proven sound approach to move expeditiously on urgent programs with minimum of fiduciary risks. In postconflict situations, alternative service delivery, including CMAs, social funds, Community-Driven Development projects, and NGOs, has been used successfully to rapidly implement large physical reconstruction programs that generally include a large share of school facilities (IEG 2006). To speed up rapid responses to crises and emergencies, the World Bank has defined specific rules to facilitate the use of procurement and project management agents, such as CMAs.[17]

DELEGATION TO NGOs

The World Bank defines NGOs as "private organizations that pursue activities to relieve suffering, promote the interest of the poor, protect the environment, provide basic social services, or undertake community development" (World Bank 1989b). NGOs vary widely in their size and activities, ranging from large-scale, northern-based charities, such as CARE or Plan International with a broad range of activities, to small, single-purpose, community-based organizations. Some focus on advocacy; others are operationally involved in implementing development programs. Operational NGOs can be classified in three main categories: *Community-based organizations* (CBOs), which are local groups of people who self-organize to achieve a specific development objective, such as a parent-teacher association; *national* NGOs, which are country-based service providers; and *international* NGOs, which are headquartered in developed countries. The OECD estimates the number of international development NGOs at about 4,000, working with 10,000 to 20,000 national NGOs and CBOs in developing countries (Hume 2004).

NGOs have been increasingly instrumental in delivering development assistance. On one hand, NGOs contribute resources that that they themselves raise, providing valuable incremental resources to bilateral and multilateral aid. Between 2001–2005, net grants by NGOs flowing to developing countries increased from US$4.7 billion to US$7.3 billion, representing an average of 5.7 percent of total net flows of Official Development Assistance from DAC countries over the period (OECD 2007). On the other hand, NGOs have also played an increasing role over time in channeling bilateral and multilateral project aid to recipient countries, particularly in weak or failed states. In the World Bank, for example, between 1973–1988, only 6 percent of World Bank–financed projects involved implementation by NGOs. This percentage grew to 28 percent by 2001[18] (World Bank 2002g).

NGOs have been engaged in school construction for many years, whether using private funds that they have raised, or using donor or government funds through management delegation. A large number of NGOs use school construction as an entry point to achieve more general community development objectives

Figure 5.8 Scheme of School Construction Implemented by NGOs

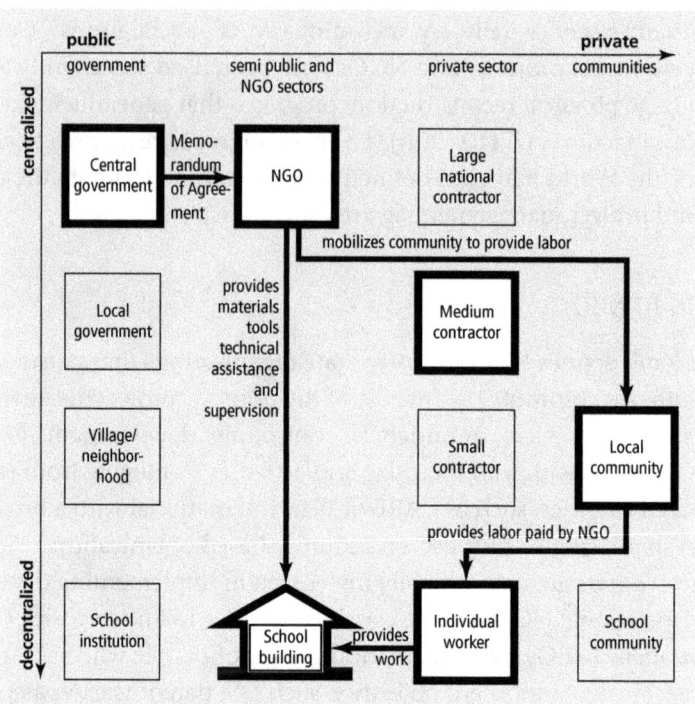

Source: Author's figure.

(Synergy 2006e). Because of their rural reach, governments and donors often consider NGOs to be more efficient in reaching the poor than the public administration. For these reasons, collaboration with NGOs has been an important feature of school construction programs since the 1970s, in which they have acted as contractors directly implementing school construction programs, or as CMAs, or have delegated construction management to communities.

Figure 5.8 illustrates a typical implementation process when an NGO acts as a school building contractor. Typically, when NGOs act as contractors, they supply the materials, and recruit and train community labor to build the school. Appendix 7 lists some NGOs operating in school construction in Africa, and shows illustrations of the implementation arrangements when NGOs act as CMAs and when they delegate construction management to communities.

Information gathered on NGO experiences in eight countries suggests that NGOs can be an appropriate solution to fill short-term capacity gaps and to increase production when the construction industry has limited reach. In Guinea, the approach resulted in a significant increase of implementation capacity allowing for double the number of classrooms to be built annually—from 600 to

1,200 between 1995–2001. In The Gambia, two NGOs—Future in Our Hands and the Christian Children's Fund—delivered 17 percent of 1,015 classrooms financed by an IDA education project (World Bank 2005k). In Mozambique, following the Peace Accords, NGOs accounted for 30 percent of the 5,000 classrooms built between 1993–98 (Synergy 2006e, World Bank 1999e). In Mali, the "community school" program launched by the government in 1994 with NGO support enrolled 10 percent of primary students in 1997–98 (Cissé et al. 2000).[19] In 1989, this country tested the use of an umbrella NGO, ACTION-ECOLE, working with 18 national NGOs to build 275 classrooms under a donor-financed project; at the end of the project, the NGOs exceeded expectations and built 670 classrooms (World Bank 1989c, 1996b).[20]

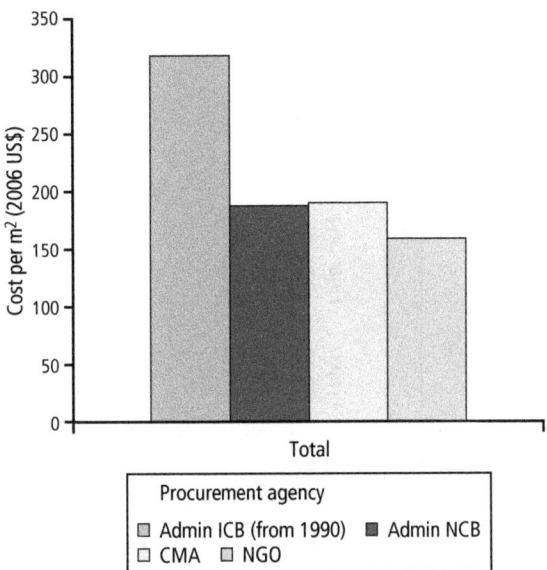

Figure 5.9 Cost per Gross m² of Classroom Works Procured by Administration, CMAs, and NGOs

Source: List of projects in SSA countries in Appendix 18.
Note: Unit costs are adjusted to 2006 prices.

From the perspective of the costs of classroom construction, Figure 5.9 shows that, on average, across countries for which data are available, and over time, the unit cost of NGO-managed construction is slightly lower than construction managed by either the central administration or a CMA using NCB procurement (the difference is statistically significant), when *NGOs act as contractors or as CMAs*. In 2006 prices, the average cost is about US$160/m², compared to US$180 and US$190 per m² for administrations (using NCB) and CMAs respectively. In this chart, the NGO column does not count projects where classrooms are built by communities under a delegation from an NGO.

Table 5.5 shows the per m² cost of classrooms built by NGOs in the eight countries for which data are available by construction approach and compared with parallel programs implemented during the same period managed by Ministries of Education or CMAs. The table aggregates the NGO projects in three groups: (1) projects managed by NGOs as contractors, (2) projects managed by NGOs as CMAs, and (3) projects managed by communities by delegation from an NGO. Although the data points are limited, they strongly suggest that NGOs have no comparative cost advantage when they implement the construction themselves. On the contrary, when NGOs construct classrooms themselves, they are 19 percent higher, compared with centrally managed construction programs using NCB

Table 5.5 Unit Costs of Classrooms Built by NGOs (3 approaches) Compared with Other Methods

					NGO management of school construction						Comparative approach				
Country	Year	Project name	Financing agency	NGO name	Procurement agency	Procurement method	Unit cost US$/m^2	Source	Project name	Financing agency	Procurement agency	Procurement method	Unit cost US$/m^2	Source
First approach: NGOs acting as contractors														
Burkina Faso	2003	n.a.	Plan Internat.	Plan Internat.	Same NGO	Direct contracting	130	a	PPTE	Gov. (PTTE)	Faso Baara	NCB	133	a
	2007	n.a.	OSEO	OSEO	Same NGO	Direct contracting	112	b						
Chad	1993–2001	BEP	IDA	SAWA	Same NGO	Direct contracting	308	c	BEP	IDA	ATETIP	NCB	193	c
Gambia, The	1997–98	SESP-TESP	IDA	FIOH-CCF	Same NGOs	Direct contracting	140	d	SESP-TESP	IDA	PIU/MoE	NCB	110	d
Guinea	1995	PASE-II Phase 1	IDA	CECI-ADRA	Same NGOs	Direct contracting	282	e	PCPEPMRG	UNESCO	UNESCO	direct contracting	181	f
	1996–97	PASE-II Phase 2	IDA	CECI-ADRA-ADIK-EUPD	Same NGOs	Direct contracting	265		n.a.	KfW	PIU/MoE	NCB	180	g
	1997–99	PASE-II Phase 3	IDA	34 NGOs	Same NGOs	Direct contracting	152		n.a.	Plan Guinée	Plan Guinée	Direct contracting	131	h
Mozambique	2000–04	n.a.	NGO	AMNDIR	Same NGO	Direct contracting	110	i	ESSP	FINNIDA	MINED/DPE	NCB	116	j
									ESSP	IDA	DCEE/DPE	NCB	173	
Senegal	1999	PUSE	CIDA	FPGL	Same NGO	Direct contracting	143	k	PDRH2	IDA	AGETIP	NCB	129	k
Average							182						152	

NGOs acting as contract management agencies

Mali	1990–95	ESCP	IDA	Large Umbrella NGO	18 small NGOs	Direct contracting	151	l	ESCP	Gov.	AGETIPE-Mali	NCB	186	l
Guinea	2000–04	EFA-I Phase 1	IDA	10 NGOs as CMAs	250 small NGOs	LCB or 3-Q	116	m	VCCP	IDA	Local Governments (VCSP)	NCB	215	o
	2004–07	Phase 2 EFA-1	IDA	5 NGOs (CMA)	5 NGOs (CMA)	NCB	125	n						
Average							179						201	

NGOs delegating to communities

Ghana	1998–2004	QUIPS	USAID	ILP	Community	Direct contracting	68	p	BESIP-PERP	IDA-AfDB	MoE (FPMU)	NCB	118	q
Burkina Faso	2007	Prog Burk	Action Aid	Action Aid	Community	LCB	89	r	PAOEB	France (FDA)	Faso Baara	NCB	150	s
Average							79						134	

Sources: (a) Group 5 2006a; (b) OSEO 2007; (c) Basic Education Project (Lecysyn 1997, World Bank 2003b); (d) Second and Third Education Sector Program (Synergy 1997), (e) Equity and School Improvement Project (Theunynck 2000); (f) Projet de construction de prototypes d'écoles primaires en milieu rural en Guinée (De Bosch, Kemper et al. 1990); (g) Lipsmeier 2000, World Bank 2001c Annex 13; (h) Plan Guinée 2001; (i) Education Sector Support Program–PASE (Group 5 2006c); (j) ESSP Education Sector Support Program (Group 5 2006c); (k) PUSE: Education Sector Support Emergency Program, FPGL Fondation Paul Gerin Lajoie (F2 Consultants 1999); (l) Education Sector Consolidation Project (World Bank 1989c, 1996b); (m) Dupety 2004 and 2005b; (n) cost information from Aide et Action 2007; (o) VSCP 2007; (p) Quality and Improvement in Primary Schools (Group 5 2006b); (q) Education Sector Investment Plan, Group 5 2006b; (r) Aide et Action 2007; (s) Group 5 2006a.

Note: Unit costs are adjusted to 2006 prices. For a complete list of acronyms, see p. xv.

n.a. Not applicable.

procurement. On the other hand, examples in Guinea and Mali show that, when NGOs act as CMAs, they can achieve significantly lower costs than AGETIP CMAs. The most cost-effective of the three approaches is when NGOs delegate construction management to communities. In Ghana, community implementation of school construction set up in 1998–2004 by an NGO resulted in a 48 percent lower unit cost per m^2 compared with centrally managed construction using NCB to employ contractors. In Burkina Faso, when communities are empowered by the NGO program, they build classrooms at 38 percent less than the CMA Faso Baara.

However, experience suggests that heavy and exclusive reliance on NGOs is not a long-term solution to the problem of scaling up for several reasons. NGOs have limited capacity, are generally not specialized in construction management, and their support is often geographically circumscribed. Most important, depending on the scope, the strategy may be counterproductive to the development of the local construction industry. For example, the scheme in Guinea frustrated many local contractors who were excluded from this market. They responded by creating storefront NGOs to access the contracts (refer to box 5.1 for the experience of Guinea). For all these reasons, NGOs can be a good short-term solution to address capacity gaps, but cannot be relied upon as a long-term solution to the problem of weak domestic construction capacity.

BOX 5.1 CONTRACTING TO NGOs—THE CASE OF GUINEA

In 1990, only 28 percent of children were enrolled in primary school; management capacity of the government was low; and the local construction sector had almost no small- and medium-size construction contractors. To mobilize all existing capacity and increase community participation in the construction process, the Ministry of Education fully delegated the management and execution of its school construction program to NGOs under a World Bank–financed project.

In a first stage, two NGOs (CECI, ADRA) were invited through sole source contracts in 1995 to build 15 classrooms. Although the NGOs delivered the classrooms, the unit cost of construction at US$228/m^2, including the cost of community participation, was high partly due to limited competition and partly to high NGO management fees of 18 percent. In a second stage, four NGOs (CECI, ADRA, ADIK, and EUPD) built 36 classrooms at a similar average cost of US$218/m^2. In a third phase, carried out in 1997–98, 34 NGOs were invited to build 570 classrooms at an established rate of US$127/m^2, including the cost of community participation (estimated at 12 percent of construction costs) and NGO contract management fees, which were capped at 10 percent of construction costs.

The program was a success. As a result, in 2000, the MoE delegated construction management of its entire school construction program to NGOs. A first layer of 10 large NGOs, mostly international with strong financial and technical capacity, were recruited to play the role of CMAs on behalf of the MoE. The 10 NGOs contracted the services of 250 smaller local NGOs, which competed for individual contracts of two to three classrooms. In 2002–04, almost 700 classrooms were delivered on time using this approach, and unit costs fell to an average of US$106 per m^2 owing to increased competition. The costs were significantly lower than the US$158 per m^2 achieved by programs centrally managed by the MoE using NCB procedures.

The program resulted in a significant increase in implementation capacity, which allowed for double the number of classrooms to be built annually from 600 to 1,200. Several problems arose, however. First, NGOs had limited experience as CMAs and the quality of construction was uneven. Second, the approach presented the potential for conflicts of interest because NGOs acting as CMAs managed contracts with NGOs with whom they had partnerships in other activities. Third, the arrangement created perverse incentives for small local contractors, who became increasingly frustrated as they watched the escalating role of NGOs in the school construction business from which they were excluded. As a result, they established storefront NGOs to access the contracts.

To address these issues, in 2004 the MoE changed the approach by reducing the number of NGOs acting as CMAs to five with proven capacity, and gave them the authority to recruit small- and medium-size contractors through NCB. This translated into a small increase in cost to US$118 per m^2 in 2007, but was still much lower than previous MoE-managed programs and lower than a Village Community Support Project implemented by local governments during the same period, which built 46 schools for the MoE at a cost of US$215 per m^2.

Although NGOs continue to play an important role in school construction in Guinea, the government is considering a recentralization of management to the MoE.

Sources: World Bank 1989c, 1998a; Synergy 1997; Ernst & Young 2001.

DELEGATION TO SOCIAL FUND AGENCIES

Increasingly, the provision of primary schools is carried out by actors other than Ministries of Education, through multisector projects, such as Social Funds. In 2005, for example, the World Bank financed 66 noneducation projects with education components, totaling almost 32 percent of total Bank lending to education, and a 75 percent increase over 2004.[21] Education components in multisector projects are especially prominent in the Africa region, where 41 percent of the projects and 30 percent of all IDA financing is channeled through multisector projects in the Social Protection Sector, and another 6 percent of operations and 20 percent of funding passes through multisector Poverty Reduction Support Credits (World Bank 2004d, 2005j).

Social Funds were initially developed in the 1980s to mitigate the effects of the structural adjustment and alleviate poverty, mainly by financing small-scale social infrastructure in rural areas to improve services and create employment. They were also seen to be an effective way to provide basic services in short-term or emergency situations, such as in postconflict countries or in weak or failed states where governance and private sector development are lacking. Social Funds offer many flexible features to work effectively in this environment and contribute to governance/empowerment structures at a local level, as basic building blocks for development.

Similar to AGETIPs, Social Funds have nonprofit status, management independent of government, and an elected board of directors that oversees operations and governance. The World Bank was a main promoter of Social Funds. The first Social Fund in Africa was created in 1989 in Guinea. By 2001, World Bank funding had scaled up rapidly to 98 projects in 58 countries totaling US$3.5 billion, and by 2007 Social Funds had been established in 21 countries (Van Domelen and El-Rashidi 2001).[22]

Social Funds differ from CMAs in several aspects. First, all social funds use a bottom-up, *demand-driven*, approach (Jack 2001). In contrast, CMAs are generally contracted by Ministries of Education or donors to deliver construction programs based on top-down planning. Second, Social Funds do not have the promotion of small- and medium-size enterprises (SMEs) as an explicit objective (Frigenti and Harth 1998). In practice, however, they have contributed to opening up the construction market to SMEs, and in particular, they have opened it up to microenterprises, which constitute the reservoir of the future local construction industry. Third, Social Funds have introduced targeting mechanisms to ensure that resources reach the poorest. Finally, Social Funds have a well-developed administrative structure that enables them to build schools, health centers, and water systems efficiently in poor and remote communities. They have typically outperformed the line ministries and CMAs in achieving these goals (World Bank 1998c).

Figure 5.10 Social Fund Operating as a Contract Management Agency for Communities

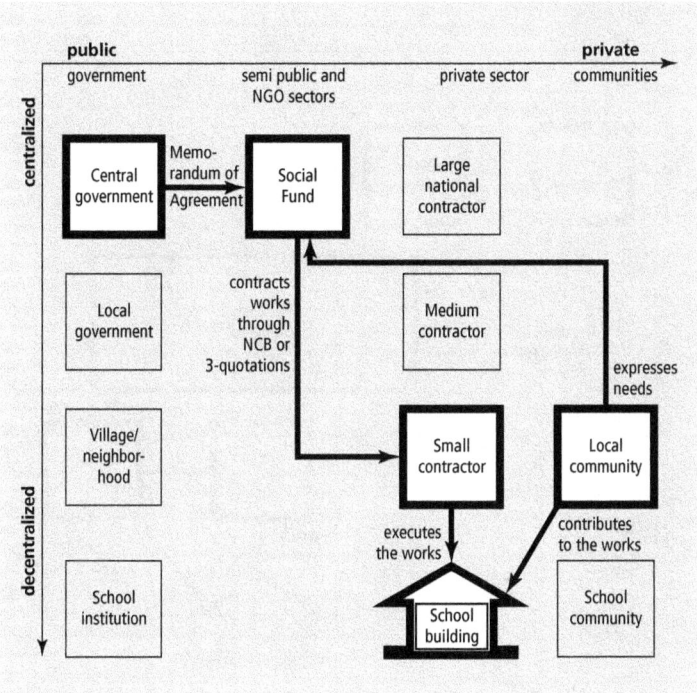

Source: Author's figure.

Similar to the involvement of NGOs in school construction, Social Fund Agencies have taken several forms. In some cases, Social Fund Agencies operate as CMAs, procuring construction services from SMEs on behalf of communities through competitive bidding. This approach is illustrated in figure 5.10 and has been used by Social Funds in Angola (FAS), Ethiopia, Eritrea, Burundi (Twitezimbere), and Madagascar (FID). We refer to this approach as *demand-driven financing* coupled with *centrally managed implementation*.

In other countries, Social Funds channel resources directly to communities empowered through a contractual financing agreement to be the implementing agencies, and manage the construction process as shown in figure 5.11. In this approach, communities have full responsibility to procure and pay labor, works, and materials on the basis of simplified procedures for community participation. This approach has been used in Social Funds in Benin (Agence de Financement des Initiatives de Base or AGeFIB), Malawi (MASAF), Madagascar (FID) Senegal (Agence de Fonds de Développement Social or AFDS), Uganda (Northern Uganda Social Action Fund or NUSAF), and Zambia (Zambia Social Investment Fund or

Figure 5.11 Social Funds Operating as a Financer of Communities to Implement Their Project

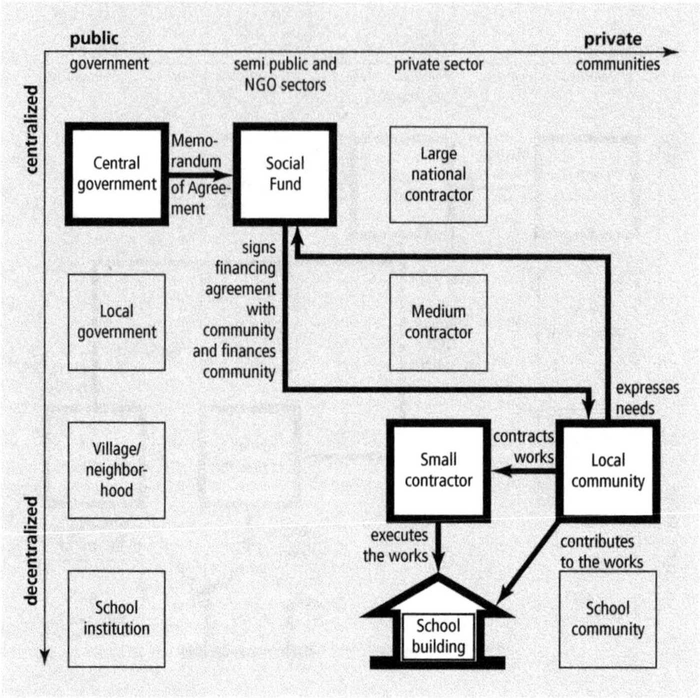

Source: Author's figure.

ZAMSIF). We refer to this approach as *demand-driven financing with community-managed implementation*. In yet other situations, communities hire labor while the Social Fund pays the invoices as done in Angola.

Experience shows that Social Funds have met an important gap in education infrastructure. Across many countries, communities have used Social Funds to finance school construction more than any other social infrastructure.[23] In Peru, between 1992 and 1998, communities used 25 percent of the FONCODES' funds to build 9,000 classrooms with a substantial impact on school attendance and completion (Paxson and Schady 1999). In Eritrea, 29 percent of the funds were disbursed to rebuild education facilities destroyed during the conflict (World Bank 2002b). In Nigeria, schools account for 30 percent of community projects financed by the Social Fund, just behind water supply and far ahead of health facilities and roads (World Bank 2001g). In Zambia, primary schools represented more than 70 percent of Social Fund projects in the 1990s, and 16 percent of the school stock was rehabilitated (Group 52 006e, World Bank 2 000). In Benin, 73 percent of projects financed by the Social Fund were invested in the construction of primary schools, which accounted for more than half of the classrooms built in the country during the period; and in the fourth Community Development Program (FID-IV) in Madagascar, more than 62 percent of community subprojects financed by the FID during 2000–2006 were for school construction (World Bank 2004c, Olivier 2004).

Ex-postevaluations of Social Funds indicate that they have been highly effective in delivering small-scale infrastructure with more than proportional benefits to the poorest. And they have produced visible results quickly. The evidence shows that Social Fund investments improved not only classroom availability but also the provision of furniture, water, and sanitation in the areas where they operate. Further, classrooms financed by Social Funds were generally higher-quality buildings compared with schools that had not received a social fund investment. Primary enrollment rates in the communities increased as a result, with a significant impact on age-for-grade (Rawings et al 2001, OED 2002).

Social Funds are also very efficient. In 2001, a review of 17 Social Funds concluded that the efficiency of Social Funds is typically superior to other delivery mechanism measured by the share of overhead and the unit cost of investment (Van Domelen 2001). One reason for this efficiency is the special status provided by the government to Social Fund agencies to manage public funds for basic infrastructure investment. Like the AGETIPs, Social Fund agencies are exempt from public procurement, financial management, and civil service rules, which allows for greater flexibility. A second explanation for this higher level of efficiency is the greater degree of accountability of Social Fund agencies to the beneficiaries who are highly involved at all stages of subproject preparation and implementation. Even when communities are not empowered to manage the works, they are at least empowered to monitor the works carried out by the contractor.

When we analyze the experience of Social Funds in school construction, compared with other delivery mechanisms, such as central governments, CMAs, and NGOs, we find, however, that the cost advantage applies only when the Social Fund supports community implementation.[24] When Social Funds use centrally managed implementation, that is, when they act as CMAs on behalf of communities, they generally do not achieve better cost results compared with other centralized agencies. Figure 5.12 shows that across countries and periods, when Social Funds apply the approach above referred as *demand-driven financing* coupled with *centrally managed implementation—that is, similar to CMAs—*they achieve unit costs of about US\$/m^2 170, close to those achieved by other agencies using the same procurement methods.

Table 5.6 shows the costs of classroom construction by this type of Social Fund in Angola, Burundi, Eritrea, and Ethiopia, which act as CMAs, and compares them with cost of classrooms built by other agencies. On average, there is no significant

Figure 5.12 Cost per Gross m² of Classrooms Procured by Administration (ICD and NCB), CMAs, NGOs, and Social Funds When They Act as CMAs

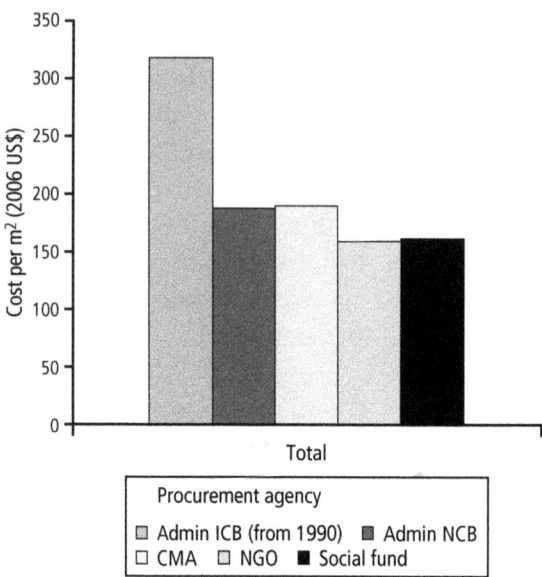

Source: List of projects in SSA countries in Appendix 18.
Note: Unit costs are adjusted to 2006 prices.

cost advantage. Classrooms built by Social Funds, when using the *demand-driven financing* coupled with *centrally managed implementation*, average US$172 per m², compared with US$198 per m² among comparator agencies using the same procurement method. Among the five country examples, two Social Funds achieved substantially higher costs compared to ministries; one (Ethiopia) achieved a slightly lower cost, and only one (Burundi) achieved substantially lower costs than other agencies, including the CMA ABUTIP. In this country, the management of the Social Fund had been delegated to a local NGO, Twitezimbere, which has a high level of community participation for the selection of subprojects and monitoring of their construction

Table 5.7 shows the unit costs of classroom construction in five countries when the Social Fund uses *community-managed implementation*, compared with other management arrangements. Cost savings are important when Social Funds use *community-managed implementation*. When communities manage the procurement process, on average, classrooms financed by Social Funds cost 44 percent less than those built by other agencies. In Zambia, similar unit costs of US$80 per m² were achieved by an EU microprojects program managed by the education districts that delegate the procurement of works to the local communities. Benin, Senegal, and Zambia are examples of good-quality work executed by local contractors through the Social Fund. Good-quality works are always the result of efficient technical site supervision. The Uganda Social Fund is an example of mixed-quality results, due to weak technical site supervision carried out by the community that lacked the necessary technical skill. On the other hand, the AFDS Social Fund in Senegal is an example of good-quality work resulting from efficient site supervision by local technicians recruited on a competitive basis by the communities themselves.[25]

Social Funds have also proven to be appropriate and effective instruments in postconflict and LICUS countries (Cliffe et al., 2003). Social Funds created in Angola, Burundi, and Rwanda are good examples. In these cases, they generally work as a CMA. The Senegalese Social Fund is an example of successful operation

Table 5.6 Cost of Classrooms Built by Social Funds Operating as Contract Management Agencies, Compared to Other Agencies

			Social fund acting as CMA					Comparative project				
Country	Year	Social fund	Financing agency	Procurement agency	Procurement method	Unit cost US$/m²	Source	Project name	Financing agency	Procurement agency	Procurement method	Unit cost US$/m²	Source
Angola	2000–04	FAS-II	IDA	FAS-II	Materials: ICB Works: NCB	**319**	a	n.a.	Donors	MPW	NCB	**296**	a
Burundi	1999–06	Twitezimbere	IDA	Twitezimbere	NCB	**115**	b	n.a.	IDA Belgium	ABUTIP Belg-Bur Fund	NCB NCB	**169** **174**	b
Eritrea	1996–01	ECDF	Belgium, Dutch, Italian IDA	ECDF	NCB	**199**	c	n.a.	n.a.	MoE	NCB	**191**	c
Ethiopia	1996–04	ESDRF	IDA	ESDRF	NCB	**141**	d	n.a.	n.a.	Non-ESDF	NCB	**147**	d
Average						194						195	

Sources: (a) Second Social Fund Project FAS-II (World Bank 2000a, 2004a); (b) Second Social Action Project (World Bank 2007); (c) World Bank 1996g, 2002a, 2002b; (d) Ethiopian Social Rehabilitation and Development Fund (World Bank 2005i).

Note: Unit costs are adjusted to 2006 prices using the U.S. GDP deflator. For a complete list of acronyms, see p. xv.

Table 5.7 Cost of Classrooms Built by Social Funds with Community Implementation, Compared to Other Agencies

			Social fund					Comparative approach			
Country	Year	Social fund	Financing agency	Procurement agency	Procurement method	Unit cost US$/m²	Source	Project name	Financing agency	Procurement agency	Procurement method	Unit cost US$/m²	Source
Benin	200–01	AGeFIB	IDA	Community	LCB	81	a	AGDS	Donors	CMA, admin.	NCB	126	b
Malawi	1998–06	MASAF	IDA	Community	3Q	66	c	n.a.	DANIDA	MoE/PCU	NCB	157	c
Mali	1999–04	GRIP	IDA	Community	LCB	120	d	ESCP	IDA	AGETIP	NCB	186	e
Senegal	2000–05	AFDS	IDA	Community	LCB	110	f	NRIP	IDA	Local gov.	LCB	140	f
								EFA-1	PTTE	MoE	NCB	141	f
								EFA-1	IDA	AGETIP	NCB	152	f
								Urb. Proj.	IDA	LG/MCA	NCB	149	g
Uganda	2000–07	NUSAF	IDA	Community	LCB	83	h	LGDP-2	IDA	Local gov.	NCB	90	i
Zambia	2000	ZAMSIF	IDA	Community	Labor: dir.	125	j	MoE	IDA	MoE	NCB	150	k
	2005				Materials: shop	80	k	MoE	Gov-HPIC	MoE	NCB	125	k
Average						95						142	

Sources: (a) AGeFIB 2001, p. 48; (b) Agence de Gestion de la Dimension Sociale du Développement, et Programme d'Investissement Public (AGeFIB 2001, p. 48); (c) EMC Jatula Associates 2003; (d) Grass-Roots Initiative Project; (e) Education Sector Consolidation Project (World Bank 1996b); (f) Diouf 2006; (g) Dupety 2005a; (h) NUSAF 2007; (i) Theurynck 2007; (j) Rawlings et al., 2001, Group 5 2000a; (k) Group 5 2006e, pp. 19–20.
Note: Unit costs are adjusted to 2006 prices using the U.S. GDP deflator. For a complete list of acronyms, see p. xv.
n.a. Not applicable.

in the postconflict region of Casamance during 2003–06, where it played an important role in rebuilding schools destroyed during the conflict, using the *community-managed implementation* approach.

Questions, however, have frequently been raised about Social Funds in terms of the sustainability of the investments. Questions regarding sustainability center around maintenance and adequate functioning of the infrastructure built. Because of the modus operandi of Social Funds as independent agencies working directly with communities, it is often assumed that a lack of coordination with line ministries affects adequate functioning of the facilities and that bypassing local governments weakens long-term sustainability (Strand et al. 2003, Kumar 2003). Experience, however, shows that these concerns are misplaced. Actually, schools built with social funds range from similar to better staffed than school comparators (Frigenti and Harth 1998, World Bank 2007e). Evidence of actual maintenance accumulated from Social Funds in Africa shows that the demand-driven approach with community empowerment for implementation results in improved community commitment to maintenance (Rawlings et al. 2001). It also shows that schools built with Social Fund financing are at least as well staffed as schools that had not benefited from the Social Fund (Rawling et al. 2001, Jorgensen cited in World Bank 2000c, Frigenti and Harth 1998, World Bank 2007e).

The concern about bypassing local governments is legitimate in some cases, but should also be seen in context. In many cases, Social Funds were established long before the creation of local governments. One example is Benin where the Social Fund was established in 1998, whereas the first elected communal councils were only established in 2003 (Kumar 2003, World Bank 2004b, World Bank 2004c). Social Funds have learned from this experience and are increasingly evolving into entities that work to provide mainstream service through local governments. Examples of this can be found in Brazil; Mexico; Colombia; in Benin since 2004; and in Senegal since 2006 (Kessides 1997, World Bank 2004b and 2006a). In Benin, the former Social Fund Agency, AGeFIB, evolved to provide fiduciary services to communes and communities in the subsequent community-driven development project (World Bank 2004b). In Senegal, the Social Fund was merged in 2006 with a Participatory Local Development Project that community-implemented projects financed through local governments.

Despite these advantages, MoEs in Africa, unlike their counterparts in Latin America, have been very reluctant to delegate resources for school construction to Social Fund Agencies. In Latin America, already in the mid-1990s, Ministries of Education in Honduras, Nicaragua, and Bolivia began to delegate resources for school construction to Social Funds. Nicaragua later delegated school construction management further down to school councils. (Walker et al. 1999). In Honduras, the government solved the problem of resistance within the Ministry of Education to delegating to the Social Fund in 1996 by closing the School Construction Division in the Ministry of Education and absorbing its activities into the Social Fund.

DECENTRALIZATION OF CONTRACT MANAGEMENT

Decentralization is one of the most important institutional shifts in African countries in recent years. Litvack et al. (1998) identify three types of decentralization—deconcentration, delegation, and devolution. *Deconcentration* occurs when central government allocates its responsibilities to its local-level branch offices, such as when the local level offices of the Ministry of Education manage school building programs on behalf of the central government. *Delegation* occurs when central government transfers responsibility for decision making and administration of public functions to local governments that may have some independence but are ultimately accountable to the central government. *Devolution* occurs when the central government transfers authority for decision making, finance, and management to quasi-autonomous local governments. Generally, these are municipalities that elect their own mayors and councils, raise their own revenues, and have independent authority to make decisions.

In this section, we review the experience of *deconcentration* of school construction management to local branch offices of the MoE on one hand, and *decentralization* to local government on the other, whether the local authorities fall under the definition of delegation or devolution.

DECONCENTRATION TO LOCAL MoE BRANCH OFFICES

In most countries, MoEs have established local offices to improve planning and provide better services. In the area of school construction, MoEs also considered delegation to local branch offices as a way to increase the construction volume by expanding capacity to manage many smaller contracts. This scheme is illustrated in figure 5.12.

Mozambique, Madagascar, Burkina Faso, Ethiopia, and Guinea have tested this approach. Mozambique tested the approach by delegating the management of one-third of the school program financed by IDA in 2000–2004 to the provincial branch offices while continuing to centrally manage the two other thirds, either through NCB or ICB. In Madagascar, the Ministry of Education delegated the responsibility for the procurement of works to the education district branch offices to implement an IDA-funded project (CRESED II) and OPEC-funded projects. More recently, starting the Ten Year Plan for Basic Education (2002–10), Burkina Faso delegated the management of its nation-wide multidonor funded program to the provincial branch offices.

Figure 5.13 Deconcentration of Implementation Responsibilities to Lower Levels of Administration

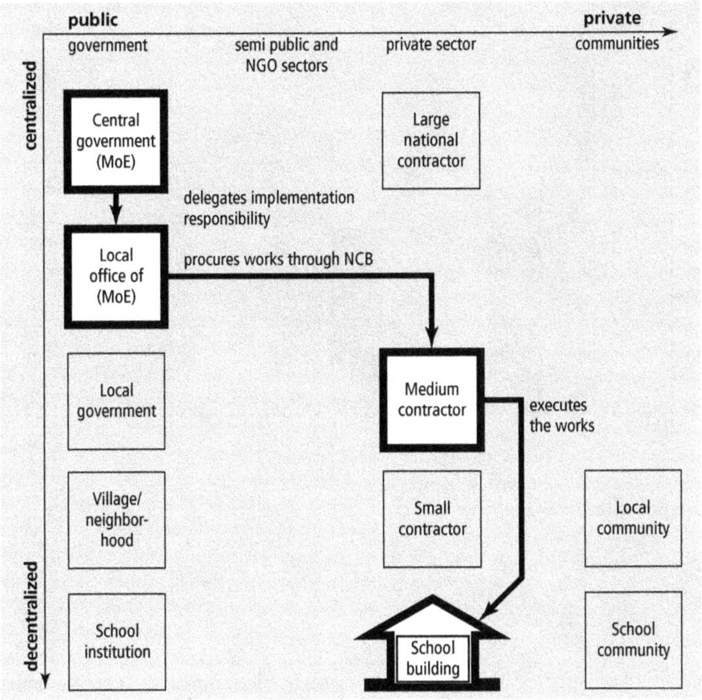

[Figure: matrix diagram with horizontal axis from public (government, semi public and NGO sectors, private sector) to private (communities), and vertical axis from centralized to decentralized. Central government (MoE) delegates implementation responsibility to Local office of (MoE), which procures works through NCB from Medium contractor, which executes the works on the School building. Other boxes shown: Large national contractor, Local government, Village/neighborhood, Small contractor, Local community, School institution, School community.]

Source: Author's figure.

Figure 5.14 shows that unit cost of classrooms procured by local branches of Ministries of Education are, on average US$175 per m^2; that is, slightly higher than units costs achieved by NGOs and Social Funds, and slightly lower than these obtained by central administrations and CMAs using NCB.

Table 5.8 shows the current unit costs of local branches of MoEs in three countries, compared with programs centrally managed by the MoE or CMA using NCB procurement in the same countries. In this sample, classrooms built by deconcentrated offices of MoEs are less expensive than those built by the central office of the MoE, CMA, or other comparable agencies, respectively by 24, 27, and 9 percent.

Despite the overall positive performance of MoE-deconcentrated offices in these countries in terms of costs, delivery capacity was highly problematic. In Madagascar, education district offices delivered only 7 percent of the program after more than 3 years of implementation under the OPEC-financed project

Figure 5.14 Cost per Gross m² of Classrooms Procured by Administration (ICB and NCB), CMAs, NGOs, SF (as CMAs), and MoE Decentralized Offices

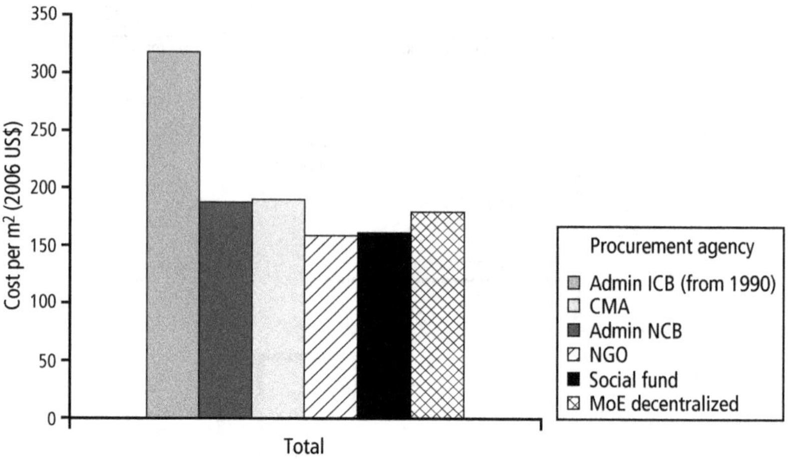

[Bar chart showing Cost per m² (2006 US$) by Procurement agency: Admin ICB (from 1990) ~315; CMA ~185; Admin NCB ~190; NGO ~155; Social fund ~160; MoE decentralized ~180]

Source: List of projects in SSA countries in Appendix 18.
Note: Unit costs are adjusted to 2006 prices.

(MENRS 2007). Under the World Bank–financed project, the slow delivery of the school construction program resulted in an unsatisfactory project rating by the World Bank in 2002, and the government turned the rest of the management over to the Social Fund (World Bank 2005m). In Burkina Faso, similar results were obtained. Because of chronic slow delivery, the MoE abandoned the approach after only 3 years and turned the construction program over to the CMA, Faso Baara, to manage. The main reason for the slow delivery has its source in weak construction management capacity of deconcentrated MoE offices. Local offices are typically charged with the management of all education matters in their jurisdiction and are staffed with former teachers and education administrators. Although local MoE staff may be committed, they simply do not have the management expertise required. Often they are also too short-staffed to tend adequately to their multiple responsibilities. Adding construction management to these responsibilities tends to weaken the focus on their education mandates.

Care should also be taken when delegating construction management to the school level for the same reasons. The experience of Philippines is instructive in this regard. During the 1980s, the Philippines delegated construction management to the school level with a high degree of success but soon abandoned the approach once officials realized that teachers were devoting more time to

Table 5.8 Cost of Classrooms Built by Deconcentrated Branches of Administration Compared with Other Agencies

| Country | Year | Government deconcentrated offices ||||| | Comparative approach |||||
		Project name	Financing agency	Procurement agency	Procurement method	Unit cost US$/m²	Source	Project name	Financing agency	Procurement agency	Procurement method	Unit cost US$/m²	Source
Burkina Faso	2000–04	SBEL	Canada, Netherlands IDA	MoE provincial offices	NCB	108	a	n.a.	Gov/HPIC	Faso Baara	NCB	133	a
								PAOEB	France (FDA)			150	
Madagascar	2000–04	CRESED II	IDA	MoE district offices (CISCO)	NCB	157	b	Edu	AfDB	MoE/PIU	NCB	248	d
						184		n.a.	BADEA	MoE/PIU	NCB	223	
	2005	n.a.	OPEP	Regional	NCB	141	c	n.a.	Gov	FID-EPT	NCB	189	
		n.a.	Gov	offices	NCB	214		n.a.	FDA	AGETIPA	NCB	301	
Mozambique	2000–04	ESSP	FINNIDA	MoE provincial offices	NCB	116	e	ESSP	IDA	MoE Central Office	NCB	173	e
		ESSP	IDA		LCB	130		RPSP	IDB		NCB	149	
					NCB	149							
	2002–06	ESSP	DANIDA		LCB	419		n.a.	AMDU (NGO)	NGO	Dir. cont.	110	
Average						180						196	

Source: (a) Development of Basic Education and Literacy (Group 5 2006a); (b) Education Sector Development Project, CRESED-II, (d) World Bank 1998b, (Group 5 2005); (c) School Construction Strategy Paper (MENRS 2007); (e) Group 5 2006c.
Note: Unit costs are adjusted to 2006 prices using the U.S. GDP deflator. For a complete list of acronyms, see p. xv.
n.a. Not applicable.

construction management than to teaching, which resulted in lower student learning outcomes.

DELEGATION BY THE MoE DIRECTLY TO COMMUNITIES

Delegation of construction management by Ministries of Education or of Finance to local communities has been implemented in Africa in Mauritania, Uganda, and Zambia and in Asia, in India, Laos , and Vietnam. Figure 5.15 illustrates this arrangement.

Results of these experiences provide solid evidence that delegation of construction management to communities can significantly increase production and lower the cost of construction, compared with centralized management approaches In all instances, the number of classrooms built exceeded expectations.

In Mauritania, which has one of the longest-running community-managed school construction programs, initially communities built 1,000 classrooms compared with the 250 expected. The capacity was immediately multiplied four times.

Figure 5.15 Delegation by Ministry of Education to Communities

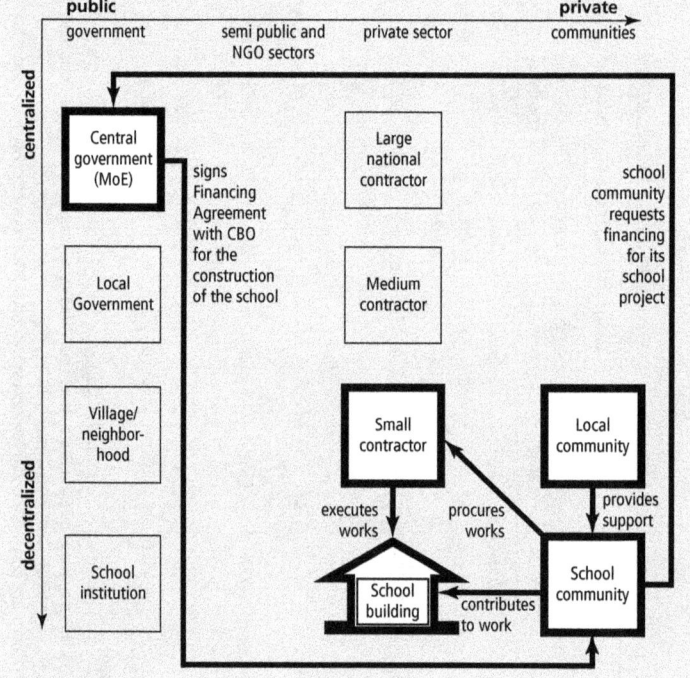

Source: Author's figure.

BOX 5.2   COMMUNITY DELEGATION IN MAURITANIA

Mauritania has one of the longest-running school construction programs using community delegation. In 1989, the Ministry of Education decided to fully delegate the management of school construction to parents' associations. An illustration of the implementation scheme is in Appendix 8.

Under this approach, communities were able to build 1,000 classrooms a year relative to the 250 planned. The approach is demand driven, and eligible projects are financed by the MoE through financing agreements monitored by a group of three engineers. Through this approach, communities have built more than 5,000 classrooms and the approach is still being used. The World Bank and the French FDA jointly support this approach.

From the beginning, classroom costs were cut by almost two-thirds, from US$18,000 when managed by the Ministry of Public Works using ICB to US$5,600. By 2000, the unit cost fell further to US$4,600 as compared to a cost of US$13,200 achieved by the CMA AMEXTIPE for the same building (Synergy 2000), and the cost savings persisted over time. Further, the strategy created a dynamic that boosted demand for education, even in the most remote villages, which was instrumental in increasing primary school enrolment from 49 percent of school-age children in 1989 to 98 percent by 2004.

Surprisingly, the quality of construction increased with the distance from the capital, with classroom masterpieces being the most remote villages because the greater social cohesion in remote communities has an impact on the governance of the school project and the management of the contractors' contract. Overall, technical audits indicate that the average quality of the construction is fair.

Sources: Mauritania: World Bank 1996c, 1998a, 2001d, 2001f; Theunynck 1993; Ould Cheikh 1994; Synergy 2000.

Cumulatively, since 1989, communities have built 5,000 classrooms through community contracting (see box 5.2). As in Mauritania, in 1998 the Ugandan MoE delegated the school construction responsibility to local communities which built 7,700 classrooms in one-and-a-half years, at a cost as low as US$52/m^2 (Kisamba-Mugerwa 2001).[26] Again, implementation capacity was immediately multiplied several times. In Zambia communities are responsible for the major part of the school construction programs. Under a basket-funding of seven donors they build about 100 classrooms per year.[27] They build similar yearly quantities from resources provided by the EU-financed microproject programs running for the past 22 years (since 1985).[28] Similar programs were successfully developed in Asia. The largest is in India, where direct transfer of responsibility to communities started in 1993 in the State of Uttar Pradesh to build schools for about 300,000 children. The program was highly successful and gradually expanded in other states to cover almost all India.

Table 5.9 shows that within five projects in the three countries, community-based management results in a 40 percent savings, compared with all parallel more centrally managed approaches using NCB. Empowering communities is a highly cost-efficient manner to invest in school construction. In addition, the example of Mauritania shows that empowering communities allows to scale up construction programs to the scope and rhythm necessary to achieve EFA objectives. It is worth noticing that, in the three countries the quality of works of community-based management projects is deemed satisfactory (Synergy 2000, EDA 2007, Kisamba-Mugerwa 2001, Group 5 2006e). Such results in Africa confirm similar results in Asia. High cost efficiency has been found more recently in Laos, where in 2004 the MoE delegated the resources for school construction to communities that built primary classrooms at US$67 per m^2 with more speed and equivalent quality, for half of the cost of classrooms previously built by the central administration through NCB (Madeco 2007, World Bank 2007c). The aforementioned India program was attractive and has been able to scale up from one state to all others because the unit cost in Uttar Pradesh was as low as US$81.5 per m^2 (World Bank 2001b). The scale-up process culminated in the nationwide Sector Investment Credit of 2004 of US$3,500 million, including large amounts of construction.

DELEGATION OF CONTRACT MANAGEMENT TO LOCAL GOVERNMENT

In many African countries, responsibility for the provision of primary education has been legally either delegated or devolved to local governments, including the responsibility for school infrastructure. Table 5.10 shows that legislation in at least nine African countries provides for the full devolution of school construction responsibilities to local governments. Appendix 8 provides a brief summary by country on the status of decentralization in education.

The rationale for decentralization is to improve basic service delivery because these services are consumed locally (Ahmad et al. 2005). Among African countries, political decentralization is progressing well, whereas administrative decentralization in Africa is progressing slowly and fiscal decentralization in Africa is far behind (Negwa 2002). For school construction, only Uganda has a legal framework that regularly channels the resources corresponding to their mandate to local governments.[29] In all other African countries, governments are still piloting

Table 5.9 Cost of Classrooms Built by Communities Compared with Other Management Arrangements

Country	Year	Project	Ministry	Community empowerment					Comparative approach				
				Financing agency	Procurement agency	Procurement method	Unit cost US$/m^2	Source	Project	Financing agency	Procurement agency	Procurement method	Unit cost US$/m^2	Source
Mauritania	1995–2000	Edu-V	MoE	IDA, FDA (France)	Community	Direct contract.	97	a	Urban Project-1	IDA	AMEXTIPE	NCB	277	c
	2000–05	PNDSE	MoE				148	b	Urban Project-2	KfW-IDA	AMEXTIPE	NCB	233	d
Uganda	1998–2000	SFG phase1	MoE	IDA	Community	LCB	52	e	LGDP-1	IDA	LG	LCB	54	f
Zambia	1999–2003	BESSIP	MoE	7 donors	Community	Labor: dir	134	g	BSCP	MoE	MoE	NCB	161	g
	2005	MPP	MoF	UE	Community	Materials: shop	84		MoE	HPIC	MoE	NCB	131	
Average							103						171	

Sources: (a) Theurynck 1999; (b) data collected by Theurynck; (c) Synergy 2000; (d) Rosso US$7,463 and Nouadhibou US$6,936, data collected by Theurynck; (e) Kisumba-Mugerwa et al. 2001; (f) World Bank 2004n; (g) Synergy 2006e.

Note: Unit costs are adjusted to 2006 prices using the US GDP deflator. For a complete list of acronyms, see p. xv.

Table 5.10 Status of Decentralization of School Construction in Selected Countries

Countries	Decentralization law or local government act (year)	Devolution of school construction to LGs
Benin	2003	yes (2003)
Burkina Faso	1998	yes (1/3 LG)
Ethiopia	1991	no
Ghana	1992	yes
Guinea	1991	no
Mali	1995	yes (2002)
Malawi	1998	no
Mauritania	1986	yes (1986)
Senegal	1996	yes (1996)
Tanzania	1990	yes (1990)
Uganda	1997	yes (1997)
Zambia	1992	yes (2005)

Source: See Appendix 8.

decentralization by transferring limited amounts to local governments for basic infrastructure investment through specific projects, as in Senegal, Mauritania, Ghana, and Benin.

Across countries, local governments have been involved in school construction through three different implementation arrangements:

- Direct implementation, by which local governments, procure, contract and pay contractors and site supervisors. Ghana, Guinea, Madagascar, and Senegal have projects piloting this approach, whereas Rwanda and Uganda have greater experience.[30] This approach is illustrated in Figure 5.16.[31]
- Delegation of construction management from local government to CMAs is currently implemented in Senegal and Mauritania, inparallel with one or two of the other approaches in urban areas under IDA-financed urban development and rural infrastructure projects.[32]
- Delegation from local governments to their local communities is also currently implemented in Benin, Ghana, and Uganda. Illustrations of the implementation arrangements for the second and third methods are in Appendix 11. In terms of costs, performances of local governments in school construction are quite similar to these of other agencies, such as central government, CMAs, NGOs, SFs, and local branches of MoEs, when they act by themselves or as CMAs or delegate to CMAs. Figure 5.17 illustrates that, on average, local governments—*when they act by themselves*—achieve slightly lower unit costs compared with contracting out the construction management to a CMA. However, costs are lowest when local governments delegate the construction management to communities.

Table 5.11 shows the comparative cost of local government management compared with CMA or other centralized approaches in six countries.

In the first group of two countries, local governments are outsourcing construction management to CMAs and achieving an average cost that is more than twice the average cost of comparator approaches. However, these averages mask

Procurement and Contract Management • 97

Figure 5.16 Devolution of School Construction to Local Governments

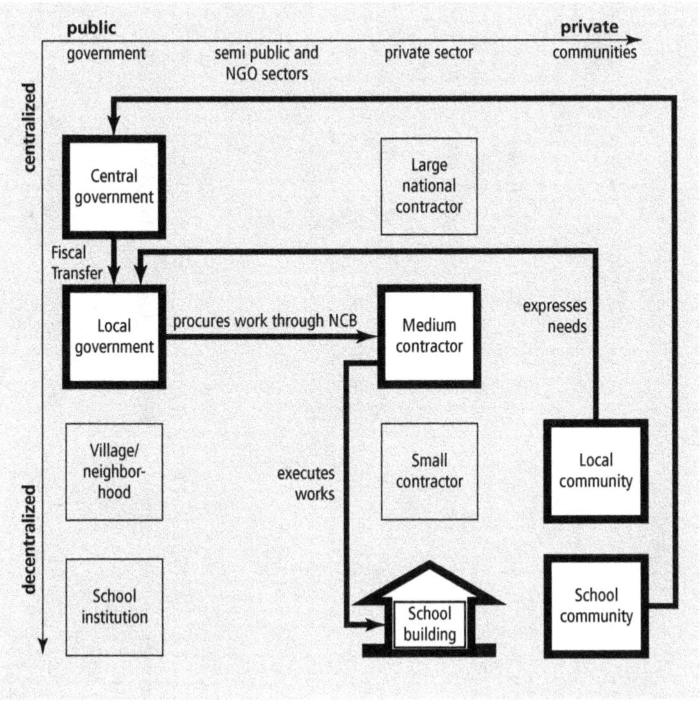

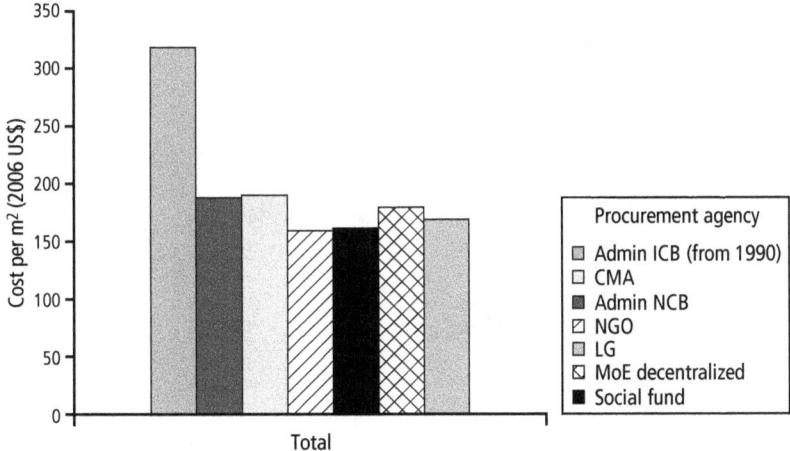

Source: Author's figure.

Figure 5.17 Cost per Gross m² of Classrooms Procured by Administration (ICB-NCB), CMAs, NGOs, SFs (as CMAs) and MoE Decentralized, and Local Governments

Source: List of projects in SSA countries in Appendix 18.
Note: Unit costs are adjusted to 2006 prices.

Table 5.11 Cost of Classroom Construction Built by Local Government through Different Modalities Compared with Other Agencies

Country	Year	Project name	Financing agency	Type of local government	Procurement agency	Procurement method	Unit cost US$/m²	Source	Project name	Financing agency	Procurement agency	Procurement method	Unit cost US$/m²	Source
Local governments out contract school construction to contract management agency														
Mauritania	1997–04	Urban Project 1	IDA	Urban LG	AMEXTIPE	NCB	277	a	Edu V	IDA/FDA	Communities	Direct contracting	97	d
	2005	Urban Project 2	IDA/KFW	Urban LG	AMEXTIPE	NCB	231	b	PNDSE	IDA/FDA	Communities	Direct contracting	148	b
Senegal	2000–05	Urban Project 1	IDA	Urban LG	AGETIP	NCB	149	c	EFA-1	Gov/HPIC	MoE	NCB	141	f
Average							219						129	
Local governments directly procure works for school construction														
Ghana	2002–05	ESSP/SU	DFID	Districts	Districts	NCB	86	g	BESIP	IDA	MoE (FPMU)	NCB	166	g
Guinea	1989–94	PASE-1	IDA	Prefects	Prefects	NCB/LCB	349	h	PCPEP	UNESCO	Donor	Direct	181	h
	2006–07	EFA/VCSP	IDA	Rural LG	Rural LG	LCB	215	i	EFA-1-2	IDA	NGO (CMA)	NCB	121	m
Senegal	2000–05	NRIP	IDA	Rural LG	Rural LG	LCB	140	j	EFA-1	IDA	CMA	NCB	152	f
Madagascar	2004–07	FID-IV	IDA	Rural LGs	Rural LG	LCB	127	k	OPEP	OPEP	MoE (PIU)	NCB	141	n
Rwanda	2004–06	HRDP	IDA	Rural LGs	Rural LG	NCB	194	l	Edu-III	AfDB	MoE (PIU)	NCB	263	o
Uganda	2004–07	LGDP-2	IDA	LGs	LGs	NCB	90	t	ESSIP	IDA	MoE (SFD)	NCB	141	u
Average							172						166	
Local governments delegate school construction to communities														
Benin	2006	NCDDSP	Gov/IDA	Rural and urban LG	Local communities	LCB	116	p	MoE	Gov	MoE	NCB	169	q
	2007						118	q						
Ghana	2000–03	MPP	UE	Rural LG	Community	Labor: dir Materials: shop	68	r	BESIP	IDA	MoE (FPMU)	NCB	166	r
Uganda	1997–07	ESIP (SWAP)	MoE/SFG	Rural LG	Community	LCB	81	s	SWAP	Gov/SFG	Cent off for urban schools	NCB	141	s
	2000–03	MPP	UE	Rural LG	Community	3 Q	92							
Average							95						159	

Sources: (a) Synergy 2000; (b) Rosso (KFW) US$11,843 and Nouadhibou (IDA) 12,500, data collected by Theurynck; (c) Urban Development and Decentralization Project (Dupety 2005a); (d) World Bank 2001e; (f) Education For All Project (Diouf 2006); (g) Education Sector Investment Plan (Group 5 2006b); (h) De Bosch Kemper et al. 1990, World Bank 1995c; (i) VCSP 2007; (j) National Rural Infrastructure Project (Diouf 2006); (k) National Community-Driven Development Support Project, data collected by Serge Theurynck; (l) Kayumba 2006, Kabuga 2001, MESTRS 2006; (m) Dupety 2004 and 2005c; (n) PNDCC 2007; (o) Kayumba 2006; (p) FID 2005a, 2005b, 2005c, 2007; (q) MENRS 2007; (r) Group 5 2006b; (s) Group 5 2006d; (t) Theurynck 2007a; (u) Group 5 2006d.

Note: Unit costs are adjusted to 2006 prices using the U.S. GDP deflator. For a complete list of acronyms, see p. xv.

different results of individual countries . In one country (Senegal) local go vernments are, through a CMA, performing just as w ell as the central go vernment, while in the second country (Mauritania), local go vernments are building classrooms, through a CMA, at a high unit cost that is more than double those achieved by communities. In this country, there is no other approach to include in the comparison.

- In the second group of six countries (including one of the first group), local governments are doing procurement b y themselv es and achieving unit costs that are, on a verage, slightly higher than those achiev ed in those countries b y central administrations or CMAs , although with large differences within individual countries.
- In the third group of three countries (including one of the second group), local governments are delegating the management of school construction to their local communities (four projects). In this group, all individual cases sho w the same result: local governments, though delegation to their communities achieve units costs that are , on a verage, less than half those of the central go vernment through NCB. The implementation scheme is illustrated in Appendix 8.

Although collected data are not sufficient to s ystematically compare the efficiency of construction management by local governments relative to other centralized approaches in the same country , data from Guinea and Senegal in table 5.1 1 suggest that local governments have no comparative advantage in terms of cost relative to central MoE management, or to management by a CMA, whereas data from Ghana, Madagascar, Rwanda, and Uganda suggest the opposite conclusion.

Data from Benin, Ghana, and Uganda suggest also that when local go vernments delegate the management of school construction projects to local communities, the latter outperform all other construction management methods. In these countries, community management lo wered the cost of construction b y between 20 to 3 0 percent, compared with direct management b y central or local go vernments or CMA. The Micro-Project Program in Ghana and the National CDD program in Benin are examples of good-quality w orks executed under community management, as a result of adequate supervision (Group 5 2006b, Bathys Consult 2007). The Benin example sho ws that proper technical supervision is effectiv e when carried out by private sector technicians hired on a competitive basis by the communities.[33] The second phase of the School F acility Grant in Uganda is an example of a wide range of quality w orks, due to inadequate site supervision b y LGs and the MoE.

However, similar to the results obtained in the Social Funds and the NGO examples of Benin, Ghana, Senegal, and Uganda, the data in table 5.12 show that community delegation outperforms all other construction management methods.

Table 5.12 Examples of Gross Unit Costs Obtained in Benin, Ghana, Senegal, and Uganda

Country	Procurement agency	US$/m²
Benin	MoE	157
	MoE delegating to CMA	156
	Communities by delegation from LG	113
Ghana	MoE	156
	LG	86
	Communities by delegation from NGO	68
Senegal	LG	140
	MoE	141
	CMA by delegation from LG	152
	Communities by delegation from SF	110
Uganda	MoE	141
	MPP by delegation to communities	83
	Communities by delegation from MoE (SFG-1)	52

Source: Preceding tables.

This result is achieved whether communities receive responsibility by delegation from an SF, an NGO, or LGs, or from MoEs, as in the examples of Mauritania and Zambia with equivalent quality of works.

COMMUNITY CONTRACTING

Of all the various management approaches, decentralized approaches to school construction management (whether by MoE branch offices, local governments, or especially communities) are the most cost effective, compared with centralized management approaches, such as the central MoE, CMAs, NGOs, and Social Funds when they act as CMAs.

Results from numerous countries—Benin, Burkina Faso, Ghana, Madagascar, Malawi, Mali, Mauritania, Senegal, Uganda, Zambia, India, Laos, and Vietnam—provide solid evidence that community delegation can significantly increase production and lower the cost of construction compared with other management strategies. They also show that community management provides good-quality construction. When we combine all community management experiences together, figure 5.18 shows that, on average, community-managed school construction achieved by far the lowest cost per classroom constructed. On average, communities built their own classrooms at US$110/m², a cost at least one-third lower than classrooms built by NGOs, CMAs, or central administration using NCB.

To further test the robustness of these results, a regression analysis was done based on data from 215 school construction projects in 30 countries, 23 of which are in Sub-Saharan Africa, and 7 in other regions (Latin America, East Asia &

Figure 5.18 Cost per Gross m² of Classrooms Procured by Administrative CMAs, NGOs, SFs (as CMAs), Local MoEs Decentralized, Local Governments, and Communities

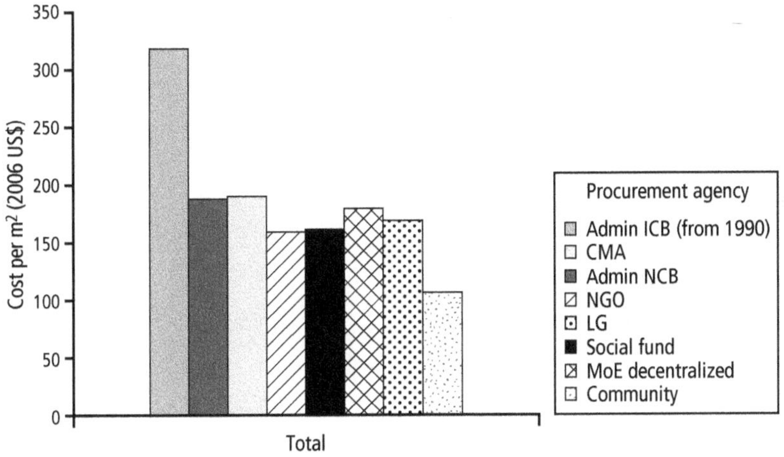

Procurement agency:
- Admin ICB (from 1990)
- CMA
- Admin NCB
- NGO
- LG
- Social fund
- MoE decentralized
- Community

Source: List of projects in SSA countries in Appendix 18.

Pacific, or South Asia). Most projects date to the past 10 years, although data from as far back as 1977 have been included for comparison. Of the 215 projects, the World Bank financed 93; NGOs, bilateral, or other multilateral donor agencies financed 104; and national governments financed 18. Unit construction costs in U.S. dollars were adjusted to 2006 prices using the U.S. GDP deflator.

Average unit cost is US$212. However, classroom construction projects invariably result in diverse construction costs across countries. Some countries might justifiably have higher unit costs because of a higher cost of labor, or longer distances between construction sites by reason of lower population density. Variations in costs may also be "random" or unexplained because every project is different and has its own set of administrative costs and overheads, or because the persons running the projects may be more or less successful at managing the procurement processes and keeping costs down.

To isolate the relative impact of procurement and management arrangements, we control for other variables that may affect costs, namely year of construction, as costs may increase or decrease over time, construction technology, financier, region, GNI per capita as a proxy for labor costs, availability of roads as a proxy for transport costs, population density that may affect both labor and transport costs, and a governance indicator to test the impact of corruption.

Table 5.13 shows the results of the regression analysis. On the left side, it shows the first model specification, including a long list of explanatory variables, some of which have a statistically significant impact on the cost and others that do not.

Table 5.13 Regression Estimates of the Impact of Project and Country-Specific Variables on the Classroom Construction Cost per Gross m² from Various Classroom Construction Projects

	Model specification 1		Model specification 2: reduced model[a]	
	Coefficient	t-statistic[a]	Coefficient	t-statistic
Intercept	121.4		192.2	
Continuous variables				
Project year[b]	−7.3	−4.4**	−7.0	−4.6**
Log (pop. density per square km)	−11.7	−1.5	−14.7	−2.1*
Log (GNI/capita)	10.3	0.5		
CPIA indicator on governance (quintile)	2.5	0.3		
Road to pop. ratio (km/m habitants)	0.0004	0.1		
Dummy variables				
Asia regions (EAP and SAS)	−83.3	−2.1*	−71.5	−2.1*
LAC region	180.1	2.1*	210.4	3.1**
Prefab	−3.2	−0.1		
Shelter	−252.3	−4.0**	−261.1	−4.3**
Bilateral or EU financing (except JICA)	69.1	3.4**	70.1	3.6**
JICA financing	346.5	7.1**	353.4	7.4**
Procurement agency = Admin ICB	80.6	2.0*	81.1	2.1*
Procurement agency = community	−70.2	−2.6*	−89.4	−4.1**
Execution of works = micro and small contractors	−28.4	−1.3		
Execution of works = large contractor	113.4	2.7**	119.7	3.4**
No. of observations	215		215	
R-square for regression	60.0%		60.0%	

Source: Kirsten Majgaards calculation.
Notes: * indicates statistical significance at the 5 percent level, ** statistical significance at the 1 percent level. (a) The reduced model only includes explanatory variables when their coefficients are significant at the 5 percent level. (b) This variable is computed as the project year minus 2006.

On the right side, the table shows a reduced model that includes only those variables that have statistically significant coefficients. The coefficient estimates can be interpreted as US$ increments in the unit cost. The analysis confirms the findings that ICB procurement is the highest-cost method of procuring construction services, whereas community management results in significantly lower costs. The empirical analysis shows that:

- Classroom construction is less costly in countries with a high population density: The higher density allows the contractor to organize work more efficiently because of the shorter distances between construction sites, and more availability

of labor and suppliers in the surroundings of each construction site. For example, the 2006 construction cost for a WB funded project in a country with a density of 14 persons per km^2 (like Zambia) would be US$153, compared to only US$121 per gross m^2 in a country with a density of 128 persons per km^2 (for example, Uganda).
- The construction cost was found to have declined over time, by about US$7 each year prior to 2006, reflecting the increased competition in the construction sector in many countries. The regional dummies indicate that—compared to Sub-Saharan Africa—costs are much higher in Latin America (the countries in our sample are Mexico and Brazil, where per capita incomes are much higher than in Africa), and a little lower in Asia (the countries included in our sample are Bangladesh, India, Laos, Pakistan, and the Philippines).
- Other than the regional differences in costs, which may be related to difference in income, there appears to be no impact from GNI per capita on the construction cost. Thus, within Sub-Saharan Africa, the poorest countries have the same structure of construction costs as the richer countries.
- No statistically significant difference was found between financing by the World Bank or other multilateral agencies, the UN, governments, or NGOs. Bilateral donors and the European Union were found to have higher costs, particularly in the case of JICA, whose costs are much higher than those of other donors.
- Shelters, not surprisingly, are significantly less costly than classic construction, while no statistical difference was found in the construction costs of classic techniques versus prefabrication.
- The indicators for governance and availability of roads had no impact on construction costs.
- When controlling for these other factors, centralized management with ICB results in significantly higher unit costs than other procurement methods—higher by US$81 per gross m^2, whereas community-based management and procurement result in significantly lower costs—lower by US$89 per gross m^2. Similarly, execution of works by large contractors is related to higher costs—higher by US$120 per gross m^2. Thus, the project design has more impact on the cost than country-specific parameters such as income per capita, availability of roads, and public sector governance.[34]

Despite these highly positive results, and the encouraging legal landscape for decentralization, the scope of decentralized management of school construction remains limited. Centralized planning and management of school construction remain the norm in most countries. Few African countries—Mauritania, Tanzania, Uganda, and South Africa being the exceptions—have devolved school construction management to local governments or communities. Table 5.14 shows that in a sample of eight African countries, centralized construction management still accounts for two-thirds of all recent school construction projects.

Table 5.14 Parallel Centralized and Decentralized Projects/Programs During 2000–04 in Selected African Countries

Country	Number of centralized projects	Number of decentralized projects	Total number of projects
Burkina Faso	9	4	13
Madagascar	10	1	11
Mauritania	0	2	2
Mozambique	9	1	10
Niger	8	0	8
Senegal	6	4	10
Uganda	0	2	2
Zambia	3	8	11
Average	6	3	8

Sources: Dupety 2005b; Group 5 2006a, c–e; Zerbo 2008; author's data.

Table 5.15 Local Government Expenditure as a Share of GDP and Government Expenditure, 1997–99

Country	Share of LG as % GDP	Share of LG expenditure/ total expenditure
Ghana	3	8
Senegal	1.8	7
Swaziland	0.6	2
Zambia	0.5	3
Zimbabwe	3	8
Uganda	4	21
Total	2.1	8
Nigeria	1.2 (6)*	5 (26)*
OECD	11	10–35

Source: Olowu 2003.
Note: *All subnational expenditures, that is, state and local governments.

Within government, the transfer of administrative and fiscal management has been slow as shown by the small proportion of resources transferred to local governments, and the proportion of resources the latter spends compared to total public spending. Table 5.15 shows that in 1999, in a sample of six countries that have enacted decentralization laws, the percentage of public expenditure spent through local governments is no more than 8 percent, compared to an average of 22.5 percent in developed countries, ranging between 40 percent in the Nordic countries, 32 percent in OECD countries, and 10 to 20 percent in Asian and Latin

Table 5.16 Status of Decentralization of School Construction in Selected Countries

Countries	Decentralization law or local government act (year)	Actual transfer of school construction from MoE to LGs in 2005	Some delegation of school construction to LGs through projects in 2005
Benin	2003	no	yes
Burkina Faso	1998	no	yes
Ethiopia	1991	no	N/A
Ghana	1992	no	yes
Mali	1995	no	yes
Malawi	1998	no	yes
Mauritania	1986	no	no
Senegal	1996	no	yes
Tanzania	1990	yes	
Uganda	1997	yes	no
Zambia	1992	no	yes

Source: See Appendix 8.

American countries (Negwa 2002). Francophone and lusophone countries, heirs of both the Roman and Napoleonic traditions based on a highly centralized state, are less likely to delegate construction management to local levels (World Bank 2004j).

Further, Ministries of Education are reluctant to release their control over school construction. Table 5.16 shows that of 11 countries that have enacted legislation that delegates school construction management to local governments, MoEs continue to manage the majority of school construction programs in nine of them. The two exceptions are Tanzania and Uganda. Appendix 8 provides further information levels of decentralization and compliance of Ministries of Education with regard to school construction.

The most common argument given by MoEs for their unwillingness to comply with the law is that local governments do not have the management capacity, and they worry that local government will not spend the resources for the purposes intended. The fact is, however, that few countries have even tried to determine how best to match fiscal and administrative arrangements to achieve efficient service delivery within devolution. As a result, across Africa, central governments, local governments, and community organizations carry out parallel school building programs with little to no coordination or harmonization. Worse, these programs are often financed by the same donors. Figure 5.19, for example, illustrates four parallel programs involving school construction undertaken in Senegal at the same time, financed by the same donor.

Figure 5.19 Simultaneous IDA-funded Projects Financing School Construction with Different Approaches in Senegal. 2005

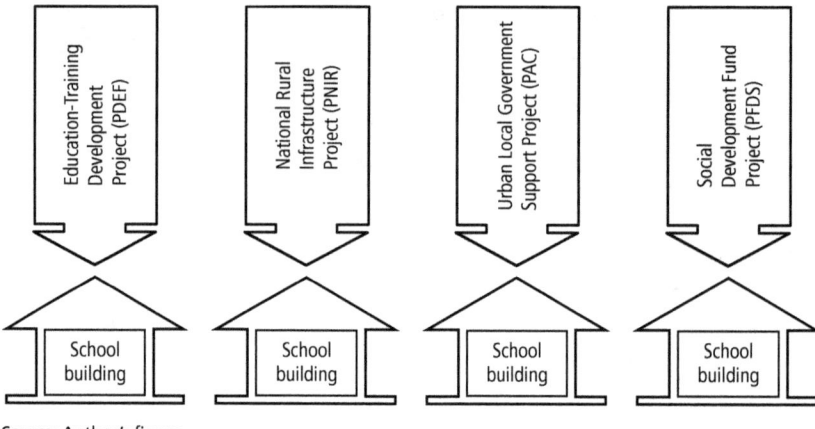

Source: Author's figure

Experience shows that reformers will have to manage resistance from MoE civil servants who fear a loss of power, or their jobs, from the shift to a community-based approach to school construction. This is clearly not the case however. Decentralization and community empowerment do not mean chipping away at the MoE. Rather, they imply a mutually beneficial joint venture among different levels of the central government, local governments, and communities in which each has specific roles to play according to their comparative advantage in a learning-by-doing approach. Building this understanding is part of the development challenge.

CONCLUSIONS

The experiences of Benin, Burkina Faso, Ethiopia, Ghana, Madagascar, Malawi, Mali, Mauritania, Senegal, Uganda, and Zambia show that community delegation has been the most effective. The notions that communities and local governments are unable to manage school construction are highly inaccurate These experiences show that communities can organize themselves quickly to diagnose local problems, identify priorities, develop solutions and action plans, and execute those plans. Communities can be trained efficiently and successfully to carry out procurement and financial management methods that ensure transparency economy, and efficiency through adapted training methods. These experiences also show that the quality of the works done by local contractors is—as in any other implementation arrangement—heavily dependent on the efficiency of the technical supervision, which is always more efficient when the technical supervision service is competitively contracted out to private sector providers. This is true whether the contract is provided by communities or any other entity such as MoEs, LGs, CMAs, or SFs. Experiences in Senegal and Benin show that communities can procure good technical supervision services and ensure good quality of the works.

Moreover, when communities are empowered with information, resources, and technical support they outperform all other construction management arrangements in terms of cost for quality and delivery time.

NOTES

1. In Senegal, classrooms procured through ICB averaged around US$14,000 in 1982. In Niger the range of cost per classroom was about US$15,500 in 1984 (World Bank 1986). In Mauritania, the cost in 1984 ranged between US$17,000 to US$30,000 per classroom (World Bank 1988, UNESCO 1984).

2. For instance, AfDB-financed PERP in Ghana during 1998–2004 (Group 5 2006b); in Zambia, the OPEC-financed Primary School Upgrading Project (Group 5 2006e).

3. The combined approach was implemented through the IDA-financed Education III (1985–94) and Education IV (1992–98).

4. The community participation strategy resulted in costs of US$120 per m^2 in 1993–1995 compared to US$93 per m^2 achieved by the Ministry of Education in 1993–1997 (World Bank 1999c, Synergy 1997).

5. Urban communities are served by the Urban Development Project, which requires contributions from local government and not from communities, whereas rural communities are served by the MoE-managed education programs whereby communities have to contribute 30 percent of the estimated cost.

6. During the 1981–1990 period, the Ministry of Public Works managed the school construction program of the first Education Project and built 60 classrooms in 3.5 years (World Bank 1981, 1996d). The IDA-financed second Education project, the Primary Education Development Project (1987–95), abandoned the full ICB approach for the combination of ICB for materials and LCB for labor by microenterprise.

7. From FCFA 4,370,000 in 1984 (Ministry of Public Works, ICB), to FCFA 2,178,000 in 1994 under MoE management through the combined approach, and FCFA 3,000,000 in 1995 after the devaluation

8. In Madagascar, AfDB- and OPEC-financed projects; in Rwanda, AfDB- and UNICEF-financed projects.

9. The 16 countries are Cape Verde (AGECABO), Chad (A TETIP), Benin (A GETUR, AGETIP, PRIMO), Burkina Faso (Faso Baara), Burundi (ABUTIP), Central African Republic, Djibouti, Gabon, Gambia (GAMWORKS), Guinea-Bissau, Madagascar, Mali (A GETIP-Mali), Mauritania (AMEXTIPE), Mozambique, Niger (NIGETIPE), and Togo. The network is AFRICATIPE.

10. In Senegal after 7 years of A GETIP activities, the number of construction firms increased fivefold (World Bank 2006j). In Mali, after 5 years of AGETIP-Mali activities, the number of enterprises boomed from 400 to 1,280 enterprises in 1996 (Bigio 1998).

11. Madagascar (Law 99-023 dated July 30, 1999); Benin (Laws 2001-07 and 2005-07 dated May 9, 2001); and Mauritania (Law 2005-020 dated January 30, 2005).

12. Burkina Faso (IDA funds), Cape Verde (IDA and AfDB funds), Chad (IDA funds), Senegal (IDA, KfW, and AfDB funds), The Gambia (IDA funds), and Madagascar (AfDB funds).

13. AGETIP first became involved in primary school construction in 1992 under an IDA-financed primary education development project. This involvement was continued under subsequent projects financed by IDA and the KfW.

14. The list includes 19 projects managed by administration through ICBs, 37 projects managed by administration through NCB, and 30 projects managed by CMAs.

15. Such results regarding comparable costs between AGETIPs and other actors are also mentioned in Diou et al. 2007, p. 30.

16. This is a case of conflict of interest. See Diou et al. 2007.

17. World Bank, Operation Manual, BP 800—Rapid Response to Crises and Emergencies, March 1, 2007.

18. 179 of a total of 644 projects approved in 2001.

19. NGOS included Save The Children, World Education, World Vision, Plan International, and 10 local NGOs.

20. Education Sector Consolidation Project financed by IDA, USAID, Norway, the French FAC and CIDA (World Bank 1989c).

21. Education components in noneducation projects totaled US$908.4 million in fiscal year 2005, compared with US$1.95 billion channeled through projects in the education sector itself.

22. Social Funds were established in Guinea in 1989, in Sao-Tome & Principe and Zambia in 1991, Madagascar and Rwanda in 1993, Comoros and Burundi in 1994, Angola, Eritea and Ethiopia in 1996, Malawi in 1997, Mali, Benin and Zimbabwe in 1998, Togo and Ghana in 1999, Angola, Lesotho and Tanzania in 2000, Nigeria and Senegal in 2001, Uganda in 2002, Kenya in 2005, and in the Central Africa Republic in 2007.

23. This pattern is common to all demand-driven approaches. The demand-driven, EU-financed Micro-Projects Program also finds that education is the first sector, absorbing 25 percent of the resources (EDA 2006).

24. The comparison is with central governments *when they used NCB,* and NGOs *when they act as contractors or CMAs.*

25. See World Bank Aide-memoires of the Project supervision missions.

26. During the first phase of the Ugandan School Facility Grant 1998–2002.

27. Danida, DFID, Finland, Ireland, Netherland, Norway and the government are commonly financing the Basic Education Sub-Sector Plan—BESSIP (Group 5 2006a)

28. The EU-financed MPP started in 1985, joined with the IDA-financed Social Recovery Project in 1991 and separated when it transformed into ZAMSIF in 2001. It disburses directly to communities.

29. And also South Africa, but this country is not part of this study.

30. In Uganda, delegation to LGs under the SGF started in 2002 after a community empowerment phase in 1998–2002.

31. In 2006, the MoE in Guinea delegated part of the school construction program to rural local governments comprising 113 classrooms and other facilities under the Village Communities Support Program (World Bank 1999d). In Senegal, this approach was implemented between 2000–06 under the IDA-financed National Rural Infrastructure Project (World Bank 1999g).

32. Local governments in Mauritania have delegated the management of infrastructure programs to AMEXTIPE since 1997. School construction represented 28 percent of the 149 projects managed by AMEXTIPE (World Bank 2002). In Senegal, under the IDA-financed Urban Development Projects, local governments have delegated their construction programs to AGETIP.

33. The technical specialist is hired before the community launches the local competitive biding for works. He plays the role of community adviser for the procurement of works, including finalization of the bidding documents; subsequently, he controls the quality and certifies the execution of the works before the community pays the contractor. The contract for works includes provisions for laboratory tests of the quality of the concrete.

34. However, a relatively large proportion of the variation in unit cost is still unexplained (R^2 is 60 percent). This suggests that there may be additional factors—project- or country-specific—that affect the costs; factors that we have not been able to capture in the regression analysis owing to very limited project information (omitted variables) or the use of proxies that reflect poorly what we are trying to measure (measurement error). It could also indicate that a fair proportion of the variation in construction costs is random, or depends on factors, such as the skills of the persons managing the processes, that are very hard to measure.

CHAPTER 6

Setting up Community Management

The evidence shows that communities have a long history of self-help and have built many of their own schools throughout the years. They are highly capable of doing much better, with some help and resource transfer.

Community-based programs can work under various management arrangements. Nevertheless, policy makers often believe that community-based approaches are too complicated to set up relative to centrally managed school construction programs and they worry about accountability and community capacity. Yet experience proves otherwise. When accountability mechanisms are adequate and when communities are empowered, community-based programs are highly successful. Experience across countries with the Community-Driven Development (CDD) approach provides useful lessons in how to set up community-based programs that address these issues.

Community-Driven Development is a term used by the World Bank to characterize investment programs that support decentralization. CDD programs aim to set up appropriate accountability mechanisms within a decentralized environment and strengthen community choice and empowerment in implementing small-scale infrastructure programs. CDD projects give more responsibility to communities than Community-Based Development (CBD), particularly over resources and decisions in projects' design and implementation. In the Bank, the proportion of CBD/CDD projects has increased from 2 to 10 percent of total lending between 1989 and 2003, with more emphasis on CDD in recent years, and their outcome ratings have been better than those of non-CBD/CDD projects. The largest share of CDD projects is in Africa, and CDD projects in education do better than in other sectors (OED 2005c). The application of the CDD model to school construction provides considerable guidance on how to set up a CDD approach that addresses the dual concerns of accountability and community empowerment. In a CDD approach, accountability is strengthened in two main ways—through a clear definition of the roles and accountabilities of the stakeholders involved, and through monitoring and evaluation and information flows. Empowerment is

Figure 6.1 The CDD Scheme for School Construction

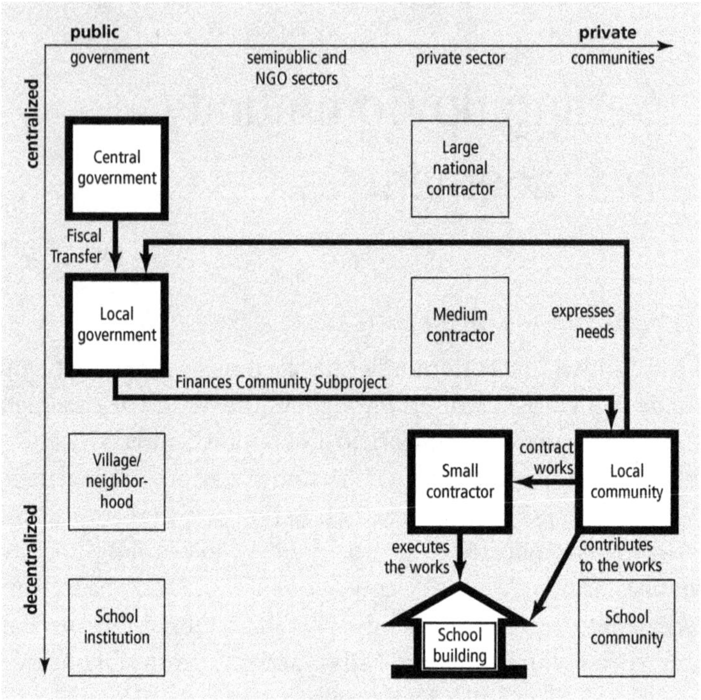

[Figure: A diagram with axes labeled "public" to "private" horizontally (columns: government, semipublic and NGO sectors, private sector, communities) and "centralized" to "decentralized" vertically. Boxes include: Central government → (Fiscal Transfer) → Local government → (Finances Community Subproject) → Local community (expresses needs); Large national contractor, Medium contractor, Small contractor; Local community contracts works to Small contractor which executes the works; Local community contributes to the works; School building; Village/neighborhood; School institution; School community.]

Source: Author's figure.

fostered through community organization, full information, appropriate procedures, and capacity development. The implementation scheme is illustrated in figure 6.1. Other specific type of implementation schemes in Uganda can be found in Appendix 8.

The use of the CDD approach for the school construction program addresses issues that may be considered within a broader policy framework. The following section discusses the role of actors, organization and procedures, and capacity building needed for this approach.

ACCOUNTABILITY

ROLES OF STAKEHOLDERS

The CDD approach considers that school construction is the coproduction of four actors—Ministries of Education (MoEs), local governments, communities, and the private sector, which is contracted by communities to build the schools

Figure 6.2 School Construction in a CDD Approach: Main Responsibilities of the Four Actors

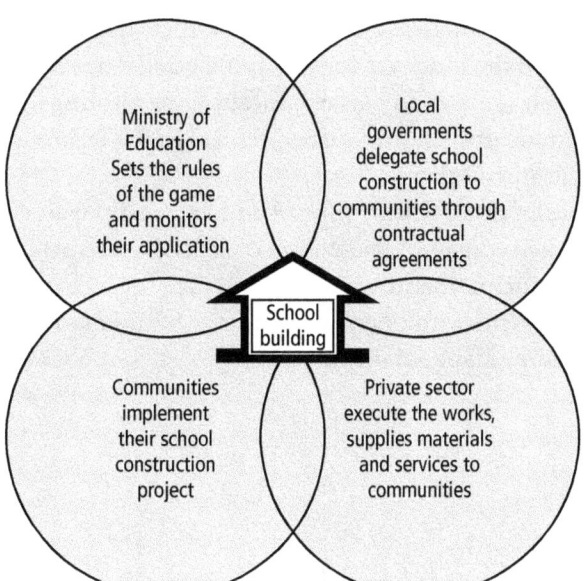

Source: Author's figure.

and provide technical supervision of the contracted works (figure 6.2). Each has its role to play in the project cycle as follows. Appendix 11 summarizes these roles according to key stages in the project cycle.

The Ministry of Education plays a strategic, policy-setting, financing, capacity-building, and regulatory role. It

- establishes norms and criteria to allocate financial and human resources to relieve obstacles to primary education for all and reduce disparities;
- establishes school planning norms, school models, and architectural and construction norms that facilitate implementation by local governments and communities. Box 6.1 shows a list of essential norms;
- adjusts the roles of MoE branch office staff from construction implementers to technical advisers of local governments and communities;
- mobilizes adequate funding for education as a whole, which requires successful negotiations with Ministries of Finance, parliaments, and donors;
- sets up reliable procurement and financial management procedures and accountability mechanisms to be followed by all actors;
- establishes appropriate targeting strategies to reach disadvantaged communities;
- establishes technical and financial norms for maintenance;

- coordinates donors to support the strategy;
- empowers local governments by (1) providing them with adequate resources according to transparent criteria; (2) ensuring that they are aware of national priority objectives and the purposes for which the budget has been allocated; and (3) building their capacity to master education monitoring indicators and planning tools, and incorporate education progress in the monitoring systems of their local development plans;
- builds capacity of local governments to work in partnership with communities, and to delegate to them the implementation of school construction according to the subsidiarity principle[1]; and
- equips local governments with operation manuals for themselves and their communities, including standard documents.

BOX 6.1 NORMS TO BE ESTABLISHED BY MoEs

School Planning Norms and School Models

- A maximum distance from home to school of less than 2 kilometers
- A minimum primary school size that maximizes the use of multigrade classes to ensure efficiency in teacher utilization and construction resources
- A standard minimum school facility package that includes office and storage space, water, latrines, and furniture
- A menu of models for urban and rural schools, including one- or two-classroom models

Architectural and Construction Norms

- A standard classroom area that allows for interactive and multigrade classes and a library area
- Classroom and latrine models that are simple and economical, that have been widely tested in the country, and that can be constructed by small local contractors
- A menu of simple and economic water supply systems adapted to different conditions
- A furniture design that allows for mobility and diversification of teaching strategies

In the CDD approach, *local governments (LGs)*

- develop and implement local development plans, incorporating the Millennium Development Goals and other national priorities in local plans;
- analyze essential information on education trends in the jurisdiction and assess the gaps;
- mobilize communities and build their capacity to identify, prepare, and submit a request for financing, and to implement school construction projects;
- enter into a financing agreement (FA) with communities to build their schools;
- appraise and approve the community projects against the norms established by the MoE and against the eligibility criteria for inclusion in the local government development plans;
- legally provide the land for the school as required;
- monitor the execution of the FA by the communities;
- incorporate the school facilities in a patrimonial accounting system; and
- budget annually for maintenance.

Communities organize themselves, identify their education needs, and prepare and implement their school construction projects through an inclusive participatory approach. They submit a request for financing their school project, sign an FA with the funding agency, manage the funds allocated, as well as the procurement of works, goods, and technical services for work supervision from the local private sector, using simplified procurement procedures. The request for financing should be based on a standard form provided by the MoE, and should include certain basic elements listed in box 6.2. They sign, monitor, and pay the contracts for works on the basis of the certification of good execution provided by the technical site supervisor. They report to the local government on the FA execution.

BOX 6.2 ESSENTIALS FOR A COMMUNITY REQUEST

- Number of classrooms and other facilities for which financing is requested
- Justifications (including estimates of need based on the school-age population), enrollment, distance to school, number of children per classroom, status of existing facilities and use of multigrade or double-shift teaching, and community commitment to enroll all children
- Standard drawings with technical specifications and estimated cost
- Composition of the Community Development Committee and the Project Management Committee, with minutes of the decision meetings for their creation

- Community bank account information
- Agreement to use simplified procurement procedures agreed upon by the MoE and LGs, and a procurement plan
- The community's contribution to the project and for maintenance

INFORMATION, MONITORING, AND EVALUATION

Maintaining an appropriate level of accountability in a CDD approach hinges to a great degree on information. First is the transparent information about the roles and responsibilities, and how the program is intended to function. Second, monitoring and evaluation provide a second source of information critical to all stakeholders. Monitoring and evaluation (M&E) are also essential in a learning-by-doing approach to provide information on areas in need of improvement.

In a CDD approach, monitoring and evaluation involve both the MoE and local governments in an integrated system. MoEs need to help local governments use education statistics and evaluate progress relative to established goals. This requires that the MoE disaggregate its data to report on education performance in each local government area and, if possible, at the ward or village level. Local governments also need to inform the MoE and communities regarding their performance. The M&E system should also track the flow of funds to local governments and communities, and conduct cost-effectiveness analyses to determine whether the government's approach is more (or less) cost-effective than comparable interventions by other actors.

MoEs should promote quantitative and qualitative evaluation. The first group should include multivariate regression analysis to control for possible observable characteristics that distinguish participant communities in school construction programs and nonparticipant ones, or *double difference analysis* (or difference-in-difference analysis) to compare participating communities with comparison communities. Qualitative studies should use focus groups, participant observation, and case studies to provide information on processes, behaviors, and conditions in participating communities.

COMMUNITY EMPOWERMENT

COMMUNITY ORGANIZATION

Community organization is a first critical step in the CDD process. To manage public resources, communities need to form legitimate community-based organizations (CBOs). CBOs may take various forms. In Mauritania, for example, this role has been played by parents' associations. In Social Fund projects, this role has been played by preexisting CBOs, such as women farmers' associations, even if education is not their main objective. Although the World Bank does not require legalization of the community group, national laws and regulations may require it to allow the CBO to receive and manage public funds (De Silva 2002).

In all countries, national legislation generally provides the formal rules that legitimate such organizations. These include decentralization laws, public works laws, delegation of public works management, and financial laws and regulations. In many countries, legislation already provides for community-based formal representative bodies to enter into formal agreements with local governments to manage public funds. These include, for example, village and ward development committees in Tanzania, village and parish councils in Uganda, and village councils in Mali (UNCDF 2006). In other countries, these laws and regulations may require amendments to allow communities to manage public funds. In Benin, for example, the laws regulating civil society organizations allowed communities to organize themselves as "associations." However, under the 2001 Public Works Contract Management Delegation Law, conceived as a framework for contract management agencies (CMAs), the management of public funds for infrastructure projects could not be delegated to community associations. As a result, the Government of Benin revised this law in 2004 to allow local community associations to act as local contract management agents for the construction of small-scale local infrastructures by delegation from communes, thus enabling the implementation of a CDD program (World Bank 2004c).[2]

An approach that has been adopted by numerous countries, and that has worked well, is for the community to organize two committees—a Community Development Committee (CDC), which acts as the CBO, and a Project Management Committee (PMC). The CDC is the legal body responsible for the school project, enters into the FA with the funding agency on behalf of the community, and is accountable for the use of the funds. The CDC also organizes a Community Tender Board, which is composed of community members with gender parity and inclusion of the disabled, and whose sessions are open to public attendance. The PMC is a small committee composed of about four people, responsible for planning, procurement, and day-to-day project management, and is accountable to the CDC and community at large. Awarded contracts are monitored by the PMC, which posts the progress of payments in a public area accessible to all community members.

APPROPRIATE PROCEDURES

An FA and simplified procurement procedures are key elements in the process of facilitating community empowerment.

The financing agreement supports community empowerment by "contractualizing" the roles and responsibilities of local governments as funders, and communities as implementers. Through the FA, the community commits itself to build the facilities according to standard drawings and within an agreed maximum cost. The community manages the funds and the procurement of goods and services. It pays the contractor on the basis of certification of works by an engineer that is also contracted by the community to supervise the site-works. In turn, the funding agency commits itself to disburse the funds to the community in installments, on the basis of progress. A summary of the content of an FA between a community and local government is displayed in box 6.3.

Simplified procurement procedures are also fundamental to a CDD approach. The main goals of procurement procedures are to ensure economy and efficiency in procurement, safeguard transparency in the procurement process, ensure eligible bidders a fair opportunity to compete, and encourage the development of domestic contracting. Some countries lack an adequate National Procurement Code, and when they have one, it lacks appropriate provisions for procurement by local government or community organizations (De Silva 2000).

Recognizing this gap, some donor agencies have developed specific procurement guidelines for community contracting. For example, the World Bank provides general and specific guidelines. Its general guidelines allow for the adaptation of the procurement procedures, specifications, and contract packaging when it is desirable to call for the participation of local communities or non-governmental organizations in the delivery of services. The guidelines also allow for situations when it is desirable to increase the utilization of local know-how or materials, or employ labor-intensive or other appropriate technologies (World Bank 2004l).[3] Consistent with this policy, the World Bank has issued several publications with specific guidance to support implementation of community contracting and fund

---

BOX 6.3   ESSENTIAL ELEMENTS OF A FINANCIAL AGREEMENT

- Standard drawings and technical specifications
- A procurement plan, including estimated contract value and simplified procurement methods
- Models of simplified bid documents and contracts with contractors and site supervisors
- A schedule for payment of the grant, in installments according to physical progress of the works
- Models of reports to be provided by the community to support its requests for payments

BOX 6.4 COMMUNITY-BASED PROCUREMENT: KEY FEATURES

Tools and Documents

- Operation manual and community handbook
- Simplified invitation to bid form
- Simplified bidding document with standard design and specifications as provided by the MoE
- Simplified contract

Procurement Methods

- Local competitive bidding with local advertisement for works
- Three price quotations for works or goods, or both
- Shortlist of consultants for site supervision (generally provided by local government or other funding agency)

Procedures

- Invitation to bid form posted in local public places (trees, buildings)
- Community Tender Board with gender parity and inclusion of handicapped people
- Public community information on offered prices and contracts awarded, including the contract amount and payments when made

management in projects it finances.[4] The key features of community procurement are described in box 6.4. These procedures should be made explicit in a program handbook for management of the program and for the participating communities (De Silva 2002).

CAPACITY BUILDING

Capacity building across all stakeholders is essential for a CDD or any community-based approach to work. Capacity building through information and specific training needs to be built in.

Ensuring broad provision of all the necessary information, such as operation manuals, standard designs, model FAs and contracts, and lists of competent local contractors and site supervisors is fundamental. Successful experiences show that several documents can

Figure 6.3 Senegal Social Fund Handbook Illustration for Training Communities in Establishing a Community Development Committee

Source: AFDS 2002; drawing by Aly Nguer.

facilitate this flow of information. These include handbooks for the MoE, local governments, and communities. Box 6.5 shows the essentials to include in these handbooks. The MoE handbook targets MoE local staff to play their new roles as technical advisers to local governments and communities, capable of training local governments and communities on school norms and standards, and efficiently participating in the local governments' appraisal committees.

BOX 6.5   HANDBOOK ESSENTIALS

The Community Handbook

- The project cycle and role of the MoE, local government, and community
- Expected community organization
- Standard drawings and specifications of the school facility
- Procurement and disbursement procedures
- How to plan for implementation of a school project
- How to operate a project account and which records to keep
- How to assess and mitigate any environmental risks
- How to manage community contributions and store materials
- Draft contracts for the procurement of goods, works, and services
- How to monitor and provide information on results
- How to provide for maintenance

The Local Government Handbook

- Simple data formats and tools to enable local governments to assess their needs
- Mechanisms to target poor communities
- Role and accountabilities of the local government relative to communities and the MoE
- Criteria for appraising a community project
- Description of the role of MoE's local representative in the project cycle
- Standard drawings and specifications of the school facilities
- Model of FA
- Description of the required accounting procedures
- Description of procedures to budget for and maintain the facilities
- How to monitor and provide information on results

The MoE Local Staff Handbook

- Methods for the collection and analysis of basic education indicators
- Methods to help local governments and communities learn about the community project cycle and norms for school construction, and to prepare and submit a school construction project for financing
- Standard designs and cost estimates for facilities
- Model of FA
- Guidelines for local MoE staff to participate in appraising project proposals
- Monitoring and reporting requirements.

The local government handbook targets the local government officials and their staff, as well as local representatives of other ministries that are involved in construction or that oversee the effectiveness of locally elected bodies. The local government handbook may be conceived and organized regardless of the sector concerned by community projects, or it may be conceived for education sector needs.

The community handbook should describe the various stages of implementation of the activities at each stage. The community handbook targets the community as a whole for monitoring and sustainability issues, the CBO, and the PMC. It should be written in simple language, translated into local languages, and should use as many illustrations as possible to facilitate easy access in communities where literacy levels are limited (De Silva 2002).

Training is the second essential element. Both the CDC and PMC need to be trained in project management and procurement. Grassroots Management Training (GMT) programs, such as those developed by the World Bank Institute, have proven highly effective in communities with limited literacy.[5] The GMT method uses role playing and discussions based on illustrations. GMT programs recruit local people as trainers, adapt training programs to the context and local knowledge, and involve the community in the design and execution of the program. Figure 6.4 shows an excerpt from the Senegal Social Fund handbook used for training a community to establish a CDC with gender parity and the inclusion of disabled members through a transparent process based on public meetings. Appendix 13 provides illustrations from the same handbook on procurement training that was used to train members of the CDC and the PMC in about 1,000 villages over 4 years, of which about 500 are now community-based procurement specialists.

Benin is an example of a successful scale-up of such capacity building programs: in 3 years, under the national CDD program, 40 percent of the targeted

Figure 6.4 Deconcentrated Planning, Community Empowerment, and Financing through Fiduciary Agency

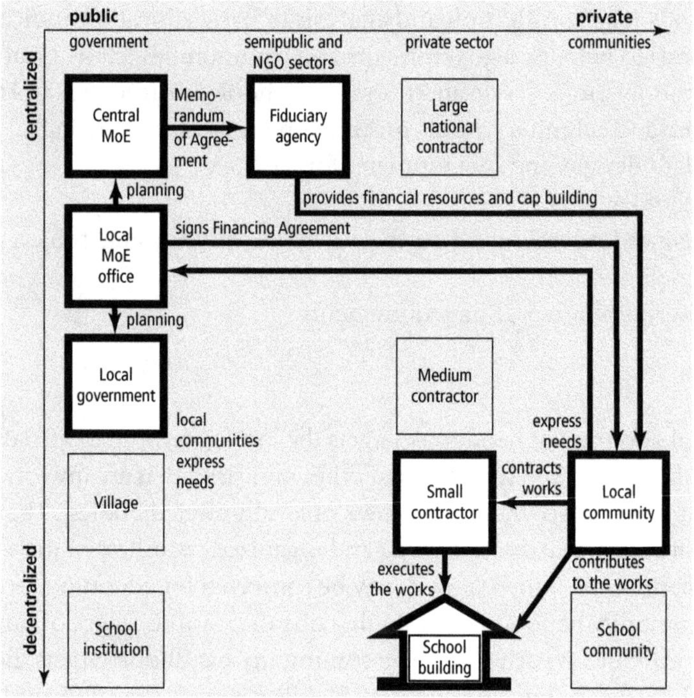

Source: Author's figure.

villages in the country received GMT training and successfully implemented local projects of their choice, 80 percent being schools (World Bank 2007a).[6] On the basis of this experience, the MoE decided in 2008 to move away from direct construction management and to use EFA-FTI funds to implement part of the school construction program using the CDD approach illustrated in figure 6.1 (Benin 2008).[7] Also, in the context of FTI, the Malagasy MoE decided in 2007 to develop a demand-driven decentralized strategy for school construction by which local governments and communities will be implementers of school construction (MENRS 2007a). The community-based program illustrated in figure 6.4 will be also used in 2008 to implement an emergency program to rebuild about 700 classrooms destroyed by cyclones in February 2008.

The CDD approach also provides a model for defining responsibilities for maintenance.

- MoEs are responsible for setting up the rules of the game for maintenance, and ensuring that an adequate volume of resources flows to the maintenance funding agencies.

- Where local governments are responsible for school maintenance and for the management of financial resources for school maintenance transferred to them by the central government, they should contract with local communities or school boards for the execution of maintenance activities including management of maintenance funds.
- Communities (or school boards) should be responsible for day-to-day maintenance and repair or rehabilitation works, using local governments' delegated financial resources, for which they are accountable to the local governments; in such a scheme, the head of school has a particular responsibility to develop the maintenance planning.
- The private sector is responsible for executing maintenance work under contracts with the communities' school boards. The chapter on maintenance of the 2004 AfDB Toolkit of Quality Education Project advises a similar approach (African Development Bank Group 2004).

NOTES

1. Subsidiarity is an organizing principle that states that matters ought to be handled by the smallest, lowest, or least centralized competent authority.
2. Laws no. 2001–07 dated May 9, 2001, and no. 2005–07 dated April 8, 2005.
3. See section 3.17.
4. See Gopal 1995, Mbungu 1999, Cavero 2000, De Silva 2002, and World Bank 2002.
5. The Grassroots Management Training (GMT) was developed in 1993 by the Economic Development Institute (EDI), now World Bank Institute, and used since by Burkina Faso, India, Mali, Malawi, Mauritania, Nigeria, Tanzania, and Senegal.
6. The targeted 40 percent number (1,500 villages).
7. The other part of the program is outsourced to CMAs.

CHAPTER 7

School Maintenance

The durability of school buildings not only results from design and quality construction, but also relies heavily on maintenance. Throughout Africa, maintenance of public facilities, including schools, is wanting. This lack of maintenance not only erodes confidence in the education system, it also results in the need for large and costly rehabilitation programs soon after the building is constructed. In African countries, classroom maintenance is compounded by the many classrooms built by communities with local nonpermanent materials that require a high level of upkeep to keep them operational. In Chad, Senegal, and Guinea, for example, the World Bank estimates that between 13–20 percent of classrooms built with nondurable materials need urgent rehabilitation (World Bank 2001c, 2003b).

There are several reasons for this lack of maintenance on the part of the government, donor, and community. On the government side, first, most countries have not established clear maintenance policies, strategies, or implementation arrangements. Second, governments rarely allocate sufficient financing for maintenance, even when they have a maintenance policy preferring to allocate resources for new construction. In Senegal, maintenance was treated as a technical problem only. The MoE developed an excellent maintenance guide in the 1980s that is still useful today. However, the cost of maintenance was never estimated, and the financing was never budgeted (DECS 1985). In other cases, to the extent that resources *are* allocated for school maintenance, they are usually included under the broader budget line of "operations and maintenance" (O&M). To start, O&M budgets represent an insignificant share of recurrent education expenditure. Once utilities, chalk, paper, travel costs, and other recurrent expenditure are paid, nothing is left for maintenance. Third, when the countries' decentralization laws devolve responsibility for maintenance to local governments, the corresponding funds are rarely transferred from the central to local governments. Finally, an important reason explaining the failure of school maintenance can be found in the lack of clarity regarding who is the owner of the land on which the school is built, particularly in a decentralized context. As a result, few African countries have ever piloted maintenance programs, but instead offload maintenance onto communities.[1]

For their part, maintenance by communities rarely materializes. Communities rarely assume this responsibility in the absence of financing because the commitment of communities to maintain buildings that are government owned is often absent as communities consider that the buildings should be maintained by the owner. This reluctance is likely to be more pronounced when the quality of construction is low, thus requiring even more maintenance. Poor communities also have difficulty mobilizing the resources required, either due to lack of organization or competing pressures on family and community budgets. If they had contributed to the construction of the school, they may feel that they have already made their contribution. Further, communities may not understand the basic rules of maintenance and how to put this into practice. According to a World Bank Impact Evaluation of Social Funds conducted in 2000, "there is a gap between the community declaring itself the owner of the project and understanding in theory the basic rules of maintenance, and putting all this knowledge into practice (OED 2002)." As a result, in projects with maintenance components with communities, results are generally far from expectations (World Bank 1979, World Bank 1982).

Finally, there are the donors. Donors pour additional resources into rehabilitation but never fix the maintenance problem. Few donor-supported projects include a maintenance component. When they do, the component is limited to capacity-building activities and limited pilots, but no project has ever succeeded in scaling up maintenance activities and streamlining them into regular postproject activities. Maintenance can hardly be financed through projects that are short-term, while maintenance is an ongoing recurrent expenditure that is best financed through the government budget to ensure sustainability. Most projects simply assign school maintenance to the government, without an assessment of its feasibility. Donors also rarely evaluate their investments 10 to 15 years later, and continue to finance rehabilitation of buildings that would not have been necessary had they been properly maintained.

The few tests that have been conducted have never lasted long and were not evaluated. Thus, experience from Africa provides few lessons. Asian and Latin American countries have some experience. Only developed countries have proper maintenance policies. Box 7.1 presents the maintenance experience in Pakistan.

Overall, there is a deep knowledge gap regarding all aspects of school maintenance, and the present study, reflecting such a gap, is not able to provide the same level of information on maintenance strategies as on construction strategies.

Maintenance, however, does not pose an insurmountable cost. In the past, maintenance was estimated to require a yearly budget of about 1 percent of the investment cost (UNESCO 1986). More recent analysis in developed and developing

BOX 7.1 BUDGETING FOR SCHOOL MAINTENANCE IN PAKISTAN

The 1972 nationalization of the primary schools ended the previous long-term community commitment to school maintenance, and it was not replaced with any clear maintenance policy. During the subsequent 15 years without maintenance, the durable classrooms ("pucca") deteriorated so much that one-third were dilapidated and unusable, and another third needed substantial repair. The World Bank subsequently financed the following solutions.

A Third Primary Education Project (1987–96) for the Punjab province included development of a maintenance policy that resulted in a plan (1996) to release funds directly to communities with significant impact on community and teacher involvement in repair and maintenance.

A World Bank–financed Primary Education Development Program (1991–95) in the Sindh Province provided an increment to the 50 percent of the maintenance budget for the rehabilitation and maintenance of about 2,000 classrooms. This raised maintenance to 2 percent of the primary education recurrent budget. Community awareness increased as a result of the establishment of PTAs empowered to manage recurrent funds, which included maintenance.

In Baluchistan province, the operation and maintenance budget (including classroom materials) was raised, in 1993, to 4 percent of the total recurrent costs managed by communities. Approximately 10,000 Parent-Teacher School Management Committees were formed. More than 2,000 were trained, and more than 4,670 opened a bank account for nonsalary operating funds.

In the North-West province, the 1995 project planned a maintenance annual budget of 1.5 percent of capital costs.

Sources: World Bank 1987c, 1990, 1993c, 1995a, 1995f, 1997, 2000b.

countries shows that maintenance needs to be assessed according to the building and the country context. In Africa, recent studies estimate yearly maintenance costs for classrooms between 1.5 and 3 percent of the investment cost (Group 5 2006a, b, c, d, and e). In developed countries, schools hardly ever budget less than 2.5 percent of the investment cost. Table 7.1 outlines a concrete approach to estimate the cost of classroom maintenance in Burkina Faso, and provides a good

Table 7.1 The Cost of Maintenance

Element and activity	Scope and interval	% of total cost	Annual maintenance cost as % of construction cost
Floor screed; repairs	20% of area, 5 years	4.00	0.16
Plaster, internal/external; repairs	10% of area, 5 years	4.00	0.08
Painting walls	50% of area, 2 years	2.00	0.50
Painting doors, windows, trusses	100%, 5 years	1.50	0.30
Painting blackboard	100%, every year	0.25	0.25
Locks, hinges, bolts; replace	100%, 5 years	1.50	0.30
Roofing screws, fix and replace	25%, 5 years	1.00	0.05
Doors; replace	50%, 10 years	3.00	0.15
Total annual maintenance cost as percentage of construction costs			**1.79**

Source: Group 5 2006a, table 12.2, p. 28.

indication of the type, cost, and schedule of each maintenance activity, which can serve as a useful guide for other countries. In this case, the cost of classroom maintenance is estimated at 1.8 percent of the initial capital investment per year. Using the same methodology, the annual cost in Ghana was estimated at 3 percent (Group 5 2006b). The CDD approach is a good model for distributing roles and responsibilities in the management of maintenance resources.

Getting maintenance back on the radar screen will require a clear strategy of educating donors, central and local governments, and communities about the significant costs that neglect imposes in terms of renovation and replacement. Adequate volume of resources need to be planned and mobilized by governments and transferred to local government budgets. The Bank and the EFA Fast Track Initiative Secretariat can play a major role in this by making detailed infrastructure plans—with adequate investment and recurrent budgets—a required component of education sector plans, with provision for regular stocktaking, preferably conducted by an independent agency.

As a first step, there is a need to build knowledge of actors and partners regarding maintenance.

NOTE

1. This is a long-standing tradition, beginning with Kenya's "Harambee" movement in the 1960s, which was emulated throughout Africa. The promise was that if communities built and maintained the schools, government would follow up with teachers and books.

CHAPTER 8

Corruption in School Construction

Throughout the world, the construction sector consistently ranks as the most corrupt of any segment of a nation's economy (Transparency International 2005b). The scale of corruption in the construction sector is magnified by the size of the sector, estimated globally at some US$3.2 trillion a year. Recent examples of corruption in developed countries include the United Kingdom and France In the United Kingdom, in 2005, the Office of Fair Trading announced its intention to introduce measures to rid the construction industry of anticompetitive behavior (Dundas & Wilson 2005). In France, major construction enterprises were convicted in 2006 for bribing to obtain public contracts for school construction and transport.[1] In New York City, past corruption in school construction is measured in the hundreds of millions of dollars (Klitgaard and Parris 2000). In Guinea, where corruption to obtain public contracts is high, construction contractors can pay an average of 20 percent of the contract value to obtain the contract. The total amount of bribes paid by private contractors to civil servants was estimated to amount to 9.3 percent of gross national income in 2003 (ANLC 2005).

One reason that community-based programs are significantly more cost effective than other approaches to school construction management may be that fewer resources are wasted through corrupt practices. Although we do not have the data to test this hypothesis, based on prevailing theory, research, and experience, we posit that the greater cost effectiveness is at least partly attributable to certain implementation aspects of community-based programs that are not present in the other management methods. These include community participation, decentralized and competitive procurement processes, the flow and transparency of information, and the ability to appoint and fire the managers for which community-based programs have developed effective mechanisms.

Becker and Stitgler 1974 (cited by Olken 2005), for example, consider community participation key to reducing corruption since community members have better incentives to monitor the progress and quality of the works than do bureaucrats because communities benefit from the service. Transparency International concludes that centralized procurement offers greater opportunity for corruption. In its 2005 Global Corruption Report, Transparency International reported that large, centralized capital-intensive projects offer decision makers more scope for kickbacks, bureaucratic control, and political prestige than decentralized community-based projects. Such projects also offer greater scope for private gain than does the rehabilitation of existing infrastructure. Further, Becker and Stigler (1974) argue that monitoring and punishment alone have not succeeded in reducing corruption because those who regulate and punish are corruptible themselves.

In school construction, corruption is also facilitated by other practices that limit competition and accountability. These include direct contracting, packaging works into large bid packages, setting qualification requirements too high, and weak public accountability. Box 8.1 contrasts these facilitating factors with community-based approaches that limit corruption more effectively.

Direct contracting, or sole-source procurement, is a method that provides the greatest scope for kickbacks because there is no competition. This approach was common in Africa during the 1980s and early 1990s. In Senegal, for example, a 1993 review of government procurement practices showed that direct contracting represented 51 percent of the contracts awarded and 59 percent of their cumulative value (World Bank 1993d). A second common procurement practice during this time, which still continues today, is the packaging of numerous schools into one or a few large bid packages. This approach limits competition because the enterprise security deposit and capital and turnover requirements need to be high to ensure that the enterprise has the capacity to deliver the full package of works. Only large enterprises that meet these requirements can compete effectively, which offers greater scope for collusion and bribery. As we saw with school construction, during the 1970s and 1980s in many African countries, public procurement for works was controlled by cartels of a few large, often foreign, contractors because the eligibility criteria were such that only they could qualify. Research done in Mauritania in the late 1980s showed that for low-cost housing, these few contractors broke down large contracts into medium-size lots (20–30 units) and (illegally) subcontracted these lots at two-thirds the initial price to medium-size contractors, who in turn subcontracted smaller lots of 3–5 units to smaller contractors in the informal sector. These in turn subcontracted some of the buildings to individual "tâcherons" who in the end built the housing units at one-fourth the initial contract price (Theunynck 1984). Examples of this can be found worldwide.

In addition to the cost advantage that results from community-based procurement, community-based programs have also achieved greater transparency and accountability throughout the construction process, from the delivery of funds to the completion of the works. Community-based programs have developed effective mechanisms to ensure a free flow of information among community

BOX 8.1   FACTORS THAT FACILITATE AND LIMIT CORRUPTION IN SCHOOL CONSTRUCTION

Facilitating factors

- Centralized procurement and corruptibility of controllers
- Direct contracting
- Large packaging, which limits competition to a few large contractors
- Administrative requirements to access public procurement leading to its capture by few contractors
- Lack of transparency
- Lack of control on the execution of public works in remote areas
- Lack of accountability

Safeguards in Community-based Approaches

At the central level

- Transparent and timely allocation of funds to local governments (LGs) or communities
- No centralized procurement

At the local government level

- Transparency of funds received from central government and of funds transferred by LGs to communities
- Upward and downward information to government and civil society about flow of funds at each level
- No procurement by LGs for primary schools

At the community level

- Transparency of funds received by communities from local governments and information provided to the whole community
- Use of acceptable, community-based procurement methods
- Transparency of all steps of the procurement process executed at the community level
- Accountability of the community's Project Management Team to the whole community regarding decisions and awards
- Information to the community regarding the results of the audit at the community level

At all levels

- Audits of all levels and disclosure of information regarding the results of the audits members regarding the funds received, the procurement process itself, how the funds were spent, and the resulting quality of the works.

Box 8.2 shows the mechanisms applied in the Senegal Social Fund implemented during 2000–05 in 1,000 villages, which was effective in limiting corruption. Five cases of misuse of funds were reported and resulted in reimbursement and blacklisting of the culprits by the communities. More than 600 procurement

---

BOX 8.2 APPROACH TO LIMIT CORRUPTION AT THE COMMUNITY LEVEL: THE SENEGAL SOCIAL FUND

General information

- Regional offices publish the list of approved community projects, including type of project and financial allocations
- Regional offices create, update, and provide to communities a list of competent expertise for site supervision

Socialization and inclusion

- Villagers learn their rights, how to exert them, and improve their management capacity though grassroots management training
- Women and handicapped villagers are systematically included in all meetings and committees

Community control and simplicity

- Communities manage the funds and the procurement process using simplified procedures
- A group of five persons, mainly female, is put in charge of controlling the respect of procedures

Transparency

- All financial information is made public and remains accessible in a public display
- Invitations to bid are locally displayed in public (rural radios, posted on trees, school doors, and so on)
- Bid evaluations are opened in public and bid evaluation and award are also made in public
- Information to community of awarded contracts and payments to contractors

Limited discretion

- All works are procured through open local competitive bidding
- All goods are procured through comparison of at least three quotations
- Technicians for site supervision are hired though competition of short-listed competent specialists accredited by the Social Fund

Accountability mechanisms

- Regular village meetings to account for funds
- A village subcommittee is assigned to monitor proper use of funds
- Sanctions by community on misusers of funds
- External audits did not qualify any community project

Monitoring and follow-up

- Regular project monitoring by community
- Training of communities on use and maintenance of facilities built

specialists were trained and about 250,000 residents were informed of the project's financial and procurement procedures. The procurement training module also included role-plays on corruption to make it appropriate to talk about, and facilitate discussion on, how to mitigate this risk.[2] In Indonesia, the Kecamatan Development Project also implemented some of these approaches in more than 20,000 villages where levels of corruption were high, with significant results in limiting corruption (World Bank 2004a). Section 7 lays out these processes in more detail.

External audits are essential to contain corruption. A 2005 experiment, conducted in Indonesia in more than 600 villages that carried out smallroad projects, showed that the threat of being audited reduced unaccounted-for expenditure by about 8 percentage points, an amount largely superior to the cost of the audit. Increased monitoring by villagers also reduced corruption on wages paid (Olken 2005).

NOTES

1. Between 1990–1997, 34 construction contractors in France, including the three largest (Bouygues, Vinci, and Eiffages) participated in price-fixing on works for schools and

transport in the region of Île-de-France. Contracts worth about 1 billion euros (US$1.2 billion) were parsed out among the three. They were convicted in March 2006 and ordered to pay 40.5 million euros (US$60 million) in fines (www.Batiactu.com, March 22, 2006). The system also involved political corruption. A levy of 2 percent on all contracts was paid to finance the major political parties in the region, including the RPR (Rassemblement pour la République, the PR (Parti Républicain), the PS (Parti Socialiste), and the PC (Parti Communiste) (unicorn@againstcorruption.org, March 17, 2005).

2. Using Grassroots Management Training methods.

CHAPTER 9

The Donor Factor

Most countries in Sub-Saharan Africa rely heavily on external aid to fund school construction. For example, foreign aid constitutes 55, 90, and 100 percent of financing for school construction in Senegal, Mauritania, and Chad, respectively. As a result, donors have exerted a significant influence on school infrastructure programs, from school designs to implementation arrangements, and are a main contributing factor to the many inefficiencies found in school construction programs throughout Sub-Saharan Africa.

With few exceptions, the bulk of aid for school construction is delivered through a multitude of stand-alone projects, characterized by project-specific school designs, procedures, unit costs, and reporting requirements. Separate Project Implementation Units (PIUs) are often an integral part of this approach. School construction programs, in particular, have historically offered some of the strongest arguments in support of PIU management, owing to the need for technically competent project management staff and flexibility to recruit them at a market wage.

The use of PIUs and the project approach more generally, however, have some proverbial weaknesses. They undermine government leadership, create high compliance costs for recipient governments, disperse limited government capacity, facilitate policy fragmentation, and duplicate efforts. Further, a 2005 World Bank report on capacity building in Africa concludes that, although PIUs have promoted rapid and efficient project implementation, they have undermined long-term institutional development (World Bank, OED 2005a). In school construction, a particularly insidious outcome of the widespread use of a project approach has been a systematic failure on the part of countries and donors to learn from experience, resulting in the perennial resurrection of failed strategies.

There has never been a more favorable time for change. Recent global commitments promise to radically transform the way most aid is delivered. The Millennium Development Goals (MDGs) adopted in 2000 set clear targets for eradicating poverty and other human deprivations, including lack of basic education. The Monterrey Consensus of 2002 stressed the mutual accountability of developed and developing nations in reaching these goals by increasing financing and improving the effectiveness of aid. The Paris Declaration on Alignment and Harmonization, signed by more than 90 countries in 2005, lays out specific commitments of developed and developing countries to improve the effectiveness of aid through progress on country ownership, donor alignment with country priorities, and donor harmonization of procedures and reporting requirements, eliminating tied aid and strengthening mutual accountability in the achievement of these goals. Finally, the Education For All-Fast Track Initiative (EFA-FTI) has translated these global agreements into a global compact among countries and development partners to reach the MDG of universal completion of primary education for all children by 2015.

Prior to these agreements, sectorwide approaches had already been taking shape in many countries. Sectorwide approaches (SWAPs) provide a framework to facilitate collaboration and harmonization with country-led priorities and country systems. SWAPs are typically characterized by strong government ownership, agreed policy and expenditure frameworks, pooled resources (often in the form of sector budget support), a focus on monitoring and results, and harmonization of partner agency and government procedures for procurement and disbursements. (Refer to box 9.1 for the characteristics of sectorwide approaches.)

These global initiatives, particularly the EFA-FTI, provide an unprecedented opportunity to transform how aid is delivered in education, including for school construction. As a result of these agreements, many donors are moving more deliberately to harmonize procedures and processes at the country level, starting at a minimum with using joint analytical work, common review and reporting requirements, and aid aligned with a country's national poverty reduction strategy. At the same time these donors work toward the use of country systems to disburse aid flows.

The 2004 EFA-FTI Status Report notes that SWAPs and budget support are an increasing trend in the education sector across countries. Of 75 international development association-eligible countries for which data were available, half (38) are reported to either have sectorwide programs or are developing one. Further, in most countries, donors are aligned around the government's sector program (EFA-FTI Secretariat 2004). A 2004 study by the Organisation for Economic Co-operation and Development Development Assistance Committee Working Party on Aid Effectiveness across 14 countries supports the conclusion that the education sector has made significant progress in aligning donor support with one national program.

BOX 9.1 CHARACTERISTICS OF SECTORWIDE APPROACHES

Comprehensive Sector Development Program that:

- Covers all programs and projects
- Is based on policy objectives for the sector, and strategies to achieve them over the medium to long term
- Has a program of specific interventions and expenditure plans for the short and medium term

An expenditure framework that:

- Links with the country's macroeconomic framework and Poverty Reduction Strategy for integration within a country's expenditure program
- Has an intrasectoral spending plan derived from program priorities

Country ownership where:

- Government takes the lead, sets priorities, coordinates the donors, and consults broadly with local stakeholders

Donor partnerships in which:

- Donors support the country in its role and align their support with the same country program

Donor harmonization where:

- Donors adopt common implementation and management structures and arrangements, preferably those of the recipient country

Source: World Bank 2001a.

Although the trends in the education sector are certainly moving in the right direction, the 2004 EFA-FTI report also notes that project approaches still remain the most prominent approach to aid delivery in the sector. Few donors at the country level have harmonized their procurement, disbursement, and financial management procedures, and fewer still use government systems. Countries and donors still have a long road to reduce the disconnect between the global commitments and corresponding action at the country level. Five necessary steps that countries and development partners must take to improve the effectiveness of aid for school construction are:

- Embrace a program-based approach to school construction, with country governments taking the lead in defining their construction strategies and donors aligning their support with this strategy.
- Phase out PIUs.
- Learn from the more than 30 years of experience in school construction within the country and make good use of communities and the private sector.
- Pool donor resources to support the strategy.
- Harmonize with the country's decentralization framework when that is appropriate.

CHAPTER 10

Framework for Action

This extensive analysis of the history of school infrastructure in Sub-Saharan Africa has shown that the availability and quality of infrastructure are a critical component of reaching the Millennium Development Goals and the scope of the needs are considerable.

To accommodate all primary school-age children in safe environments, we estimated that the 33 International Development Association-eligible countries in Sub-Saharan Africa will need to construct an estimated 2 million classrooms by 2015 (table 10.1). They will also need to equip new schools with adequate latrines and water, while retrofitting about half the existing ones to the required level, and with a minimum of auxiliary facilities, such as offices and storages. They will need to adapt all classrooms and one sanitation box in each school for access and use by handicapped children.

Figure 10.1 illustrates the projection of the required increase in classroom stock for the 33 countries. The needs are front-loaded, assuming that all will be met by 2015. Thereafter, construction requirements will be driven by the need to accommodate increases in the school-age population and to replace the buildings when they have reached the end of their useful life. Appendix 16 provides details on this projection.

Table 10.2 shows estimates of the financing required to close the school facility gap over the next 10 years in the 33 African countries. Two scenarios are estimated on two different assumptions. In the high-cost scenario, it is assumed that countries make no change in the way school construction activities are currently carried out. It uses an average of US$9,150 per classroom, or the average across African countries when school construction is managed centrally by the ministry of education (MoE) or a contract management agencies (CMAs). The low-cost scenario is based on the assumption that all countries harmonize school construction strategies and shift to the community-contracting approach. The low estimate applies the average cost across countries of community-managed school construction: US$6,800 per classroom.

Table 10.1 School Construction Needs, 2005–15, for 33 African IDA Countries

	Increases classroom stock	Total construction needs 2005–15	%
Construction of **additional** classrooms	Yes	1,200,000	60
Replacement of **temporary/substandard** classrooms	No	500,000	25
Replacement of **overaged** classrooms	No	300,000	15
Total		2,000,000	100

Source: Author's calculation. See Appendix 16.

Figure 10.1 Total Classroom Construction Needs for 33 African IDA Countries

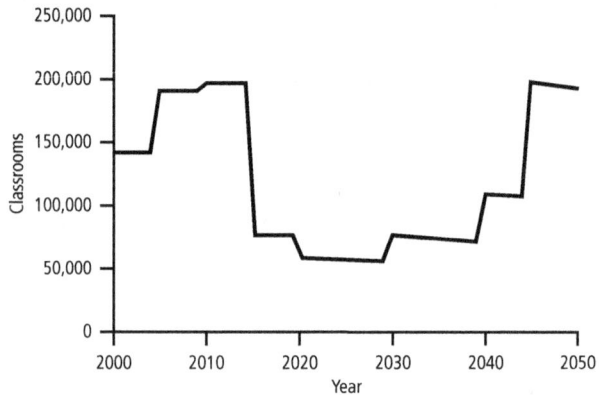

Source: Kirsten Majgaard's calculation.

In both scenarios, the net space norm applied is that of the African average of 56 m². Both estimates include the cost of a minimum facility package consisting of classrooms, latrines, a water supply, and some office and storage space. For office or storage, the area is assumed at the cross-country average of 20 percent of the area of a classroom, and the unit cost per gross m² is the average unit cost for a classroom. For latrines and furniture in the high-cost scenario, the unit costs applied are the cross-country averages. In the low-cost scenario, we assume cost savings similar to those obtained for classroom construction under a community-based strategy. The unit cost of water supply has been kept at the cross-country average in both scenarios.

Based on these assumptions, the financial requirements are estimated between a low of US$23.3 billion and a high of US$30.5 billion from now to the year 2015, **or between US$2.9–3.8 billion per year** (table 10.2). The potential cumulative

Table 10.2 Financing Needs for EFA in 2015 in 33 African Countries

	Structure of unit cost	Units	High-cost scenario (tendency sustained)	Low-cost scenario (all shift to communities)	Difference as % of high-cost scenario
Unit cost per classroom	classroom	US$/Classroom	9,150	6,800	26
	Office/storage	20%[a]	1,830	1,360	26
	Furnishing	US$/classroom	1,600	1,189	26
	Latrines	US$/classroom	1,300	966	26
	Water supply	US$/classroom	1,350	1,350	0
Classrooms to be built 2005–15		Number	2,000,000	2,000,000	
Total financing need between 2005 and 2015 classroom	Classrooms	Billion USD	18.3	13.6	26
	Office/storages	20%[a]	3.7	2.7	26
	Furnishing	US$ billions	3.2	2.4	26
	Latrines	US$ billions	2.6	1.9	26
	Water supply	US$ billions	2.7	2.7	0
	Total	US$ billions	30.46	23.33	23

Source: Author's calculations.
a. of U.S. classroom.

savings from community management can be very significant, averaging almost US$1 billion a year. This is a greater amount than many overly optimistic estimates would suggest,[1] but within the range of what countries at the Gleneagles conference have promised to provide.[2]

To this amount should be added the cost of maintenance. Table 10.3 shows the estimated cost of infrastructure maintenance, assumed at a rate of 2 percent annually of the initial investment and 5 percent for furniture. Under these assumptions, the financing required for maintenance averages between US$540 million and US$710 million per year. The low estimates assume that, similar to the investment activities, the management of maintenance activities would be, in this option, delegated to communities rather than being carried out centrally, either by MoEs, CMAs, or LGs.

Combining maintenance with the initial infrastructure investment brings the financing requirements between US$23.8 billion and US$37.6 billion over the next 8 years, or US$3 to US$4.7 billion annually.

Table 10.3 Estimated Annual Cost of Maintenance of the Programs to Be Built in the 33 African Countries During 2005–15

	Total investment cost			Annual maintenance cost	
	High-cost scenario (tendency sustained)	Low-cost scenario (all shift to communities)	% investment cost	High-cost scenario (tendency sustained)	Low-cost scenario (all shift to communities)
Classroom	18.3	13.6	2	0.37	0.27
Office/storage	3.7	2.7	2	0.07	0.05
Furnishing	3.2	2.4	5	0.16	0.12
Latrines	2.6	1.9	2	0.05	0.04
Water supply	2.7	2.7	2	0.05	0.05
Total	30.5	23.3		0.71	0.54

Source: Author's calculations.

WHAT COUNTRIES SHOULD DO

Countries should take charge, learn from experience, and lead the process to ensure that school facility needs will be satisfied. For this purpose, they should complete a stock-taking exercise and harmonize planning norms, processes, school models, architectural and construction standards and implementation strategy; develop tools and handbooks; build capacity of the various actors; develop a communication strategy; and ensure sound monitoring and evaluation of the implementation of the process.

COMPLETE A STOCK-TAKING EXERCISE

Ministries of Education should conduct a stock-taking exercise that analyzes (a) current and projected infrastructure needs to reach the MDG of complete quality primary education for all by 2015; (b) current planning norms and processes and flow of funds for school construction; (c) the national context regarding decentralization, the construction industry, water and sanitation policies, public procurement rules, and the environment; and (d) the past and current programs in terms of who did or does what, how, and at what cost in the provision of school facilities. Box 10.1 mentions the essential elements needed for the exercise. Table 10.4 shows an example of such an exercise with data from Ghana to organize the information on who does what, how, and with what result. Appendix 17 provides other examples. The stock-taking exercise is intended to provide a basis for harmonizing norms, management, and implementation arrangements, and achieving better unit costs. It provides a sound basis for unit costs to be used for education expenditure projections. It may usefully complement the Education

BOX 10.1   ESSENTIAL ELEMENTS OF STOCKTAKING EXERCISE

Assessing Current Status and Needs

- School-age population (current and forecast) and geographical distribution, urban/rural, proportion of handicapped children
- Enrollments: GER—national, by region, by gender, disabled children
- Retention/dropout rates, by regions; urban/rural, by cycle
- Use of multigrade teaching
- Pupils per classroom ratio (PCR): national, by region, urban/rural
- Schools with incomplete education: national, by region, urban/rural
- Number of classrooms and other facilities (latrines, water, office, storage, furniture)
- Geographical distribution, identification of inequities between regions, urban/rural, gender disparities
- Status of buildings (fair, needing repair, dilapidated beyond repair, nonpermanent)
- Classroom and other school facilities needs assessment to reach EFA by 2015

Assessing Planning and Financing

- Planning norms and standards for school creation and expansion, maximum distance from home to school
- Size and distribution of villages, maximum size of school
- Targeting strategy, priorities
- Planning process: who does what, when, and how?; top-down versus bottom-up approaches
- Projected financing from all sources
- Actual expenditures for school investment and maintenance

Knowing Context

- Status of administrative and fiscal decentralization
- Construction industry: modern sector, informal sector
- Transport issues for materials and impact on cost
- Water supply policy and strategy by Ministry of Water
- Sanitation policy and rules by Ministry of Health and Sanitation
- Public procurement code status, openness for community procurement
- Environmental issues related to school construction

> **Knowing Who Does What, How, and With What Result, for Each Program or Project**
> - Norms and standard designs for each type of facility
> - Overall management of each program
> - Implementation mechanisms, including flow of funds, procurement arrangements, contracting out, delegations, payment of contractors, and supervision arrangements
> - Maintenance arrangements
> - Unit costs for each type of facility
> - Cross-comparison of efficiency and cost efficiency
> - Potential for harmonization across projects

Country Status Report carried out by many countries, and may be combined with it if applicable, as did Burkina Faso in 2008. Madagascar carried out its stock-taking exercise in 2007 for the preparation of its submission to EFA-FTI.

HARMONIZE AND ADOPT PLANNING NORMS, PROCESSES, SCHOOL MODELS, ARCHITECTURAL AND CONSTRUCTION STANDARDS, AND DEVELOP A SCHOOL CONSTRUCTION STRATEGY

The process should be fully participatory, managed by the MoE with involvement of all stakeholders, including other key ministries involved in school construction, water, sanitation, or small- and medium-size enterprise development; local governments; staff of education construction projects or multisector projects financing school construction, such as social funds or decentralization projects; donors; and civil society. Chapters 2, 3, and 4 provide indications regarding the planning elements to be harmonized. Chapter 5 provides information and guidance regarding the more cost-efficient implementation and procurement strategies. Appendix 13 provides illustrations of toolkits for harmonization. Chapter 6 provides information on norms to be established by MoEs.

DEVELOP TRAINING TOOLS AND HANDBOOKS AND BUILD CAPACITY

Chapter 6 provides information regarding tools and handbooks for MoEs at the central and local levels, local governments, and communities that are useful for community management of the school construction. To the extent possible, MoEs may build on existing experienced programs in their own country and adapt their

Table 10.4 A Stock-taking Exercise on Who Does What and How in Primary School Construction: Example with Ghana

Project	WHO DOES WHAT?	Donor	Centralized/deconcentrated approaches					Decentralized approaches				
			Ministry			Agency		NGOs		Local govern-ments	Private sector	Communities	
			Central office	Local office	School staff	Central office	Local office	Central office	Local office			empower-ment	partici-pation
BESSIP - Basic Education Strategic Investment Program												
Financing agency		IDA											
Number of classrooms:		750											
Years		1997–02											
PIU		yes											
Coverage		nation											
Year of cost data		2002											
$/classroom		10,433											
Gross m² per classroom		69.00											
US$ per m²		97.00											
Community participation		No											
source		Group 5											
	1. Proposes planning		GES										
	2. Decides planning		PIU								Districts			
	3. Standard design												
	4. Signs Financing Agmt		NCB											
	5. Sets DAO standard docs		PIU											
	6. Invites to bid		PIU											
	7. Awards contracts		PIU											
	8. Signs contracts												
	9. Monitors works										Dist. Eng.			
	10. Pays works		PIU											
	11. Executes works											SME		
	12. Hands over building		GES											
ESSP-SU - School Upgrading Program												
Financing agency		DFID											
Number of classrooms:		560											
Years		2002–now											
PIU		yes											
Coverage		2 regions											
Year of cost data		2004											
$/classroom		10,727											
Gross m² per classroom		51.00											
US$ per m²		85.00											
Community participation		No											
source		Group 5											
	1. Proposes planning										Districts			
	2. Decides planning										Districts			
	3. Standard design					MoE								
	4. Signs Financing Agmt										NCB			
	5. Sets DAO standard docs										Districts			
	6. Invites to bid										Districts			
	7. Awards contracts										Districts		Par. Ass.	
	8. Signs contracts													
	9. Monitors works													
	10. Pays works										Districts			
	11. Executes works											Small Ent		
	12. Hands over bldg										Districts			
Primary School construction Program												
Financing agency		Plan Int.											
Number of classrooms:		90											
Years		2002–now											
PIU		NGO											
Coverage		3 regions											
Year of cost data		2004											
$/classroom		7,500											
Gross m² per classroom		50.60											
US$ per m²		60.70											
Community participation		Yes											
source		Group 5											
	1. Proposes planning	Plan Int												
	2. Decides planning	Plan Int												
	3. Standard design					MoE								
	4. Signs Financing Agmt	Plan Int												
	5. Sets DAO standard docs													
	6. Invites to bid													
	7. Awards contracts	Plan Int												
	8. Signs contracts													
	9. Monitors works	Plan Int												
	10. Pays works													
	11. Executes works											artisan	Comm.	labor
	12. Hands over bldg					MoE								

Source: Table from the author with data from Group 5b

training tools and handbooks. They may also learn for other countries' experience through international workshops or country visits. Capacity-building programs may take advantage of experienced non-governmental organizations (NGOs) and local experts.

COMMUNICATION STRATEGY

A national information education communication strategy will be needed to ensure national access to program information by all stakeholders and the civil society. The IEC (Information education communication) system should find the information required to form a sound monitoring and information system. It should ensure transparency through public availability of all information regarding the school construction program, including decision-making processes and results, flow of funds, procurement activities, and results. The strategy should target different audiences with different tools: central authorities with general reports and scorecards, local authorities with specific reports and scorecards. At the community level, information on resources, procurement decisions, and payments of contracts should be displayed in public places and subject to information-sharing sessions in community meetings. Chapter 8 provides information on the efficiency of transparency mechanisms to curb corruption.

BUILD OR DEVELOP SOUND MONITORING AND EVALUATION OF THE SCHOOL CONSTRUCTION PROGRAM

Monitoring capacity should be built within the MoE and particular attention paid to developing evaluation capacity in the universities.

Monitoring mechanisms should be based on a clear set of data and performance indicators, with a clear chain of data collection. Tracked indicators may be translated into scorecards to be disseminated to concerned audiences and disclosed to the public through the communication system. Examples of monitoring scorecards for local governments were developed in 2007 by the Nigeria Community-Driven Development (CDD) project and in 2008 by the Benin CDD project.

The **Evaluation system** should include annual *financial audits* and *technical audits* that provide ex-postevaluation of cost efficiency of each project or program, and the value for money obtained during the past period; and *beneficiary assessments* that provide the management with feedback from all actors (Salmen 1995, 1998; Owen and Van Domelen 1998). When different programs with different strategies are implemented simultaneously in the country, the M&E system should cover all programs, measure their performances with the same tools and indicators, and inform all stakeholders of the comparative efficiency and cost efficiency of the different programs.

BOX 10.2 TECHNICAL AUDIT AND BENEFICIARY ASSESSMENT: KEY FEATURES

Technical Audit
- Covers all projects and programs
- Sample statistically valid by project/program and region
- Assess appropriateness of design and conformity of works to design
- Capacity of management, contractor, and site supervisor
- Actual unit cost per m^2 of contract prices and value for money in each project/program
- Assess achievement of school project objective
- Sustainability of operations and maintenance of facilities

Beneficiary Assessment
- Consultation with beneficiaries and stakeholders
- Representative sample
- In-depth interviews around key themes and topics
- Focus group discussions
- Direct observation and participant observation

WHAT DONORS SHOULD DO

Donors should implement the Paris Declaration, taking their support to school construction as a specific subject of harmonization. In this area, they should develop formal joint agreements to secure harmonized partner support and assist each donor in internally negotiating the changes needed for its own support.

In each country, donors should support the country leadership and agree on a detailed agenda toward school construction harmonization with time-bound benchmarks. The agenda may include (a) donor support to develop a national country-led school construction strategy; (b) adoption of revised school mapping approaches that ensure access to EFA for all children; (c) consensus on norms and standard designs; (d) agreement to finance the national minimum package of facilities including furniture, water, and sanitation; (e) agreement to move toward a harmonized implementation arrangement and procedures based on best practices allowing large and rapid scale-up, and the most cost-effective implementation modalities; (f) agreement to help MoEs realign their modus operandi, along with decentralization of school construction to local governments when needed, and streamline CDD approaches for school construction to increase cost efficiency and transparency; (g) consensus to finance investment subject to the incorporation of a sound maintenance strategy into the program; (h) phasing out PIUS and relying on reinforced MoEs structures; and (i) acceptance of a country-led Monitoring and Evaluation system that covers all programs regardless of origin of funds. Donors should reach agreement between themselves and the country on what is essential to improve efficiency of aid in school construction.

At the global level, under the umbrella of the EFA-FTI Secretariat, donors may agree on a global agenda covering some or all of the items above, with time-bound benchmarks to measure global progress toward harmonization in the area of school construction. The EFA-FTI Secretariat may put more focus in this area by requesting a sound school construction strategy when FTI resources are expected to finance school buildings.

AREAS FOR FURTHER RESEARCH

This review revealed important knowledge gaps that need further research:

- **Maintenance of facilities.** The lack of information on maintenance practices is abysmal. No maintenance programs have ever been evaluated. There is an urgent need to build minimum knowledge and identify best practices, if any, to support a dialogue on maintenance strategies.
- **Impact of water and sanitation** on access, retention, and learning performance of girls. In this matter, the literature is full of anecdotal information and advocacy, but statistical analysis remains to be done.
- **Minimum School Facility Package.** Little is known of the impact of canteens, staff housing, libraries on students' access and retention, and their learning outcomes. Specific analysis is also to be carried out.
- **Roles of local governments in education.** Decentralization and devolution of some educational competencies to local governments is a global evolution. Little is known about the impact of decentralization on the performances of the education sector.
- **School planning, village development planning, and local development planning.** Knowledge needs to be more systematically developed about the impact of bottom-up versus top-down planning of school construction programs, particularly in the context of decentralization.
- **National procurement rules and community-based procurement.** Community participation in procurement is allowed in World Bank Procurement Guidelines; however, national procurement codes never include provisions for such types of procurement. Many countries are currently revising their procurement code, often with the Bank's assistance, with little or no consideration of community participation in procurement.

NOTES

1. Earlier estimates suggested an average of US$1.1 billion per year during the 2005–15 period for 47 Sub-Saharan Africa countries, including an average of US$0.8 billion per year to cover rehabilitation needs and 0.3 billion for expansion countries (Burns , Mingat and Rakotomala 2003).

2. In the 2005 Global Policy Forum of Gleneagles (United Kingdom), the G8 countries and other Official Development Assistance donors promised to provide an extra US$50 billion to Africa by 2010.

APPENDIX 1

School Infrastructure Matters: The Research Evidence

Impact on Student Enrollment and Retention. The research evidence is unambiguous—the closer the school is to home, the more likely children are to attend, and enroll at the appropriate age. Based on household survey data, the World Bank Country Status Reports have examined the relation between distance to school and enrollment in a large number of Sub-Saharan African countries: the enrollment rate is consistently lower, the farther the children live from the school, but the size of the impact varies from one country to another.[1] In Mali, the enrollment rate is almost 30 percentage points higher for children who live less than 30 minutes from school than for children who live more than 45 minutes from the nearest school, whereas in Burundi, the difference in enrollment rate for the same two groups is 10 percentage points. Schaffner (2003) found that each additional kilometer from home to school reduces school enrollment by 2 to 3 percentage points in Ethiopia. And in Eritrea, primary school participation rates grew by 191 percent when the average distance to home was more than halved (Van Domelen and El-Rashidi 2001). In Lesotho, it was found that reducing the time needed to reach school from one hour to 15 minutes led parents to send their children to school at a younger age, thereby reducing the probability that the children would drop out (World Bank 2005a).

Distance to school is important, not only because it taxes the stamina of children, but also because a longer trip to school is less safe. In a study covering Chad, Guinea, and Niger, Lehman (2004) found that enrollment rates drop precipitously when children are expected to attend school in a village other than their own, even if that village is nearby. A World Bank study (2005m) on Pakistan finds that safety concerns are a major factor explaining why many parents do not send their girls to school, particularly in rural areas where villages do not have school facilities and the girls would be forced to travel outside of their communities. Kane (2004) reported that distance has a negative effect on school enrollment for girls in Côte d'Ivoire and Ghana, and that girls are often taken out of school at puberty in Zambia. Distance also poses an additional challenge for children with disabilities. Thus, the evidence is overwhelming that having an extensive network of primary schools with schools located as close as possible to where children live is essential for achieving universal primary enrollment.

The quality of the school infrastructure and facilities available at the school have also been found to impact school enrollment. Many studies have found an impact of water and latrines on enrollment and retention. Sey (2001) found that the availability of water and sanitation was important for the retention of girls in Senegal. Chaudhury, Christiaensen, and Asadullah (2006) found that the availability of water and sanitation in the nearest school increased the probability of male enrollment by 15 percent for water and 7 percent for latrines in Ethiopia (girls' enrollment was very low with or without latrines). In Pakistan, the construction of separate latrines for girls has had a major effect on girls' enrollment in primary schools (World Bank 2004o). In India, a UNICEF assessment estimated that the provision of potable water and sanitary facilities would increase girls' enrollments from 47 to 66 percent in the targeted schools (Sey et al. 2003). The condition of the school buildings has been found to affect completion in several studies, including Mason (1994) and Glewwe and Jacoby (1996). They found that poor quality of school buildings in Indonesia and Vietnam lowered the probability of completion of primary school.

Impact on Teacher Motivation and Absenteeism. Teachers show greater motivation and dedication when the infrastructure is more welcoming. A study of teacher absenteeism in Bangladesh, Ecuador, India, Indonesia, Peru, and Uganda found that teachers in schools with the best infrastructure have absenteeism rates 10 percentage points lower than teachers in schools with the worst infrastructure (Chaudhury, Hammer et al. 2005). In particular, lack of toilets was correlated with high rates of teacher absenteeism (which ranged between 11 and 27 percent). Infrastructure was even found to have a stronger impact on teacher absenteeism than the teacher's salary level or administrative tolerance of absence.

Impact on Learning Outcomes. Finally, the research provides evidence that the condition of the school infrastructure has an impact on learning outcomes. In a review of 96 production function studies on developing countries, Hanushek (1995) found 34 studies that investigated the impact of physical facilities (such as quality buildings and libraries) on student learning. A large majority of the studies found a positive effect of high-quality school infrastructure on learning achievement.

Similarly, Michaelowa and Wechtler (2005) found that the condition of school buildings has an impact on learning, based on the SACMEQ student learning achievement survey covering 14 Sub-Saharan African countries. The authors found a strong positive relationship between the condition of the school building and learning outcomes. A change from a school in extremely bad condition to one in good condition resulted in an increase of about 10 percent of a standard deviation in learning achievement. This effect is about as strong as, and in some cases stronger than, the effect of some instructional equipment (12 percent for high-tech equipment and 7 percent for teacher manuals) and equivalent to the gain in literacy scores (10 percent) from having a school library. However, the authors underscore the possibility that these results may suffer from an endogeneity problem: Because the condition of school buildings and availability of high-tech equipment are highly visible signals of a rich school environment, parents who are wealthy, have greater interest in their children's education, or have children who are brighter than average are more likely to select better-equipped schools in better physical condition. SACMEQ data (unlike PASEC) do not allow for controlling for initial knowledge, as they do not include pupils' test scores from the beginning of the year.

Other studies have also found an impact on learning from having adequate equipment in schools. In the Tan, Lane and Coustere (1997) study on first graders in the Philippines, lack of adequate furniture was found to be associated with a drop of –0.32 standard deviations in math and –0.29 standard deviations in reading. In the study by Glewwe and Jacoby (1994), repairing leaking roofs in Ghanaian middle schools produced an estimated increase of 2.0 standard deviations in reading scores and 2.2 in math scores; the availability of blackboards raised reading scores by 1.9 standard deviations and mathematics scores by 1.8. Adding a library led to smaller increases. Likewise, Michaelowa and Wechtler (2005) found that the availability of blackboards and chalk had a positive impact on student learning in mathematics.

Many more studies have demonstrated the positive impact on enrollment, completion, and learning from having adequate school infrastructure. However, many studies concur that other types of school inputs have a greater impact, particularly when compared to their costs (several studies found that the most cost-effective inputs are textbooks and teacher manuals). Infrastructure is hugely expensive, but a certain basic level of infrastructure and equipment is necessary for schools to function and learning to take place Yet, in a context of relatively low per student spending, beyond the basic infrastructure level, resources may be better spent on other learning inputs. While the existing body of research has demonstrated that school infrastructure matters, the existing research appears to be less useful in providing guidance as to how and where to spend the funds directed to infrastructure improvement. Given that most projects cannot cover an entire country at one time, we need to know more about what types of infrastructure investments are most cost-effective in improving enrollment, retention and learning. Carrying out more production function type studies may not be the right way forward, for the two reasons discussed below.

Problems with data. One reason may be on the data side: it requires a lot of variables to adequately describe the quality of school infrastructure. The quality of school infrastructure encompasses both the availability of certain facilities, such as libraries, sanitation facilities, furniture, etc., but also the quality of the buildings in terms of materials used and condition of repair or disrepair. But quality also depends on aspects such as cleanliness, spaciousness, and appearance. When data on infrastructure exist, they mostly focus on the availability of certain facilities, and sometimes on the condition of school buildings, but ignore the other aspects. Spending on infrastructure may be used as a proxy, but these data are even harder to come by. Some empirical studies deal with the complexity of describing school infrastructure by combining available information into an infrastructure quality index. But very little is known about the extent to which these indices correctly measure the infrastructure quality.

Endogeneity bias. The second problem with this type of study is that production function studies are prone to have endogeneity problems. For example, if schools with good infrastructure are systematically located in richer areas than schools with poor infrastructure, we may be capturing the effect of rich/poor household, rather than of good/poor infrastructure. For example, if school maintenance is funded by parents, schools in better-off areas are likely to be in a better condition that schools in poorer areas. Thus, there are likely systematic differences between schools that we do not completely understand. Because we do not understand them, it may be impossible to control for these differences in regressions (omitted variable bias). Another related problem is that of a possible selection bias: when given the choice, parents may choose to enroll their children in a school that has a better quality infrastructure, other things equal. This can lead to two statistical problems: 1) the better equipped schools have a higher enrollment, leading to a deterioration of their pupil: teacher ratio, and other measures of per-pupil spending, and can actually lead to a decline in learning outcomes, or 2) the student composition may change, for example if mostly resourceful families move their children to better equipped schools, learning outcomes may improve, not because the school is better, but because the student body has changed composition. Therefore, additional production function studies are not likely to provide much more information on the effect of infrastructure.

Project impact evaluations present another source of evidence on the impact of the quality of school infrastructure on learning. Despite the many school construction and rehabilitation programs funded by the World Bank over the years, very few impact evaluations have been carried out. What is more, unless the schools benefiting from the projects were selected randomly (with a control group), the impact evaluations are likely flawed (omitted variable bias again) and their results unreliable. Two useful evaluations have been carried out in recent years. A review of the World Bank's assistance to education programs in Ghana concluded that the improvements in the availability and quality of school infrastructure had resulted in higher primary school enrolment and an increase in English and math scores. Whereas in 1988, only half of all classrooms were usable when it rained, by 2003, two-thirds were able to function normally thereby increasing the amount of instructional and learning time (World Bank 2004d). Further, a 1999 World Bank study of the social fund in Peru showed that investment made in school facilities had a significantly positive impact on school attendance rates for both younger and older children (but no effect on the likelihood of children being at the right grade level for age, or on the time it takes to travel to school).

More randomized trials are needed in school infrastructure investments. Kremer (1995), in a commentary to Hanushek (1995), pointed out that project evaluations using randomized trials have indicated high payoffs to education expenditures. However, there are only a few such project evaluations, and none yet of World Bank–funded infrastructure projects. Unlike retrospective studies, randomized trials are not subject to bias from omission of variables correlated with educational outcomes. The design of a randomized trial requires that the schools benefiting from improvements be randomly selected, in order to have an "identical" control group for later statistical analysis of project effects. (If it is not politically feasible to deny investments in one group, the two groups could receive different improvements or the same improvements at different dates). According to Kremer (1995), schools in developing countries are particularly well suited for randomized trials because relatively small investments can make a big difference in school budgets.

NOTE

1. See: World Bank 2001d, 2003c, 2004e, 2004f, 2005a, 2005e, 2005f, 2005h, 2005i, 2005s, 2006c, 2006i, 2006d, and 2007h.

APPENDIX 2

Architectural Design of Primary Schools: Examples of 2- and 3-Classroom Blocks

THE GAMBIA

FIOH Project (section)

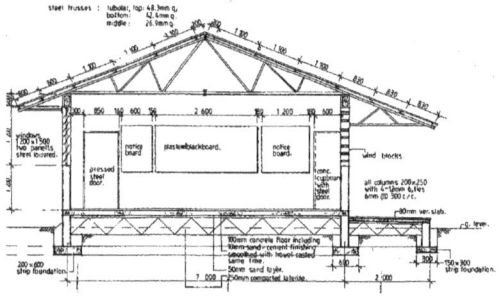

FIOH Project

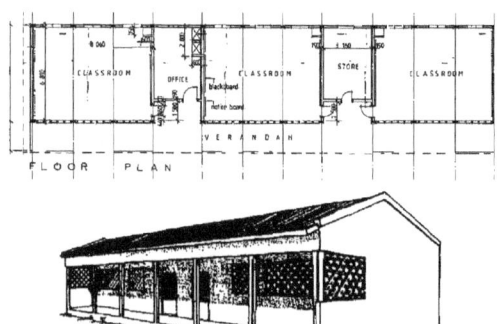

IDA project

BURKINA FASO

Common basket

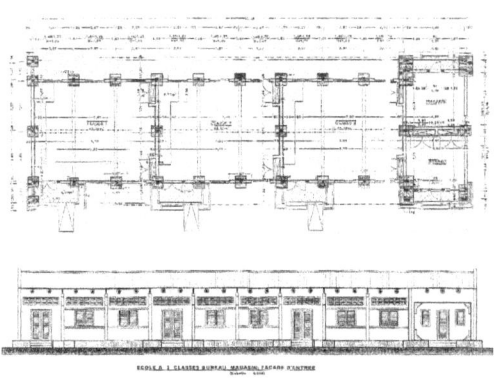

Common basket

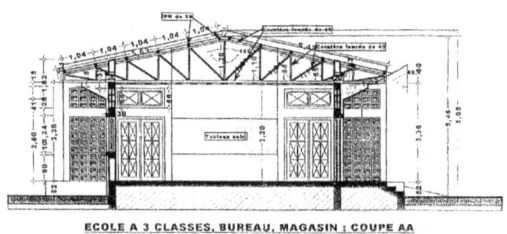

Architectural Design of Primary Schools: Examples of 2- and 3-Classroom Blocks • 157

ZAMBIA

ZAMSIF

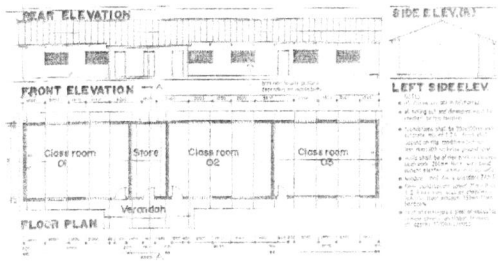

Education Rehabilitation Project

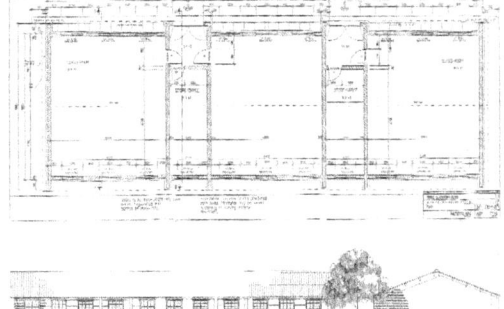

BESSIP

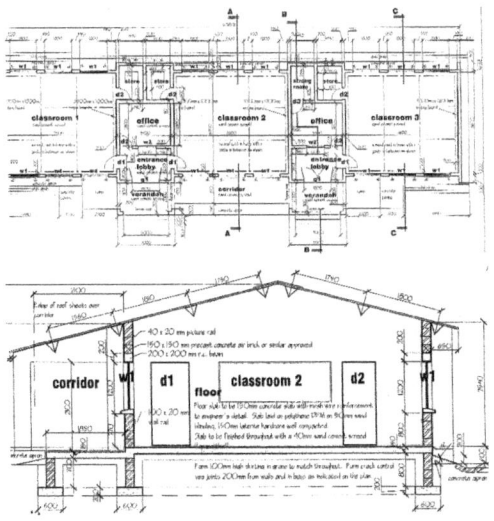

MOZAMBIQUE

Rural Primary School 2002

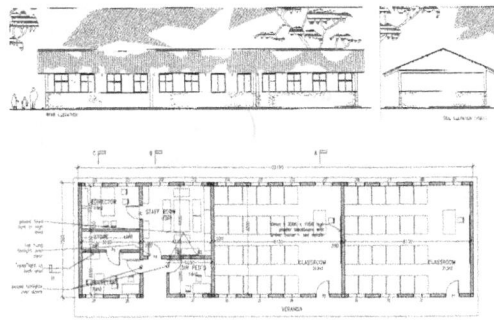

DCEE-MINED classroom (section)

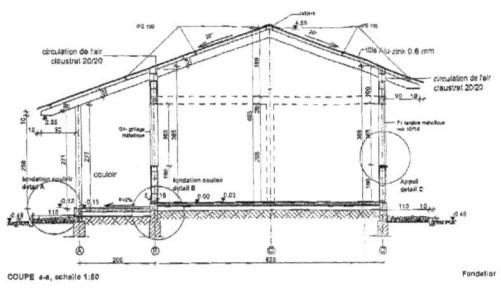

Madagascar: New Construction Strategy 2008–2010

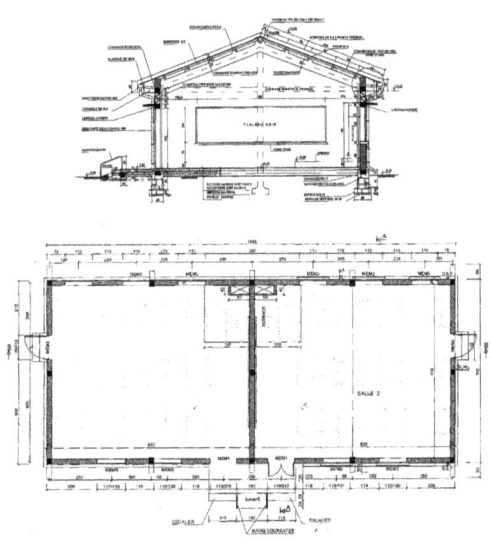

BENIN
MEMP

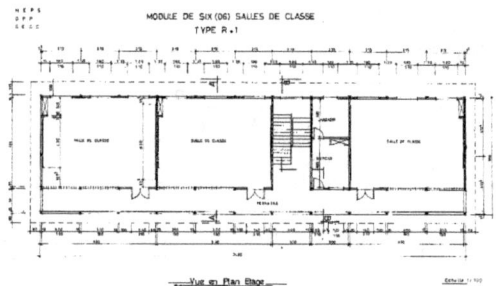

AGETUR

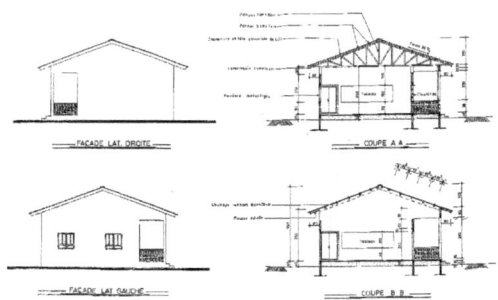

Guinea: Classroom-Block Model

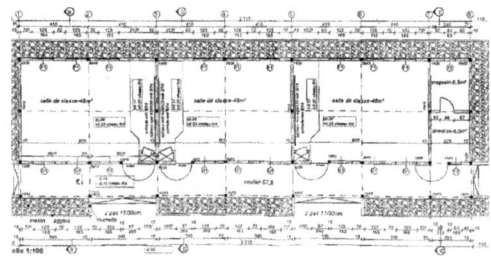

Uganda School Facility Grant

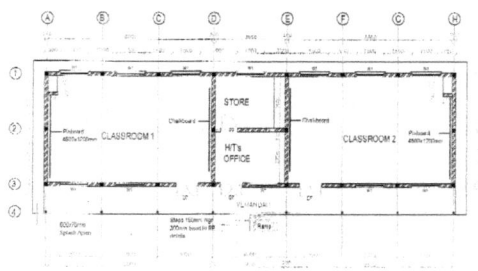

Chad Education Project

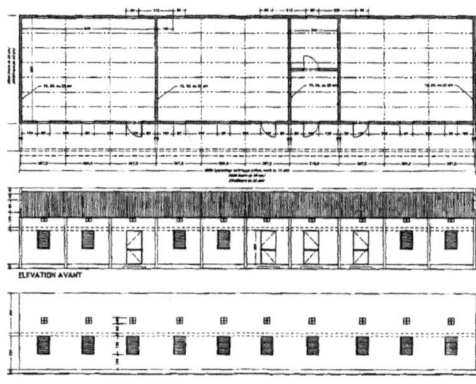

Ghana Micro-Project (EU)

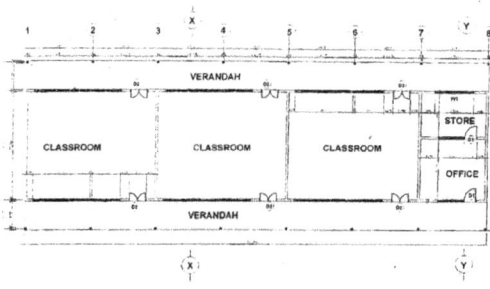

APPENDIX 3
Examples of Appropriate Technology Schools

Other examples of schools built using local materials include the literacy center in Chikal, Niger, built in 1980 by the NGO Development Workshop which used pure earth bricks only. Other approaches included the use of compressed and cement-stabilized earth bricks as well as plaster (gypsum) construction. The illustrations below show typical examples of appropriate technology construction. Figure A3.6 shows the typical implementation process used by international NGOs in implementing local materials construction.

Figure A3.1 The Koranic School of Malika, Senegal 1978: Sand-Cement Vault Technology

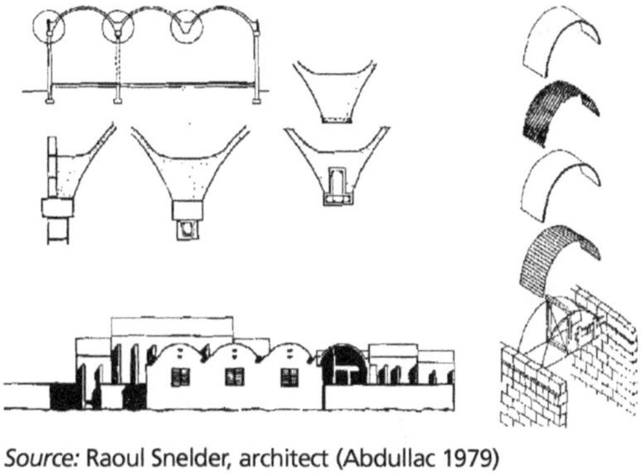

Source: Raoul Snelder, architect (Abdullac 1979)

Figure A3.2 Rosso (Mauritania) 1979: School Built with Earth and Vault Technology by the NGO ADAUA

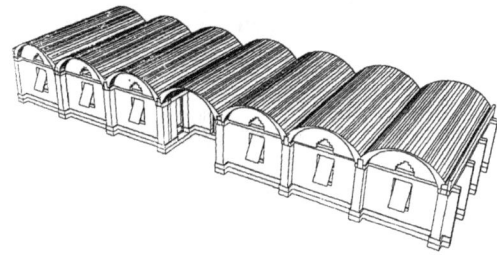

Source: Photo by Serge Theunynck, 2008.

Figure A3.3 Diaguily School, Mauritania, 1988: Sand-Cement Vault Technology by UNESCO

Source: Ministère de l'Education Natiionale.

Figure A3.4 Earth-built School in Niger (1986–87) by MoE with World Bank Assistance

Source: Photo by Christian Rey, cited in Theunynck 1994.

Figure A3.5 Primary Schools with Stabilized Earth Bricks, Senegal, 1984

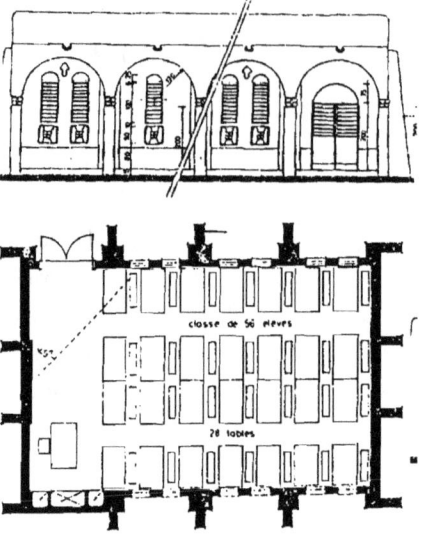

Source: Patrick Dujarric, Birahim BNiang, IDA Second Education Project

Figure A3.6 Typical Implementation Scheme for International NGOs Using Local Materials Construction

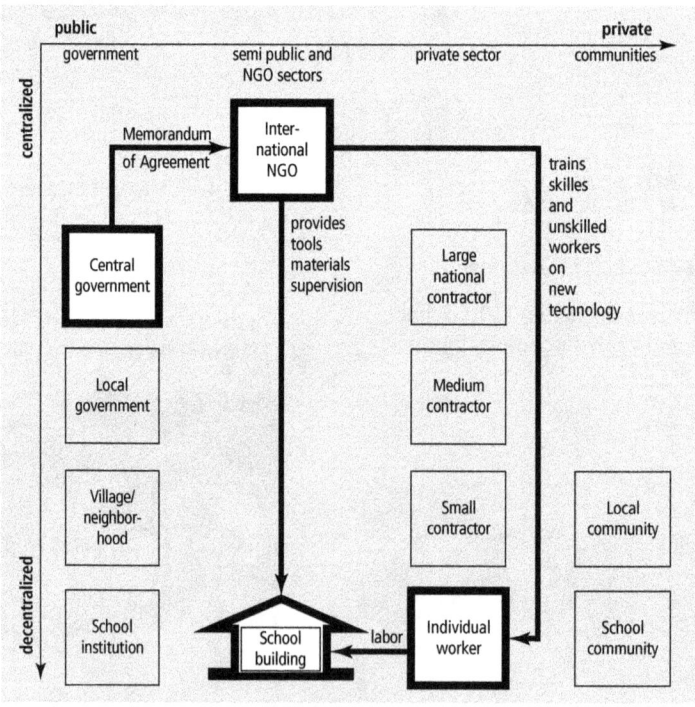

Source: Author's figure.

APPENDIX 4

Examples of Latrine Technology

The Dry Pit Latrine: An Example from Mozambique

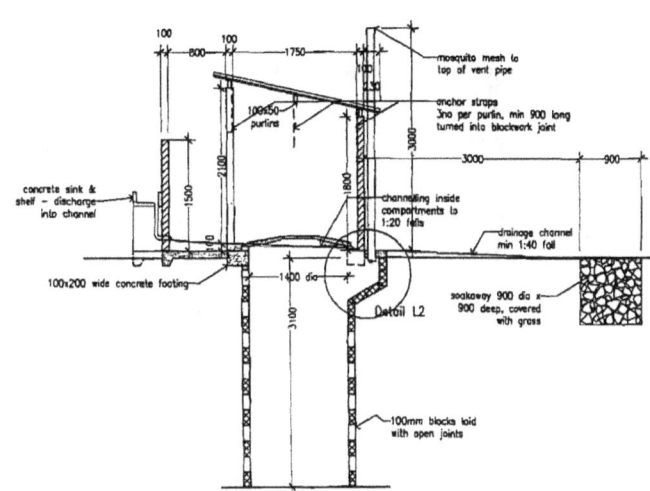

Source: World Bank 1993d.

The Dry pit Latrine: An Example from Mali

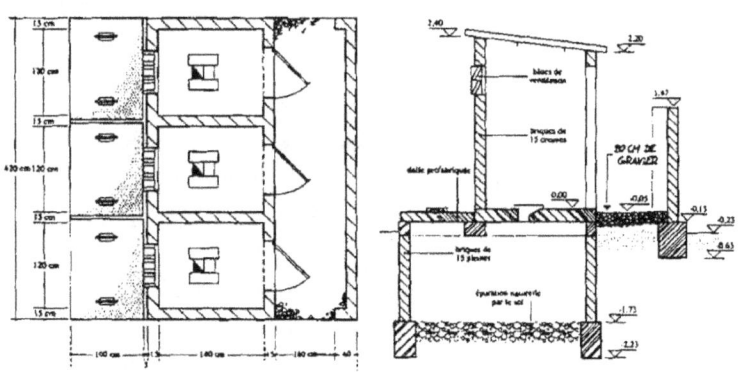

Source: World Bank 1993d.

161

APPENDIX 5

A Brief History of Industrialization in the Construction Industry Worldwide

The term *prefabrication* means that large portions of buildings are factory-produced off-site and assembled on-site. Compared with traditional construction, prefabrication requires significantly different capital requirements, logistical arrangement, and specialized skills. Capital costs include either the cost of importing the prefabricated building segments or the cost of the investment to erect an industrial plant to fabricate the building segments. Logistics involve transporting large prefabricated building segments to the construction sites, compared to the logistics of traditional construction, such as moving cement, lumber, and roofing sheets. These logistics become more complex when the school construction sites are dispersed, building segments are large, and road networks and transport systems are poor. The site assembly crews typically needs to be more knowledgeable and competent than traditional construction crews, because the building foundation needs to be more exactly precise and because specific know-how is required to assemble the prefabricated segments.

Off-site prefabrication and mass-marketing of prefabricated construction started in the U.S. during the nineteenth century as a modern way to mass-produce inexpensive housing for the middle classes. Prefabrication also became popular during the gold rush in the mid-nineteenth century, when large numbers of buildings were needed for mushrooming towns. Mass-merchandisers, led by Sears and Roebuck, sold housing packages by the tens of thousands through catalogs. The popularity of prefabricated housing, however, faded along with the economic downturn and Great Depression in 1930.

When prefabrication faded in the US, ironically, it became increasingly popular in Europe (Richman 1994), where the prefabricated movement began in 1928 with the founding of the Congres Internationaux d'Architecture Moderne (CIAM) in France by the architect le Corbusier and other modernist architects. CIAM, a major source of avant-garde ideas in architecture, promoted the industrialization of construction sector, embraced new technologies, and touted the efficiency of the automotive industry as a model for the construction industry. Soon thereafter, the Groupement d'Etudes pour une Architecture Industrialisée (GEAI) was established in the 1930s. Engineers affiliated with the GEAI, such as Marcel Lods and Jean Prouvé, developed light steel structures to support prefabricated segments for low-cost housing and adapted the production methods of the automobile and airplane industries. During the post-war reconstruction period of 1945–75 in France, large low-cost housing complexes were constructed using this method in Sottevile-les-Rouen (1948–1955), Maly le Roy (1957–59), and La Grand-Mare in Rouen (1969–1978).

The European movement toward prefabrication also included the German Bauhaus, founded in 1919 by Walter Gropius and closed in 1933 by Mies Van der Rohe. The Bauhaus group's objective was to blend art, craft, and modern technology in housing production by drawing on the mass production technology of the automobile industry. The Swedish school of architects promoted room area normalization to facilitate the fabrication of standardized components and provide flexibility in plans. Finally, in Great Britain during the 1950s and 1960s, architects promoted a technology called the Large Panel System which was an earlier Danish invention, to provide large numbers of housing units (DTI 2001).

Despite these many attempts to industrialize housing construction, industrialization never generated the anticipated cost-savings. The complexity in the design, production, delivery and assembly of prefabricated buildings exceeded the savings expected from the reduction of time, labor and materials (Koskela and Vrijboef 2001). A recent study conducted in Israel concludes that industrialization is more likely to be efficient for the construction of large multistory buildings or a a large number of units on the same site, as opposed to few and small buildings on multiple sites (Kun 2004). Further, the flexibility of traditional small- and medium-size on-site construction enterprises allowed them to remain highly competitive with industrialized builders. Studies conducted in many countries confirm these results. In the United States, the labor economist Finkel (1997) notes, that despite its important contribution to the U.S. economy of about US$400 billion per year, the construction industry has failed to generate productivity gains and attain the efficiencies of large-scale production. Output per hours increased only by 16 percent in over three decades. He states, "[T]he rapid firm entry into the building market, the low capital requirements, and minimal licensing restrictions have created a competitive market system composed of small units of capital. The Mom-and-Pop shops, the one-person firm, and the itinerant contractor have been the commonplace participants since the earliest beginning of market-based construction" (Finkel 1997). And it is still the case. The United States has about 2 million construction firms, the majority of which are small enterprises. Similarly, in France, nearly 90 percent of the 342,000 construction enterprises registered in 2004 were small, often family owned, enterprises with fewer than nine employees (INSEE 2004). In 1997, Japan had a total of 565,000 construction firms, of which 99 percent were small and medium-sized firms (Sugii 1998).

APPENDIX 6

Unit Costs of Some Contract Management Agencies in School Construction

- In Chad, the CMA A TETIP was created in 1993 to manage a school construction program financed by the World Bank. Although the agency built classrooms of acceptable quality, the unit cost was 22 percent higher than the planned costs. The agency's services were subsequently cancelled in 1998 (World Bank 1993a, 2003b).
- In Burkina Faso, the CMA Faso Baara managed school construction programs financed by the government through HIPC resources and by the AFD. Faso Baara filled an important gap and contributed enormously to expanding access. The agency built 37 percent of a total of 3,650 classrooms constructed nationwide between 2001–05 (Group 5 2006a). However, the unit costs achieved by Faso Baara, at between US$127–143 per m^2, were marginally higher than costs of the NGO Plan International (US$125/m^2) and 21 percent higher than costs achieved by provincial governments (US$103/m^2).
- In Cape Verde, the MoE delegated the management of an IDA-financed school construction program from the PIU to the CMA AGECABO. AGECABO successfully built the schools at only 60 percent of the cost of classrooms constructed by the PIU, which averaged CVEsc 4.12 million. This success swayed the MoE to adopt AGECABO's procurement procedures of three quotes in lieu of national competitive bidding. As a result, the MoE achieved similar savings and the approach was later adopted by local governments as well (World Bank 2005d).
- In Madagascar, the unit cost of AGETIPA managed classroom construction (US$322/m^2 was 60 percent higher than the cost of projects managed by the central Ministry of Education utilizing national competitive bidding procedures which averaged US$196/m^2 under an AfDB-financed project, and almost double the cost of construction carried out by the Social Fund Agency.
- In Mauritania, AMEXTIPE built classrooms through urban development projects in secondary towns at much higher cost than those built by the MoE through its community-based construction program. A technical audit showed that AMEXTIPE built a school in the town of Selibaby at a per classroom cost of US$13,200, three times higher than classrooms built by

communities (US$4,600) (Synergy 2000, World Bank 2001f). In 2005, AMEXTIPE built primary schools in the towns of Rosso and Nouadhibou at US$219/m² and US$231/m², respectively. In contrast, communities in Rosso and Nouadhibou built schools at US$155/m² and US$128/m², respectively.

- In Senegal, between 1994 and 1998, AGETIP built about 2,000 classrooms on behalf of the MoE and brought unit costs down by almost half—from US$8,100–13,200 per classroom to US$6,700 (World Bank 2000d). By 2001, the unit cost fell further to US$6,400. Between 2000 and 2004, AGETIP built 27 percent of a total of 7,950 new classrooms constructed throughout the country by different agencies (Dupety 2005a).

APPENDIX 7

Implementation Schemes for School Construction Projects Sponsored by NGOs

EXAMPLES OF NGOs OPERATING IN SCHOOL CONSTRUCTION IN AFRICA

Burkina Faso: Action Aid, Borne Foonden, CRS Cathwel, Plan International, OSEO, Save the Children

Gambia: Christian Children Fund (CFF), Future in Our Hands (FIOH)

Guinea Centre Canadien d'Etudes et de Coopération Internationale (CECI), Eglise Advantiste de Secours et de Développement (ADRA)

Mozambique: German Agro Action (AAA), IBIS (Danish), Mozambican Association for Urban Development (AMDU). Rural Development Program (PRODER), Unit for Development of Basic Education (UDEBA), World Vision

Senegal: ENDA Tiers Monde, Fondation Paul Gerin Lajoie, Plan International

EXAMPLES OF IMPLEMENTATION SCHEMES

Guinea, 2001: Implementation Scheme of a School Construction Program

This figure illustrates the implementation scheme in Guinea in 2001, under the IDA-financed Education for All project (World Bank 2001c). In this example, school construction is carried out by large NGOs acting as CMA for smaller NGOs.

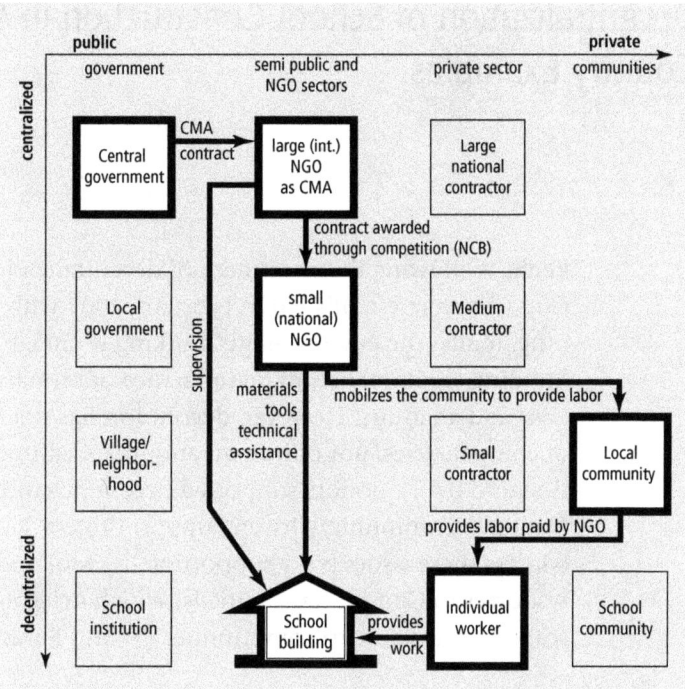

Source: Author's figure

Burkina Faso, 2007: Implementation Scheme of a School Construction Program

This figure illustrates the implementation scheme in Burkina Faso in 2007 by the NGO Action Aid. In this example, the NGO delegates school construction to communities.

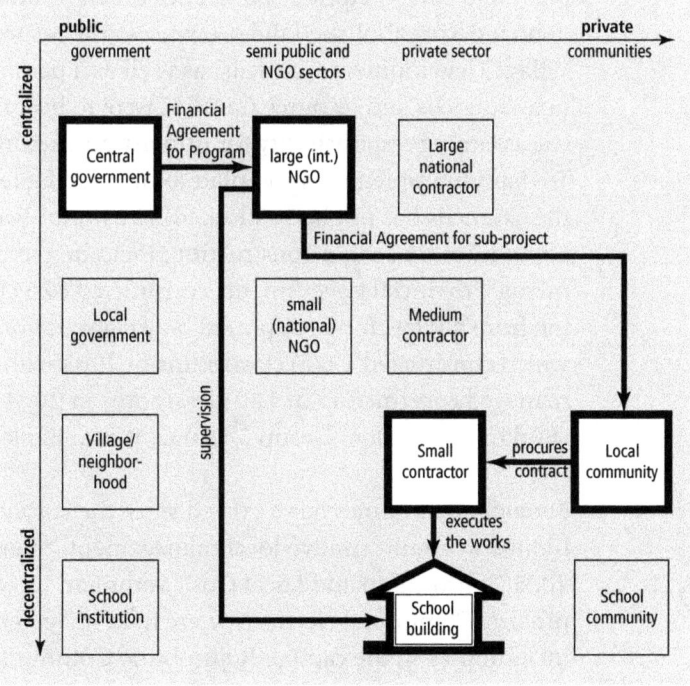

Source: Author's figure.

APPENDIX 8

Decentralization of School Construction in Africa: Country Examples

Benin. Following the enactment of decentralization laws in 1999, 77 Communal Councils were established in February 2003 with a mandate for communal planning, roads, the environment, drinking water, hygiene and sanitation, literacy, building, equipment and maintenance of primary schools, health centers, markets, and abattoirs. However, devolution has not been accompanied by a transfer of competencies, nor of human and financial resources. Nevertheless, 22 projects financed by 12 donors supported decentralization in 2004. An IDA-financed National Community-Driven Support Project, launched in 2005, was intended to address these issues by supporting the MoE in realigning and transferring resources to Communal Councils, which delegate the implementation of small-scale infrastructure to communities (World Bank 2004b).

Burkina Faso. Decentralization laws were first enacted in 1998, creating 45 provinces and 33 elected communes, each headed by a mayor. In 2004, a presidential decree abolished the provinces and created rural communes with elected Village Development Councils, as well as a permanent fund to assist them. The new Councils and resource transfers were to become effective in 2005, with Councils assuming responsibility for primary and secondary school facilities in 2008. To date, an implementation plan to transfer the responsibilities and resources to the Councils has not been adopted. Thus, the MoE continues to utilize various approaches for school construction, including management by provincial governments. Provincial governments constructed 876 classrooms in 2003 with financing from a PRSC fund supported by eight donors; management by Faso Baara, which constructed 1,050 classrooms in 2003 with HIPC funds; and MoE centrally managed construction of 120 classrooms in 2004 financed by domestic resources (Burkina Faso 2004; Group 5 2006a; World Bank 2005g, 2006a).

Burundi. Communes have existed since the colonial period, but with mandates limited to administrative local management. After a decade of civil crisis, the new 2005 Constitution and Local Government Law boosted the decentralization process. Communal elections were held in September 2005 in 123 communes, including 13 in the capital, Bujumbura. Communal competencies are still limited and central control important. IDA- and UNDP-financed projects have supported pilots providing more responsibilities to communal committees. To date, the transfer of competencies has been limited to administration. School construction and maintenance have not been effectively transferred (Demante Sidibe 2006).

Cameroon. Decentralization laws were enacted in 2004, creating communes and regions for local development. In 1996, Cameroon counted 338 communes with elected councils, each headed by a mayor. Communes are responsible *only* for the management, equipment, and maintenance of preschools and primary schools. School construction remains a central MoE responsibility. (Cameroon 2004; Kamto 2002).

Chad. Chad is not decentralized. However, the school system is co-managed by the MoE and the Federation of Parents Associations.

Ethiopia. In 1991, the central government devolved responsibilities to 11 regional governments. School construction is centrally funded and regionally administered with some school contributions (Gershberg and Winkler 2003).

Ghana. The Local Government Act of 1992 divided the country into 103 districts with elected District Assemblies. The District Assembly is legally responsible for primary and secondary school facilities. However, resources and commitment have not followed. Although six out of thirteen donor-financed school construction projects between 2000 and 2004 were managed by the districts, a 2006 review noted that both the Ministry of Education and the development partners have been reluctant to entrust districts with the responsibility for education due to weak capacity.

Guinea. A 1991 law created 38 Urban Communes with elected councils headed by a mayor, and 303 Development Rural Communes with elected councils headed by a Council President.

Mali. The Local Government Code was issued in 1995, creating 701 communes with elected councils headed by a mayor. Elections were held during 1998–99. In 2002, a government decree transferred the management of preschool and primary school construction to local governments (SNV and CEDELO 2004).

Malawi. A Local Government Act was passed in 1989 with the aim of gradually devolving school construction to elected District Assemblies. Elections took place in 2000. Nevertheless, a variety of school construction programs are carried out with no involvement of the District Assemblies. In 2003, Malawi launched a decentralized governance program in the southern part of the country by which

District Assemblies decide on priorities, in consultation with communities, and mobilize resources to carry them out. Germany, Norway, the United States and the UNDP have contributed US$12 million in financing for the pilot project. (UNDP 2003; Van Donge 2000).

Mauritania. The 1986 decentralization law created 48 urban and 163 rural Local Governments and devolved responsibility to them for basic education, including construction, equipment, and maintenance of primary schools. Funds for primary school infrastructure are largely managed by the MoE, which has delegated the implementation of school construction and maintenance to Parents' Associations. In addition, school construction is managed by urban local governments through urban development projects, which in turn delegated the management to AMEXTIPE.

Mozambique. In 1997, municipal legislation created a legal framework for elected governments in 33 municipalities. The 128 rural districts, which contain 70 percent of the population, are subject to state administration (World Bank 2003f).

Niger. As of 2006 Niger was not decentralized.

Nigeria. A 2002 review noted that although local governments are legally responsible for school construction, both federal and state governments claim they have this function, and local governments rarely receive capital investment funds (Gershberg and Winkler 2003).

Senegal. A 1996 Local Government Act created 110 urban local governments (*Communes*) and 330 rural local governments (*Communautés Rurales*), giving them responsibility for primary school construction and maintenance. By 2006, financial transfers were limited, most responsibilities remained within the MoE, and local governments still had weak planning and implementation capacity. The recent IDA-financed Participatory Local Development Project is expected to address these issues (World Bank 2006i).

Tanzania. A decentralization law was enacted in 1984, and local governments were elected in 1990. Local governments include 20 regional units, 113 Local Government Authorities, and about 11,000 wards and villages. Primary school construction is centrally funded, regionally administered, and overseen and implemented by Local Government Authorities and schools. (Gershberg and Winkler 2003).

Uganda. The 1995 Constitution and the 1997 Local Government Act decentralized the provision of school facilities to 45 districts with elected councils and

800 counties. In 1999, Uganda developed a School Facility Grant Program that continues today, in which District Councils administer and oversee school construction projects implemented by school communities. Funds are transferred to districts and municipalities to be used in accordance with the Poverty Action Fund's general guidelines issued by the Ministry of Finance, Planning, and Economic Development. School communities are represented by a School Management Committee, which prepares a community's application for funding and contracts and supervises the construction (Gershberg and Winkler 2003; Group 5 2006d).

Zambia. A Local Government Act was adopted in 1992, followed by local elections. Local authorities carry out a limited range of tasks such as managing markets and advising on road maintenance. The Ministry of Works and Supplies is responsible for all public infrastructures, including school construction. The Ministry of Local Government oversees the relationship between the line ministries and the local authorities. A 2005 study notes an absence of coordination between the central ministries and local governments. At the district level, coordination varies depending on vision, commitment, and capacity. The Social Fund, ZAMSIF, has been working with the local governments to foster decentralization (Group 5 2006e; Van Donge 2000).

APPENDIX 9

The CDD Implementation Process in Benin and Uganda

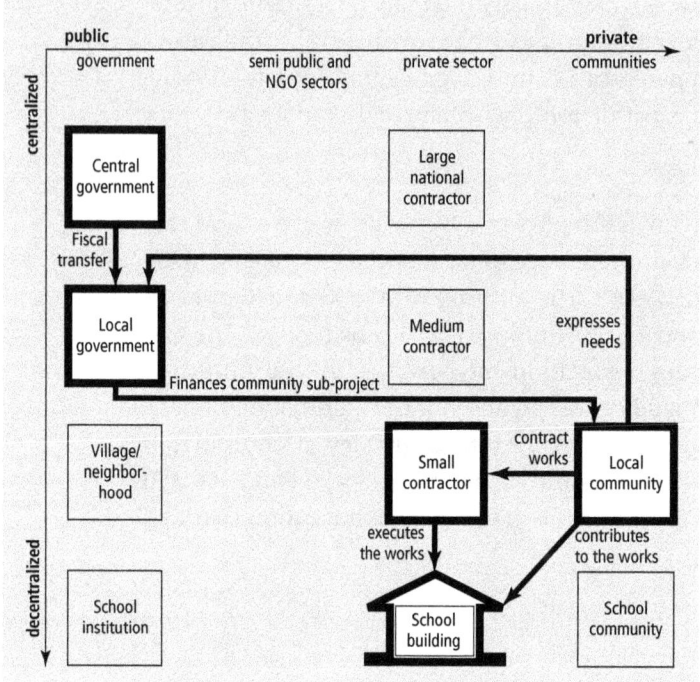

Benin: Implementation Scheme of the CDD Approach for Primary School Construction

Since 2005, Benin has been implementing the scheme illustrated here. Communities financed through their local governments have built thousands of classrooms and latrines, with savings of 30 percent compared to more centralized approaches. Since 2009, the Ministry of Education has been using this scheme to build EFA/FTI-financed school facilities.

Source: Author's figure

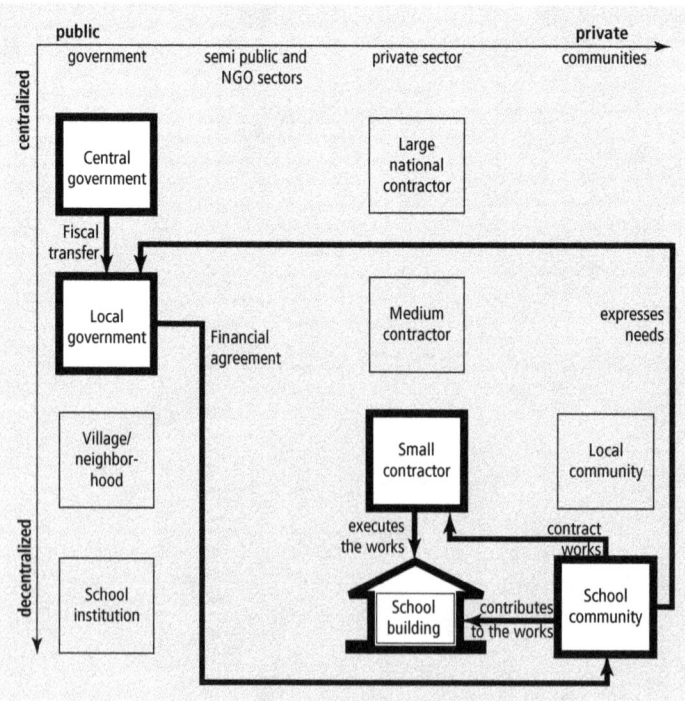

Uganda: Implementation Scheme of the CDD Approach for Primary School Construction

From 1999 to 2003, the SFG program used the scheme shown here to provide more than 21,000 classrooms (5,300 per year), 20,000 latrines, 325,000 desks, and 556 teacher houses. This is the most important single construction program ever executed in an African country for primary classroom and sanitation in schools. After 2003, the program was centralized at the local government level.

Source: Author's figure

APPENDIX 10

School Construction by Local Government Implementation Arrangements

Direct implementation of school construction by local government is illustrated in figure A10.1. It has been implemented in Ghana, Guinea, Mauritania, and Senegal. Delegation from local government to CMAs is illustrated in figure A10.2. It has been implemented in Senegal and Mauritania, in parallel with direct management by local governments in urban areas under IDA-financed urban development, as well as rural infrastructure projects. Delegation from local governments to communities is illustrated in figure A10.3. Uganda and Benin provide examples of this approach.

Figure A10.1 Devolution to Local Governments that Directly Implement School Construction

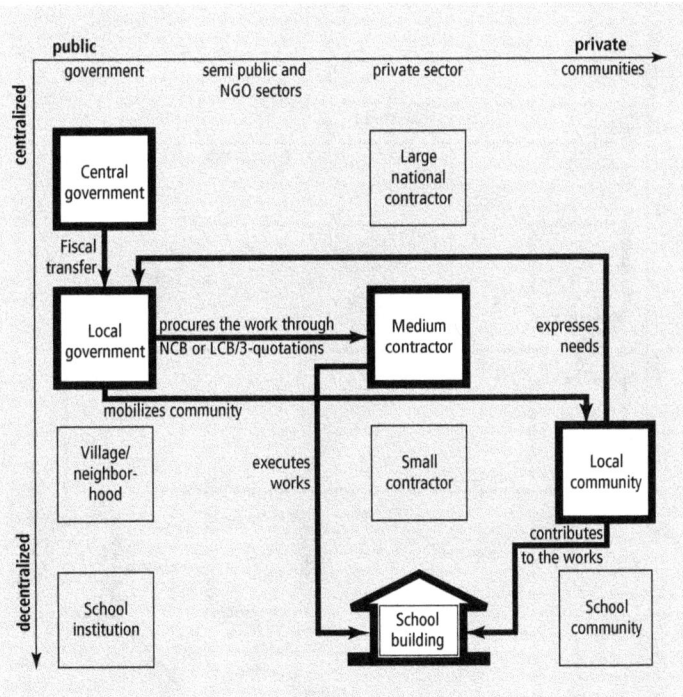

Source: Author's figure

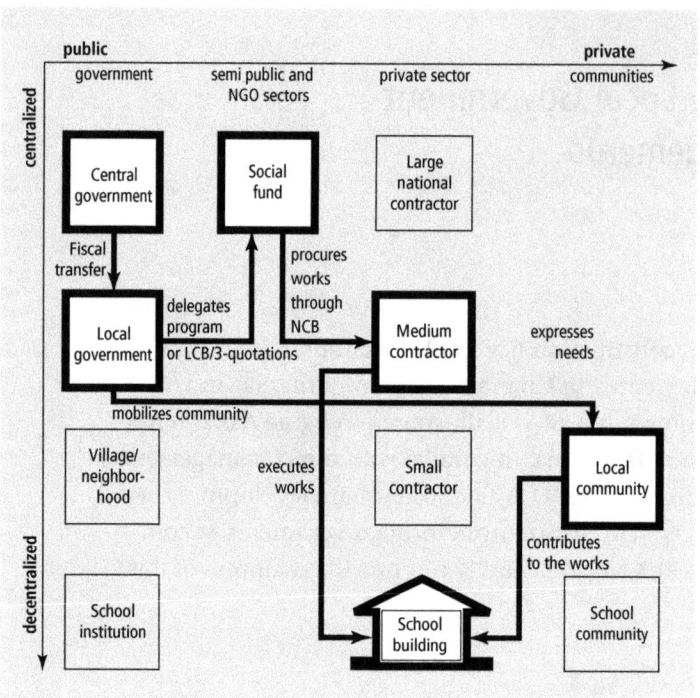

Figure A10.2 Delegation to Local Government and Subsequent Delegation to CMAs

Source: Author's figure

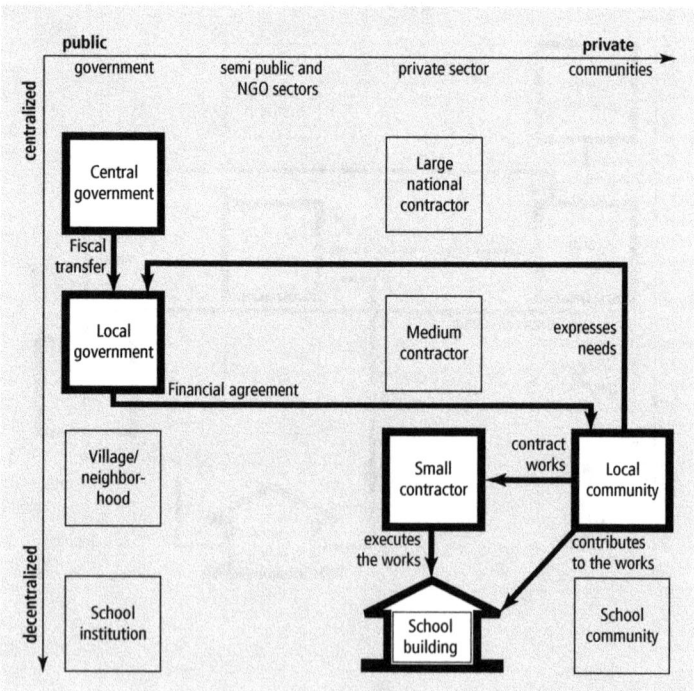

Figure A10.3 Devolution to Local Governments and Subsequent Delegation to Local Communities

Source: Author's figure

APPENDIX 11

Stakeholder Roles for Primary School Construction in a CDD Approach

	Ministry of Education (MoE)	Local Governments (LGs)	Communities (Com)	Private Sector (PS)
Financing the works of a primary school	• Mobilize adequate funding for the national program of schools. • Ensure transfer of funding to LGs.	• Receive funds from central government. • Transfer funds to Com through Financial Agreement (FA).	• Receive funds from LG to implement their primary school project.	• Is informed about the school construction program.
Planning a primary school project	• Inform LGs on sector priorities and planning norms. • Provide LG with planning toolkits and train them. • Participate in LG's appraisal to ensure respect of MoE's norms and standards by LGs and Com.	• Target poor and unserved communities. • Inform communities of opportunities and provide them with toolkits. • Appraise and approve the communities' primary school project.	• Organize Community Development Committees (CDC). • Identify school needs and priorities. • Submit a primary school project to LG.	• Expresses interest in contracts with communities for school construction and provides information on their qualifications. • Ensures that MoE and communities are informed of their expressions of interest.
Contracting between partners	• Design a model of contract (Financial Agreement—FA) between LGs and communities.	• Sign FA with eligible communities to finance approved primary school project.	• Sign FA with LG to implement primary school project; receive funds and report on project execution.	

(Table continues on the following page.)

(Table continued)

	Ministry of Education (MoE)	Local Governments (LGs)	Communities (Com)	Private Sector (PS)
Organizing the primary school project implementation	• Ensure LG receives toolkits and training for community project cycle management. • Ensure Com receives toolkit and training on project management.	• Receive training on community project-cycle management (financing communities, monitoring communities' performance).	• Set up a Project Management Committee (PMC). • Receive training on procurement, financial management, and participatory monitoring.	
Procuring works, goods and services, and managing contracts		• Supervise execution of FA by communities	• Procure contracts for works, furniture, and site supervision through local competition	• Execute works, furniture procurement, and site supervision through contracts with communities.
Monitoring execution of contracts		• Hand over newly built school facility if it conforms to FA, and register into LG property file.	• PMC monitors contracts and reports to CDC and community.	• Engineers/executes site supervision through contracts with community.
Maintaining facilities	• Ensures adequate funding is provided to LGs for maintenance.	• Sign FA with communities to cofinance maintenance of schools.	• Sign FA with LG to execute proper maintenance of schools (self maintenance + outcontracting).	• Executes maintenance contracts with communities (painting, civil work, and furniture repairs).

Source: Author's elaboration.

APPENDIX 12

Toolkits to Harmonize Norms and Standards and Implementation Strategies

Table A12.1 Norms and Standards

		Project 1	Project 2	Project 3	Project 4	Project 5	Project 6	Project 7	Project 8	Harmonization
	What Do We Need to Put in a Toolkit for Donor Harmonization Regarding Norms and Standards? An Example of a Simplified Table									
Planning norms	Maximum distance home to school									
	Maximum school size									
	Small "rural friendly" model									
	Urban multistory school model									
	Minimum School Facility Package									
School model and standard designs	Standard norm for primary classroom area									
	Ratio for area of office and storage									
	Standard designs for a menu of classroom blocs									
	Standard design for latrines and water									
	Standard design for flexible furniture									

Table A12.2   Toolkit for Donor Harmonization in Implementation Strategies

		Project 1	Project 2	Project 3	Project 4	Project 5	Project 6	Project 7	Project 8	Ideal model
Managing the overall school construction project	Ministry									X
	NGO									
	MCA									
	Local Gov.									
	Community									X
	Private sector									
Planning a primary school project	Ministry									
	NGO									
	MCA									
	Local Gov.									
	Community									
	Private sector									
Contracting between partners	Ministry									
	NGO									
	MCA									
	Local Gov.									X
	Community									X
	Private sector									
Organizing primary school project implementation	Ministry									
	NGO									
	MCA									
	Local Gov.									
	Community									X
	Private sector									
Procuring works, goods and services, managing contracts	Ministry									
	NGO									
	MCA									
	Local Gov.									
	Community									X
	Private sector									
Monitoring execution of contracts	Ministry									
	NGO									
	MCA									
	Local Gov.									
	Community									
	Private sector									X
Maintaining facilities	Ministry									
	NGO									
	MCA									
	Local Gov.									X
	Community									X
	Private sector									

APPENDIX 13

Illustrations from the Senegal Social Fund Community Handbook

Constituting the Project Management Committee

Advertising the Invitation to Bid Process through rural radio

Advertising the Invitation to Bid through postings

The Bid Deposit Process

The Bid Evaluation Process

Transparency of the financial monitoring

Source: AFDS 2003b. Drawings by Aly Nguer.

APPENDIX 14

Detailed Projections of the Classroom Needs

The current classroom gap for the period 2005–15 is important: almost 200,000 classrooms per year for 33 African countries. Of the total deficit in classroom capacity, 60 percent represents the need for additional classrooms, 25 percent represents classrooms to replace substandard existing facilities, and 15 percent presents classrooms to replace overaged structures. Furthermore, the actual classroom gap may be higher than indicated by earlier estimates.[1] The following paragraphs offer more details on how the construction need was estimated for each of these three categories.

New estimates for the 2005–15 classroom gap. By comparing the *actual* number of classrooms in the 14 countries with how many classrooms are needed by 2015, it is possible to get a new estimate of the 2005–15 classroom gap. For 5 of the 14 countries, this new estimate is close to the 2005–15 gap estimated in 2003, but for the other 9 countries, the new gap is significantly higher. On average for the 14 countries, the new gap is 20 percent more than the previously estimated gap.

This analysis leads us to the conclusion that *the need for additional classrooms in the 33 African countries, between 2005 and 2015, is a total of 1.17 million classrooms, or 117,000 classrooms per year*. After 2015, the need for increasing the primary education classroom stock will be driven by the growth in school-age population. Figure A14.1 illustrates a projection of the required increase in classroom stock for the 33 countries.

The need to replace temporary and substandard classrooms. The 2005–15 classroom gap cannot be equated with how many new classrooms need to be built every year. In practice, when new schools and classrooms are built, they often replace existing classrooms built from nonpermanent materials, or classrooms that have collapsed. Obviously, classrooms that replace older classrooms do not add to

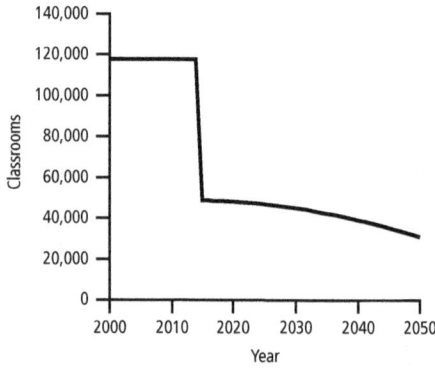

Figure A14.1 Additional Classrooms Needed for 33 African IDA Countries

Source: Kirsten Majgaard's calculation.

the stock. It is a fair assumption that the entire stock of temporary classrooms will need to be replaced within the next 10 years, as these are built of nondurable materials. We assume that 25 percent of the classrooms in the 33 countries fall in this category (table 1 above suggests 28 percent in the 14 countries). Figure A14.2 illustrates the temporary classroom replacement need. *Between 2005 and 2015, an estimated 480,000 temporary classrooms need to be replaced. This amounts to 48,000 classrooms per year.* After 2015, the analysis assumes that all temporary classrooms have been replaced.

Between 2005 and 2015, around 30,000 overaged classrooms should be replaced every year. Permanent classrooms, even when built according to international standards, also need replacement at the end of their useful life. Such a need is never considered by Ministries of Education when forecasting their construction needs. Assuming that the average life expectancy for a classroom built from permanent materials is 40 years (an internationally accepted standard), classrooms built in the 60s need replacement in the current decade 2000-2010; classrooms built in the 70s need replacement in the 2010s, and so on. Figure A14.3 shows how the need for replacement of permanent classrooms will increase in the coming years, as the system is maturing (average age of the classroom stock is rising).

Between 2005 and 2015, the primary classroom construction need peaks at 200,000 per year, as shown in figure 14.4. The total need for classroom construction, requirements combines are a sum of the need for increasing to increase the classroom stock with and the needs for replacement of to replace temporary and permanent classrooms. Although figure A14.4 is based on a highly simplified projection, it serves to illustrate how the need for classroom construction may decline after 2015 (if the targets are met) and then subsequently increase as the classroom stock ages and needs replacement. The focus will then shift from increasing the classroom stock due to enrollment growth

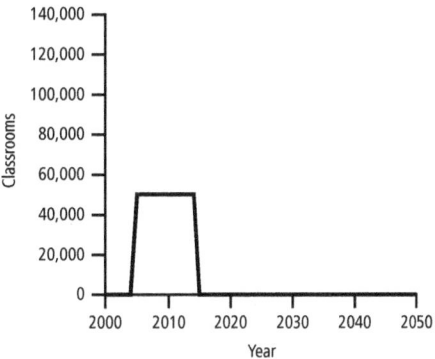

Figure A14.2 Need for Replacement of Temporary Classrooms for 33 African IDA Countries

Source: Kirsten Majgaard's calculation.

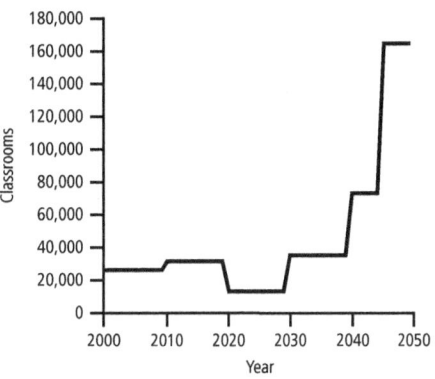

Figure 14.3 Need for Replacement of Overaged Classrooms for 33 African IDA Countries

Source: Kirsten Majgaard's calculation.

Figure A14.4 Total Classroom Construction Needs for 33 African IDA Countries

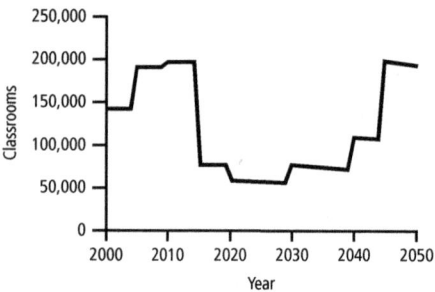

Source: Kirsten Majgaard's calculation.

to the replacement of an ageing classroom stock. All new school construction should, as a rule, be replaced 40 years later. Therefore, the estimated 2005–15 peak will recur in 2045–55, as shown in figure A14.4. Between the two peaks, primary classroom construction demand will be 50,000–100,000 per year.

NOTE

1. The 2003 gap assessment assumed that there were 41 pupils per classroom in 2000.

APPENDIX 15

Summary of the Various Implementation Schemes

Schemes to implement school construction programs

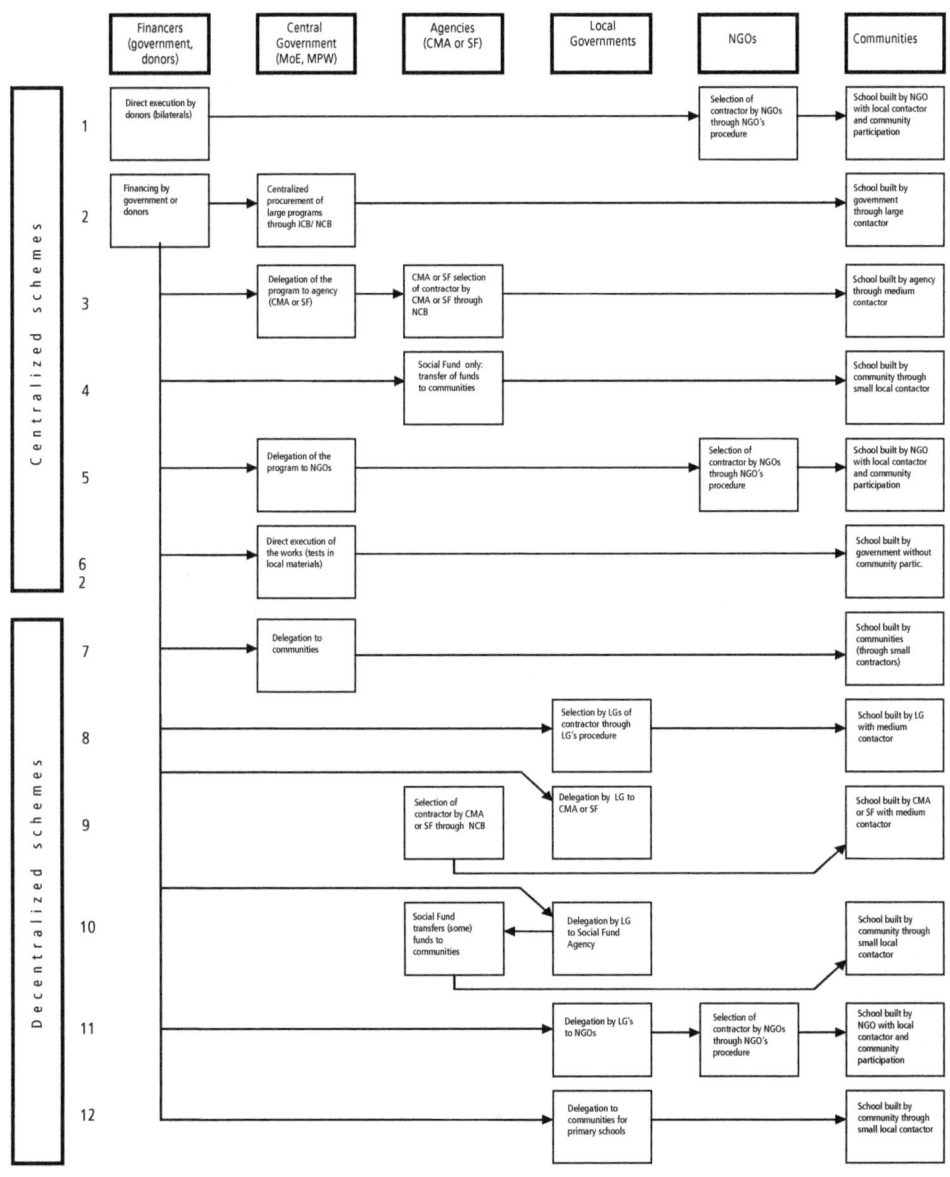

APPENDIX 16

The Situation of School Construction Programs in Selected African Countries: Who Does What and How

Burkina Faso: Who does What and How for primary school construction in 2006?

Project		WHO DOES WHAT?	Donor	Centralized approaches including deconcentrated and outsourcing approaches						Decentralized approaches				
				Ministry			Agencies (CMA/SF)		NGOs		Local Governments	Private sector	Communities	
				Central Office	Regional/ District	School staff	Central Office	Deconcen-trated Offices	Central Office	Deconcen-trated Offices			Community empowerment	Community participation

National Program

Fin	Government	1 Proposes planning		DEP/MEBA										
Nb clrs	120/year	2 Decides planning		DEP/MEBA										
Years	current	3 Standard Design		DEP/MEBA										
PIU	No 0	4 Financing Agreement		DAF/MEBA										
coverage	National	5 DAO standard doc		NCB										
Year	2005	6 Invitation to bid		Commission for Bidding Awards/MEBA										
$ clrm		7 Awards contract		DAF/MEBA										
m2/clrm		8 Signs contract			Reg Staff/MEBA									
$/m2		9 Monitors works		DAF/MEBA										
Comm.p.	0 0	10 Pays works												
S/O, L,W	0 0 0	11 Executes works										SME		
Source:	Group5 2005	12 Handovers building		MEBA										

Common Basket Fund during 2002–2005 (World Bank. Canada, The Netherlands)

Fin	Multiple	1 Proposes planning			Provinces									
Nb clrs	1,263	2 Decides planning			Provinces									
Years	2002–03	3 Standard Design		BPE/MEBA										
PIU	No 0	4 Financing Agreement												
coverage	National	5 DAO standard doc		BPE/MEBA										
Year	2002–2004	6 Invitation to bid			NCB									
$ clrm	5,962	7 Awards contract			Commission for Local Bidding Award (CAMloc)									
m2/clrm	77.21	8 Signs contract			DPEBA									
$/m2	103	9 Monitors works			Provincial Staff									
Comm.p.	0 0	10 Pays works			DPEBA									
S/O, L,W	0 0 774	11 Executes works										SME		
Source:	Group5 2005	12 Handovers building			DPEBA									

Common Basket Fund after 2005 (World Bank. Canada, The Netherlands)

Fin	Multiple	1 Proposes planning		DAF/MEBA										
Nb clrs	1,263	2 Decides planning		DAF/MEBA										
Years	2002–03	3 Standard Design		MEBA										
PIU	No 0	4 Financing Agreement		MEBA/Faso-Baara										
coverage	National	5 DAO standard doc		DAF/MEBA			MEBA/Faso-Baara							
Year	2002–2004	6 Invitation to bid					Faso Baara's PIM							
$ clrm	5,962	7 Awards contract					NCB							
m2/clrm	77.21	8 Signs contract					Faso Baara's Tender Board							
$/m2	103	9 Monitors works					Faso Baara							
Comm.p.	0 0	10 Pays works					Faso Baara							
S/O, L,W	0 0 774	11 Executes works										Contract with Faso-Bara SME		
Source:	Group5 2005	12 Handovers building		MEBA										

(Table continues on the following page.)

Burkina Faso: Who does What and How for primary school construction in 2006? (continued)

		Centralized approaches including deconcentrated and outsourcing approaches							Decentralized approaches				
		Donor	Ministry			Agencies (CMA/SF)		NGOs		Local Governments	Private sector	Communities (CBOs/PTAs)	
Project	WHO DOES WHAT?		Central Office	Regional/ District	School staff	Central Office	Deconcen-trated Offices	Central Office	Deconcen-trated Offices			Community empowerment	Community participation
PPTE/HIPC													
Fin Government	1 Proposes planning		DAF/MEBA										
Nb clrs 1050	2 Decides planning		DAF/MEBA										
Years 2000–2003	3 Standard Design		MEBA										
PIU Yes 1	4 Financing Agreement		MEBA/Faso-Baara			MEBA/Faso-Baara							
coverage National	5 DAO standard doc					Faso Baara's PIM							
Year 2003	6 Invitation to bid		DAF/MEBA			NCB							
$ clrm 4,147	7 Awards contract					Faso Baara's Tender Board							
m2/clrm 64.40	8 Signs contract					Faso Baara					Contract with Faso-Bara		
$/m2 127	9 Monitors works												
Comm.p. 0	10 Pays works					Faso Baara					SME		
S/O, L, W N/A N/A N/A	11 Executes works												
Source: Group5 2005	12 Handovers building		MEBA										
Projet d'Appui à l'Organisation de l'Enseignement de Base—PAOEB (France)													
Fin AFD	1 Proposes planning		MEBA										
Nb clrs 297	2 Decides planning		MEBA										
Years 2002–2004	3 Standard Design		MEBA										
PIU No 0	4 Financing Agreement		MEBA/Faso-Baara			MEBA/Faso-Baara							
coverage Provinces	5 DAO standard doc					Faso Baara's PIM							
Year 2004	6 Invitation to bid					NCB							
$ clrm 4,147	7 Awards contract					Faso Baara's Tender Board							
m2/clrm 64.40	8 Signs contract					Faso Baara					Contract with Faso-Bara		
$/m2 143	9 Monitors works					Faso Baara							
Comm.p. 0	10 Pays works										SME		
S/O, L, W N/A N/A N/A	11 Executes works												
Source: Group 5 2005	12 Handovers building		MEBA										
JICA Project (Japan)													
Fin JICA	1 Proposes planning	Jica's Project Office											
Nb clrs N/A	2 Decides planning	Jica's Project Office											
Years N/A	3 Standard Design	Jica's Project Office											
PIU Yes 1	4 Financing Agreement												
coverage N/A	5 DAO standard doc	Jica's Project Office											
Year N/A	6 Invitation to bid	ICB											
$ clrm N/A	7 Awards contract	Jica's Project Office											
m2/clrm N/A	8 Signs contract	Jica's Project Office											
$/m2 N/A	9 Monitors works												
Comm.p. 0	10 Pays works												
S/O, L, W N/A N/A N/A	11 Executes works										Japanese Consultancy Firms		
Source: Group5 2005	12 Handovers building		MEBA								Large Contractors		

Basic Education Support Program—PASEB (European Union)							
Fin	EU	1 Proposes planning	DEP/MEBA				
Nb clrs	60	2 Decides planning	DEP/MEBA				
Years	2004	3 Standard Design	DEP/MEBA				
PIU	Yes 1	4 Financing Agreement					
coverage	5 Provinces	5 DAO standard doc	DAF/MEBA				
Year	N/A	6 Invitation to bid	NCB				
$ clrm	N/A	7 Awards contract	Commission for Bidding Awards/MEBA				
m2/clrm	N/A	8 Signs contract	DAF/MEBA				
$/m2	N/A	9 Monitors works		Reg Staff/MEBA			
Comm.p.	0 0	10 Pays works	DAF/MEBA				
S/O, L, W	N/A N/A N/A	11 Executes works			SME		
Source:	Group5 2005	12 Handovers building	MEBA				
Islamic Development Bank—IDB (BID II and BID III)							
Fin	IDB	1 Proposes planning	BPE/MEBA				
Nb clrs	454	2 Decides planning	BPE/MEBA				
Years	2002–2004	3 Standard Design	BPE/MEBA				
PIU	No 0	4 Financing Agreement					
coverage	Provinces	5 DAO standard doc	BPE/MEBA				
Year	N/A	6 Invitation to bid	NCB				
$ clrm	N/A	7 Awards contract	BPE/MEBA				
m2/clrm	N/A	8 Signs contract	BPE/MEBA				
$/m2	N/A	9 Monitors works	BPE/MEBA				
Comm.p.	0 0	10 Pays works					
S/O, L, W	N/A N/A N/A	11 Executes works			Large Contractor		
Source:	Group5 2005	12 Handovers building	MEBA				
UNICEF Project (implementation data non available)							
Fin	UNICEF	1 Proposes planning					
Nb clrs	168	2 Decides planning					
Years	2001–2004	3 Standard Design					
PIU	No 0	4 Financing Agreement					
coverage	13 Province	5 DAO standard doc					
Year	2004	6 Invitation to bid					
$ clrm	N/A	7 Awards contract					
m2/clrm	N/A	8 Signs contract					
$/m2	N/A	9 Monitors works					
Comm.p.	1	10 Pays works					
S/O, L, W	N/A N/A N/A	11 Executes works					
Source:	Group5 2005	12 Handovers building					

(Table continues on the following page.)

Burkina Faso: Who does What and How for primary school construction in 2006? (continued)

Project	WHO DOES WHAT?	Donor	Centralized approaches including deconcentrated and outsourcing approaches							Decentralized approaches				
			Ministry			Agencies (CMA/SF)		NGOs		Local Governments	Private sector	Communities (CBOs/PTAs)	
			Central Office	Regional/ District	School staff	Central Office	Deconcen-trated Offices	Central Office	Deconcen-trated Offices			Community empowerment	Community participation

Plan International, Burkina Faso Project

Fin	Plan													
Nb clrs	55													
Years	2003–2004													
PIU	Yes 1													
coverage	N/A													
Year	2004													
$ clrm	4,147													
m2/clrm	64.40													
$/m2	125													
Comm.p.	1 N/A													
S/O, L, W	N/A N/A N/A													
Source:	Group5 2005													

1 Proposes planning	NGO	MEBA
2 Decides planning	NGO	
3 Standard Design	NGO/MEBA	NGO/MEBA
4 Financing Agreement	NGO	
5 DAO standard doc	NGO	
6 Invitation to bid	NGO	
7 Awards contract	NGO	
8 Signs contract	NGO	
9 Monitors works	NGO	
10 Pays works	NGO	
11 Executes works	NGO	Micro-contractor
12 Handovers building	NGO	MEBA — Community

OSEO

Fin	NGO	
Nb clrs		
Years		
PIU	Yes 1	
coverage	Provinces	
Year		
$ clrm	17,089	
m2/clrm	78	
$/m2	219	
Comm.p.	1 N/A	
S/O, L, W	0 0 0	
Source:	OSEO	

1 Proposes planning	NGO	MEBA
2 Decides planning	NGO	
3 Standard Design	NGO/MEBA	NGO/MEBA
4 Financing Agreement	NGO	
5 DAO standard doc	NGO	
6 Invitation to bid	NGO	
7 Awards contract	NGO	
8 Signs contract	NGO	
9 Monitors works	NGO	
10 Pays works	NGO	
11 Executes works	NGO	Micro-contractor
12 Handovers building	NGO	MEBA — Community

Other NGOs: CRS Cathwell, OSEO, Save the Children, Born Fenden

Fin	NGO	
Nb clrs	163	
Years	2004	
PIU	Yes 1	
coverage	Provinces	
Year	N/A	
$ clrm	N/A	
m2/clrm	N/A	
$/m2	N/A	
Comm.p.	1 N/A	
S/O, L, W	N/A N/A N/A	
Source:	Group5 2005	

1 Proposes planning	NGO	MEBA
2 Decides planning	NGO	
3 Standard Design	NGO/MEBA	NGO/MEBA
4 Financing Agreement	NGO	
5 DAO standard doc	NGO	
6 Invitation to bid	NGO	
7 Awards contract	NGO	
8 Signs contract	NGO	
9 Monitors works	NGO	
10 Pays works	NGO	
11 Executes works	NGO	Micro-contractor
12 Handovers building	NGO	MEBA — Community

School Construction by Local Councils—FODECOL Funds

Fin	N/A						
Nb clrs	N/A						
Years	N/A						
PIU	No 0						
coverage	Provinces						
Year	N/A						
$ clrm	N/A						
m2/clrm	N/A						
$/m2	N/A						
Comm.p.	1						
S/O, L, W	N/A N/A N/A						
Source:	Group5 2005						

Step			
1 Proposes planning			Local Councils
2 Decides planning			Local Councils
3 Standard Design	MEBA		
4 Financing Agreement	MEBA		
5 DAO standard doc			LCB
6 Invitation to bid			Local Councils
7 Awards contract			Local Councils
8 Signs contract			Local Councils
9 Monitors works			Local Councils
10 Pays works			
11 Executes works			
12 Handovers building	MEBA		SME

School Construction by Local Councils—FICOM

Fin	N/A						
Nb clrs	N/A						
Years	N/A						
PIU	No 0						
coverage	Provinces						
Year	N/A						
$ clrm	N/A						
m2/clrm	N/A						
$/m2	N/A						
Comm.p.	1						
S/O, L, W	N/A N/A N/A						
Source:	Group5 2005						

Step			
1 Proposes planning			Local Councils
2 Decides planning			Local Councils
3 Standard Design	MEBA		
4 Financing Agreement			
5 DAO standard doc		Faso Baara's PIM	
6 Invitation to bid		NCB	
7 Awards contract		Faso Baara's Tender Board	
8 Signs contract		Faso Baara	
9 Monitors works			
10 Pays works		Faso Baara	
11 Executes works			Contract with Faso-Bara
12 Handovers building	MEBA		SME

Mauritania: Who does What and How for primary school construction in 2006?

Project	WHO DOES WHAT?	Donor	Centralized approaches including deconcentrated and outsourcing approaches							Decentralized approaches					Comments
			Ministry			Agencies (CMA/SF)		NGOs		Local Governments	Private sector	Communities (CBOs/PTAs)			
			Central Office	Regional/ District	School staff	Central Office	Deconcentrated Offices	Central Office	Deconcentrated Offices			Community empowerment	Community participation		
National Ten-Year Education and Training Program (PNDSE)															
Fin		IDA/AFD													DPEF is successfully managing the MoE's program since 1989
Nb clrs	1 Proposes planning	5,000	DPEF												
Years	2 Decides planning	1989–2006	DPEF												
PIU	3 Standard Design	1 DPEF													
coverage	4 Financing Agreement	National	btwn DPEF and Parents Ass.									Parents Association			
Year	5 DAO standard doc	2001	DPEF's Operation Manual												
$ clrm	6 Invitation to bid	7,678										btwn DPEF and Parents Ass.			
Gross m²	7 Awards contract	53.25										3Q or DC			
Gross $/m²	8 Signs contract	144	DPEF's engineers									Parents Association			
Comm.-p.	9 Monitors works	30%										Parents Association			
S/O, L, W	10 Pays works	1 1 0									Micro-contractor				
Source:	11 Executes works	PNDSE/ST	MoE												
	12 Handovers building														
Urban Development Project															
Fin		IDA													The Project is using the same model as DPEF
Nb clrs	1 Proposes planning	N/A								Local Government					
Years	2 Decides planning	1995–2006								Local Government					
PIU	3 Standard Design	0 No	MoE (similar to DPEF)												
coverage	4 Financing Agreement	Urban	btwn MoE and AMEXTIPE			btwn MoE and AMEXTIPE									
Year	5 DAO standard doc	2002				AMEXTIPE's Operation Manual									
$ clrm	6 Invitation to bid	12,325				National Competitive Bidding									
Gross m²	7 Awards contract	53.25				AMEXTIPE's Tender Board									
Gross $/m²	8 Signs contract	231				AMEXTIPE					Contract with AMEXTIPE				
Comm.-p.	9 Monitors works	0 No				AMEXTIPE									
S/O, L, W	10 Pays works	1 1 0									SME				
Source:	11 Executes works	PNDSE/ST	MoE												
	12 Handovers building														

Niger: Who does What and How for primary school construction in 2006?

Project	WHO DOES WHAT?	Donor	Centralized approaches including deconcentrated and outsourcing approaches						Decentralized approaches			Communities (CBOs/PTAs)	
			Ministry				Agencies (CMA/SF)		NGOs		Local Governments	Private sector	Community empowerment	Community participation
			Central Office	Regional/ District	School staff	Central Office	Deconcentrated Offices	Central Office	Deconcentrated Offices				
PPTE													
Fin Government Nb clrs Years PIU coverage Year $ clrm 56.00 m2/clrm — $/m2 Comm.p. AB, L, W 1 1 0 Source: Soul. Zerbo	1 Proposes planning 2 Decides planning 3 Standard Design 4 Financing Agreement 5 DAO standard doc 6 Invitation to bid 7 Awards contract 8 Signs contract 9 Monitors works 10 Pays works 11 Executes works 12 Handovers building												
PADEB (classic)													
Fin IDA Nb clrs Years PIU coverage Year $ clrm 8,257 m2/clrm 56.00 $/m2 147.44 Comm.p. AB, L, W 1 1 0 Source: Soul. Zerbo	1 Proposes planning 2 Decides planning 3 Standard Design 4 Financing Agreement 5 DAO standard doc 6 Invitation to bid 7 Awards contract 8 Signs contract 9 Monitors works 10 Pays works 11 Executes works 12 Handovers building		Planning Directorate Planning Directorate Infrastructure Directorate national NCB doc (adapted) 	MoE Regional Directorate (NCB) Regional Tenderboard MoE Regional Directorate Contractual agent of Reg MoE Dir MoE Regional Directorate MoE Regional Directorate							SME		
PADEB (shelter)													
Fin IDA Nb clrs Years PIU coverage Year $ clrm 3,457 m2/clrm 56.00 $/m2 61.73 Comm.p. AB, L, W 0 1 0 Source: Soul. Zerbo	1 Proposes planning 2 Decides planning 3 Standard Design 4 Financing Agreement 5 DAO standard doc 6 Invitation to bid 7 Awards contract 8 Signs contract 9 Monitors works 10 Pays works 11 Executes works 12 Handovers building		Planning Directorate Planning Directorate Infrastructure Directorate national NCB doc (adapted) 	MoE Regional Directorate (NCB) Regional Tenderboard MoE Regional Directorate Contractual agent of Reg MoE Dir MoE Regional Directorate MoE Regional Directorate							SME		

(Table continues on the following page.)

Niger: Who does What and How for primary school construction in 2006? (continued)

			Centralized approaches including deconcentrated and outsourcing approaches						Decentralized approaches			
			Ministry			Agencies (CMA/SF)		NGOs				Communities (CBOs/PTAs)
Project	WHO DOES WHAT?	Donor	Central Office	Regional/ District	School staff	Central Office	Deconcen-trated Offices	Central Office	Deconcen-trated Offices	Local Governments	Private sector	Community empowerment	Community participation

AFD-funded project (name ?)

Fin AFD
Nb clrs
Years
PIU
coverage
Year
$ clrm
m2/clrm 56.00
$/m2 -
Comm.p.
AB, L, W 1 1 0
Source: Soul. Zerbo

1 Proposes planning
2 Decides planning
3 Standard Design
4 Financing Agreement
5 DAO standard doc
6 Invitation to bid
7 Awards contract
8 Signs contract
9 Monitors works
10 Pays works
11 Executes works
12 Handovers building

KfW-funded Project (name ?)

Fin KfW
Nb clrs
Years
PIU
coverage
Year
$ clrm
m2/clrm 56.00
$/m2 -
Comm.p.
AB, L, W 0 1 0
Source: Soul. Zerbo

1 Proposes planning
2 Decides planning
3 Standard Design
4 Financing Agreement
5 DAO standard doc
6 Invitation to bid
7 Awards contract
8 Signs contract
9 Monitors works
10 Pays works
11 Executes works
12 Handovers building

PAEFAN (name ?)

Fin ???
Nb clrs
Years
PIU
coverage
Year
$ clrm
m2/clrm 56.00
$/m2 -
Comm.p.
AB, L, W 1 1 0
Source: Soul. Zerbo

1 Proposes planning
2 Decides planning
3 Standard Design
4 Financing Agreement
5 DAO standard doc
6 Invitation to bid
7 Awards contract
8 Signs contract
9 Monitors works
10 Pays works
11 Executes works
12 Handovers building

Senegal: Who does What and How for primary school construction in 2006?

			Centralized approaches including deconcentrated and outsourcing approaches								Decentralized approaches			
			Ministry			Agencies (CMA/SF)		NGOs		Local Govern-ments	Private Sector	Communities (CBOs/PTAs)		Comments
Project	WHO DOES WHAT?	Donor	Central Office	Regional/ District	School Staff	Central Office	Decon-cen-trated Offices	Central Office	Decon-cen-trated Offices			Community Empowerment	Community Participation	

1. AFDS (Agence du Fonds de Développement Social)

Fin	IDA													
Nb clrs	115					1 Proposes planning						Community		Communities have proven they have the capacity to carry out school construction
Years	2002–06					2 Decides planning						Community		
PIU	0					3 Standard Design								
coverage	5 regions					4 Financing Agreement						between AFDS and Comm.		
Year	2006					5 DAO standard doc								
$ clrm	7,498					6 Invitation to bid						LCB		
m2/clrm	65.20					7 Awards contract						Community's Tender Board by Comm.		
$/m2	115.00					8 Signs contract						contract with comm.		
Comm.p.	1 5%					9 Monitors works						by Comm.		
O/S, L, W	1 1 1					10 Pays works								
						11 Executes works						micro-contractor.		
Source:	Dupety/Sow					12 Handovers building	Same as AGETIP between AFDS and Comm. in the PIM				according to Law			

Education Project III (AfDB III)

Fin	AfDB													
Nb clrs	0 (rehab)		1 Proposes planning	DCES										At the end of the program, 45 classrooms are subject to contract management issues
Years	2001–04		2 Decides planning	DECS										
PIU	0		3 Standard Design	DECS										
coverage			4 Financing Agreement											
Year			5 DAO standard doc	NCB/DCES										
$ clrm			6 Invitation to bid	DCES										
m2/clrm			7 Awards contract	National Tender Board										
$/m2	#VALUE!		8 Signs contract	DCES										
Comm.p.			9 Monitors works	DCES										
AB, L, W			10 Pays works	DCES										
			11 Executes works								SME			
Source:	Dupety 2005		12 Handovers building	MoE										

Investment Consolidated Budget (BCI)

Fin	Government													
Nb clrs	4,804		1 Proposes planning	DCES										During the consultant's review, 97 clas-roooms were uncompleted because of contract issues
Years	2002–06		2 Decides planning	DECS										
PIU	0		3 Standard Design	DECS										
coverage	National		4 Financing Agreement											
Year	2005		5 DAO standard doc	NCB/DCES										
$ clrm	8,473		6 Invitation to bid	DCES										
m2/clrm	67.34		7 Awards contract	National Tender Board										
$/m2	125.83		8 Signs contract	DCES										
Comm.p.	0 0		9 Monitors works	DCES										
O/S, L, W	0 0 0		10 Pays works	DCES										
			11 Executes works								SME			
Source:	Dupety 2005		12 Handovers building	MoE										

(Table continues on the following page.)

Senegal: Who does What and How for primary school construction in 2006? (continued)

			Centralized approaches including deconcentrated and outsourcing approaches								Decentralized approaches				
			Ministry			Agencies (CMA/SF)		NGOs		Local Govern-ments	Private sector	Communities (CBOs/PTAs)		Comments
Project	WHO DOES WHAT?	Donor	Central Office	Regional/ District	School Staff	Central Office	Decon-cen-trated Offices	Central Office	Decon-cen-trated Offices			Community empowerment	Community participation	
JICA IV														
Fin: JICA	1 Proposes planning	JICA												All the program is managed by JICA. The consultant could not collect information on cost
Nb clrs: 323	2 Decides planning	JICA												
Years: 2002–04	3 Standard Design	JICA												
PIU: 0	4 Financing Agreement	JICA												
coverage: Urban	5 DAO standard doc	JICA												
Year: N/A	6 Invitation to bid	JICA												
$ clrm: N/A	7 Awards contract	JICA												
m2/clrm: N/A	8 Signs contract		DCES											
$/m2: 0	9 Monitors works		DCES											
Comm.p.: 0	10 Pays works													
O/S, L, W: 0 0 0	11 Executes works										Large Contractor			
Source: Dupety 2005	12 Handovers building		MoE											
OPEP III														
Fin: OPEP	1 Proposes planning		DCES											
Nb clrs: 125	2 Decides planning		DECS											
Years: 2003–04	3 Standard Design		DECS											
PIU: 0	4 Financing Agreement													
coverage:	5 DAO standard doc		NCB/DCES											
Year: 2004	6 Invitation to bid		DCES											
$ clrm: 9,206	7 Awards contract		National Tender Board											
m2/clrm: 67.34	8 Signs contract		DCES											
$/m2: 136.71	9 Monitors works		DCES											
Comm.p.: 0	10 Pays works		DCES											
O/S, L, W: 0 0 0	11 Executes works										SME			
Source: Dupety 2005	12 Handovers building		MoE											
Commune Support Project (PAC)														
Fin: IDA	1 Proposes planning		DCES											
Nb clrs: 15	2 Decides planning		DCES											
Years: 2000–02	3 Standard Design					AGETIP								
PIU: 0	4 Financing Agreement					Btwn AGETIP and LG				Btwn AGETIP and LG				
coverage: Sec. Towns	5 DAO standard doc					AGETIP's Operation Manual								
Year: 2002	6 Invitation to bid					AGETIP's Tender Board								
$ clrm: 9,079	7 Awards contract					AGETIP's Tender Board								
m2/clrm: 63.38	8 Signs contract					AGETIP's Tender Board								
$/m2: 143.24	9 Monitors works					AGETIP								
Comm.p.: 0	10 Pays works										contract with AGETIP			
AB, L, W: 0 0 0	11 Executes works										SME			
Source: Dupety 2005	12 Handovers building		MoE with LG							with MoE				

Projet d'Amélioration de l'Offre Educative au Senegal (PAOES)					
Fin	AFD	1 Proposes planning	DCES		
Nb clrs	345	2 Decides planning	DCES		
Years	2002–03	3 Standard Design			
PIU	0	4 Financing Agreement			Btwn AGETIP and LG
coverage	N/A	5 DAO standard doc		Btwn AGETIP and LG	
Year	2003	6 Invitation to bid		AGETIP's Operation Manual	
$ clrm	12,696	7 Awards contract		AGETIP's Tender Board	
m2/clrm	65.17	8 Signs contract		AGETIP's Tender Board	
$/m2	195	9 Monitors works		AGETIP	contract with AGETIP
Comm.p.	0 0	10 Pays works		AGETIP	
AB, L, W		11 Executes works			SME
Source:	Dupety 2005	12 Handovers building	MoE with LG		with MoE

Education For All Project (PEQT)					
Fin	IDA	1 Proposes planning	DCES		
Nb clrs	1,000	2 Decides planning	DCES		
Years	2000–05	3 Standard Design		AGETIP	
PIU	0	4 Financing Agreement		Btwn AGETIP and LG	Btwn AGETIP and LG
coverage	National	5 DAO standard doc		AGETIP's Operation Manual	
Year	2005	6 Invitation to bid		AGETIP's Tender Board	
$ clrm	10,823	7 Awards contract		AGETIP's Tender Board	
m2/clrm	65.17	8 Signs contract		AGETIP	
$/m2	166.07	9 Monitors works		AGETIP	contract with AGETIP
Comm.p.	1 5%	10 Pays works			
AB, L, W	1 1 1	11 Executes works			SME
Source:	Dupety 2005	12 Handovers building	MoE with LG		with MoE

Islamic Development Bank's Project (BID)					
Fin	IDB	1 Proposes planning	DCES		
Nb clrs	500	2 Decides planning	DCES		
Years	2000–04	3 Standard Design			
PIU	1	4 Financing Agreement			
coverage		5 DAO standard doc	PIU		
Year	2004	6 Invitation to bid	PIU		
$ clrm	17,983	7 Awards contract	National Tender Board		
m2/clrm	67.34	8 Signs contract	PIU		
$/m2	267.04	9 Monitors works			contract with PIU
Comm.p.	0 0	10 Pays works			
AB, L, W	0 0 0	11 Executes works	PIU		SME
Source:	Dupety 2005	12 Handovers building			

(*Table continues on the following page.*)

Senegal: Who does What and How for primary school construction in 2006? (continued)

Project	WHO DOES WHAT?	Donor	Centralized approaches including deconcentrated and outsourcing approaches								Decentralized approaches				Comments
			Ministry			Agencies (CMA/SF)		NGOs		Local Govern-ments	Private sector	Communities (CBOs/PTAs)			
			Central Office	Regional/ District	School Staff	Central Office	Decon-cen-trated Offices	Central Office	Decon-cen-trated Offices			Community empowerment	Community participation		
National Rural Infrastructure Project (PNIR)															
Fin IDA	1 Proposes planning									LG				LG have proven they have the capacity to carry out School Construction
Nb clrs 67	2 Decides planning									LG				
Years 2000–05	3 Standard Design		PIU/PNIR											
PIU 1	4 Financing Agreement		Between PIU and LG							Between PIU and LG				
coverage 5 Regions	5 DAO standard doc		NCB from PNIR's PIM											
Year 2005	6 Invitation to bid									3 Quotations				
$ clrm 9,575	7 Awards contract									LG's Tender Board				
m2/clrm 65.20	8 Signs contract									LG	contract with LG			
$/m2 146.86	9 Monitors works													
Comm.p. 0 0 0	10 Pays works									LG				
AB, L, W 0 0 0	11 Executes works										SME			
Source: Dupety 2005	12 Handovers building									LG				

Zambia: Who does What and How for primary school construction in 2006?

Project	WHO DOES WHAT?	Donor	Centralized approaches including deconcentrated and outsourcing approaches							Decentralized approaches					Comments
			Ministry			Agencies (CMA/SF)		NGOs		Local Governments	Private sector	Communities (CBOs/PTAs)		
			Central Office	Regional/ District	School staff	Central Office	Deconcentrated Offices	Central Office	Deconcentrated Offices			Community empowerment	Community participation	

Basic Education Sub-Sector Investment Plan—BESSIP (DANIDA, DFID, Finland, Ireland Aid, Netherland, Norway and GRZ)

Project	WHO DOES WHAT?													
Fin		Multiple												The Present program ESSP III (1999–2003) followed ESSP II but since 2000 is fully integrated into the MoE program.
Nb clrs/year		27												
Years		2000–2003												
PIU	1 Proposes planning	0	SIS/DP/MoE	Province										
	2 Decides planning	No		Province										
	3 Standard Design													
coverage	4 Financing Agreement	National												
Year	5 DAO standard doc	2003	MoE											
$ clrm	6 Invitation to bid	6,500												
Gross m²	7 Awards contract	59.80										LS/DC Community		
Gross $/m²	8 Signs contract	108.70	SIS/DP/MoE	District Building Officer								Community Comm. Mangmt. Committee		
Comm.p.	9 Monitors works	1											Community	
S/O, L, W	10 Pays works	0 1 0									Jobbers			
	11 Executes works													
Source:	12 Handovers building	Group5 2005e		Province										

Basic Education Support Program—BESP (Ireland Aid)

Fin		Ireland												Same mechanism as BESSIP. Funds are deposited into the "pool, but earmarked for Northern Provinces
Nb clrs/year		30												
Years		2000–2002												
PIU	1 Proposes planning	0	SIS/DP/MoE	Province										
	2 Decides planning	No		Province										
	3 Standard Design													
coverage	4 Financing Agreement	North Prov												
Year	5 DAO standard doc	2002	MoE											
$ clrm	6 Invitation to bid	6,500												
Gross m²	7 Awards contract	59.80										LS/DC Community		
Gross $/m²	8 Signs contract	108.70	SIS/DP/MoE	District Building Officer								Community Comm. Mangmt. Committee		
Comm.p.	9 Monitors works	1											Community	
S/O, L, W	10 Pays works										Jobbers			
	11 Executes works													
Source:	12 Handovers building	Group5 2005		Province										

Basic School Construction Program—BSCP (World Bank)

Fin		IDA												
Nb clrs/year		70												
Years		2002–2003												
PIU	1 Proposes planning	0	SIS/DP/MoE	Province										
	2 Decides planning	No		Province										
	3 Standard Design													
coverage	4 Financing Agreement	Rural	MoE											
Year	5 DAO standard doc	2003	National Competitive Bidding											
$ clrm	6 Invitation to bid	7,800	MoE											
Gross m²	7 Awards contract	59.80	MoE											
Gross $/m²	8 Signs contract	130	SIS/DP/MoE	District Building Officer										
Comm.p.	9 Monitors works	0	MoE											
S/O, L, W	10 Pays works	N/A N/A N/A									SME			
	11 Executes works		MoE											
Source:	12 Handovers building	Group5 2005												

(Table continues on the following page.)

Zambia: Who does What and How for primary school construction in 2006? (continued)

Project		Donor	Centralized approaches including deconcentrated and outsourcing approaches							Decentralized approaches				Comments
	WHO DOES WHAT?		Ministry			School staff	Agencies (CMA/SF)		NGOs		Local Governments	Private sector	Communities (CBOs/PTAs)	
			Central Office	Regional/ District			Central Office	Deconcentrated Offices	Central Office	Deconcentrated Offices			Community empowerment	Community participation	
Education III (AfDB)															
Fin	AfDB														
Nb dlrs/year	94														
Years	2002–2003														
PIU	0 No		1 Proposes planning	SIS/DP/MoE											
coverage	National		2 Decides planning	SIS/DP/MoE											
Year	2003		3 Standard Design	MoE											
$ clrm	7,300		4 Financing Agreement	MoE											
Gross m²	59.80		5 DAO standard doc	International Competitive Bidding											
Gross $/m²	122		6 Invitation to bid	MoE											
Comm.p.	0 No		7 Awards contract	MoE											
S/O, L, W	1 1 1		8 Signs contract	SIS/DP/MoE											
Source: Group5 2005			9 Monitors works	MoE	District Building Officer										
			10 Pays works	MoE											
			11 Executes works									Large Contractors			
			12 Handovers building	MoE											
Primary School Upgrading Project—OPSUP (OPEC)															
Fin	OPEC		1 Proposes planning	ZEPIU											
Nb dlrs/year	44		2 Decides planning	ZEPIU											
Years	N/A		3 Standard Design	ZEPIU											
PIU	1 ZEPIU		4 Financing Agreement												
coverage	P		5 DAO standard doc	ZEPIU for materials											
Year			6 Invitation to bid	ICB for materials											
$ clrm	5,700		7 Awards contract	ZEPIU for materials									Direct contracting for labor		
Gross m²	63.25		8 Signs contract	ZEPIU for materials									Communities for labor		
Gross $/m²	90		9 Monitors works	ZEPIU for all works and materials									Communities for labor		
Comm.p.			10 Pays works	ZEPIU									Communities for labor		
S/O, L, W			11 Executes works									Large Suppliers and micro contractors	Communities for labor		
Source: Group5 2005			12 Handovers building	MoE											
Urban School Construction Project (JICA)															
Fin	JICA	Jica's Project Office	1 Proposes planning												Essentially in Lusaka and potentially the Copperbelt
Nb dlrs/year	92	Jica's Project Office	2 Decides planning												
Years	2000–2001	Jica's Project Office	3 Standard Design												
PIU	1 Jica PO		4 Financing Agreement												
coverage	Urban	Jica's Project Office	5 DAO standard doc												
Year		ICB	6 Invitation to bid												
$ clrm	24,750	Jica's Project Office	7 Awards contract												
Gross m²	63.25	Jica's Project Office	8 Signs contract									Japanese Consultancy Firms			
Gross $/m²	391		9 Monitors works												
Comm.p.			10 Pays works												
S/O, L, W			11 Executes works									Large Contractors			
Source: Group5 2005			12 Handovers building	MoE											

School Facility Construction and Rehabilitation Project (HIPC)

Fin	Government	1 Proposes planning	MoE	District Edu. Office	
Nb clrs/year	N/A	2 Decides planning		District Edu. Office	As MoE is not sure at what time funds will be received and does not make predictable planning.
Years	2001–Now	3 Standard Design	MoE		
PIU	0	4 Financing Agreement			
coverage	No	5 DAO standard doc	MoE		
Year		6 Invitation to bid			
$ clrm	6,500	7 Awards contract			No
Gross m²	59.80	8 Signs contract			DC/labor, LS/materials
Gross $/m²	109	9 Monitors works		District Building Officer	Communities
Comm.p.		10 Pays works			Communities
S/O, L, W		11 Executes works			Jobbers/Micro-Suppliers
Source:	Group5 2005	12 Handovers building		Province	

Micro-Projects Project—MPP (European Union)

Fin	EU	1 Proposes planning		District Committee	
Nb clrs	400	2 Decides planning	Micro-Project Unit		An estimated 80% of Micro-Projects are education-related ones. The MPP started in 1985, joined with ZAMSIF between 1991 and 2001 and then separated
Years	1999–2002	3 Standard Design	Micro-Project Unit		
PIU	1 MPU	4 Financing Agreement			
coverage	National	5 DAO standard doc	Micro-Project Unit		
Year	2002	6 Invitation to bid			
$ clrm	4,200	7 Awards contract			DC/labor, LS/materials
Gross m²	59.80	8 Signs contract			Community
Gross $/m²	70	9 Monitors works			Community
Comm.p.	25%	10 Pays works			Contract with MPU
S/O, L, W	1	11 Executes works			Community
Source:	Group5 2005	12 Handovers building		District Committee	Jobbers/Micro-Suppliers

(Table continues on the following page.)

Zambia: Who does What and How for primary school construction in 2006? (continued)

Project	WHO DOES WHAT?	Donor	Centralized approaches including deconcentrated and outsourcing approaches							Decentralized approaches					Comments
			Ministry			Agencies (CMASF)		NGOs		Local Governments	Private sector	Communities (CBOs/PTAs)			
			Central Office	Regional/ District	School staff	Central Office	Deconcentrated Offices	Central Office	Deconcentrated Offices			Community empowerment	Community participation		
Zambia Social Investment Fund—ZAMSIF (World Bank)															
Fin	IDA														ZAMSIF succeeds the Social Recovery Project (SRP). 70% of projects are for primary schools.
Nb clrs/year	225														
Years	2000–2005					1 Proposes planning						Community			
PIU	1 MPU					2 Decides planning						Community			
coverage	National					3 Standard Design	ZAMSIF								
Year	2005					4 Financing Agreement	btwn ZAMSIF and communities					btwn ZAMSIF and communities			
$ clrm	4,200					5 DAO standard doc	ZAMSIF								
Gross m²	59.80					6 Invitation to bid						Community			
Gross $/m²	70					7 Awards contract						Community			
Comm.p.	1 20–25%					8 Signs contract	ZAMSIF					Community			
S/O, L, W	N/A N/A N/A					9 Monitors works						Project Management Committee			
Source:	Group5 2005					10 Pays works						Community			
						11 Executes works	ZAMSIF				Jobbers/Micro-Suppliers				
						12 Handovers building									
Zambia Community School Movement															
Fin	Communities														The Community School Movement started in 1996 in spontaneous peri-urban utli-poor settlements. In 2003, there war 1,200 community schools
Nb clrs/year	150					1 Proposes planning						Community			
Years	1996–2003					2 Decides planning						Community			
PIU	1 ZCSS					3 Standard Design						ZCSS			
coverage	Poorest com					4 Financing Agreement									
Year	N/A					5 DAO standard doc						Community			
$ clrm	N/A					6 Invitation to bid						Community			
m²/clrm	N/A					7 Awards contract						Community			
$/m²	N/A					8 Signs contract						Community			
Comm.p.	1 100%			District Building Officer		9 Monitors works						Community			
S/O, L, W	N/A N/A N/A					10 Pays works						Community			
Source:	Group5 2005					11 Executes works					Jobbers/Micro-Suppliers				
						12 Handovers building						Community			

Ghana: Who does What and How for primary school construction in 2006?

Project	WHO DOES WHAT?	Donor	Centralized approaches including deconcentrated approaches					Decentralized approaches				
			Ministry				Agencies (CMA/SF)		NGOs		Local Governments	Private sector	Communities (CBOs/PTAs)	
			Central Office	Regional/ District	School staff		Central Office	Deconcentrated Offices	Central Office	Deconcentrated Offices			Community empowerment	Community participation

BESSIP—Basic Education Strategic Investment Program

Fin		IDA												
Nb clrs		750												
Years		1997–2002												
PIU		1												
coverage		nationwide												
Year		10,433												
$ clrm		59.00												
m2/clrm		97.00												
$/m2		Group 5												
Source:	1 Proposes planning		GES											
	2 Decides planning		GES								Districts			
	3 Standard Design													
	4 Financing Agreement													
	5 DAO standard doc		NCB (max 6 schools/lot)											
	6 Invitation to bid		PIU -FPPMU											
	7 Awards contract		PIU -FPPMU											
	8 Signs contract		PIU -FPPMU											
	9 Monitors works										District Engineer			
	10 Pays works		PIU -FPPMU											
	11 Executes works											SME		
	12 Handovers building		GES											

PERP—

Fin		AfDB												
Nb clrs		1,500												
Years		1998-on go												
PIU		1												
coverage		nationwide												
year		9,267												
$ clrm		52.00												
m2/clrm		106.00												
$/m2														
Com part														
Source:	1 Proposes planning	Group 5	GES											
	2 Decides planning										Districts			
	3 Standard Design													
	4 Financing Agreement													
	5 DAO standard doc		ICB 150 schools											
	6 Invitation to bid		ICB											
	7 Awards contract		PIU -FPPMU											
	8 Signs contract		PIU -FPPMU											
	9 Monitors works											Consultant		
	10 Pays works		PIU -FPPMU											
	11 Executes works											large contractor		
	12 Handovers building		GES											

ACVF—Aid Counter Value Fund Program

Fin		JICA												
Nb clrs		15												
Years		1 year												
PIU		1												
coverage		nationwide												
year														
$ clrm														
m2/clrm														
$/m2														
Com part														
Source:	1 Proposes planning	Group 5												
	2 Decides planning													
	3 Standard Design													
	4 Financing Agreement													
	5 DAO standard doc		NCB											
	6 Invitation to bid		PIU -FPPMU											
	7 Awards contract		PIU -FPPMU											
	8 Signs contract		PIU -FPPMU											
	9 Monitors works										District Engineer			
	10 Pays works		PIU -FPPMU											
	11 Executes works											Medium contractor		
	12 Handovers building		GES											

(Table continues on the following page.)

Ghana: Who does What and How for primary school construction in 2006? (continued)

			Centralized approaches including deconcentrated approaches						Decentralized approaches			
			Ministry			Agencies (CMA/SF)		NGOs		Local Governments	Private sector	Communities (CBOs/PTAs)	
Project	WHO DOES WHAT?	Donor	Central Office	Regional/ District	School staff	Central Office	Deconcentrated Offices	Central Office	Deconcentrated Offices			Community empowerment	Community participation
Non-Project Assistance Fund													
Fin		USAID											
Nb clrs		51											
Years		1 year											
PIU													
coverage	1 Proposes planning												
year	2 Decides planning												
$ clrm	3 Standard Design												
	4 Financing Agreement		Direct contracting										
	5 DAO standard doc		PIU -FPPMU										
	6 Invitation to bid		PIU -FPPMU										
$/m2	7 Awards contract		PIU -FPPMU										
	8 Signs contract												
$/m2	9 Monitors work		PIU -FPPMU										
	10 Pays works												
Com part	11 Executes works										Medium contractor		
Source:	12 Handovers building	Group 5	GES										
Rehabilitation of Schools Project													
Fin		UNICEF											
Nb clrs		534											
Years													
PIU													
coverage	1 Proposes planning												
year	2 Decides planning										Districts		
$ clrm	3 Standard Design										Districts		
	4 Financing Agreement										???		
	5 DAO standard doc	procures materials									???		
	6 Invitation to bid										procures sand and blocks		
$/m2	7 Awards contract												
	8 Signs contract												
$/m2	9 Monitors work										Districts		
	10 Pays works												
Com part	11 Executes works												skill and unskilled labor
Source:	12 Handovers building	Group 5									Districts		
ESSP-SU—School Upgrading Program													
Fin		DFID											
Nb clrs		560									Districts		
Years		2002–now									Districts		
PIU		1	????								???		
coverage	1 Proposes planning	2 regions									NCB max 2 schools/lot		
year	2 Decides planning										Districts—NCB		
$ clrm	3 Standard Design	10,727									Districts		
	4 Financing Agreement												
m2/clrm	5 DAO standard doc	51	????								Districts		
	6 Invitation to bid												
$/m2	7 Awards contract	85											
	8 Signs contract												
	9 Monitors work												
Com part	10 Pays works												
Source:	11 Executes works	Group 5									Districts		Parents Teach. Ass.
	12 Handovers building												

HIPC

Fin	Government		1 Proposes planning		Districts	
Nb clrs	1,400		2 Decides planning		Districts	
Years	2002–now		3 Standard Design		???	
PIU			4 Financing Agreement		LCB	
coverage	nationwide		5 DAO standard doc		Districts—LCB	
year			6 Invitation to bid		Districts	
$ clrm			7 Awards contract		Districts	
m2/clrm	53		8 Signs contract		District Engineer	
$/m2			9 Monitors work		Districts	
Com part			10 Pays works			
Source:	Group 5		11 Executes works		District	Small contractor
			12 Handovers building			

Ghana Education Trust Fund (GET Fund)

Fin	Government		1 Proposes planning		Districts	
Nb clrs			2 Decides planning		Districts	
Years			3 Standard Design		???	
PIU			4 Financing Agreement		NCB	
coverage			5 DAO standard doc		Districts - NCB	
year			6 Invitation to bid		Districts	
$ clrm			7 Awards contract		Districts	
m2/clrm			8 Signs contract		District Engineer	
$/m2			9 Monitors work		Districts	
Com part			10 Pays works			
Source:	Group 5		11 Executes works		District	Medium contractor
			12 Handovers building			

Micro Project Program

Fin	EU		1 Proposes planning			apply for project
Nb clrs	1,440		2 Decides planning			
Years	2000–2003		3 Standard Design	EU	DA	
PIU	1		4 Financing Agreement			
coverage	6 regions		5 DAO standard doc			
year			6 Invitation to bid			
$ clrm	7,067		7 Awards contract			
m2/clrm	62		8 Signs contract			
$/m2	64		9 Monitors work		District	with local artisans
Com part	25%		10 Pays works			
Source:	Group 5		11 Executes works		District	local artisans
			12 Handovers building			artisan provides labor

(Table continues on the following page.)

Ghana: Who does What and How for primary school construction in 2006? (continued)

Project		WHO DOES WHAT?	Donor	Centralized approaches including deconcentrated approaches							Decentralized approaches					
				Ministry			Agencies (CMA/SF)		NGOs			Local Governments	Private sector	Communities (CBOs/PTAs)		
				Central Office	Regional/ District	School staff	Central Office	Deconcentrated Offices	Central Office	Deconcentrated Offices				Community empowerment	Community participation
QUIPS—Quality Improvement in Primary Schools																
Fin	USAID	1 Proposes planning	PIU with District									Districts				
Nb clrs	632	2 Decides planning										Districts				
Years	1998–2004	3 Standard Design														
PIU	US NGO	4 Financing Agreement												procures materials		
coverage		5 DAO standard doc										procures labor				
year		6 Invitation to bid										direct contract				
$ clrm		7 Awards contract										District				
$/m2		8 Signs contract	PIU													
$/m2		9 Monitors work										District				
Com part	25%	10 Pays works											labor			
Source:	Group 5	11 Executes works										District				
		12 Handovers building														
Primary School Construction Program																
Fin	Plan Internat	1 Proposes planning	Plan Int													
Nb clrs	90	2 Decides planning	Plan Int													
Years		3 Standard Design	Plan Int											with Plan Int		
PIU	1	4 Financing Agreement	Plan Int with Community													
coverage	3 regions	5 DAO standard doc														
year		6 Invitation to bid														
$ clrm <	7,500	7 Awards contract												with local artisans		
m2/clrm	50–60	8 Signs contract												site supervision		
$/m2	60–70	9 Monitors work												local artisans		
Com part		10 Pays works												provides labor		
Source:	Group 5	11 Executes works											artisan			
		12 Handovers building		Central												

204

Grant Assistance to Grassroots Projects

Fin	Japan Embassy	1 Proposes planning	Embassy			
Nb clrs	64	2 Decides planning	Embassy			
Years	2000–2002	3 Standard Design				
PIU		4 Financing Agreement				
coverage		5 DAO standard doc				
year		6 Invitation to bid				
$ clrm		7 Awards contract				
$/m2		8 Signs contract				
$/m2		9 Monitors work		District Engineer		with local artisans
Com part		10 Pays works				local artisans
Source:	Group 5	11 Executes works			artisan	provides labor
		12 Handovers building				

Education Investment Plan

Fin	World Vision	1 Proposes planning	with DA			
Nb clrs	765	2 Decides planning				
Years		3 Standard Design				
PIU		4 Financing Agreement				
coverage		5 DAO standard doc				
year		6 Invitation to bid				
$ clrm		7 Awards contract				
$/m2		8 Signs contract				
$/m2		9 Monitors work	Zonal Program Officer	with WV		with local artisans
Com part		10 Pays works				local artisans
Source:	Group 5	11 Executes works			artisan	provides labor
		12 Handovers building				

Madagascar: Who does What and How for primary school construction in 2006?

Project		WHO DOES WHAT?	Centralized approaches including deconcentrated approaches						Decentralized approaches					General Comments on the Project performance
			Ministry			Agencies (CMA/SF)		NGOs		Local Governments	Private sector	Communities (CBOs/PTAs)		
			Central Office	Regional/District	School staff	Central Office	Deconcentrated Offices	Central Office	Deconcentrated Offices			Community empowerment	Community participation	
CRESED II regular program														
Fin	IDA	1 Proposes planning		CISCO										Difficulty to coordinate community participation. MoE abandoned approach and shifted to FID
Nb clrs	556	2 Decides planning	MoE											
Years	2000–04	3 Standard Design	PIU											
PIU	1	4 Financing Agreement			School with CISCO									
Year	2002	5 DAO standard doc		CISCO										
$/clrm	7,711	6 Invitation to bid	PIU-IDA											
$/m3	144	7 Awards contract		CISCO										
Year	2004	8 Signs contract		CISCO										
$/clrm	9,500	9 Monitors works	PIU-IDA											
$/m3	176	10 Pays works	PIU-IDA											
Source:	Group 5	11 Executes works										SME/small contracts		10%
		12 Handovers building	MoE											
CRESED II Post Cyclonic sub-program														
Fin	IDA	1 Proposes planning	MoE											High Unit costs resulting from re-centralization and "emergency" contracting procedures
Nb clrs	472	2 Decides planning	MoE											
Years	2004–05	3 Standard Design	PIU											
PIU	1	4 Financing Agreement												
$/clrm	9,500	5 DAO standard doc	PIU-IDA											
m2/clrm	54.2	6 Invitation to bid	PIU-IDA or Tender Board?											
$/m2	264	7 Awards contract	PIU-IDA											
Source:	Group 5	8 Signs contract	PIU-IDA											
		9 Monitors work	PIU-IDA											
		10 Pays works	PIU-IDA											
		11 Executes works										SME/small contracts		10%
		12 Handovers building	MoE											
FID IV														
Fin	IDA	1 Proposes planning	MoE								with ZAP			Good delivery time and the lowest unit cost. Needs large support of FID at local level
Nb clrs	1200	2 Decides planning				FID								
Years	2002–03	3 Standard Design				FID								
PIU	0	4 Financing Agreement	MoE with FID			FID with MoE								
$/clrm	7,983	5 DAO standard doc				FID								
m2/clrm	46.9	6 Invitation to bid									with FID support			
$/m2	170	7 Awards contract									with FID support			
Source:	Group 5	8 Signs contract									with FID support			
		9 Monitors work									with FID support			
		10 Pays works												
		11 Executes works										SME/small contracts		10%
		12 Handovers building	MoE											

FID-EPT Program for prefabricated industrialized construction (CMI)

Fin	multi-donor			
Nb clrs	1,400			
Years	2004–06			
PIU	0			
$/clrm	11,402			
m2/clrm	47			
$/m2	243			
source	Group 5			
$/clrm	9,000			
S$/m2	191			
Source:	ST			
1 Proposes planning	MoE			
2 Decides planning	MoE			
3 Standard Design		FID-EPT CMI specific		
4 Financing Agreement	MoE with FID-EPT	FID-EPT with MoE		
5 DAO standard doc		FID-EPT (big size contract 1400 sdc with proc issues)		
6 Invitation to bid	97380000	FID-EPT		
7 Awards contract	8999.753621	FID-EPT		
8 Signs contract	10820.29621	FID-EPT		
9 Monitors work		FID-EPT (through MoF)		
10 Pays works			One Large contract	
11 Executes works				Time delivery and unit costs higher than FID/IV resulting from bulk procurement
12 Handovers building	MoE			

FID-EPT Classic construction program

Fin	multi-donor			
Nb clrs	1200			
Years	2002–03			
PIU	0			
$/clrm	8,248			
m2/clrm	47			
$/m2	175			
Source:	ST			
1 Proposes planning	MoE			
2 Decides planning	MoE			
3 Standard Design		FID-EPT classic (specific)	with ZAP	
4 Financing Agreement	MoE with FID-EPT	FID-EPT with MoE		
5 DAO standard doc		FID		
6 Invitation to bid		FID-EPT small contracts		
7 Awards contract		FID-EPT		
8 Signs contract		FID-EPT		
9 Monitors work		?	???	
10 Pays works		FID-EPT	SME/small contracts	10%
11 Executes works				Good delivery time and the lowest unit cost. Needs large support of FID at local level
12 Handovers building	MoE			

AfDB-financed project

Fin	AfDB			
Nb clrs	1200			
Years	2003–07			
PIU	1			
$/clrm	10,327			
m2/clrm	52.8			
$/m2	196			
Source:	Group 5			
1 Proposes planning	MoE	CISCO		
2 Decides planning	idem CRESED II			
3 Standard Design				
4 Financing Agreement	by PIU on basis AGETIPA/AFD bid doc			
5 DAO standard doc	PIU with small contract size (2 sdc)			
6 Invitation to bid	Central Tender Board			
7 Awards contract	PIU-AFDB			
8 Signs contract			contract with PIU	
9 Monitors work				
10 Pays works	PIU-AFDB			
11 Executes works			Small	Long bidding process due to slow tenderboard. Low quality offers.
12 Handovers building	MoE			

(Table continues on the following page.)

Madagascar: Who does What and How for primary school construction in 2006? (continued)

			Centralized approaches including deconcentrated approaches						Decentralized approaches					General Comments on the Project performance
			Ministry			Agencies (CMA/SF)		NGOs		Local Governments	Private sector	Communities (CBOs/PTAs)		
Project		WHO DOES WHAT?	Central Office	Regional/ District	School staff	Central Office	Deconcentrated Offices	Central Office	Deconcentrated Offices			Community empowerment	Community participation	
BADEA-financed project														
Fin	BADEA	1 Proposes planning	MoE											Delays during procurement of supervision and payments. High unit cost (centralized approach)
Nb clrs	1,170	2 Decides planning	MoE											
Years	2003–06	3 Standard Design	idem CRESED II											
PIU	1	4 Financing Agreement	idem CRESED II											
$/clrm	29,626	5 DAO standard doc	PIU with DAO with small size contract											
m2/clrm	52.8	6 Invitation to bid	Central Tender Board											
$/m2	561	7 Awards contract	PIU-BADEA											
Source:	Group 5	8 Signs contract									cont with PIU			
		9 Monitors work	PIU-BADEA											
		10 Pays works									SME			
		11 Executes works												
		12 Handovers building	MoE											
OPEP-financed project														
Fin	OPEP	1 Proposes planning	MoE											Delays during procurement of supervision and payments. High unit cost (centralized approach)
Nb clrs	155	2 Decides planning	MoE											
Years	2003–06	3 Standard Design	idem CRESED II											
PIU	1	4 Financing Agreement												
$/clrm	N/A	5 DAO standard doc		CISCO										
m2/clrm	N/A	6 Invitation to bid		CISCO										
$/m2	N/A	7 Awards contract	Central Tender Board											
Source:	Group 5	8 Signs contract	?	?							cont with PIU			
		9 Monitors work	PIU-OPEP											
		10 Pays works									SME			
		11 Executes works												
		12 Handovers building	MoE											
BIT/Norway-financed project														
Fin	Norway	1 Proposes planning	MoE											Small scale training system. Not possible to scale up. Low cost by hidden BIT costs not included
Nb clrs	81	2 Decides planning	MoE											
Years	2003–07	3 Standard Design	BIT-Norway specific design											
PIU	1	4 Financing Agreement												
$/clrm	8,683	5 DAO standard doc	PIU-BIT											
m2/clrm	43.5	6 Invitation to bid	Central Tender Board											
$/m2	200	7 Awards contract	PIU-BIT											
Source:	Group 5	8 Signs contract	PIU-BIT											
		9 Monitors work	PIU-BIT											
		10 Pays works												
		11 Executes works	BIT trains with workers locally hired and with community participation					community organization			individuals			
		12 Handovers building	MoE											

AFD-financed Project

Fin	AFD			
Nb clrs	195			
Years	2003-07			
PIU	0			
$/clrm	19,113			
m2/clrm	59.4			
$/m2	322			
Source:	Group 5			
		1 Proposes planning	MoE	
		2 Decides planning	MoE	
		3 Standard Design	AFD specific design	
		4 Financing Agreement	AFD with AGETIPA	
		5 DAO standard doc		AGETIPA with AFD
		6 Invitation to bid		WB standard doc
		7 Awards contract		AGETIPA with small size contract
		8 Signs contract		AGETIPA	contract with AGETIP
		9 Monitors work	AFD	AGETIPA	SME
		10 Pays works	AFD		
		11 Executes works				Very high unit costs resulting mainly from centralized implementation approach
		12 Handovers building	MoE		

JICA-financed Project

Fin	JICA			
Nb clrs	343			
Years	2005-06			
PIU	0			
$/clrm	32,190			
m2/clrm	57.4			
$/m2	561			
Source:	Group 5			
		1 Proposes planning	MoE	
		2 Decides planning	MoE	
		3 Standard Design	JICA specific design	
		4 Financing Agreement		
		5 DAO standard doc	JICA standard doc (all bulked in one contract to Japanese contractor)	
		6 Invitation to bid	by JICA in Japan	
		7 Awards contract	Gov of Japan Tender Board	
		8 Signs contract	JICA with Japanese contractor who, in turn sub-contracts to Malagasi contractors		Japanese engineering firm
		9 Monitors work	JICA standard doc (all bulked in one contract to Japanese contractor)		large contract + subcontracts to SME
		10 Pays works	JICA		
		11 Executes works			Very high unit costs resulting from bulk procurement to international firm and subcontracts to national ones
		12 Handovers building	MoE		

Mozambique: Who does What and How for primary school construction in 2006?

Project	WHO DOES WHAT?	Donor	Centralized approaches including deconcentrated approaches — Ministry			Agencies (CMA/SF)		NGOs		Decentralized approaches — Local Governments	Private sector	Communities (CBOs/PTAs)		General Comments on the Project performance
			Central Office	Regional/ District	School staff	Central Office	Deconcentrated Offices	Central Office	Deconcentrated Offices			Community empowerment	Community participation	
Education Sector Support Program (ESSP)—modality through DPE and LCB (1 third of the program)														
Fin: IDA	1 Proposes planning			DDE (District Directorate of Education)										Deconcentrated procurement to Provincial Directorate and use of Local biddings translates in cost savings compared to centralized NCB
Nb clrs: 600	2 Decides planning		DCEE											
Years: 2000–04	3 Standard Design		std 2000											
PIU: DCEEex PIU	4 Financing Agreement													
Year: 2003	5 DAO standard doc													
$ clrm: 6,901	6 Invitation to bid			DPE (Provincial Directorate of Education through LCB)										
$/m2: 55.65	7 Awards contract			DPE (through LCB)										
$/m2: 124.00	8 Signs contract			DPE (through LCB)										
Source: Group 5	9 Monitors works			DPE supervisor										
	10 Pays works			DPE										
	11 Executes works										SME			
	12 Handovers building		DCEE											
Education Sector Support Program (ESSP)—modality through DCEE and NCB (1 third of the program)														
Fin: IDA	1 Proposes planning			DDE (District Directorate of Education)										Centralized NCB approach results in cost 34% higher then deconcentrated management and use of LCB
Nb clrs: 600	2 Decides planning		DCEE											
Years: 2000–04	3 Standard Design													
PIU: DCEEex PIU	4 Financing Agreement													
Year: 2003	5 DAO standard doc													
$ clrm: 9,267	6 Invitation to bid		DCEE through NCB											
$/m2: 55.65	7 Awards contract		DCEE through NCB											
$/m2: 166.52	8 Signs contract		DCEE											
Source: Group 5	9 Monitors works			DPE										
	10 Pays works		DCEE											
diff/LCB 2,366 34%	11 Executes works										Large enterprise			
	12 Handovers building		DCEE											
Education Sector Support Program (ESSP)—modality through DCEE and ICB (1 third of the program)														
Fin: IDA	1 Proposes planning			DDE (District Directorate of Education)										Not yet started
Nb clrs: 600	2 Decides planning		DCEE											
Years: 2000–04	3 Standard Design													
PIU: DCEEex PIU	4 Financing Agreement													
Year: 2003	5 DAO standard doc													
$ clrm: -	6 Invitation to bid		DCEE through ICB											
$/m2: 55.65	7 Awards contract		DCEE through IICB											
$/m2: -	8 Signs contract		DCEE											
Source: Group 5	9 Monitors works			DPE										
	10 Pays works		DCEE											
	11 Executes works										Large enterprise			
	12 Handovers building		DCEE											

Rural Primary School Project IDB								
Fin	IDB	1 Proposes planning					DDE (District)	
Nb clrs	220	2 Decides planning					DPE (Province)	
Years	No	3 Standard Design						
PIU		4 Financing Agreement						
$/clrm	7,928	5 DAO standard doc	NCB					
m2/clrm	55.83	6 Invitation to bid	DCEE					
$/m2	142	7 Awards contract	DCEE					
Source:	Group 5	8 Signs contract	DCEE				DPE	
		9 Monitors work						
		10 Pays works	DCEE					SME
		11 Executes works						
		12 Handovers building	DCEE					

Emergency Program (Royal Netherland Embassy)								
Fin	RNE	1 Proposes planning	DCEE				DPE	
Nb clrs	360	2 Decides planning						
Years		3 Standard Design						
PIU	0	4 Financing Agreement						
$/clrm	26,464	5 DAO standard doc	ICB					
m2/clrm	58.16	6 Invitation to bid						
$/m2	455	7 Awards contract						Firms
Source:	Group 5	8 Signs contract						
		9 Monitors work						
		10 Pays works	DCEE					
		11 Executes works						International Supplier
		12 Handovers building	DCEE					

Education Sector Support Program—PASE								
Fin	Finnida	1 Proposes planning					Provincial Directorate	
Nb clrs	237	2 Decides planning					DPE	
Years	1998–2005	3 Standard Design						
Coverage	Maputo Prov	4 Financing Agreement	PASE					
PIU	1	5 DAO standard doc					DPE/LCB	
$/clrm	7,394	6 Invitation to bid					DPE/LCB	
m2/clrm	62.14	7 Awards contract					DPE	
$/m2	119	8 Signs contract					?	
Source:	Group 5	9 Monitors work					DPE	
		10 Pays works	PIU					
		11 Executes works						micro contactor
		12 Handovers building	DCEE					

(Table continues on the following page.)

Mozambique: Who does What and How for primary school construction in 2006? (continued)

Project		Donor	Centralized approaches including deconcentrated approaches							Decentralized approaches			Communities (CBOs/PTAs)		General Comments on the Project performance
			Ministry			Agencies (CMASF)		NGOs		Local Governments	Private sector	Community empowerment	Community participation		
			Central Office	Regional/ District	School staff	Central Office	Deconcentrated Offices	Central Office	Deconcentrated Offices						
Danish Support to the Education Sector Strategic Plan—through local contractors															
Fin	DANIDA			Provincial Directorate											
Nb clrs	300			DPE											
Years	2002–07		std 1998												
PIU	1														
Coverage	3 prov.			DPE/LCB											
$/clrm	22332			DPE/LCB											
m2/clrm	56			DPE											
$/m2	400			DPE											
Source:	Group 5			DPE											
			PIU												
				DPE											
Danish Support to the Education Sector Strategic Plan—modality with community participation															
Fin	DANIDA			Provincial Directorate											
Nb clrs	300			DPE											
Years	2002–07			with community									with DPE		
PIU	1														
Coverage	3 prov.														
$/clrm	4466														
m2/clrm	56														
$/m2	80														
Source:	Group 5		PIU								SME		community		
				DPE											
Primary School Construction Project in Maputo Town															
Fin	JICA		PIU/JICA												
Nb clrs	100		PIU/JICA												
Years	2003	JICA													
PIU	1	Japan													
$/clrm	30,660	JICA													
m2/clrm	58.4	JICA													
$/m2	525	JICA													
Source:	Group 5											Japanese consultant			
			PIU/JICA									large contractor			
			DCEE												

Row headers (WHO DOES WHAT?): 1 Proposes planning; 2 Decides planning; 3 Standard Design; 4 Financing Agreement; 5 DAO standard doc; 6 Invitation to bid; 7 Awards contract; 8 Signs contract; 9 Monitors work; 10 Pays works; 11 Executes works; 12 Handovers building

NGOs: AAA, PRODER, UDEBA, IBIS, World Vision, AMDU

Fin	NGOs						
Nb clrs	2600						
Years	1998–02						
PIU							
$/clrm							
m2/clrm							
$/m2							
Source:	Group 5						
1 Proposes planning				NGO			
2 Decides planning				NGO			
3 Standard Design				NGO			
4 Financing Agreement				NGO with communities			
5 DAO standard doc				NGO			
6 Invitation to bid							
7 Awards contract							with NGO
8 Signs contract			DPE	NGO			
9 Monitors work					SME		
10 Pays works							
11 Executes works							to work
12 Handovers building							

KfW

Fin	KfW						
Nb clrs							
Years							
PIU							
$/clrm							
m2/clrm							
$/m2							
Source:	Group 5						
1 Proposes planning							Not yet started
2 Decides planning							
3 Standard Design							
4 Financing Agreement							
5 DAO standard doc							
6 Invitation to bid							
7 Awards contract							
8 Signs contract							
9 Monitors work							
10 Pays works							
11 Executes works							
12 Handovers building							

Fundo de Apoio ao Sector de Educacao / FASE (EFA/FTI)

Fin	multi-donor						
Nb clrs	45000						
Years	2003–2013						
PIU	No						
$/clrm							
m2/clrm							
$/m2							
Source:	Group 5						
1 Proposes planning							Not yet started
2 Decides planning							
3 Standard Design							
4 Financing Agreement							
5 DAO standard doc							
6 Invitation to bid							
7 Awards contract							
8 Signs contract							
9 Monitors work							
10 Pays works							
11 Executes works							
12 Handovers building							

Uganda: Who does What and How for primary school construction in 2006?

Project		WHO DOES WHAT?	Donor	Centralized approaches including deconcentrated approaches							Decentralized approaches				
				Ministry			Agencies (CMA/SF)		NGOs		Local Governments	Private sector	Communities (CBOs/PTAs)		
				Central Office	Regional/ District	School staff	Central Office	Deconcentrated Offices	Central Office	Deconcentrated Offices			Community empowerment	Community participation
SFG School Facility Grant															
Fin	multi donor	1 Proposes planning		MOES									School Managmt Committee	
Nb clrs	20,000	2 Decides planning												
Years	1998–2003	3 Standard Design												
PIU		4 Financing Agreement												
coverage	nationwide	5 DAO standard doc		MOES										
rural		6 Invitation to bid									District proposes to MOEs		SMC – 3 quotations	
$ clrm	3,885	7 Awards contract												
m2/clrm	51.8	8 Signs contract									District tender board		SMC	
$/m2	75	9 Monitors works									District engineer		SMC	
urban		10 Pays works										Micro-enterprise		
$/m2	135	11 Executes works												
Source:	Group 5	12 Handovers building											SMC	
Micro Project Program															
Fin	EU	1 Proposes planning		PIU – MP									School Managmt Committee	
Nb clrs	400	2 Decides planning											SMC assisted by PIU	
Years	2000–03	3 Standard Design												
PIU	1	4 Financing Agreement		PIU – MP										
coverage	nationwide	5 DAO standard doc												
year		6 Invitation to bid											SMC	
$ clrm		7 Awards contract											SMC	
m2/clrm	97	8 Signs contract		PIU + SMC									SMC	
$/m2	15%	9 Monitors works											SMC + PIU	
Com part		10 Pays works											SMC	
Source:	Group 5	11 Executes works										Micro-enterprise		
		12 Handovers building											SMC	

APPENDIX 17
List of Projects Reviewed

				date of		Project overall management agency				Procurement	Procurement	type of	Unit cost per m²		
Country	Project name	Acronym	Project period	cost info	Financing Agency	Head	Directorate	Delegation	Technology	Agency	method	contractor	current	2006	Source
Africa															
Angola															
1 NA			2000–04	2003	donor	MoE	MPW		classic	MPW	NCB	medium	275	296	World Bank 2000a, 2004a
2 Second Social Fund Project		SSFP	2000–04	2003	IDA	SF	FAS-II		classic	CMA	ICB/NCB	large/small	297	319	World Bank 2000a, 2004a
Benin						type	name								
3 Social Fund Project		SFP	2000–01	2001	IDA	FS	AGeFIB Direct.	community	classic	community	3-quot	jobbers	73	81	AGeFIB 2001, p. 48
4 Investment Program		PIP	2000–01	2001	Gov	Admin.	Direct.		classic	Admin.c	NCB	Medium	113	126	World Bank 2004c
5 N/A		AGDS		2001	donor	CMA	AGDS		classic	CMA	NCB	Medium	113	126	World Bank 2004c
6 National Community-Driven Project		PNDCC	2005–10	2006	IDA	PIU	SE-PNDCC	community	classic	community	LCB	Medium	116	116	Theurynck
7 National Community-Driven Project		PNDCC	2005–10	2007	IDA	PIU	SE-PNDCC	community	classic	community	3-quot	jobbers	117	117	PNDCC 2007
8 National Community-Driven Project		PNDCC	2005–10	2007	IDA	PIU	SE-PNDCC	community	classic	community	LCB	micro	120	118	PNDCC 2007
9 regular Program MoE		MoE	2007	2007	Gov	MoE			classic	Admin. Cent.	NCB	medium	172	169	PNDCC 2007
Burkina Faso															
10 Government program			1985–94	1990	donor	Admin.			classic	Admin.c	ICB	large	250	349	World Bank 1991a, 1995a
11 Education III Project			1985–94	1990	IDA	MoE			classic	PIU	ICB/CW	large/com	125	175	World Bank 1991a, 1995a
12 10-Year Plan for Basic Edu and Lit.		PDDEB	2002–10	2004	basket/l	MoE	PCU	prov. Off.	classic	Admin.d	NCB	medium	103	108	Group 5 2006a, tab 7.4a
13 Projet Appui à Org Ens de Base		PAOEB	2002–10	2004	FDA			Faso Baara	classic	CMA	NCB	medium	143	150	Group 5 2006a, tab 7.4a
14 Government program (HPIC)		HPIC		2004	Gov			Faso Baara	classic	CMA	NCB	medium	127	133	Group 5 2006a, tab 7.4a
15 N/A				2004	JICA										
16 Plan International Program		PI		2004	Plan Int	Plan Int			classic	NGO	direct	jobbers	124	130	Group 5 2006a, tab 7.4a
17 OSEO Program		OSEO		2007	OSEO	OSEO			classic	NGO	direct	micro	114	112	OSEO 2007
18 Program Burkina		AeA		2007	Action Aid	AA		community	classic	community	LCB	micro	91	89	cost info from AA 2007
Burundi															
19 Second Social Action Project		SSAP	1999–06	2005	IDA	SF	Twitezimbere		classic	SF	NCB	small	113	115	World Bank 2007b
20 Second Social Action Project		SSAP	1999–07	2006	IDA	SF	Twitezimbere		classic	SF	NCB	small	176	176	Dupety 2006
21 Public Works and Employ. Creation Proj		PWECP	1999–06	2005	IDA	ABUTIP			classic	CMA	NCB	medium	166	169	World Bank 2007b
22 Public Works and Employ. Creation Proj		PWECP	1999–07	2006	IDA	ABUTIP			classic	CMA	NCB	medium	182	182	Dupety 2006
23 Belgian Burundi Fund		BBF		2005	Belgium/Gov	Belg/Bur Fund			classic	SF	NCB	medium	171	174	World Bank 2007b
24 N/A		AFD		2005	FDA				classic	Admin/cent	NCB	medium	104	106	Dupety 2006
25 N/A		UNCHR		2005	UNCHR				classic	NGO	direct	small	134	137	Dupety 2006
26 N/A		UNICEF		2005	UNICEF				classic	community	direct	small	59	60	Dupety 2006
Cape Verde															
27 Edu. and Training Cons. and Mod. Proj		PROMEF	2000–02	2002	IDA	MoE	PIU		classic	Admin/cent	NCB	medium	325	355	Siri and Goovaert 2002
28 Social Sector Development Project		SSDP	2001–06	2004	IDA	AGECABO			classic	CMA	NCB	medium	243	247	Theurynck 2005a, World Bank 1999b
29 Education Project II Ecole				2004	Gov	MoE	DPEE		classic	Admin/cent	3-Q	small	260	265	Theurynck 2005a
30 SDDP Ecole Belavista		SSDP	2001–06	2001	IDA	AGECABO	CMA		classic	CMA	NCB	medium	278	308	Theurynck 2005a

#	Project		Dates									Refs
Central Africa												
31	Construction of a classroom in Bangui	RESEN	2007	N/A	N/A		classic	Admin/cent	NCB	medium	305	299	World Bank 2008c
32	Construction of a classroom in Sibut	RESEN	2007	N/A	N/A		classic	Admin/cent	NCB	medium	457	448	World Bank 2008c
33	Construction of a classroom in Lobaye	RESEN	2007	N/A	N/A		classic	NGO	direct	jobbers	233	229	World Bank 2008c
Chad												
34	Education Rehabilitation Project	ERP	1988–94	1986	donor	State	PCU	classic	admin/cent	ICB	Large	327	524	World Bank 1993a, annex 13
35	Basic Education Project Phase 1/3	BEP	1993–01	1995	IDA	MoE	ATETIP/NGO	classic	NGO/2	direct	micro	249	308	Lecsyn 1997, World Bank 2003b
36	Basic Education Project Phase 2/4	BEP	1993–01	1996	IDA	MoE	ATETIP	classic	CMA	NCB	medium	159	193	Lecsyn 1997, World Bank 2003b
37	KfW Project		1998–00	2000	KfW	PIU(consul)	Hydroplan	classic	admin/cent	NCB	medium	138	157	World Bank 2003b, annex 13
Congo												
38	N/A			2005	N/A			classic	admin/cent	NCB	medium	179	183	World Bank 2005e
Eritrea												
39	Community Development Fund Project	ECDF	1996–01	2000	Mutiple/6	SF	ECDF	classic	SF	NCB	medium	175	199	World Bank 1996a, 2002a, 2002b.
40	N/A		1996–01	2000	donor	MoE		classic	admin/cent	NCB	medium	168	191	World Bank 1996a, 2002a, 2002b.
Ethiopia												
41	School construction program		2000–04	2004	donor	Provincial LG		classic	admin/decon	NCB	medium	850	890	World Bank 2005i
42	School construction program		2000–04	2004	donor	MPW		classic	admin/cent	NCB	medium	275	288	World Bank 2005j
43	Ethiopian Social Rehab and Dev Fund	ESRDF	2000–04	2003	IDA	SF		classic	SF	NCB	medium	131	141	World Bank 2005i
44	N/A (non ESDRF)		2000–04	2003	donor	Admin		prefab	admin/cent	NCB	medium	137	147	World Bank 2005i
45	Education Sector Development Project	ESDP1	1998–04	2002				prefab	ICB	large	255	279	Theisen 2002
46	Education Sector Development Project	ESDP1	1998–04	2002				classic	ICB	large	164	179	Theisen 2002
Gambia (The)												
47	Second Edu. Sector Proj. – phase 1	SESP	1993–95	1994	IDA	MoE	PCU	classic	PCU	ICB/CW	large/com	120	152	Synergy 1997, World Bank 1999c
48	Second Edu. Sector Proj. – phase 2	SESP	1996–00	1998	IDA	MoE	PCU	classic	PCU	NCB	medium	93	110	World Bank 1995g
49	Second and Third Education Project	SESP/TESP	1999–05	1997	FIOH	FIOH		classic	NGO	direct	small	117	140	Synergy 1997
50	Second and Third Education Project	SESP/TESP	1999–05	1997	CCF	CCF		classic	NGO	direct	small	117	140	Synergy 1997
51	Action Aid Program	AA	1997	Action Aid	Action Aid		classic	NGO	direct	jobbers	97	116	Synergy 1997
52	Basic Education in The Gambia	BEG	2002	MoE		Gamworks	classic	CMA	NCB	medium	182	199	Sinke 2003

(Table continues on the following page.)

Table (continued)

			Project period	date of cost info	Financing Agency	Project overall management agency			Delegation	Technology	Procurement Agency	Procurement method	type of contractor	Unit cost per m²		Source
Country	Project name	Acronym				Head	Directorate							current	2006	
Ghana																
53	Basic Education Strategic Invest. Prog	BESIP	1999–02	2003	IDA	MoE	FPMU			classic	admin/cent	NCB	medium	154	166	Group 5 2006b, p. 24
54	Primary Education ... Project	PERP	1998–2004	2001	AfDB	MoE	FPMU			classic	admin/cent	ICB	large	106	118	Group 5 2006b, p. 18
55	School Upgrading Program	ESSP-SU	2002–05	2003	DFID	MoE			Districts (LG)	classic	local gov	NCB	medium	80	86	Group 5 2006b, p. 18
56	HPIC program	HPIC		2004	Gov	Districts (LG)				classic	local gov	NCB	medium			
57	Quality Improvement in Primary Schools	QUIP	1998–04	2004	USAID	NGO	ILP			classic	community	direct	small	65	68	Group 5 2006b
58	Primary School Development Project	PSDP	1980–96	1996	IDA	MoE	PIU			shelter	admin/cent	ICB	small	60	73	Group 5 2006b, p. 18
59	Micro-Project Program (fifth)	MPP	2000–03	2003	EU	MoF	MPP		Districts	classic	community	direct/LS	small	64	69	Group 5 2006b
60	UNICEF	UNICEF	1990–04	2003	UNICEF					classic	donor	NCB/CW	small	65	70	Group 5 2006b
Guinea																
61	Education Sector Support Project 1	PASE-1	1989–94	1990	IDA	MoE			Prefectures (LG)	classic	loca gov	shopping	jobbers	250	349	De Bosch Kemper, Barry, and Bumke 1990, World Bank 1995c
62	Proj. Const. Prototypes Ec. Prim	PCPEPMRG	1989	1989	UNESCO	UNESCO				classic	donor	direct	small	125	181	De Bosch Kemper, Barry, and Bumke 1990
63	Equity and School Improv. Proj (phase 1)	PASE-2	1995	1995	IDA	MoE	PIU		NGO/8	classic	NGO	direct	small	228	282	Theurynck 2000
64	Equity and School Improv. Proj (phase 2)	PASE-2	1996–97	1996	IDA	MoE	PIU		NGO/9	classic	NGO	direct	small	218	265	Theurynck 2000
65	Equity and School Improv. Proj (phase 3)	PASE-2	1997–99	1997	IDA	MoE	PIU		34 NGOs	classic	NGO	direct	small	127	152	Theurynck 2000
66	Equity and School Improv. Proj (addit. Clrms)	PASE-2		2001	GTZ	MoE			GTZ	classic	donor	NCB	medium	94	105	Dupety
67	Equity and School Improv. Proj (addit. Clrms)	PASE-2		2001	AeA	MoE			Aide et Action	classic	NGO	direct	small	118	131	Dupety
68	KfW Project	KfW	1996–00	2000	KfW	MoE	PIU			classic	admin/cent	NCB	medium	158	180	Lipsmeier 2000, World Bank 2001c, Annex 13
69	Plan Guinea Program	PG	1997–00	2000	Plan Guinea	NGO		Plan Guinea		classic	NGO	direct	small	115	131	Plan Guinea 2001
70	Education For All -1 (phase 1)	EFA-1	2000–04	2002	IDA	MoE			NGO/CMA/10	classic	NGO	NCB	small	106	116	Dupety 2004 and 2005b
71	Education For All -1 (phase 2)	EFA-1	2004–07	2006	IDA	MoE			NGO/CMA/11	classic	NGO	NCB	small	125	125	Dupety 2004 and 2005b
72	Village Community Support Project	VSCP	2004–07	2006	IDA	MPC			Local Gov	classic	Local Gov	NCB	small	215	215	VSCP 2007
73	Aide et Action's Program	AeA			AeA	AeA				classic	NGO	direct	small	91	108	voir SAR Guinea
Madagascar																
74	Education Sector Develop. Program - I	CRESED-I	2000–02	2000	IDA	MoE				classic	admin/cent	NCB	medium	129	147	World Bank 2005m
75	Government Program		1987	1987	donor	MoE/MPW		MPW		classic	admin/cent	ICB	large	582	906	World Bank 1987a
76	Education Sector Develop. Program - II	CRESED-II	2002–04	2002	IDA	MoE			Districts	classic	admin/decon	NCB	medium	143	157	Group 5 2005
77	Education Sector Develop. Program - II	CRESED-II	2000–04	2004	IDA	MoE			Districts	classic	admin/decon	NCB	medium	176	184	MENRS 2007
78	OPEP project	OPEP	2006	2006	OPEP	PIU			Districts	classic	admin/decon	NCB	medium	141	141	MENRS 2007
79	BADEA' project	BADEA	2006	2006	BADEA	PIU				classic	admin/cent	NCB	medium	223	223	MENRS 2007
80	AfDB's project	AfDB	2005–06	2006	AfDB	MoE				classic	admin/cent	NCB	medium	248	248	MENRS 2007
81	Industrialized Modular Const. Proj.	CMI	2004–07	2006	Gov	MoE			CMA/FID-EPT	prefab.	CMA	ICB	large	214	214	MENRS 2007
82	Classic const program	FID-EPT	2005–06	2006	Gov	MoE			CMA/FID-EPT	classic	CMA	NCB	medium	185	185	MENRS 2007
83	Programme FID	FID	2005–05	2005	Gov	MoE			CMA/FID-IV	classic	CMA	LCB	medium	184	188	FID 2007
84	Programme FID	FID	2005–06	2006	Gov	MoE			CMA/FID-IV	classic	Local Gov	LCB	medium	154	154	FID 2007
85	Programme FID	FID	2005–07	2007	Gov	MoE			CMA/FID-IV	classic	community	LCB	medium	168	165	FID 2007
86	BIT's const program	BIT	2005–06	2006	BIT/Norway	BIT				classic	donor	NCB	medium	141	141	MENRS 2007
87	Government Program		2006–07	2007	Gov	MoE			Regions	classic	admin/decon	NCB	medium	218	214	MENRS 2007
88	JICA's project		2004	2004	JICA	JICA				classic	donor	reserved	large	528	553	MENRS 2007

#	Project	AGETIPA		FDA/France	CMA	AGETIPA								
89	AGETIPA's program	AGETIPA		2004	CMA	AGETIPA		classic	CMA	NCB	medium	288	301	MENRS 2007
90	Aide et Action - Antananarivo	AeA		2001	NGO	AeA		classic	NGO	LCB	small	52	58	Aide et Action 2007
91	Aide et Action Tulear	AeA		2004	NGO	AeA		classic	NGO	LCB	small	82	86	Aide et Action 30 mai 2007
92	FID (DRT) Projet EPP Iavoambony	FID-IV		2003	FID			classic	community	LCB	medium	96	103	FID 2003a
93	FID (DRT) Projet EPP Morarano Anrongona	FID-IV		2003	FID			classic	community	LCB	medium	94	102	FID 2003b
94	FID (DRT) Projet CEG Nandihizana	FID-IV		2005	FID			classic	local gov	LCB	medium	185	189	FID 2005c
95	FID (DRT) Projetlycée Soanindrariny	FID-IV		2004	FID			classic	CMA	LCB	medium	146	153	FID 2004d
96	FID (DRT) Projet CEG Ambogamarina	FID-IV		2005	FID			classic	local gov	LCB	medium	65	66	FID 2005a
97	FID (DRT) Projet EPP Antanimenabe	FID-IV		2005	FID			classic	local gov	LCB	medium	98	100	FID 2005b
98	FID (DRT) Projet EPP Andranomasina	FID-IV		2004	FID			classic	community	LCB	Medium	72	75	FID 2004c
99	FID (DRD) Projet Ecole FJKM Andapa	FID-IV		2003	FID			classic	CMA	RCB	medium	177	190	Olivier 2004
100	FID (DRN) Projet Ecole NDDLP Ambohianatrika	FID-IV		2003	FID			classic	CMA	RCB	medium	141	152	Olivier 2004
101	FID (DRU) Projet EPP Ranavo (access diff)	FID-IV		2003	FID			classic	community	RCB	medium	104	112	Olivier 2004

Malawi 177.16

#	Project													
102	Second Social Development Fund	MAZAF	1998–06	2003	MAZAF			classic	community	3O	small	62	66	EMC Jatula Associates 2003
103	N/A	DANIDA		2003	PIU			classic	admin.	NCB	medium	146	157	EMC Jatula Associates 2003
104	Plan International Program	PI	2003–06	2006	NGO			classic	NGO	direct	small	101	101	Plan International Data
105	Micro Project Program	MPP	2004–06	2006	MPP	PIU		classic	community	direct/LS	jobbers	134	134	Majgaard data
106	Micro Project Program	MPP	2004–06	2006	MPP	PIU		classic	community	direct/LS	jobbers	121	121	Majgaard data
107	Malwi UNICEF program	UNICEF	2004–06	2006	donor			classic	community	direct/LS	jobbers	90	101	Majgaard data
108	MAZAF Program	MAZAF		2001	MAZAF			classic	community	3O	small	63	70	Majgaard data
109	Building Department	BD		2001	donor			classic	admin/cent	NCB	medium	100	111	Majgaard data
110	Malawi DFID Program (urban)	DFID	2004–06	2004	donor			classic	admin/cent	NCB	medium	107	112	Majgaard data
109	Malawi DFID Program (rural)	DFID	2004–06	2004	donor			classic	admin/cent	NCB	medium	101	106	Majgaard data
110	Malawi DFID Program (urban)	DFID		2006	donor			classic	admin/cent	NCB	medium	125	125	Majgaard data
111	Malawi DFID Program (rural)	DFID		2005	donor			classic	admin/cent	NCB	medium	118	118	Majgaard data

Mali

#	Project													
112	Primary schools		1982–87	France	NGO	AFVP		local mat	NGO	direct	jobbers	41		Derisbour et al 1987
113	Low-cost housing proj. Banconi		1982	France	NGO	ACA		local mat	NGO	direct	jobbers	98	178	ACA 1982, p. 58
114	Training Center Gabriel Cisse Segou			1987	Church	NGO	Altech		local mat	NGO	direct	jobbers	115	179	Houben and Guillard 1989, pp. 69–87
115	Government Program			1985	donor	donor		classic	donor	ICB	large	356	583	World Bank 1989c
116	Community Schools		1994–00	1998	NGOs	NGOs		classic	NGO	direct/LS	small	128	193	Cissé et al. 2000
117	Education Sector Consolidation Proj	ESCP	1990–95	1990	IDA	MoE	AGETIP-Mali	classic	CMA	NCB	medium	133	186	World Bank 1989c, 1996b
118	Education Sector Consolidation Proj	ESCP	1990–95	1990	IDA	MoE	NGOs	classic	NGO	direct	micro	108	151	World Bank 1989c, 1996b
119	Grassroots Initiative Project	GRIP		1990	IDA	Admin.	PIU	classic	community	LCB	small	105	120	voir e-mail Sverrir

(Table continues on the following page.)

Table (continued)

Country	Project name	Acronym	Project period	date of cost info	Financing Agency	Project overall management agency - Head	Project overall management agency - Directorate	Delegation	Technology	Procurement Agency	Procurement method	type of contractor	Unit cost per m² current	Unit cost per m² 2006	Source
Mauritania															
120	Low-cost housing projet Rosso		1977–81	1980	multiple	NGO	ADAUA		local mat	NGO	direct	jobbers	70	148	Theunynck 1994, p. 809
121	Primary school in Diaguily		1987–88	1988	UNESCO	donor	BREDA		local mat	donor	direct	jobbers	98	148	UNESCO 1988, pp. 6–7
122	FED program		1973–77	1977	UE	MPW			classic	admin/cent	ICB	large	500	1334	UNESCO 1984, p. 27
123	Government Program RIM 78		1978	1978	Irak, Koweit	MPW			classic	admin/cent	ICB	large	387	965	UNESCO 1984, p. 28
124	Government Program			1984	donor	MPW			classic	admin/cent	ICB	large	370	624	World Bank 1988
125	Urban Project 1 (school in Selibaby)			2000	IDA	MoF	ADM	AMEXTIPE	classic	CMA	NCB	medium	243	277	Synergie 2000y
126	Urban Project 2 (Nouadhibou)			2005	IDA	MoF	ADM	AMEXTIPE	classic	CMA	NCB	medium	227	231	Theunynck 2007
127	Urban Project 2 (Rosso)			2003	KFW	MoF	ADM	AMEXTIPE	classic	CMA	NCB	medium	219	235	Theunynck 2007
128	Urban Project 2 (Nema)			2001	IDA	MoF	ADM	AMEXTIPE	classic	CMA	NCB	medium	165	184	Theunynck 2007
129	Education III Project	Edu-III	1989–95	1991	IDA-FDA	MoE	PIU	community	classic	community	direct	small	104	140	Theunynck 1999
130	Education III Project	Edu-III	1989–96	1995	IDA-FDA	MoE	PIU	community	classic	community	direct	small	113	139	Theunynck 1999
131	Education III Project	Edu-V	1989–97	1999	IDA-FDA	MoE	PIU	community	classic	community	direct	small	117	136	Theunynck 1999
132	Education V Project	Edu-V	1995–00	2000	IDA-FDA	MoE	PIU	community	classic	community	LCB	small	85	97	World Bank 2001f
133	Edu. Sector Nat. Support Program (Rosso)	PNDSE	2000–10	2001	IDA-FDA	MoE	PIU	community	classic	community	LCB	small	53	58	data collected by S. Theunynck
134	Edu. Sector Nat. Support Program (Ndbou)	PNDSE	2000–10	2001	IDA-FDA	MoE	PIU	community	classic	community	LCB	small	77	85	data collected by S. Theunynck
135	Edu. Sector Nat. Support Program (Rosso)	PNDSE	2000–10	2002	IDA-FDA	MoE	PIU	community	classic	community	LCB	small	135	148	data collected by S. Theunynck
136	Edu. Sector Nat. Support Program (Ndbou)	PNDSE	2000–11	2003	IDA-FDA	MoE	PIU	community	classic	community	LCB	small	119	128	data collected by S. Theunynck
137	Urban school in Nyiad, Dar Naim	Urb. Proj		2002	IDA	Local Gov		AMEXTIPE	classic	CMA	NCB	medium	192	210	data collected by S. Theunynck
Mozambique															
138	Second Education Projet	SEP	1991–98	1998	IDA	MoE		NGO	classic	NGO	FA	jobbers	116	137	World Bank 1999f para 23–24
139	Education Sector Strategic Program	ESSP	2000–04	2004	IDA	MoE	DCEE		classic	admin/cent	NCB	medium	165	173	Group 5 2006c
140	Education Sector Strategic Program	ESSP	2000–04	2004	IDA	MoE		Provinces	classic	admin/decon	LCB	small	124	149	Group 5 2006c
141	Rural Primary School Project	RPSP	2000–04	2004	IDB	MoE		Provinces	classic	admin/decon	NCB	medium	142	149	Group 5 2006c
142	Education Support Program	PASE	1995–05	2003	FINNIDA	MoE		Provinces	classic	admin/decon	LCB	small	108	116	Group 5 2006c
143	Danish Support to the ESP	ESSP	2002–06	2004	DANIDA	MoE		Provinces	classic	MoE/decon	LCB	medium	400	419	Group 5 2006c
144	Danish Support to the ESP	ESSP	2002–06	2004	DANIDA	MoE		Provinces	classic	community	direct	jobbers	80	84	Group 5 2006c
145	Primary School Construction Proj			2004	JICA	donor	JICA		classic	donor	reserved	large	525	550	Group 5 2006c
146	Emergency Program			2004	IDA	MoE	PIU		prefab	admin/cent	ICB	large	455	506	Group 5 2006c
147	AMDU Program			2004	NGO	NGO	AMDU		classic	NGO	direct	small	105	110	Group 5 2006c
148	Lutheran World Federation project	LWF		2005	NGO	NGO			classic	NGO	direct	small	173	176	Group 5 2006c
149	PRONES	PRONES		2005	UNICEF				classic						Group 5 2006c
Niger															
150	Literacy Center in Chical			1980	UNDP	NGO	ACA		local mat	NGO	direct	jobbers	322	638	DMN 1980, p. 7
151	Education III Project			1986	IDA	MoE	PIU		local mat	admin/cent	direct	jobbers	160	256	Theunynck 1994, p. 807
152	Government Program			1984	donor	MoE/MPW			classic	admin/cent	ICB	large	378	638	World Bank 1996d
153	Government Program			1984	Gov	MoE			classic	admin/cent	ICB	large	214	361	World Bank 1986
154	First Education Project (test 60 clrms)	FEP	1981–90	1986	IDA	MPW			classic	admin/cent	ICB	large	143	228	World Bank 1992b

#	Project													Source
155	First Education Project (MPW for MoE))	FEP	1981–91	IDA	MPW			classic	admin/cent	ICB	large	208	323	World Bank 1992b
156	Primary Edu. Develop. Projet (Edu-II)	PEDP	1987–95	IDA	MoE	PIU		shelter	admin/cent	ICB/com	large	66	102	World Bank
157	Primary Edu. Develop. Projet (Edu-II)	PEDP	1987–95	IDA	MoE	PIU		shelter	admin/cent	ICB/com	large	66	99	World Bank 1996d
158	Basic Education Project	PADEB	2003–08	IDA	MoE	PIU		shelter	admin/cent	ICB/com	large	62	63	Zerbo 2008
159	Basic Education Project	PADEB	2003–08	IDA	MoE	PIU		classic	admin/cent	NCB	medium	147	150	Zerbo 2008
160	AFD Program	FDA	2005	FDA	MoE	PIU	Nigetipe	classic	CMA	NCB	medium	172	175	Zerbo 2008
161	KfW Program	KfW	2005	KfW	MoE	PIU		classic	donor	NCB	medium	157	160	Zerbo 2008

Rwanda

162	Human Resource Development Project	HRDP	2000–07	IDA	MoE	PIU	Local Government	classic	local gov	NCB	medium	220	231	Kayumba 2006a
163	Education III Project	EDU-III	2000–06	AfDB	MoE	PIU		classic	admin/cent	NCB	medium	263	263	Kayumba 2006a
164	Construction et Rehab. Ecoles Primaires	CREP	2003–09	Belgium	MoE	PIU		classic	admin/cent	NCB	medium	125	125	CREP 2006
165	HRDP Marché Ville Kabuga-Ent Ecotibat	HRDP	2000–07	IDA	MoE	PIU	Local Government	classic	local gov	NCB	medium	145	156	Kabuga 2001
166	HRDP Marché Rubavu-Ent Kazoza	HRDP	2000–08	IDA	MoE	PIU	Local Government	classic	local gov	NCB	medium	209	209	MESTRS 2006

Senegal

167	Training Center in Nianning		1977	UNESCO	donor	BREDA		local mat	donor	direct	medium	56	149	Delilcour and AI, 1978
168	School of Derkle in Dakar		1983	EU	donor	EU		local mat	donor	direct	medium	131	230	Theunynck 1974, p. 719
169	Coranic School of Malika		1979	NGO	NGO	Daara		local mat	NGO	direct	medium	132		Abdullac 1979, p. 37
170	Third Education Project	TEP	1983	IDA	Gov	PIU		local mat	admin.	direct	medium	117		World Bank 2000d, annex 12
171	Third Education Project	TEP	1982	IDA	Gov	PIU		classic	admin.	direct	medium	203	369	World Bank 2000d, annex 13
172	Gov Programs			donors	Gov			classic	admin/cent	ICB	large	593	828	Verspoor, Looked, p. 179
173	Aide et Action Program	AeA	1982	NGO	NGO			classic	NGO	direct	small	162	294	Aide et Action 1994, p. 20
174	Government Program		1984	donor	MoE	MPW		classic	admin/cent	ICB	large	293	494	World Bank 1993e
175	Primary Edu. Develop Proj, Phase1	PEDP-1	1987–89	IDA	MoE	PIU		classic	admin.	ICB/com	large/com	210	316	World Bank 1995g
176	Primary Edu. Develop Proj, Phase2	PEDP-1	1989–95	IDA	MoE		AGETIP	classic	CMA	NCB	medium	177	233	World Bank 1995g
177	Education IV		1988–90	EU	MoE	DCES		classic	admin/cent	NCB	large	237	331	World Bank 2000d
178	PDRH-2	PDRH-2	1990	Gov	MoE	DCES		classic	admin cent	NCB	medium	143	185	World Bank 2000d
179	Government Program (BCI)		1993	Gov	MoE	DCES		classic	admin.	direct	medium	129	152	World Bank 2000d
180	Human Resource Dev. Project II	PDRH-2	1995–98	IDA	MoE		AGETIP	classic	CMA	NCB	medium	109	129	Dupety 2005b
181	Edu. Sector Emergency Program	PUSE	1998	CIDA	NGO	FPGL		classic	NGO	direct	jobbers	123	143	F2 Consultants 1999
182	Gov Program (1020 classrooms)		1998–99	Gov /BCI	MoE	DCES		classic	admin/cent	NCB	medium	126	149	World Bank 2000d
183	Gov Program (1000 classrooms)		1999	Gov /BCI	MoE	DCES		classic	admin/cent	NCB	medium	80	93	World Bank 2000d
184	School Construction Project III	OPEP-III	2000–04	OPEP	MoE	PIU		classic	admin.	NCB	medium	135	141	Dupety 2005a
185	School Construction Project		2000–04	IDB	MoE			classic	admin/PIU	ICB	large	264	277	Dupety 2005a
186	School Construction Project IV	JICA-IV	2000–04	JICA	JICA			classic	donor	reserved	large	731	766	World Bank 2005j
187	Education For All Project -1	EFA-1	2000–04	IDA	MoE		AGETIP	classic	CMA	NCB	medium	145	152	Diouf 2006
188	Education For All Project -2	EFA-2	2002–05	IDA	MoE		AGETIP	classic	CMA	NCB	medium	138	141	Dupety 2005a
189	Education Improvement Proj for Senegal	PAOES	2003	FDA	MoE		AGETIP	classic	CMA	NCB	medium	162	174	Dupety 2005a
190	BID Program	BID	2001–04	IDB	MoE	DCES		classic	admin/cent	NCB	medium	221	231	Dupety 2005a
191	OPEP Program	OPEP-III	2003–04	OPEP	MoE	DCES		classic	admin/cent	NCB	medium	136	142	Dupety 2005a
192	Third Education Project	Edu-III	2001–04	AfDB	MoE	PUI		classic	admin/cent	NCB	large	137	144	Dupety 2005a
193	National Rural Infrastructure Proj.	NRIP	2003	IDA	Min Rural D		Local Gov	classic	local gov	LCB	medium	122	132	Dupety 2005a
194	National Rural Infrastructure Proj.	NRIP	2000–04	IDA	Min Rural D		Local Gov	classic	local gov	LCB	medium	134	140	Diouf 2006
195	Edu. Supply Improvement Proj.	PAOES	2000–04	FDA/France	AGETIP			classic	CMA	NCB	medium	193	202	Dupety 2005a

(Table continues on the following page.)

Table (continued)

Country	Project name	Acronym	Project period	date of cost info	Financing Agency	Project overall management agency - Head	Project overall management agency - Directorate	Delegation	Technology	Procurement Agency	Procurement method	type of contractor	Unit cost per m² current	Unit cost per m² 2006	Source
196	Communal Support Project	PAC	2000–04	2004	IDA	MoLD	ADM	AGETIP	classic	CMA	NCB	medium	142	149	Dupety 2005a
197	Social Development Fund Project	PFDS	2001–05	2004	IDA	FS	AFDS	community	classic	community	LCB	small	105	110	Diouf 2006
198	Government Program (HIPC)	HPIC	2000–05	2004	Gov	MoE	DCES		classic	amdmin/cent	NCB	medium	135	141	Diouf 2006
199	Government Program (BCI)	BCI	2000–04	2004	Gov	MoE	DCES		classic	admin/cent	NCB	medium	125	131	Dupety 2005a
200	Japan Education Program			2002	JICA	Donor			classic	JICA	reserved	large	357	391	GAZD 2002
201	AFDS FatickNiassene	PFDS		2003	IDA	FS		community	classic	community	LCB	small	95	102	contract
202	EFA1- AGETIP Fatick Gossas	EFA-1		2003	IDA	MoE		AGETIP	classic	CMA	NCB	medium	119	128	contract

Uganda

203	Education Strategic Investment Plan	ESSIP	2000–06	2003	MoE/SFD/LG	MoE		SFD/local gov	classic	community	LCB	small	75	81	Group 5 2006d
204	Edu. Strategic Invest. Plan (urban schools)	ESSIP	2000–07	2004	MoE/SFD/LG	MoE		SFD/local gov	classic	admin/cent	NCB	small	135	141	Group 5 2006d
205	Micro-Project Program	MPP	2000–03	2002	UE	MoF	MPP	Local Gov	classic	local gov	direct/LS	small	97	92	Group 5 2006d
206	Micro-Project Program	MPP	2000–05	2005	UE	MoF	MPP	Local Gov	classic	local gov	direct/LS	small	109		EU 2005, p. 45
207	Northern Uganda Social Action Fund	NUSAF	2000–07	2007	IDA	Prime Min		Community	classic	community	LCB	medium	49.5		World Bank 2004n
208	Local Government Development Program	LGDP-I	2000–04	2002	IDA	MoLG	PIU	Local Gov level 3	classic	local gov	NCB	medium	63		PKF Consulting 2003, p. 124
209	Local Government Development Program	LGDP-1	2000–04	2003	IDA	MoLG	PIU	Local Gov level 4	classic	local gov	NCB	medium	92		Theunynck 2007a
210	Local Government Development Program	LGDP-2	2004–07	2007	IDA	MoLG	PIU	Local Gov level 4	classic	local gov	NCB	medium	59		PKF Consulting 2003
211	School Facility Grant - ESSP	SFG-ESSP	2000–03	2003	multidonor	MoE	CMU	Sch. Mngm. Com.	classic	community	LCB	small			

Zambia

212	Primary School Upgrading Program	OPSUP-1		1993	OPEP	PIU	ZEPIU		classic	PIU	ICB/CW	large/com	167	215	Group 5 2000a
213	OPEC Primary School Upgrading Project	OPSUP-2	2000–03	2003	OPEC	MoE/PIU	ZEPIU		classic	PIU	ICB/CW	large/com	131	141	Group 5 2006e, pp. 19–20
214	Social Recovery Project	SRP	1992–03	1993	WB/EU	PIU	MPU		classic	community	direct	jobbers	125	161	Group 5 2000a
215	Education Sector Support Project III	ESSP-III	1992–03	2000	Finland	MoE			classic	community	direct/LS	jobbers	125	142	Group 5 2006e, pp. 19–20
216	Community Implementation Program	BESSIP	1999–03	2003	Pool/7	MoE	DPI		classic	community	direct/LS	jobbers	125	134	Group 5 2006e, pp. 19–20
217	Basic School Construction Program	BSCP	2002–05	2003	IDA	MoE	SIS		classic	admin/cent	NCB	medium	150	161	Group 5 2006e, pp. 19–20
218	Education III	Edu-III	1999–01	2000	AfDB	MoE	SIS		classic	admin/cent	ICB	large	337	384	Rawling et al 2001, Group 5 2000a
219	Education III	Edu-III	2002–05	2003	AfDB	MoE	SIS		classic	admin/cent	ICB	large	140	151	Group 5 2006e, pp. 19–20
220	Urban School Construction	USCP	2000–05	2000	JICA	MoE	PIU		classic	donor	reserved	large	450	513	Group 5 2006e, pp. 19–20
221	Zambia Social Investment Fund	ZAMSIF	1999–05	2000	WB	SF			classic	community	direct/SL	jobbers	125	142	Rawling et al 2001, Group 5 2000a
222	Zambia Social Investment Fund	ZAMSIF	1999–05	2004	WB	SF	SIS		classic	community	direct/LS	jobbers	80	84	Group 5 2006e, pp. 19–20
223	Government Program (HPIC)	HPIC	2004	2004	Gov	MoE			classic	admin/cent	NCB	medium	125	131	Group 5 2006e, pp. 19–20
224	Micro-Projects Program	MPP	1985–06	2004	EU	MPU	Microproj Unit		classic	community	direct/LS	jobbers	80	84	Group 5 2006e, pp. 19–20

Asia

Philippines

225 Second Education Projet	SEEP	1990–97	1992	Gov	MoE			prefab	admin/cent	NCB	large	173	229	World Bank 1996e

Bangladesh

226 Second Primary Education Project (rural)	SPEP	1985–90	1985	IDA	MoE		local gov	classic	admin/decon	LCB	small	59	97	World Bank 1985a
227 Second Primary Education Project (urban)	SPEP	1985–90	1985	IDA	MoE			classic	admin/cent	LCB	medium	89	145	World Bank 1985a
228 General Education Project (Rural)	GEP	1990–96	1996	IDA	MoE		local gov	classic	admin/decon			98	119	World Bank 1997a
229 General Education Project (urban)	GEP	1990–96	1996	IDA	MoE			classic	admin/cent			128	155	World Bank 1997a
230 Fourth Education	Edu-IV	1980–90	1980	IDA	MoE			classic	admin/cent	ICB/LCB	large/small	47	99	World Bank 1980, p. 28
231 Fourth Education	Edu-IV	1980–90	1990	IDA	MoE			classic	admin/cent	ICB/LCB	large/small	58	80	World Bank 1990a

India

232 Raj. District Pri. Edu. Project (1st)	RDPE-1	1999–04	2004	IDA	MoE			classic	community	3-Q	small	61	64	World Bank 2005u
233 Utah Pradesh Primary Edu. Project (1st)	UPPEP	1993–00		IDA	MoE			classic	community	3-Q	small	82	97	World Bank 1993g

Laos

234 Basic Education Project	BEGP	1992–99	1999	ADB	MoE	PIU		classic	admin/cent	NCB	medium	88	102	Madecor 2007
235 Second Education Quality Improvement Proj.	EQIP-II	1999–07	2002	ADB	MoE	PIU		classic	admin/cent	NCB	medium	115	126	Madecor 2007
236				JICA	Donor			classic	donor	reserved	large	250	291	Madecor 2007
237 Education Development Project	EDP-I	1993–00	1999	IDA	MoE			classic	admin/cent	NCB	medium	120	140	Madecor 2007
238 Second Education Development Project	EDP-II	2004–10	2007	IDA	MoE			classic	community	LCB	small	67	66	Madecor 2007
239 Second Education Development Project	EDP-II	2004–11	2007	IDA	MoE			classic	community	LCB	small	62		World Bank 2007e
240 Poverty Reduction Fund	PRF	2003–07	2007	IDA	SF			classic	community	LCB	small	65		World Bank 2007e
241 Girls Education Project	GEP			ADB	MoE			classic	admin/cent	NCB	medium	96		World Bank 2007e
242 Second Educ. Quality Improvement Proj.	EQIP-II	1999–07		ADB	MoE			classic	admin/cent	NCB	medium	115		World Bank 2007e

Pakistan

243 Second Elementary Education Proj.	SEEP	1985–93	1987	IDA	Gov/PCU			prefab.	PCU	ICB	large	194	303	World Bank 1995f (7000$/clrm)
244 Fourth Education Project	Edu-IV	1979–87	1985	IDA	Gov/PCU			classic	PCU	LCB	small	138	226	World Bank 1987b, Annex 16
245 Sindh Primary Education	SPEDP	1990–99	1990	IDA	MoE			classic	admin/cent	LCB	164.7	204	285	World Bank 1990c
246 Sindh Primary Education	SPEDP	1990–99	1990					classic	admin/cent	LCB	203.8	139	195	World Bank 1990c

Latin America

Brazil

247 Innovation in Basic Education	IBE		1991	IBRD	MoE			classic	admin/cent	NCB	large	442	596	World Bank 2000e

Mexico

248 Primary Education (4states)	PE		1991	IBRD	MoE			classic	admin/cent	NCB	large	473	638	World Bank 1994b
249 Second primary Education	SPE		1994	IBRD	MoE			classic	admin/cent	NCB	large	465	587	World Bank 1994b
250 Primary Education	PE		1998	IBRD	MoE			classic	admin/cent	NCB	large	336	397	World Bank 1999h

References

Abdullac, Samir. 1979. *L'utilisation des techniques et matériaux locaux: Quatre études de cas—la grande mosquée de Niono; l'école coranique de Malika; l'école rurale de Nigde; l'école maternelle de Clesse*. Dakar, Senegal: R egional Bureau for Education in Africa, United Nations Educational, Scientific, and Cultural Organization.

Abeillé, Bernard, and Jean Marie Lantran. 1993a. "Social Infrastructure Construction in the Sahel." Discussion Paper No. 200, World Bank, Washington, DC.

Ablo, Emmanuel, and Ritv a Reinikka. 1998. "Do Budgets R eally Matter? Evidence from Public Spending on Education and Health in Uganda." Policy Research Working Paper 1926, World Bank, Washington, DC.

Adam, Sarah. 2005. "Evaluating Social Fund Impact: A Toolkit for Task Team and Social Fund Managers." Social Protection Discussion Paper 0611, World Bank, Washington, DC.

ACA. 1982. *Projet Bamako: Bilan*. P aris: Programme Interministériel de Coopération, Rexcoop. August.

ADE [Aide à la Decision Économique]. 2 006. "Ev aluation of European Commission Support to Micro-Projects Programmes under the European Development Fund in ACP Countries: Final Report." ADE, Louvain-la-Neuve, Belgium, August.

AFDS [Agence du F onds de Développement Social]. 2 003a. *L'organisation et la dynamique communautaire: Guide illustré*. Dakar, Senegal: AFDS.

———. 2 003b. *La passation des marchés par les communautés de base: Guide illustré*. Dakar, Senegal: AFDS.

———. 2 006. "État d'a vancement des micro-projets et sous-projets dans la Région de Ziguinchor." Zinguinchor Regional Branch, AFDS, November.

African Development Bank Group. 2 004 "Improving the Quality of Projects —Quality of Infrastructure, Maintenance and Sustainability —Quality of Education." T oolkit for Quality in Education Projects, Tunis-Belvedère, Tunisia, December.

Ahmad, Junaid Kamal, Shantayanan Devarajan, Stuti Khemani, and Shekhar Shah. 2 005. "Decentralization and Service Deliv ery." Policy Research Working Paper 3603, World Bank, Washington, DC.

AGeFIB [Agence de Financement des Initiatives de Bases]. 2001. "Evaluation d'impacts des approches et actions de l'AGeFIB." Projet de Fonds Social de Lutte contre la Pauvreté au Bénin, réalisation LIFAD, Cotonou, Benin. June.

AGETIP [Agence d'Exécution des Travaux d'Intêret Public]. 2004a. "Rapport annuel 2003." AGETIP, Dakar, Senegal. January.

Aide et Action. 1984. "Sénégal: Rapport d'activité." Aide et Action, Dakar, Senegal.

———. 2005. "Programme Burkina: Démarche de maîtrise d'ouvrage déléguée." Includes a contract between the Parents' Association of Doundougou and the contractor EMJF/BTP. Aide et Action, Paris, November 4.

———. 2007. "Proforma d'un bâtiment en 2001." Document remis à Serge Theunynck lors de sa mission à Madagascar. April 2007.

ANLC (Agence Nationale de Lutte contre a Corruption et de Moralisation des Activités Économiques et Financières). 2005. "Enquête nationale sur la corruption et la gouvernance en Guinée (ENACOG 2003): Résumé du rapport final." ANLC, Conakry, Guinea, June.

Ansley, James. 2000. "Creating Accessible Schools." National Clearinghouse for Educational Facilities, Washington, DC, June.

Association for the Development of Education in Africa. 2003. "Study of the Provision of Physical Infrastructure and Its Impact on Quality Improvement in Primary Education in Lesotho." Country case study prepared for the Association for the Development of Education in Africa's Sixth Biennial Meeting, Grand Baie, Mauritius, December 3–6.

Bagayoko, Mamadou. 2005. "Expériences éducatives novatrices pour l'éducation des enfants et jeunes ruraux au Burkina Faso." Paper prepared for the Ministerial Seminar on Education for Rural People in Africa: Policy Lessons, Options, and Priorities, Food and Agricultural Organization, held by the Association for the Development of Education in Africa, and the United Nations Educational, Scientific, and Cultural Organization, Addis Ababa, Ethiopia, September 7–9.

Baquer, Ali, and Anjali Sharma. 2005. *Disability: Challenges vs. Responses*. New Delhi, India: Concerned Action Now. http://www.healthlibrary.com/reading/ncure/disability.

Barthélémy, Gérard. 1986. *Artisanat et développement*. Paris: Gret.

BATHYS Consult. 2007. "Rapport d'audit technique et financier des sous-projets financés par le PNDCC." Projet National d'Appui au Développement Conduit par les Communautés, Ministère de la Microfinance, de l'Emploi des Jeunes et des Femmes et des Petites et Moyennes Entreprises, Cotonou, Benin.

Batiactu. 2007. "Artisanat du Bâtiment: Bilan 2006 positif et année 2007 prometteuse." Bactiactu, Paris, January 11. http://www.batiactu.com/edito/artisanat-du-batiment—bilan-2006-positif-et-anne-5036.php.

BEC Engineering. 2005. "Northern Uganda Social Action Fund (NUSAF): Technical Audit of Community Assets—Final Report." BEC Engineering, South Perth, Australia, December.

Becker, Gary S., and Georges J. Stigler. 1974. "Law Enforcement, Malfeasance, and Compensation of Enforcers." *Journal of Legal Studies* 3 (1): 1–18.

Benin. 2008. "Programme de l'Accord de Don: Fast-Track/FCB." Working draft, Coutonou, Benin, February.

Beynon, John. 1998. "Installations et bâtiments éducatifs: Ce que les planificateurs doivent savoir." Principes de la planification de l'éducation 57, International Institute for Educational Planning, Paris.

Bigio, Anthony G., ed. 1998. *Social Funds and Reaching the Poor: Experiences and Future Directions*. Washington, DC: World Bank.

Binswanger, Hans, and Tuu Van Nguyen. 2005. "Scaling Up Community-Driven Development: A Step-By-Step-Guide." World Bank, Washington, DC, April 5.

———. 2006. "Scaling Up Community-Driven Development for Dummies." World Bank, Washington, DC, April 14.

Blundo, Giorgio. 2001. "Dessus-de-table: La corruption quotidienne dans la passation des marchés publics locaux au Sénégal." *Politique Africaine* 83 (October): 79–97.

Bruns, Barbara, Alain Mingat, and Ramahatra Rakotomalala. 2003. *Achieving Universal Primary Education by 2015: A Chance for Every Child*. Washington, DC: World Bank.

Burkina Faso. 2004. *Loi No. 055-2004/AN Portant Code Général des Collectivités Territoriales, au Burkina Faso*. In *Journal Officiel*, special issue 02, April 20, 2005.

Burns, Barbara, Alain Mingat, and Ramahatra Rakotomalala. 2003e. *Achieving Universal Primary Education by 2015: A Chance for Every Child*. Washington, DC: World Bank.

Bussat, Pierre, Heimo Mantynen, Jørgen Sønderberg, and Mohamed El-Ghannam. 1973a. "Flexible Short-Span Structures for Low-Cost Educational Buildings." Regional Office for Education in the Arab States, United Nations Educational, Scientific, and Cultural Organization, Beirut, Lebanon.

Cameroon. 2004. *Loi No. 2004/018 du 22 juillet 2004 fixant les règles applicables aux communes*. Yaoundé, July.

CAPEB [Confédération de l'Artisanat et des Petites Entreprises du Bâtiment]. 2007. *Livre blanc*. Montpellier, France: CAPEB.

Carassus, Jean. 1987. *Economie de la filière construction*. Paris: Presses de l'École Nationale des Ponts et Chaussées.

Cassimatis, Peter J. 1969. *Economics of the Construction Industry*. Studies in Business Economics 111. Washington, DC: National Industrial Conference Board.

Cavero Uriona, Jorge A. 2000. "Guide for Task Teams on Procurement Procedures Used in Social Fund." World Bank, Washington, DC.

Cerna, Michael M. 1998. "Nongovernmental Organizations and Local Development." Discussion Paper 40, World Bank, Washington, DC.

Chad. 2002. *Revue des dépenses publiques dans le secteur de l'education*. Final report, Commission Technique pour la Revue et le Suivi des Dépenses Publiques dans le Secteur de l'Education, Direction Générale, Ministère de l'Education, N'Djamena, Chad, January.

Chaudhury, Nazmul, Luc Christiaensen, and Mohammad Niaz Asadullah. 2006. "Schools, Household, Risk, and Gender: Determinants of Child Schooling in Ethiopia." Paper presented at the Centre for the Study of African Economics Annual Conference, St. Catherine's College, Oxford, U.K., March 19–21.

Chaudhury, Nazmul, Jeffrey Hammer, Michael Kremer, Karthik Muralidharan, and F. Halsey Rogers. 2006. "Missing in Action: Teacher and Health Worker Absence in Developing Countries." *Journal of Economic Perspectives* 20 (1): 91–116.

Chaudhury, Nazmul, and F. Halsey Rogers. 2004. "Measuring and Understanding Teacher Absence." PowerPoint presentation, Education Sector Board, World Bank, Washington DC, May.

Christian Blind Mission and International Center for Eye Health. 2006. *Rapid Assessment of Musculoskeletal Impairment in Rwanda: Preliminary Report for the Ministry of Health*. London: Christian Blind Mission and International Center for Eye Health, London School of Hygiene and Tropical Medicine.

Cissé, Morifing, Abel Diarra, Jacques Marchand, and Sékou Traoré. 2000a. *Les écoles communautaires au Mali*. Paris: Institute for International Economic Planning.

Cliffe, Sarah, Scott Guggenheim, and Markus Kostner. 2003. "Community-Driven Reconstruction as an Instrument in War-to-Peace Transitions." Center for Policy Research Working Paper 7, Social Development Department, Environmentally and Socially Sustainable Development Network, World Bank, Washington, DC, August 2003.

Collier, Paul, and Anke Heffier. 2005. "The Economic Costs of Corruption in Infrastructure." In *Global Corruption Report 2005*, ed. Transparency International, 12–19. London: Pluto Press.

Congo, Republic of. 2003. *Loi No. 10-2003 du 6 février 2003 portant transfert de competences aux Collectivités Locales*. Brazzaville, Republic of Congo, February 6.

CRATerre. 1989. *Bulletin d'Information du CRATerre* 2 (April–June). École d'Architecture de Grenoble, France.

DCES [Direction des Constructions et de l'Equipement Scolaires]. 1985. *Entretenons notre école: Guide d'entretien à l'usage des instituteurs et des élèves des établissements publics d'enseignement élémentaire et des parents d'élèves*. Dakar, Senegal: DCES, Direction de l'Administration Générale et de l'Equipement, Ministère de l'Education Nationale.

———. 1997. *Pour une école appropriée: Guide de programmation et de conception des écoles élémentaires*. Dakar, Senegal: DCES, Direction de l' Administration Générale et de l'Equipement, Ministère de l'Education Nationale.

De Bosch Kemper, Jan, T. O. Barry, and S. Bumke. 1990. "Projet de construction de prototypes d'écoles primaires en milieu rural en Guinée." Regional Bureau for Education in Africa, United Nations Educational, Scientific, and Cultural Organization, Dakar, Senegal, March 5.

Dellicour, Oswald, Kamal El Jack, Chris Posma, and Paul de Walick. 1978. "Vers une meilleure utilisation des ressources locales en construction: Le centre de formation agricole de Nianing." Regional Bureau for Education in Africa, United Nations Educational, Scientific, and Cultural Organization, Dakar, Senegal.

Demante, Marie Jo, and Abdoulaye Sidibe. 2006. *Evaluation du thème "Appui à la decentralization et gouvernance locale."* Étape 2: Études de terrain, le Burundi. Cepia, International Institute for Environment and Development, African Institute for Community-Driven Development, Institut de Recherches et d'Applications des Méthodes de Développement, Service Public Féderal et Coopération au Développement, La Coopération Belge au Développement, Paris, France.

Derisbourg, François, and AET A. 1987. *Au Mali: Un programme de construction en banco stabilisé*. Monographie de Projet Association Française des Volontaires du Progès, Ministère de la Coopération, Bamako, Mali, March.

De Silva, Samantha. 2000. "Community-Based Contracting: A Review of Stakeholder Experience." World Bank, Washington, DC.

———. 2002. *Communities Taking the Lead: A Handbook on Direct Financing of Community Subprojects*. Washington, DC: World Bank.

DIAL [Développement Institutions & Analyses de Long Terme]. 2007. "Youth and Labour Markets in Africa: A Critical Review of Literature." Working Paper 49, DIAL, Paris, October.

Diou, Christian, Michel Henry, and Babaly Deme. 2007. *La délégation de maîtrise d'ouvrage en Afrique en 2007: Bila, enjeux et perspectives*. Public-Private Infrastructure Advisory Project, Dakar, Senegal, April.

Diouf, Mame Sémou. 2006. *Rapport d'évaluation des coûts unitaires des constructions scolaires réalisées par le Projet Fonds de Développement Social*. Agence du Fonds de Développement Social, Dakar, Senegal, May.

DMN [Direction de la Météorologie Nationale]. 1980. "Station agrométéorologique de Chikal." Projet PNUD/OMM/NER/77/002, DMN, Niamey, Niger.

DPEF [Direction des Projets Education et Formation]. 1994a. *Atlas Info RIM, Tome 1: Sites*. Ministère de l'Education Nationale, Ministère du Plan, Nouakchott, Mauritania.

———. 1994b. *Atlas scolaire: Données par collectivité*. Appui aux collectivités pour la construction de salles de classe de l'Enseignement Fondamental, Projets Education III et V, Direction des Projets Education et Formation, Direction de la Planification et de la Coopération, Ministère de l'Education Nationale, Ministère du Plan, Nouakchott, Mauritania, December 21.

DTI [U.K. Department of Trade and Industry]. 2001. *Current Practice and Potential Use of Prefabrication*. Project Report 203032, Construction Industry Directorate, DTI, London.

Duflo, Esther. 2001. "Schooling and Labor Market Consequences of School Construction in Indonesia: Evidence from Unusual Policy Experiment." *American Review* 91 (4): 795–813.

Dundas & Wilson. 2005. "EU and Competition." Dundas & Wilson bulletin. http://www.dundas-wilson.com.

Dupety, Daniel. 2003. *Evaluation des travaux de genie-civil: Mission Daniel Dupety du 18 juillet au 3 aôut 2003*. Projet Équité et Amélioration des Écoles (IDA Cr 2719-GUI), Composante Construction et Réhabilitation des Écoles Primaires, Conakry, Guinea, September 9.

———. 2004. "Revue du volet génie civil: Rapport de mission (05 au 15 février 2004)." Projet Equité et Amélioration des Ecoles (IDA Cr 2719-GUI), Programme Education pour Tous (IDA Cr 3552-GUI), Conakry, Guinea.

———. 2005a. "Construction scolaire: Évaluation des travaux de génie-civil de la première phase." Mission report, Senegal, March 16–April 10.

———. 2005b. "Revue du volet génie civil: Rapport de mission (10 au 19 avril 2005)." Programme Education pour Tous (IDA Cr 3552-GUI), Conakry, Guinea.

———. 2005c. "Revue du volet génie civil: Rapport de mission (1 au 13 septembre 2005)." Programme Education Pour Tous (Cr 3552-GUI), Conakry, Guinea.

———. 2006. "Aide-mémoire: Contribution de Daniel Dupety, mission de pré-évaluation, 6–18 février 2006." Programme d'appui à la reconstruction du système educatif du Burundi, Bujumbura, Burundi.

Edward, Michael, and Alan Fowler, eds. 2004. *The Earthscan Reader on NGO Management*. London: Earthcan Publications.

EMC Jatula Associates. 2003. "Malawi Social Fund Consultancy Services for Review of Cost-Effectiveness and Technical Design Standards." Final Report, EMC Jatula Associates Consulting Engineers, Lilongwe, Malawi, June.

Ernst & Young. 2001. "Projet Équité et Amélioration des Écoles (PEAE): Rapport sur la mission de contrôle des procédures d'appel d'offres." Conakry, Guinea, September.

EU [European Union]. 2005. "8th EDF Microprojects Programme, Project No. 8, ACP UG 013: Completion Report—2000–2005." Kampala, Uganda.

F2 Consultants. 1999. "Étude comparative de salles de classe." F2 Consultants, Ministère de l'Education Nationale, Direction des Constructions et de l'Equipement Scolaires, Agence d'Exécution des Travaux d'Intêret Public, Dakar, Senegal.

Faso Baara. 2006. "Rapport annuel exercice 2005." Faso Baara, Ouagadougou, Burkina Faso.

FCGA [Fédération des Centres de Gestion Agréés]. 2007. *Activités et tendances*. 11th ed. Paris: FCGA, June.

FID [Fonds d'Intervention pour le Développement]. 2003a. "Travaux de construction de deux bâtiments respectivement à deux salles de classe et à deux salles de classe avec bureau pour EPP Iavo Ambony." Contrat entreprise Hasina, Antananarivo, Madagascar, April 5.

———. 2003b. "Travaux de construction de l'EPP Morarano Antongona." Contrat entreprise EETMa." Antananarivo, Madagascar, August 28.

———. 2004a. "Construction de 3000 salles de classe: '2700 EPP et 700 CEG avec la fourniture de mobilier scolaire.'" Rapport de synthèse: Programme–Prospection–Études DCE–Consultation des Entreprises–Passation des Marchés, établi le 12 mars 2004 par SBLT Consultant, Antananarivo, Madagascar.

———. 2004b. "Programme Education pour Tous (EPT), Financement Ministère de l'Education Nationale et de la Recherche Scientifique: Dossier d'appel d'offres." Hexaport International, FID. Ministère de l'Education Nationale et de la Recherche Scientifique, Antananarivo, Madagascar, July 13.

———. 2004c. "Travaux de construction de l'E.P.P. Andranomasina." Contrat entreprise E.M.M, Antananarivo, Madagascar, April 26.

———. 2004d. "Travaux de construction du lycée Soanindrariny." Contrat 1497/ENT/DRT/04, Entreprise Dina, Antananarivo, Madagascar, November 21.

———. 2005a. "Exécution des travaux de construction CEG Ambongamarina." Contrat 04/CR-AMG-03, Entreprise Arena, Antananarivo, Madagascar, June 9.

———. 2005b. "Travaux de construction de l'EPP Antanimenabe." Contrat entreprise Toandro, Antananarivo, Madagascar, April 25.

———. 2005c. "Travaux de construction du CEG à 4 salles de classes avec bibliothèque et bureau à Nandihizana." Contrat C01, Entreprise Andry-H, Antananarivo, Madagascar, Septermber 5.

———. 2007. "Coût moyen des infrastructures scolaires." Estimation provided by FID to Serge Theunynck during a mission, Antananarivo, Madagascar, April 2007.

FID-EPT [Fonds d'Intervention pour le Développement–Education Pour Tous]. 2005a. *Convention de Maîtrise d'Ouvrage Déléguée entre le Ministère de L'Education Nationale et de Recherche Scientifique (MENRS) et le Fonds d'Intervention pour le Développement—Education Pour Tous (FID-EPT).* Convention No. 01/2005, MENRS/FID-EPT, Antananarivo, Madagascar, January 18.

———. 2005b. "Memorandum: Marché FID/EPT–Hexaport International, construction 1.400 salles de classe, composante 'founitures,' composante 'travaux,' services connexes." Antananarivo, Madagascar, November.

Filmer, Deon. 2004. "If You Build It, Will They Come? School Availability and School Enrollment in 21 Poor Countries." Policy Research Working Paper 3340, World Bank, Washington, DC.

Finkel, Gerard. 1997. *The Economics of the Construction Industry.* Armonk, NY: M.E. Sharpe.

Foster, Andrew D., and Mark R. Rosenzweig. 1996. "Technical Change and Human Capital Returns and Investments: Evidence from the Green Revolution." *American Economic Review* 86 (4): 932–53.

Frigenti, Laura, and Alberto Harth. 1998. *Local Solutions to Regional Problems: The Growth of Social Funds and Public Works and Employment Projects in Sub-Saharan Africa.* Washington, DC: World Bank.

Gershberg, Alec Ian, and Donald R. Winkler. 2003. "Education Decentralization in Africa: A Review of Recent Policy and Practice." World Bank, Washington, DC.

Glewwe, Paul, and Hanan G. Jacoby. 1994. "Student Achievement and Schooling Choice in Low-Income Countries: Evidence from Ghana." *Journal of Human Resources* 29 (3): 834–64.

———. 1996. "School Enrollment and Completion: An Investigation of Recent Trends." In *Household Welfare and Vietnam's Transition,* ed. David Dollar, Paul Glewwe, and Jennie Litvack, 201–34. Washington, DC: World Bank.

Glick, Peter, and David E. Sahn. 2006. "The Demand for Primary Schooling in Madagascar: Process, Quality, and the Choice between Public and Private Providers." *Journal of Development Economics* 79 (1): 118–45.

Gopal, Gita. 1995. *Bank-Financed Projects with Community Participation: A Manual for Designing Procurement and Disbursement Mechanisms.* Washington, DC: World Bank.

Gould, William T. S. 1978. "Guidelines for School Location Planning." Staff Working Paper 308, World Bank, Washington, DC.

Group 5 Consulting Engineers. 2000. "Zambia Primary School Infrastructure Study: Final Report." Group 5 Consulting Engineers, Rotterdam, Netherlands.

———. 2005. "Review of Primary School Construction Standards, Cost, and Construction Management Capacity in Madagascar." Group 5 Consulting Engineers, Rotterdam, Netherlands.

———. 2006a. "Country Report: Burkina Faso." In *School Construction Study: A Comparative Analysis of Primary School Construction in Burkina Faso, Ghana, Mozambique, Uganda, Zambia.* Rotterdam, Netherlands: Group 5 Consulting Engineers.

———. 2006b. "Country Report: Ghana." In *School Construction Study: A Comparative Analysis of Primary School Construction in Burkina Faso, Ghana, Mozambique, Uganda, Zambia*. Rotterdam, Netherlands: Group 5 Consulting Engineers.

———. 2006c. "Country Report: Mozambique." In *School Construction Study: A Comparative Analysis of Primary School Construction in Burkina Faso, Ghana, Mozambique, Uganda, Zambia*. Rotterdam, Netherlands: Group 5 Consulting Engineers.

———. 2006d. "Country Report: Uganda." In *School Construction Study: A Comparative Analysis of Primary School Construction in Burkina Faso, Ghana, Mozambique, Uganda, Zambia*. Rotterdam, Netherlands: Group 5 Consulting Engineers.

———. 2006e. "Country Report: Zambia." In *School Construction Study: A Comparative Analysis of Primary School Construction in Burkina Faso, Ghana, Mozambique, Uganda, Zambia*. Rotterdam, Netherlands: Group 5 Consulting Engineers.

Gurney, Beth. 2004. *Sand and Soil: Earth's Building Blocks*. New York: Crabtree Publishing.

Haan, Hans Christian. 2001. *Training for Work in the Informal Sector: Fresh Evidence from Eastern and Southern Africa*. Turin, Italy: International Training Center, International Labour Organization.

Habitat Forum Berlin. 1987. *Learning from One Another*. Proceedings of Habitat Forum Berlin 1987, International Conference on Housing and Local Development, Urbanization Processes, and Development Options, Berlin, June 1–11.

Hammarskjöld, Dag. 1975. "Que faire? Un autre développement" [French translation]. Report prepared for the Seventh Extraordinary Session of the United Nations, New York.

Hanushek, Eric A. 1995. "Interpreting Recent Research on Schooling in Developing Countries." *World Bank Research Observer* 10 (2): 227–46.

Harris, E. C., and KPMG. 1995. "Construction Industry Development Study." Stage 1 Report, December 21.

Houben, Hugo, and Hubert Guillard. 1989. *Modernité de l'architecture de terre en Afrique: Réalisations des années 80*. Grenoble, France: CRATerre.

IEG [Independent Evaluation Group]. 2006a. *Engaging with Fragile States: An IEG Review of World Bank Support to Low-Income Countries under Stress*. Washington, DC: World Bank.

———. 2006b. *Malawi: Country Assistance Evaluation*. Report 36862. Washington, DC: World Bank.

ILO [International Labour Office]. 1982. *Pour une politique d'emploi au Sénégal: Esquisse d'une stratégie concertée et intégrée*. Addis Ababa, Ethiopia: ILO.

———. 2002a. *Decent Work and the Informal economy: Sixth Item on the Agenda*. Report VI, International Labour Conference, 90th Session. Geneva: ILO.

INSEE (Institut National de la Statistique et des Études Économiques). 2004. Statistics from website (http:////www.insee.fr).

Jack, William. 2001. "Social Investment Funds: An Organizational Approach to Improved Development Assistance." *World Bank Research Observer* 16 (1): 109–24.

Jadin, Olivier. 2004. "La situation des personnes handicapées au Bénin: Diagnostic préliminaire et propositions d'action." World Bank, Washington, DC. http://siteresources.worldbank.org/DISABILITY/Resources/Regions/Africa/BeninJadin.pdf.

Johanson, Richard K., and Arvil V. Adams. 2004. *Développement des qualifications professionnelles en Afrique subsaharienne*. Washington, DC: World Bank.

Kabuga. 2001. "Projet de construction du centre scolaire de Rusheshe." Mairie de Kabuga, Rwanda, December.

Kamto, Maurice. 2002. "Decentralisation communale et développement local au Cameroun: Étude critique juridique et propositions." Final Report, 2nd ed., Programme National de Développement Participatif, July.

Kane, Eileen. 2004. "Girls' Education in Africa: What Do We Know about Strategies That Work?" Africa Region Human Development Working Paper 73, World Bank, Washington, DC.

Kaufmann, Daniel, Aart Kraay, and Pablo Zoido-Lobatón. 2000. "Governance Matters: From Measurement to Action." *Finance and Development* 37 (2): 10–13.

Kayumba. 2006. Project Education III interoffice memorandum dated March 10.

Kessides, Christine. 1997. "World Bank Experience with the Provision of Infrastructure Services for the Urban Poor: Preliminary Identification and Review of Best Practices." Transportation, Water, and Urban Development Department, World Bank, Washington, DC.

Kingdon, Geeta. 1996. "The Quality and Efficiency of Public and Private Schools: A Case Study of Urban India." *Oxford Bulletin of Economics and Statistics* 58 (1): 55–80.

Kisamba-Mugerwa, Christine, Yakobo Moyini, Erissa Ochieng, and Henk Meijerink. 2001. "Uganda, SFG Evaluation." Final Report, Ministry of Education and Sports, Kampala, Uganda, March.

Klitgaard, Robert. 1998. *Controlling Corruption*. Santa Monica, CA: University of California Press.

Klitgaard, Robert, Ronald Maclean-Abaroa, and H. Lindsey Parris. 2000. *Corrupt Cities: A Practical Guide to Cure and Prevention*. Oakland, CA: ICS Press.

Knapp, Eberhard, Kaj Noschis, and Çelen Pasalar, eds. 2007. *School Building Design and Learning Performance with a Focus on Schools in Developing Countries*. Lausanne, Switzerland: Comportements.

Koskela, Lauri, and Ruben Vrijhoef. 2001. "The Prevalent Theory of Construction Is a Hindrance for Innovation." TNO Building and Construction Research, Delft, Netherlands.

Kremer, Michael. 1995. "Research on Schooling: What We Know and What We Don't—A Comment on Hanushek." *World Bank Research Observer* 10 (2): 247–54.

Kumar, Nalini. 2003a. "Community-Driven Development: Lessons from the Sahel—An Analytical Review." Working Paper, Operations Evaluation Department, World Bank, Washington, DC.

Kun, George. 2004. "Low Labor-Input Technology Utilization in the Construction Industry." Central Bureau of Statistics, Jerusalem, Israel.

Laking, Rob. 2006. "Agencies: Their Benefit and Risks." *OECD Journal on Budgeting* 4 (4): 9–30.

Langley, Philip, with Nazaire Sadom, Jean Gbedo, Zourkaïnén y Adamou, Boniface Fade, and Saraf Dine Ogbon. 2002. "Le développement dirigé par les communautés: Un bilan sommaire des actions menées au Bénin." Centre for Environment and Development in Africa, Cotonou, Benin.

Lavy, Victor Chaim. 1996. "School Supply Constraints and Children's Educational Outcomes in Rural Ghana." *Journal of Development Economics* 51 (2): 291–314.

Lecysyn, René. 1997. "Tchad évaluation technique de la première phase du volet 'constructions scolaires' du Projet de l'Enseignement Fondamental: Rapport deuxième partie." Direction des Projets Education, Ministère de l'Education Nationale, N'Djamena, Chad.

Lehman, Douglas. 2004. "Selected Implementation Strategies: Options for Accelerating Progress to EFA in Ethiopia." Paper prepared for the Ethiopia Education Forum, September 2004.

Lehman, Douglas, Piet Buys, Gaiwé François Atchina, Léo Laroche, and Bob Prouty. 2004. *The Rural Access Initiative: Shortening the Distance to Education for All in the African Sahel*. Washington, DC: World Bank.

Lesotho. 2005. "Kingdom of Lesotho Education Sector Strategic Plan, 2005–2015." Ministry of Education and Training, Maseru, Lesotho.

Levačić, Rosalind, and Peter Downes. 2004. *Formula Funding of Schools, Decentralization, and Corruption: A Comparative Analysis.* Paris: Institute for International Economic Planning.

Lewis, Maureen A., and Marlaine E. Lockheed. 2006. *Inexcusable Absence: Why 60 Million Girls Still Aren't in School and What to Do about It.* Washington DC: Center for Global Development.

Lipsmeier & Partner Architects. 2000. "Drawings and Costs." Documents collected by Serge Theunynck, Lipsmeier & Partner Architects.

Litvack, Jennie, Junaid Ahmad, and Richard Bird. 1998. "Rethinking Decentralization in Developing Countries." World Bank, Washington, DC.

Lloyd, Cynthia B., Sahar El Tawila, Wesley H. Clark, and Barbara S. Mensch. 2003. "The Impact of Educational Quality on School Exit in Egypt." *Comparative Education Review* 47 (4): 444–67.

Lo, Fu-Chen, and Yue-Man Yeung, eds. 1998. *Globalization of the World of Large Cities.* Tokyo: United Nations University Press.

Lockheed, Marlaine E., and Adriaan M. Verspoor. 1991. *Improving Primary Education in Developing Countries.* Washington, DC: Oxford University Press.

Ly, Serigne. 1992. "Problématique des constructions scolaires au Sénégal." Ingénieur Génie Civil, Chef de la Division des Constructions et de l'Equipement Scolaires, Dakar, Senegal.

Lynch, James. 1994. "Provision for Children with Special Educational Needs in the Asia Region." Asia Technical Paper 261, World Bank, Washington, DC.

Maclean, Andrew. 2005. *Review of DFID Technical Assistance to the Unit for Construction and Equipment of Schools (UCES).* London: DFID.

Madagascar. 2006. "Rapport de suivi du Plan Education pour Tous." First draft, Antananarivo, Republic of Madagascar, March 15.

Madecor Career System. 2007. "Second Education Development Project (Grant No H0840-LA) Component 1: Evaluation of Impact of Community-Based Interventions—Mid-Term Evaluation." Madecor Career System, Vientiane, Lao PDR.

Manikowski, Stanislaw, and Ibrahima Hathié. 2005. "Projet National d'Infrastructures Rurales Première Phase (PNIR1): Rapport d'achèvement." École National d'Économie Appliquée, Dakar, Senegal.

Mason, Andrew D. 1994. "Schooling Decisions, Basic Education, and the Poor in Rural Java." PhD thesis, Food Research Institute, Stanford University, Stanford, CA.

Mason, Andrew D., and Scott D. Rozelle. 1998. *Schooling Decisions, Basic Education, and the Poor in Rural Java.* Washington, DC: World Bank.

Mauritania. 2006. "Cadre Global de Dépenses à Moyen Terme 2007–2009." Draft Zero, Ministère des Affaires Economiques et du Développement, Ministère des Finances, Nouakchott, Mauritania.

May, John, Soumana Harouna, and Jean-Pierre Guengant. 2004o. "Nourrir, éduquer et soigner tous les Nigériens: La démographie en perspective." Africa Region Human Development Working Paper 63, World Bank, Washington, DC.

Maynard, Kimberly. 2005f. "Community-Driven Conflict Recovery: From Reconstruction to Development." World Bank, Washington, DC.

Mbungu, Mbuba. 1999. "Procurement and Financial Procedures Manual for Use by Community-Based Organizations." World Bank, Accra Ghana.

Meadows, Donella H., Dennis L. Meadows, Jørgen Randers, and William W. Behrens. 1972. *The Limits to Growth.* Washington DC: Potomac Associates.

MEMP [Ministère de l'Enseignement Maternel et Primaire]. 2007. "Enseignement primaire 2005–2006: Public et privé." Ministère de l'Enseignement Maternel et Primaire, Cotonou, Benin.

MENRS [Ministère de l'Education Nationale et de la Recherce Scientifique]. 2007. "Programme Éducation pour Tous: Stratégie de construction d'écoles." MENRS, Antananrivo, Madagascar.

MESTRS [Ministère de l'Éducation, de la Science, de la Technologie et de la Recherche Scientifique]. 2006. Documents remis par le MESTRS à la mission. World Bank, Rwanda, October.

Michaelowa, Katharina, and Annika Wechtler. 2005. "The Cost-Effectiveness of Inputs in Primary Education: Insights from the Literature and Recent Student Surveys for Sub-Saharan Africa." Background paper for the Association for the Development of Education in Africa biennial meeting, January 2006. Operations Evaluation Department, World Bank, Washington, DC.

Mingat, Alain. 2003. "Eléments analytiques et factuels pour une politique de la qualité dans le primaire en Afrique subsaharienne dans le contexte de l'Education pour Tous." World Bank, Washington, DC, October.

Mingat, Alain, Ramahatra Rakotomalala, and Jee-Peng Tan. 2002a. "Financing Education for All by 2015: Simulations for 33 African Countries." Africa Region Human Development Working Paper, World Bank, Washington, DC.

Mingat, Alain, and Bruno Suchaut. 1998. "Une analyse économique comparative des systèmes éducatifs africains." Rapport réalisé pour le compte du Ministère Français de la Coopération et du Développement. Institut de Recherche sur l'Économie de l'Éducation, Université de Bourgogne, Dijon, France, November.

NaCSA [National Commission for Social Action]. 2003. *Community-Driven Programme: Direct Community Financing.* Freetown, Sierra Leone: NaCSA.

Narayan, Deepa. 2003. *Autonomisation et reduction de la pauvreté.* Montreal, QC: Editions Saint-Martin.

Ndegwa, Stephen N. 2002. "La décentralisation en Afrique: Vue d'ensemble." World Bank, Washington, DC, November.

NISER [Nigerian Institute of Social and Economic Research]. 2004. "Background Study for the Mid-Term Review of the Community-Based Poverty Reduction Project." Study conducted for the National Planning Commission and the World Bank, NISER, Niamey, Niger.

Neufert, Ernst. 2006. *Les éléments des projets de construction.* 9th ed. Paris: Dunod.

NMFA [Netherlands Ministry of Foreign Affairs]. 2003. *Local Solutions to Global Challenges: Towards Effective Partnership in Basic Education, Joint Evaluation of External Support to Basic Education in Developing Countries.* The Hague, Netherlands: NMFA. http://www.dfid.gov.uk/pubs/files/basic-education-final-report.pdf.

Norton, John. 1997. *Building with Earth: A Handbook.* 2nd ed. London: ITDG Publishing.

NUSAF [Northern Uganda Social Action Fund]. 2007. "Northern Uganda Social Action Fund: CDI Sub-projects Funded as at 31st July 2007." NUSAF, Kampala, Uganda.

OECD [Organisation for Economic Co-operation and Development]. 2007. "Statistical Annex." In *Development Co-operation Report 2006.* Table 2. Paris: OECD.

OED [Operations Evaluation Department]. 2002. "Social Funds: A Review of World Bank Experience." Report 23668. OED, World Bank, Washington, DC.

———. 2004. *Books, Buildings, and Learning Outcomes: An Impact Evaluation of World Bank Support to Basic Education in Ghana.* Washington, DC: World Bank.

———. 2005a. *Capacity Building in Africa: An OED Evaluation of World Bank Support.* Washington, DC: World Bank.

———. 2005b. "Niger: First Education Project (Cr 1151-NIR), Primary Education Development Project (Credit 1740-NIR), Basic Education Sector Project (Hybrid) (Credit 2618-NIR)—Project Performance Assessment Report." Report 31657, World Bank, Washington, DC.

———. 2005c. *The Effectiveness of World Bank Support of Community-Based and-Driven Development: An OED Evaluation*. Washington, DC: World Bank. http://www.worldbank.org/oed/cbdcdd.

Okidi, John A., and Madina Guloba. 2006. "Decentralization and Development: Emerging Issues from Uganda's Experience." Occasional Paper 31, Economic Policy Research Centre, Kampala, Uganda.

Olivier, Franco. 2004. "Audit technique du Programme de Développement Communautaire (FID IV) à Madagascar: Rapport final." Fonds d'Intervention pour le Développement, Antananarivo, Madagascar.

Olken, Benjamin A. 2005. "Monitoring Corruption: Evidence from a Field Experiment in Indonesia." Harvard University and National Bureau of Economic Research, Cambridge, MA.

Olowu, Dele. 2003. "Local Democracy, Taxation, and Multi-level Governance in Africa." Paper prepared for the Norwegian Association for Development Research Annual Conference on Politics and Poverty, Workshop on Taxation, Accountability, and Poverty, Oslo, Norway, October 23–24.

OSEO [Oeuvre Suisse d'Entraide Ouvrière]. 2007. "Devis estimatif pour la réalisation d'un complexe scolaire." Représentation au Burkina Faso. Document remis à Serge Theunynck. February 2007.

Ould Cheik, Abdel Weddoud. 1994. *Mission pour l'identification des mécanismes de financement des constructions scolaires des collectivités*. Rapport de mission, Ministère du Plan, Projet de Restructuration du Secteur de l'Éducation, Bureau de Coordination du Projet, Nouakchott, Mauritania, March.

Oumarou, Boubacar. 1993. "Stratégie de construction des classes primaires." Présentation de la délégation du Niger au séminaire sur les pratiques de construction des infrastructures sociales dans les pays du Sahel à Dakar. October 19–22.

Owen, Daniel, and Julie Van Domelen. 1998. "Getting an Earful: A Review of Beneficiary Assessment of Social Funds." Social Protection Discussion Paper 9816, World Bank, Washington, DC.

Parajuli, Dilip. 2001. "What Is Driving Educational Ineffectiveness in Kenya? The Role of Economic Inefficiency, Institutional Corruption, and Poverty." Transparency International–Kenya, Nairobi, Kenya.

Paxson, Christina, and Norbert Schady. 1999. "Do School Facilities Matter? The Case of the Peruvian Social Fund (FONCODES)." Policy Research Working Paper 2229, World Bank, Washington, DC.

Pichvai, Ahita. 2004. "Assessment of School Infrastructure Needed to Support the Expansion of Basic Education." CfBT Education Trust, Rwandan Education Sector Support Program, Ministry of Education, Science, Technology, and Scientific Research, Kigali, Rwanda.

PKF Consulting. 2003. "SFG Programme: Value for Money Audit." Draft Report, PKF Consulting, Kampala, Uganda.

Plan Guinée. 2001. *Constructions dans les Zones de Yomou et Bowe: Détail des coûts*. Plan Guinée, Conakry, Guinea, January 13.

PNDCC [Projet National d'appui au Développement Conduit par les Communautés]. 2007. "Comparaison de prix par mètre carré par type de financement." Executive Secretariat, PNDCC, Cotonou, Benin, June 27.

Ratcliffe, Mike, and Murray Macrae. 1999. "Sector Wide Approaches to Education: A Strategic Analysis." Education Research, Serial 32, U.K. Department for International Development, London.

Rawlings, Laura, Lynne Sherburne Benz, and Julie Van Domelen. 2001. "Letting Communities Take the Lead: A Cross-Country Evaluation of Social Fund Performance." World Bank, Washington, DC.

Richman, Judah Lee. 1994. "Accelerated Methods of Residential Construction: Prefabrication Re-evaluated." M.S. thesis, Massachusetts Institute of Technology, Cambridge, MA.

Salmen, Lawrence F. 1995. "Beneficiary Assessment: An Approach Described." Social Assessment Paper 23, World Bank, Washington, DC.

Salmen, Lawrence F., assisted by Misgana Amelga. 1998. "Implementing Beneficiary Assessment in Education: A Guide for Practitioners (with Examples from Brazil)." Social Development Paper 25, World Bank, Washington, DC.

Schaffner, Julie. 2003. "The Determinants of Schooling Investments among Primary School-Aged Children in Ethiopia." Human Development Department, Africa Region, World Bank, Washington, DC.

SCHL [Société Canadienne d'Hypothèque et de Logement]. 2003. *Guide des codes de construction résidentiels des États-Unis à l'intention des exportateurs canadiens*. Kanata, ON: SCHL.

Schumacher, Ernst Friedrich. 1973. *Small Is Beautiful: Economics as If People Mattered*. London: Harper Perennial.

———. 1980. *Good Work*. Paris: Editions du Seuil.

Sey, Haddy. 2001. "Quality Education for All in Senegal: Including the Excluded." Background paper for the Quality Education for All Project, World Bank, Washington, DC.

Sey, Haddy, Sudesh Mukhpadhyay, Evelyne Laurin, and Sourav Banerjee. 2003. *Enhancing Educational Opportunities for Vulnerable People: Exploring UNICEF SWASTHH for Support—A Rapid Assessment*. Washington, DC: Creative Associates International.

Sinke, Leo. 2003. "The Gambia: Third Education Project—Contribution to the Aide Memoire." World Bank, Washington DC.

Siri, Gabriel, and Piet Goovaerts. 2002. "Analysis of the Costs and Benefits of Public Works Programs in Cape Verde." National Poverty Alleviation Program, Social Sector Development Project, Praia, Cape Verde.

SNIES [Service National des Infrastructures et Equipements Scolaires]. 1990. *Programme experimental d'écoles avec les collectivités rurales*. SNIES, Ministère de l'Enseignement Pré-Universitaire et de l'Education Civique, Conakry, Guinea.

———. 1999. " Atelier sur la rehabilitation des infrastructures scolaires, du 3 au 7 mai 1999." Documents préparatoires aux travaux de l'atelier. SNIES, Ministère de l'Enseignement Pre-Universitaire et de l'Education Civique, Conakry, Guinea.

SNV and CEDELO [Netherlands Development Organization and Centre de Developpement Local]. 2004. "La décentralisation au Mali: du discours à la practique." Décentralisation et gouvernance locale bulletin 358, Institut Royal des Tropiques, Amsterdam, May 4.

SP-SRP [Secrétariat Permanent de la Stratégie de la Pauvreté]. 2005. "Deuxième rapport de mise en œuvre de la stratégie de réduction de la pauvreté." SP-SRP, Ministère de l'Economie et des Finances, Conakry, Guinea.

Steinfeld, Edward. 2005. "Education for All: The Cost of Accessibility." Education Notes, World Bank, Washington, DC.

Strand, Arne, Hege Toje, Alef Morten Jerve, and Ingrid Samset. 2003. "Community-Driven Development in Contexts of Conflicts." Concept paper, Chr. Michelsen Institute, Bergen, Norway.

Sugii, Takashi. 1998. "The Construction Sector Suffers from Declining Labor Productivity." Industrial Research Department, NLI Research Institute, Tokyo.

Synergy International. 1995. "Rapport de mission d'audit technique du volet 'construction de salles de classe' couvrant la période novembre 1995." Synergy International, Brussels, Belgium.

———. 1997. "Preparation of a Nation-Wide Classroom Construction Program under the Third Education Project." Synergy International, Brussels, Belgium, and Ministry of Education, Banjul, The Gambia.

_____. 2000. "Rapport de mission d'audit technique du volet 'construction de salles de classe,' couvrant la période novembre 1995–June 2000." Synergy International, Brussels, Belgium.

Tan, Jee-Peng, Julia Lane, and Paul Coustere. 1997. "Putting Inputs to Work in Elementary Schools: What Can Be Done in the Philippines?" *Economic Development and Cultural Change* 45 (4): 857–79.

Theisen, Gary. 2002. "Education Sector Development Project: Ethiopia." Supervision Mission, October 22–November 10, Addis Ababa, Ethiopia.

Theunynck, Serge. 1987. *Economie de la construction à Nouakchott*. Paris: L'Harmattan.

_____. 1993. "Création d'une capacité nationale de réalisation des infrastructures sociales de base." Rapport general, Direction des Projets Éducation-Formation, Nouakchott, Mauritania.

_____. 1994. *Economie de l'habitat et de la construction au Sahel*. Vols. 1 and 2. Paris: L'Harmattan.

_____. 1995. "Preparation of the Third Elementary Education Project." Annex to the aide memoire for civil works, World Bank, Washington, DC, February–March.

_____. 1999. "Coût des constructions scolaires: Recueil de données par pays et par projet." Projet d'Appui aux Collectivités pour la Construction de Salles de Classe, Direction des Projets Éducation-Formation, Nouakchott, Mauritania, October 25.

_____. 2000. "Projet PASE-II: Supervision Report." Technical Note, World Bank, Washington, DC.

_____. 2002. "School Construction in Developing Countries: What Do We Know?" World Bank, Washington, DC.

_____. 2005. "Note technique sur les performances de l'AGECABO." Projet de Développement du Secteur Social, World Bank, Washington, DC.

_____. 2006. "Note sur l'approche construction modulaire industrialisée (CMI)." Projet d'Appui à la Réduction de la Pauvreté, Construction de Salles de Classe, World Bank, Washington, DC.

_____. 2007. "Universal Secondary Education (USE): Universal Primary Education and Training (UPPET)." Aide memoire, mission regarding school construction in Uganda, World Bank, Washington, DC.

Transparency International. 2002. "Corruption Fighters' Tool Kit: Civil Society Experiences and Emerging Strategies." Transparency International, Berlin.

_____. 2005a. *Un avenir dérobé: La corruption dans l'éducation—Dix experiences vécues à travers le monde*. Berlin: Transparency International

_____. 2005b. *Global Corruption Report 2005: Special Focus—Corruption in Construction and Post-conflict Reconstruction*. Berlin: Transparency International.

UNCDF [United Nations Capital Development Fund]. 2006. *Delivering the Goods: Building Local Government Capacity to Achieve the Millennium Development Goals—A Practitioner's Guide for UNDCF Experience in Least Developed Countries*. New York: UNCDF.

UNCHS [United Nations Center for Human Settlements]. 2001. *Cities in a Globalizing World. Global Report on Human Settlements 2001*. London: Earthscan.

UNESCO [United Nations Educational, Scientific, and Cultural Organization]. 1984. "UNESCO-FADES Feasibility Study on the Development of Low-Cost Educational Buildings and Facilities in Djibouti, Mauritania, Somalia, Sudan, PDR Yemen, and Yemen AR." UNESCO, Noukachott, Mauritania, and Dakar, Senegal.

_____. 1986. *Normes et standards des constructions scolaires*. Paris: Division des Politiques et de la Planification de l'Education, UNESCO.

_____. 1990. "Projet de construction de prototypes d'écoles primaires en milieu rural en Guinée." Final report, UNESCO Regional Bureau, Dakar, Senegal et la Direction de la

Coopération Technique et des Projets, Ministère de l'Education Nationale, Conakry, Guinea.

———. 2005. *EPT: Repères pour l'action—Éducation pour tous en Afrique*. Senegal, Dakar: Bureau Régional à Dakar, UNESCO.

United Nations. 2002. *Report of the International Conference on Financing for Development: Monterrey, Mexico, March 18–22*. New York: United Nations.

———. 2005. "2005 World Summit Outcome." Resolution 60/1, adopted by the General Assembly, 60th Session, United Nations, New York, October 24.

Vajpeyi, Kabir. 2005. "Building as Learning Aid: Developing School Space as a Learning Resource." Education Group, Human Resource Network, South Asia Human Development Sector, World Bank, Washington, DC.

Van Domelen, Julie, and Randa El-Rashidi. 2001. "A Review of Social Funds in Africa: Implementation Experience and Issues for the Future." Human Development Network, World Bank, Washington, DC.

Van Donge, Jankees. 2000. "Nurtured from Above and Growing from the Roots: Social Funds and Decentralization in Zambia and Malawi." Institute of Social Studies, The Hague, Netherlands.

Van Imschoot, Marc. 2004a. "Rapport du premier audit technique de la sous-composante d'intervention sur les dégâts cycloniques." Fonds d'Intervention pour le Développement, Antananarivo, Madagascar, October 1–19.

———. 2004b. "Rapport du 2ème audit technique de la sous-composante d'intervention sur les dégâts cycloniques." Fonds d'Intervention pour le Développement, Antananarivo, Madagascar, October 1–19.

Varghese, N. V. 1995. "School Facilities and Learner Achievement: Towards a Methodology of Analysing School Facilities in India." *Perspectives in Education* 11 (2): 97–108.

VSCP [Village Community Support Project]. 2007. Data received via personal communication, March 2007.

Wade, Magatte. 2004. "Overview of Senegal's AGETIP Model for Jobs Creation," Paper presented at the Meeting on Youth and Employment in West Africa, Goree Institute, Goree Island, Senegal, February 12–13.

Walker, Ian, Rafael del Cid, Fidel Ordoñez, and Florencia Rodríguez. 1999. "Ex-Post Evaluation of the Honduran Social Investment Fund (FHIS2)." ESA Consultores, Tegucigalpa, Honduras.

Wilson, Michael. 2006a. "Family and Community Contributions to School Construction and Maintenance: A Review of the Fast Track Initiative Countries." World Bank, Washington, DC.

———. 2006b. "The Fast Track Initiative and School Facilities: Achieving the Second Millennium Development Goals." PowerPoint briefing presented at the 12th Architecture and Behaviour Colloquium, Lausanne, Switzerland, March 29–April 1.

———. 2006c. "Moving Towards Free Basic Education: Policy Issues and Implementation Challenges." United Children's Fund and World Bank, Washington, DC, January 2006.

Wolfskill, Lyle A., Waine A. Dunlop, and Bob M. Galloway. 2005. *Handbook for Building Homes of Earth*. Honolulu, HI: University Press of the Pacific.

World Bank. 1979. "Pakistan: Primary Education Project, Credit 892-PAK—Staff Appraisal Report." Report 2307-PAK, World Bank, Washington, DC.

———. 1980. "Bangladesh: Fourth Education Project (1980–90)—Staff Appraisal Report." Report 2964-BD, World Bank, Washington, DC, May 27.

———. 1981. "Niger: Education Project—Staff Appraisal Report." Report 3047-NIR, World Bank, Washington, DC, May 4.

———. 1985a. "Bangladesh: Second Primary Education Projects." Report 5363-BD, World Bank, Washington, DC.

_____. 1985b. "Pakistan: Second Primary Education Project (Cr. 1602-PAK)—Staff Appraisal Report," Report 5363-PAK, World Bank, Washington, DC, May 1.

_____. 1986. "Niger: Primary Education Development Project, Credit 1740-NIR—Staff Appraisal Report." Report 6115-NIR, World Bank, Washington, DC, October 28.

_____. 1987a. "Madagascar: Second Education Project (Credit 663-MAG)—Project Completion Report." Report 6774-MAG, World Bank, Washington, DC, May 22.

_____. 1987b. "Pakistan: Fourth Education Project/Primary Education Project (Cr. 892-PAK)—Project Completion Report." Report 6827-PAK, World Bank, Washington, DC, June 19.

_____. 1987c. "Pakistan: Third Primary Education Project, Credit 1821-PAK—Staff Appraisal Report." Report 6492-PAK, World Bank, Washington, DC.

_____. 1988. "Mauritania: Education Sector Restructuring Project—Staff Appraisal Report." Report 7213-MAU, World Bank, Washington, DC, June 28.

_____. 1989a. "Brazil: Northeast Basic Education (Loan 1867-BR) Project Completion Report." Report 8266-BR, World Bank, Washington, DC, December 29.

_____. 1989b. "Involving Nongovernmental Organization in Bank-Supported Activities." Operational Directive 14.70, World Bank, Washington, DC.

_____. 1989c. "Mali: Education Sector Consolidation Project—Report and Recommendation of the President of the International Development Association." World Bank, Washington, DC, Report P-25010-MLI, May 17.

_____. 1990a. "Bangladesh: Fourth (Primary) Education Project (Credit 1054-BD)—Project Implementation Report." Report 8355-BD, World Bank, Washington, DC, February 6.

_____. 1990b. "The Gambia: Education Sector Project—Staff Appraisal Report." Report 8359-GM, World Bank, Washington, DC, April 30.

_____. 1990c. "Pakistan: Sindh Primary Education Development Program—Staff Appraisal Report." Report 8178-PAK, World Bank, Washington, DC, February 6.

_____. 1990d. "Philippines: Second Education Project—Staff Appraisal Report." Report 8395-PH, World Bank, Washington, DC, May 30.

_____. 1991a. "Burkina Faso: Fourth Education Project, Cr. 244-BUR—Staff Appraisal Report." Report 9119-BUR, World Bank, Washington, DC, April 24.

_____. 1991b. "Senegal: Second Human Resource Development Project—Implementation Completion Report." Report 21474-SE, World Bank, Washington, DC.

_____. 1992a. *Étude sectorielle régionale: Pratiques de construction des infrastructures sociales dans les pays du Sahel*. Vol. 1, Report 10294-AFR. Washington, DC: World Bank. April 6.

_____. 1992b. "Niger. First Education Project (Credit 1151-NIR): Project Completion Report." Report 10786, World Bank, Washington, DC, June 26.

_____. 1993a. "Chad: Basic Education Project (Education V), Credit 2501-CD—Staff Appraisal Report." Report 11680-CD, World Bank, Washington, DC, April 16.

_____. 1993b. *Guide des pratiques de construction des infrastructures sociales dans les pays du Sahel: Draft du nouveau guide suite au séminaire de Dakar, Région Afrique, Département du Sahel*. Divisions Population et Resources Humaines et Infrastructures and Synergy International, Brussels, Belgium.

_____. 1993c. "Pakistan: Baluchistan Primary Education Program—Staff Appraisal Report." Report 11403-PAK, World Bank, Washington, DC.

_____. 1993d. "Rapport d'évaluation des procédures de passation de marchés au Sénégal." World Bank, Dakar, Senegal.

_____. 1993e. "Senegal: Second Human Resource Development Project (Education V)—Staff Appraisal Report." Report 11254-SE, World Bank, Washington, DC, February 11.

_____. 1993f. "Vietnam: Primary Education Project (1993-2001), Cr. 2548-VN—Staff Appraisal Report." Report 12203, World Bank, Washington, DC.

_____. 1993g. "India. Uttar-Pradesh Basic Education Project. Staff Appraisal Report." Report No. 11746-IN, World Bank, Washington, DC.

_____. 1994a. "Niger: Basic Education Sector Project (Hybrid)—Report and Recommendation of the President." Report P-6328-NIR, World Bank, Washington, DC, May 5.

_____. 1994b. "Mexico. Basic Education Development Project. Project Appraisal Document." Report No. 17535, World Bank, Washington, DC.

_____. 1995a. "Burkina Faso: Primary Education Development Project—Education III (Cr. 1598-BUR)." Report 14464-BUR, World Bank, Washington, DC, May 4.

_____. 1995b. "Guinea: Education Sector Adjustment Credit (Credit 2155-GUI)—Implementation Completion Report." Report 14617-GUI, World Bank, Washington, DC, June 16.

_____. 1995c. "Guinea. Equity and School Improvement Project: Staff Appraisal Report." Report 13472-GUI, World Bank, Washington, DC, April 7.

_____. 1995d. "Malawi: Primary Education Project—Staff Appraisal Report." Report 15127-MAI, World Bank, Washington, DC, December 21.

_____. 1995e. "Mauritania: General Education Project (Cr-MAU), PAD." Report 13569, World Bank, Washington, DC.

_____. 1995f. "Pakistan: Second Primary Education Project (Cr. 1602-PAK), Project Completion Report." Report 14218-PAK, World Bank, Washington, DC, April 3.

_____. 1995g. "Senegal: Primary Education Development Project (Credit 1735-SE)—Project Implementation Report." Report 14443-SE, World Bank, Washington, DC, May 4.

_____. 1995h. *Working with NGOs: A Practical Guide to Operational Collaboration between the World Bank and Non-governmental Organizations.* Washington, DC: Operation Policy Department, World Bank.

_____. 1996a. "Eritrea: Community Development Fund Project—Staff Appraisal Report." Report 14937-ER, World Bank, Washington, DC, January 30.

_____. 1996b. "Mali: Education Sector Consolidation Project (Cr. 2054-MLI)—Implementation Completion Report." Report 15720-MLI, World Bank, Washington, DC, June 10.

_____. 1996c. "Mauritania: Education Restructuring Project (Cr 1943-MAU)—Implementation Completion Report." Report 15739-MAU, World Bank, Washington, DC.

_____. 1996d. "Niger: Primary Education Development Project (1986–95), Cr. 1740-NIR—Implementation Completion Report." Report 15748-NIR, World Bank, Washington, DC, June 14.

_____. 1996e. "Philippines: Second Elementary Education Project (Cr. 3244-PH)—Implementation Completion Report." Report 16177-PH, World Bank, Washington, DC, December 30.

_____. 1996f. "Philippines: Third Elementary Education Project—Staff Appraisal Report." Report 15888-PH, World Bank, Washington, DC, October 25.

_____. 1997. "Bangladesh: General Education Project (Credit 2118-BD)—Implementation Completion Report." Report 16729-BD, World Bank, Washington, DC, June 19.

_____. 1998a. "The Gambia: Third Education Sector Program—Project Appraisal Document." Report 17903-GM, World Bank, Washington, DC, August 7.

_____. 1998b. "Madagascar: Education Sector Development Project—Project Appraisal Document." Report 16666-MAG, World Bank, Washington, DC, February 13.

_____. 1998c. "The Use of Social Investment Funds as an Instrument for Combating Poverty." Strategy Paper POV-104, World Bank, Washington, DC.

_____. 1999a. "Burkina Faso: Education IV Project (Credit 2244-BUR)—Implementation Completion Report." Report 19485-BUR, World Bank, Washington, DC, June 28.

_____. 1999b. "Cape Verde: Education and Training Consolidation and Modernization Project (PROMEF)—Project Appraisal Document." Report 18581-CV, World Bank, Washington, DC, April 30.

_____. 1999c. "The Gambia: Education Sector Project (Credit 2142-GM)—Implementation Completion Report." Report 19269-GM, World Bank, Washington, DC, June 29.

_____. 1999d. "Guinea: Village Communities Support Program (Phase 1)—Project Appraisal Document." Report 17934-GUI, World Bank, Washington, DC, January 27.

_____. 1999e. "Mozambique: Education Sector Strategic Program (ESSP)—Project Appraisal Document." Report 18681-MOZ, World Bank, Washington, DC, January 22.

_____. 1999f. "Mozambique: Second Education Project (Credit 2200-MOZ)—Implementation Completion Report." Report 19524-MOZ, World Bank, Washington, DC, June 18.

_____. 1999g. "Senegal: National Rural Infrastructure Program—Project Appraisal Document." Report No. 19663-SE, World Bank, Washington, DC, December 20.

_____. 1999h. "Mexico. Second Primary Education Project. Project Appraisal Document." Report No. 12529. World Bank, Washington, DC.

_____. 2000a. "Angola: Second Social Action Fund Project (FAS-II)—Project Appraisal Document." Report 20474-ANG, World Bank, Washington, DC, May 26.

_____. 2000b. "Mali: Education Sector Expenditure Program." World Bank, Washington, DC.

_____. 2000c. "Second Conference of Social Funds." World Bank, Washington, DC, June 5–7.

_____. 2000d. "Senegal: Quality Education for All Program in Support of the First Phase of the Ten-Year Education and Training Program (PDEF)—Project Appraisal Document." Report 19610-SE, World Bank, Washington, DC, March.

_____. 2000e. "Brazil. Second Northeast Education Project. Project Completion Report." Report No. 8266-BR, World Bank, Washington, DC.

_____. 2001a. *Education and Health in Sub-Saharan Africa: A Review of Sector-Wide Approaches*. Washington, DC: World Bank.

_____. 2001b. "India: Uttar Pradesh Basic Education Project, Cr. 25090-IN—Implementation Completion Report." Report No. 21754-IN, World Bank, Washington, DC.

_____. 2001c. "Guinea: Education for All Project in Support of the First Phase of the Education for All Program—Project Appraisal Document." Report 20405-GUI, World Bank, Washington, DC.

_____. 2001d. "Le système éducatif Mauretanien: Eléments d'analyse pour instruire des politiques nouvelles." Africa Region Human Development Working Paper 15, World Bank, Washington, DC, November.

_____. 2001e. "Malawi: Primary Education Project—Implementation Completion Report." Report No. 22167-MAI, World Bank, Washington, DC, June 28.

_____. 2001f. "Mauritania: Education Sector Development National Program in Support of the First Phase of the Ten-Year Education Program—Project Appraisal Document." Report 22529-MAU, World Bank, Washington, DC, September 26.

_____. 2001g. "Nigeria: Community-Based Poverty Reduction Project—Project Appraisal Document." Report 21396-UNI, World Bank, Washington, DC, September.

_____. 2001h. "Senegal: Second Human Resources Development Project (Education V, PDRH2)—Implementation Completion Report." Report No. 21472, World Bank, Washington, DC, March.

_____. 2002a. "Eritrea: Community Development Fund Project (Cr. 28230)—Implementation Completion Report." Report 22694, World Bank, Washington, DC, May 6.

_____. 2002b. "Eritrea: Community Development Fund Project (Cr. 28230)—Project Performance Assessment Report." Report 24418, World Bank, Washington, DC, June 24.

_____. 2002c. "Fiduciary Management for Community-Driven Development Projects: A Reference Guide." World Bank, Washington, DC.

_____. 2002d. "Mauritania: Urban Infrastructure and Pilot Decentralization Project—Implementation Completion Report." Report 24302-MAU, World Bank, Washington, DC, June 24.

_____. 2002e. "Niger: Basic Education Sector Project (Hybrid)—Implementation Completion Report (DA-26180). Report 24311-NIR, World Bank, Washington, DC, June.

_____. 2002f. "Senegal: Primary Education Development Project (Credit 1735-SE), Second Resources Development Project (Credit 2473-SE)—A Review of Investments in Education and Performance Assessment Reports." Report 23715-SE, World Bank, Washington, DC, February 21.

_____. 2002g. "World Bank–Civil Society Collaboration: Progress Report for Fiscal Years 2000 and 2001." World Bank, Washington, DC.

_____. 2003a. "Anticorruption Guide: Developing an Anti-Corruption Program for Reducing Fiduciary Risks in New Projects—Lessons from Indonesia." Jakarta, Indonesia, World Bank, March 15.

_____. 2003b. "Chad: Education Sector Reform Project—Project Appraisal Document." Report 23797-CD, World Bank, Washington, DC, February 14.

_____. 2003c. *Education in Rwanda: Rebalancing Resources to Accelerate Post-conflict Development and Poverty Reduction*. Washington, DC: World Bank.

_____. 2003d. "Guinea: 20 Years of IDA Assistance: Second Education Project—Education Sector Adjustment Credit, Higher Education Management Support Project, Pre-service, Pre-service Teacher Education Project." Report 26245-GUI, World Bank, Washington, DC, June 26.

_____. 2003e. "Guinea: Equity and School Improvement Project—Implementation Completion Report." Report 25808-GUI, World Bank, Washington, DC, June 18.

_____. 2003f. "Mozambique: Decentralized Planning and Financing Project—Project Appraisal Document." Report 26365-MOZ, World Bank, Washington, DC, October 15.

_____. 2003g. "Niger: Basic Education Project—Project Appraisal Document." Report 25688-NIR, World Bank, Washington, DC, June 20.

_____. 2003h. "Recommendations visant à renforcer le Programme Anti- Corruption: Mali." Africa Region, World Bank, Washington, DC, March.

_____. 2004a. "Angola: Second Social Action Fund Project (FAS-II)—Implementation Completion Report." Report 29162, World Bank, Washington, DC, August 17.

_____. 2004b. Benin: National Community-Driven Development Support Project (PNDCC)—Project Appraisal Report." Report 29165-BJ, World Bank, Washington, DC, September 9.

_____. 2004c. "Benin: Social Fund Project—Implementation Completion Report." Report 29078, World Bank, Washington, DC, June 7.

_____. 2004d. *Books, Buildings, and Learning Outcomes: An Impact Evaluation of World Bank Support to Basic Education in Ghana*. Washington, DC: Operations Evaluations Department, World Bank.

_____. 2004e. "Cost, Financing, and School Effectiveness in Malawi: Country Status Report." Africa Region Human Development Working Paper 78, World Bank, Washington, DC.

_____. 2004f. *Education in Ethiopia: Strengthening the Foundation for Sustainable Progress*. Washington, DC: World Bank.

_____. 2004g. "Fighting Corruption at the Local Level: The Case of Kecamatan Development Project." PowerPoint presentation prepared for the Local Development Conference, World Bank, Washington, DC, June 17.

_____. 2004h. "La dynamique des scolarisations au Niger: Evaluation pour un développement durable." Africa Region Human Development Working Paper, World Bank, Washington, DC, July.

_____. 2004i. "Local Development Discussion Paper." Paper prepared for the International Conference on Local Development, Human Development, Social Development, and Public Sector Management Networks, World Bank, Washington, DC, June 16–18.

_____. 2004j. "Madagascar: First Poverty Reduction Support Project." Report 29376-MAG, World Bank, Washington, DC, June 23.

_____. 2004k. "Mainstreaming Anti-Corruption Activities in World Bank Assistance, A Review of Progress Since 1997." Report No. 29620, Operations Evaluation Department, World Bank, Washington, DC, July 14.

_____. 2004l. *Procurement Guidelines under IBRD Loans and IDA Credits*. May 2004, Revised October 1, 2006. Washington, DC: World Bank.

_____. 2004m. *Strategic Framework for Assistance to Africa: IDA and the Emerging Partnership Model*. Washington, DC: World Bank.

_____. 2004n. "Uganda: Local Government Development Program— Implementation Completion Report." Report 30284, World Bank, Washington, DC, November 23.

_____. 2004o. *World Bank Development Report 2004: Making Services Work for Poor People*. Washington, DC: World Bank.

_____. 2005a. "Building on Free Primary Education: Primary and Secondary Education in Lesotho—A Country Status Report." Africa Region Human Development Working Paper 101, World Bank, Washington, DC.

_____. 2005b. "Burkina Faso: Administration Capacity Building Project— Project Appraisal Document." Report 29909-BF, Africa Region, World Bank, Washington, DC, February 17.

_____. 2005c. "Burkina Faso: Fifth Poverty Reduction Support Operation— Program Document." Report 31342-BF, World Bank, Washington, DC, April 7.

_____. 2005d. "Cape Verde: Social Sector Development Project—Implementation Completion Report." World Bank, Washington, DC, August 22.

_____. 2005e. *Education in the Democratic Republic of Congo: Priorities and Options for Regeneration*. Washington, DC: World Bank.

_____. 2005f. *Education in Ethiopia. Strengthening the Foundation for Sustainable Progress*. Washington, DC: World Bank.

_____. 2005g. *The Effectiveness of World Bank Support for Community-Based and Demand-Driven Development*. Advance conference ed. Washington, DC: Operations Evaluation Department, World Bank.

_____. 2005h. "Eléments de diagnostic du système éducatif tchadien pour une politique nouvelle." World Bank, Washington, DC, July.

_____. 2005i. "Ethiopia: Ethiopian Social Rehabilitation and Development Fund—Implementation Completion Report." Report 32321, World Bank, Washington, DC, June 24.

_____. 2005j. *Fiscal Year 2005 Retrospective: Summary of Key Achievements*. Washington, DC: World Bank.

_____. 2005k. "The Gambia: Third Education Sector Project—Implementation Completion Report (TF-22573, IDA-31280 TF-54182)." Report 33169-GM, World Bank, Washington, DC, December 19.

_____. 2005l. "Le système éducatif guinéen: Diagnostic et perspectives pour la politique éducative dans le contexte des contraintes macro-économiques fortes et de la réduction de la pauvreté." Africa Region Human Development Working Paper 90, World Bank, Washington, DC, November.

———. 2005m. "Madagascar: Education Sector Development Project—Implementation Completion Report." Report 33345-MAG, World Bank, Washington, DC, October 24.

———. 2005n. "Mozambique: Second Poverty Reduction Support Operation—Program Document." Report 32890-MZ, World Bank, Washington, DC, August 4.

———. 2005o. "Note technique sur les performances de l'AGECABO." Mission de supervision, Projet de Développement du Secteur Social, World Bank, Washington, DC, March 23–30.

———. 2005p. "Organizational Effectiveness Task Force: Final Report." SecM2005-0064, World Bank, Washington, DC, February 25.

———. 2005q. "Pakistan Country Gender Assessment: Bridging the Gender Gap—Opportunities and Challenges." Report 32244-PAK, World Bank, Washington, DC.

———. 2005r. "Primary and Secondary Education in Lesotho: A Country Status Report." Africa Region Human Development Working Paper 101, World Bank, Washington, DC.

———. 2005s. "Rapport d'état du système éducatif ivoirien: Eléments d'analyse pour instruire une politique educative nouvelle dans le contexte de l'EPT et du PRSP." Africa Region Human Development Working Paper 80, World Bank, Washington, DC, September.

———. 2005t. "Senegal: Urban Development and Decentralization Program—Implementation Completion Report." Report 32408-SE, World Bank, Washington, DC, June 28.

———. 2005u. "India. Rajasthan District Primary Education Project, Staff Appraisal Report." Report No. 21955-IN, World Bank, Washington, DC.

———. 2006a. "Burkina Faso: Fifth Poverty Reduction Support Financing." Report 31342-BF, Africa Region, World Bank, Washington, DC.

———. 2006b. "Développements récents et sources de financement du budget de l'état: Revue des dépenses publiques." Report 36497-SN, World Bank, Washington, DC.

———. 2006c. *Eléments de diagnostic du système éducatif burundais*. Washington, DC: World Bank. June 2006.

———. 2006d. *Eléments de diagnostic du système éducatif malien: Le besoin d'une politique éducative nouvelle pour l'atteinte des objectifs du millénaire et la réduction de la pauvreté*. Washington, DC: World Bank. January 2006.

———. 2006e. "The Gambia: Third Education Project, Phase 2—Project Appraisal Document." Report 35-797-GM, World Bank, Washington, DC, May 8.

———. 2006f. "Mali: Second Education Sector Investment Program—Project Appraisal Document." Report 36189-MLI, World Bank, Washington, DC, June 23.

———. 2006g. "Managing Risks in Rural Senegal: A Multi-Sectoral Review of Efforts to Reduce Vulnerability." Report 33435-SN, Human Development 2, Africa Region, World Bank, Washington, DC.

———. 2006h. "Rapport sur l'état du système éducatif national." Version de travail, Ministère des Enseignements Fondamental et Secondaire, Ministère des Affaires Economiques et du Développement. World Bank, Washington, DC, January 2006.

———. 2006i. "Senegal: Participatory Local Development Program (PDLP) in Support of National Local Development Program—Project Appraisal Document." Report 35459-SN. World Bank, Washington, DC, April 3.

———. 2006j. *World Bank Development Report 2007: Development and the Next Generation*. Washington, DC: World Bank.

———. 2007a. "Benin: Aide mémoire de la 6ème mission de supervision." National Community-Driven Development Program, World Bank, Washington, DC, September 16–18.

_____. 2007b. "Burundi: Second Social Action Project—Implementation Completion and Results Report (BELG-24242, IDA-32870, IDA-H0330)." Report ICR000045, World Bank, Washington, DC.

_____. 2007c. *Community Driven Approaches in Lao PDR: A Review of the Poverty Reduction Fund and Selected Community-Driven Livelihood Projects.* Washington, DC: World Bank.

_____. 2007d. "Elements de diagnostic du système éducatif centrafricain (RESEN): Contraintes et marges de manoeuvre dans la perspective de la réduction de la pauvreté." Version provisoire, World Bank, Washington, DC, February.

_____. 2007e. "Senegal: Social Development Fund Project—Implementation Completion and Results." Report ICR000106, World Bank, Washington, DC, January 31.

_____. 2008a. "Rapport d'étape du système éducatif national (RESEN)." World Bank, Washington, DC: World Bank.

_____. 2008b. "Diagnostic de la pauvreté." Département de la Réduction de la Pauvreté et de la Gestion de l'Economie, avec la collaboration de l'Agence Nationale de la Statistique et de la Démographique, World Bank, Washington, DC, June 9.

_____. 2008c. "Le système éducatif centrafricain." Contraintes et marges de manœuvre pour la reconstitution du système éducatif dans la perspective de réduction de la pauvreté. Document de travail de la Banque Mondiale No. 144. Série de Développement Humain en Afrique. World Bank, Washington, DC.

Wyss, Urs. 2005a. "La construction en "matériaux locaux": État d'un secteur à potentiel multiple." Swiss Agency for Development and Cooperation, Ougadougou, Burkina Faso.

_____. 2005b. "Projet dissémination des techniques de construction et de toitures économiques et non consommatrices de bois au Burkina Faso." Ministère des Affaires Étrangères, Ouagadougou, Burkina Faso.

Yars, Samuel. 1999. "MIHU-CNUEH-HABITAT-PNUD Projet LOCOMAT BKT 07/013/99: Rapport de mission d'évaluation." Ministry of Infrastructure, Housing and Urbanism, Ouagadougo, Burkina Faso.

Zerbo, Souleymane. 2008. E-mail message to author dated May 11.

Index

absenteeism of teachers, 5, 152
ABUTIP. *See* Agence Burundaise des Travaux d'Intérêt Public (ABUTIP)
accessibility, for children with physical disabilities, 15–16, 26–27
accountability
  and community-driven development, 112–16, 123n1
  in reaching MDGs, 136
  in school construction, 130, 131b8.1, 132b8.2
achievement
  impact of lack of water and sanitation facilities on, 5
  impact of multiple shifts on, 9–10
  impact of substandard structures on, 3–4
  link to classroom size, 20
  link to school roofs, 4
ACTION-ECOLE, 75
AfDB. *See* African Development Bank (AfDB)
AFDS. *See* Agence de Fonds de Développement Social (AFDS)
African Development Bank (AfDB), 58, 68, 107n2
AFRICATIPE, 67, 107n9
AGECABO. *See* Cabo Verdean Agency for Public Works
AGeFIB. *See* Agence de Financement des Initiatives de Base (AGeFIB)
Agence Burundaise des Travaux d'Intérêt Public (ABUTIP), 84, 85t5.6
Agence de Financement des Initiatives de Base (AGeFIB), 81, 86t5.7, 87
Agence de Fonds de Developpement, 68
Agence de Fonds de Développement Social (AFDS), 81, 84, 86t57

Agence d'Exécution des Travaux d'Intérêt Public, Madagascar (AGETIPA), 164–65
Agences d'Exécution des Travaux d'Intérêt Public (AGETIPs), 31–32b3.1, 61
  contract management delegated to, 67–73, 107–8nn9–16, 109n32
  See also contract management agencies (CMAs)
Agences Mauitanienne d'Execution des Travaux d'Intérêt Public pour l'Emploi (AMEXTIPE), 18, 68, 93b5.2, 109n32, 164–65
agencies
  and capacity of government, 72, 108n16
  overview of delegation of contract management to, 66–67
  See also contract management agencies (CMAs); non-governmental organizations (NGOs); social funds
AGETIPA. *See* Agence d'Exécution des Travaux d'Intérêt Public, Madagascar (AGETIPA)
AGETIPs. *See* Agences d'Exécution des Travaux d'Intérêt Public (AGETIPs)
air flow in classrooms, 20, 21, 27n3, 39–40, 50n13
allocation of resources
  inefficiency of, 10–11
  and school location planning, 15–16
AMEXTIPE. *See* Agences Mauitanienne d'Execution des Travaux d'Intérêt Public pour l'Emploi (AMEXTIPE)
"Another Development", 36, 49n5
antiques dealers, and prefabricated buildings, 45, 50n18

appropriate technology classrooms,
  35–40, 49–50nn4–13
 conclusions concerning, 48–49, 50n19
 examples of, 159–60
architects and architecture
 architectural design of schools, 156–58
 architectural norms, 113, 114b6.1
 and prefabrication, 40, 50n15
Architecture for the Poor, 37–38, 49n6
attendance, link to distance to school,
  6–8, 13nn9–10
audits, 133, 146–47
auxiliary purpose-built facilities, 21–24

Bala initiative, 22b2.1
Basic Education Sub-Sector Investment
  Program (BESIP), Ghana, 35b3.2
Basic Education Sub-Sector Plan (BESSIP),
  Zambia, 108n27
Benin, 168, 172
BESIP. *See* Basic Education Sub-Sector
  Investment Program (BESIP), Ghana
BESSIP. *See* Basic Education Sub-Sector
  Plan (BESSIP), Zambia
bidding process, 81
 bid packages and CMAs, 72
 corruption in, 130
 and prefabricated classrooms,
  46–47b3.3
 See also international competitive
  bidding (ICB); local competitive
  bidding (LCB); national competitive
  bidding (NCB)
budgets
 and education sector, 136
 and maintenance of schools, 125, 126,
  127b7.1, 128n1
 Pakistan, 126, 127b7.1
 for school construction, 65
Building as a Learning Air, 22b2.1
buildings. *See* classrooms and buildings
bulk procurement, 56, 58–63
Burundi, 168–69

Cabo Verdean Agency for Public Works,
  69–70, 71t5.4, 72, 164
Cameroon, 169
capacity building, 119–23, 123nn5–7,
  144, 146
Cape Verde, 164
catchment areas, 15–19, 27n1

CBD. *See* community-based
  development (CBD)
CBOs. *See* community-based
  organizations (CBOs)
CDCs. *See* Community Development
  Committees (CDCs)
CDD. *See* community-driven
  development (CDD)
central governments, 83, 108n24
centralized management, 81–83, 85t5.6,
  108n23
 inefficiencies of, 24–25
 and procurement through ICB, 55–63,
  107nn1–5
 and procurement through NCB, 63–66,
  107n8
Chad, 164, 169
Christian Children's Fund, 75
classic classroom model, 29–32,
  33t3.1, 49n1
 architectural design examples, 30,
  156–58
 conclusions concerning, 48–49, 50n19
 costs compared to prefabricated
  classrooms, 42, 45t3.3
 See also classrooms and buildings
classroom construction. *See* school
  construction
classrooms and buildings
 architectural design of, 156–58
 class size, 8–10
 conclusions concerning appropriate
  technology in, 48–49, 50n19
 distance norms, 16–19, 27n1
 growth trend in, 1–2, 12–13n1
 and industrialized prefabrication,
  40–42, 46–47b3.3, 50nn15–18
 inefficient use of, 10–11
 life span of, 12, 13n12
 link to population, 17–19, 27n1
 local materials and appropriate
  technology classrooms, 35–40,
  48–49, 49–50nn4–13
 maintenance of, 122–23, 125–28,
  128n1, 141–42
 multiple shifts in, 8–10
 need for, 12–13n1, 102, 139–41, 180–82
 number and condition of, 2–3
 one-classroom schools, 17–19, 27n2
 prefabrication of, 40–45, 46–47b3.3,
  50nn15–18, 50n18, 162–63

sanitation for, 4–5, 13*n*4, 51–53, 152
school shelter model, 32, 34–35, 49*nn*2–3
size of classroom, 16–19, 20–21, 27*n*1, 27*nn*3–4
speed of construction, 12, 13*n*11
two-classroom schools, 17–19
water supply for, 4–5, 13*n*4, 17, 53–54, 152
See also classic classroom model; costs; procurement; school construction
CMAs. *See* contract management agencies (CMAs)
Cointereaux, François, 36, 49*nn*6–11
communication, development of strategy for, 146
communities, 75
community cost recovery, 61
community-managed school construction, 3, 84, 86*t*5.7, 87, 100–103, 108*n*34
corruption in school construction, 129–33, 133–34*nn*1–2
delegation by MoEs of contract management to, 92–94, 95*t*5.9, 108*nn*26–28
and demand-driving financing, 81–83, 108*n*23
empowerment of, 116–23, 123*n*2, 123*nn*5–7
handbooks for, 120*b*6.5, 121
and maintenance of school buildings, 126
performance of construction management methods, 99–100
role in CDD school construction projects, 115–16, 175–76
Senegal Social Fund Community Handbook, 179
community-based development (CBD), 111
community-based organizations (CBOs), 73, 116–17
Community Development Committees (CDCs), 115*b*6.2, 117
community-driven development (CDD), 111–16, 123*n*1, 175–76
Community Handbook, 120*b*6.5, 121
Community Tender Board, 117
competition, and procurement, 56–58
compressed earth bricks, 36, 49*n*6

construction industry, 11
and centralized management with procurement through ICB, 55–63, 107*nn*1–5
and CMAs, 67–73, 107*nn*9–16
conclusions concerning appropriate technology in, 48–49, 50*n*19
construction norms, 113, 114*b*6.1
and demand-driven financing with community participation, 82–83
direct contracting, 130
improvements in, 68
informal sector in, 30–32, 49*n*1
modern construction model, 45, 47–48
and prefabrication, 40–45, 46–47*b*3.3, 50*nn*15–18
and use of local materials, 35–40, 49–50*nn*6–13
worldwide historical perspective, 162–63
See also contract management; school construction
construction technology, 16
classic classroom, 29–32, 33*t*3.1, 49*n*1
industrialized prefabrication, 40–42, 46–47*b*3.3, 50*nn*15–18
local materials and appropriate technology classrooms, 35–40, 49–50*nn*4–13
and modern construction model, 45, 47–48
school shelter model, 32, 34–35, 49*nn*2–3
contract management, delegation of
to CMAs, 67–73, 107*nn*9–16
community contracting of, 100–106, 108*n*34
conclusions concerning community delegation, 106–7
and decentralization, 88–106, 108–9*nn*30–33, 168–71
to local governments, 94, 96–100, 108–9*nn*30–33
to local MoE branch offices, 88–92
by MoEs directly to communities, 92–94, 95*t*5.9, 108*nn*26–28
to NGOs, 73–79, 108*nn*18–20
overview of delegation to agencies, 66–67
to social fund agencies, 80–88, 108*nn*21–24

contract management agencies (CMAs),
    56–57, 68–73, 108nn12–16
  compared to social fund agencies,
    80–82
  delegation of construction management
    from local governments to, 96–99,
    108n32
  and financing of school construction,
    139–42, 149nn1–2
  limitations of, 70, 72–73
  Madagascar, 47b3.3
  management of public funds, 117
  and NGOs, 74–79
  unit costs of CMA's in school
    construction, 164–65
  See also specific agencies
contractors, 68, 74–75, 107n10
corrugated-iron roofed rooms, 49n10
corruption in school construction,
    129–33, 133–34nn1–2
costs, 72
  of classic classroom technology, 32,
    33t3.1
  of classroom construction by local
    governments, 96–99
  of classrooms procured by local MoE
    branch offices, 89–92
  to close school facility gap in Africa,
    140–42, 149nn1–2
  of community-managed school
    construction, 100–103, 109n34
  and delegation of contract management
    to communities, 93–94
  of earth-built facilities, 37
  of furniture, 6, 13nn6–7
  in Ghana, 35b3.2
  in Guinea, 78–79b5.1
  and ICB procurement, 55–63, 64–66,
    70–72, 89–92, 107nn1–7,
    108nn14–15
  latrines, 52–53
  of local material technology compared
    to informal sector, 37–39
  of maintenance, 125–28, 128n1, 141–42
  in Mauritania, 93b5.2
  and NCB procurement, 64–66, 70–72,
    108nn14–15
  of NGO-managed classroom construction,
    73–78, 78–79b5.1
  prefabricated classrooms, 42–48

rural vs. urban communities, 61, 107n5
  of school shelter model, 34, 35b3.2
  social funds and centrally managed
    implementation, 83–84, 86t5.7
  and stock-taking exercise, 142–44,
    145t10.4, 149n1
  of teacher housing, 24
  using CMAs, 70–72, 108nn14–15, 164–65
  water wells, 53–54
craftsmen, 30, 49n1
CRATerre, 37, 49nn7–10

data, and school infrastructure, 153–54
decentralization of contract management,
    88–106, 108–9nn30–33, 168–71
delivery delays, 66, 90, 107n8
demand-driven financing, 81–83, 85t5.6,
    87, 108n23
development assistance, 73
distance norms, 16–19, 27n1
distance to school, 6–8, 13nn9–10,
    16–19, 151
donor assistance, 6, 13n1
  and coordination of school
    construction, 105–6
  and ICB, 56
  influence on school construction, 135–38
  for local materials technology, 36, 39
  and maintenance of school
    buildings, 126
  and procurement guidelines for
    community contracting, 118
  role of donors in school construction,
    147–48
  and school construction
    strategies, 48–49
  shift from ICB to NCB procurement, 65
  and water and sanitation technologies, 54
double difference analysis, 116
dropout rates, link to distance to school, 7
dry-pit latrines, 51–53
durability, of earth-built construction,
    37, 49n9

earth bricks, 36, 49n6, 159
Economic Development Institute (EDI),
    123n5
economies of scale
  and distance norms, 16–17
  and prefabricated buildings, 41–42, 50n17

EDI. *See* Economic Development Institute (EDI)
Education for All (EFA), 1, 20, 25, 31–32*b*3.1, 94
Education for All-Fast Track Initiative (EFA-FTI), 1, 122, 136–38
Education Sector Consolidation Project (ESCP), 70, 71*t*5.3, 108*n*20
EEC, and procurement, 58, 107*n*2
EFA. *See* Education for All (EFA)
EFA-FTI. *See* Education for All-Fast Track Initiative (EFA-FTI)
efficiency
  of centralized planning, 24–25
  high cost of, 94
  of resource allocations, 10–11
  and school location planning, 15–16
  of social funds, 83
emergencies, 20, 27*n*5
empowerment of communities, 116–23, 123*n*2, 123*nn*5–7
endogeneity bias in research, 154–55
enrollment
  expenditures as function of, 17
  in Guinea, 78–79*b*5.1
  impact of school infrastructure on, 151–52
  link to distance to school, 7
  and NGO support, 75, 108*n*19
  and prefabricated classrooms, 47*b*3.3
  in school shelters in Ghana, 35*b*3.2
environmental issues, and earth-built construction, 39–40, 50*n*13
ESCP. *See* Education Sector Consolidation Project (ESCP)
Ethiopia, 169
European Union (EU), 84, 94, 108*n*28
European Union Fund, 45, 47–48
evaluation. *See* monitoring and evaluation (M&E)
Executing Agencies for Construction in the Public Interest, 31–32*b*3.1, 61, 67–73, 107–8*nn*9–16, 109*n*32
expenditures, 17, 104–5
  See also costs

FAS. *See* Social Funds in Angola (FAS)
Faso Baara, 59, 107*n*3, 164, 168
Fast Track Initiative (FTI), 122
  See also Education for All-Fast Tract Initiative (EFA-FTI)

FCFA. *See* Franc Communauté Financière Africaine (FCFA)
FID. *See* Fonds d'Intervention pour le Développement (FID)
financing, 26, 62, 139–41, 149*nn*1–2
  See also donor assistance
financing agreements (FAs), 117, 118*b*6.3, 120–21*b*6.5
fired bricks, 39, 50*n*13
Fonds d'Intervention pour le Développement (FID), 47*b*3.3
  Madagascar, 81
Franc Communauté Financière Africaine (FCFA), 107*n*7
France, corruption in school construction, 129, 133–34*n*1
FTI. *See* Fast Track Initiative (FTI)
furniture, 5–6, 13*nn*6–7
Future in Our Hands, 75

GAMWORKS, 69–70
GEAI. *See* Groupement d'Etudes pour une Architecture Industrialisée (GEAI)
Ghana, 35*b*3.2, 169
girls, distance to school as barrier to attendance, 7
Gleneagles, 141, 149*n*2
GMT. *See* Grassroots Management Training (GMT) programs
GNI. *See* gross national income (GNI)
Grassroots Management Training (GMT) programs, 121–22, 123*nn*5–7, 133, 134*n*2
Gropius, Walter, 40
gross national income (GNI), 101, 103
Groupement d'Etudes pour une Architecture Industrialisée (GEAI), 50*n*15
Guinea, 78–79*b*5.1, 169

habitation-to-school distance, 8, 13*n*10
handbooks, 119*f*6.3, 120–21
  development of, 144, 146
  Senegal Social Fund Community Handbook, 179
Harambee movement, 126, 128*n*1
harmonization
  and school construction strategies, 144
  toolkits to harmonize norms and standards, 177–78
health of students, 3–4, 5

heavily indebt poor country (HIPC), 168
home construction industry, 41

ICB. *See* international competitive bidding (ICB)
IDA. *See* International Development Association (IDA)
IEC. *See* information education communication (IEC)
IIEP. *See* International Institute for Education Planning (IIEP)
ILO. *See* International Labor Organization (ILO)
implementation schemes
   CDD process in Benin and Uganda, 172
   for construction projects sponsored by NGOs, 166–67
   and cost of classrooms, 32, 33*t*3.1, 43*t*3.3
   increase in capacity of, 79*b*5.1
   by local governments, 173–74
   PIUs, 135
   and social funds, 83–84, 86*t*5.7, 87
   summary of, 183
   toolkits to harmonize norms and standards, 177–78
imported materials, 58–59, 62–63
industrialization, in construction industry worldwide, 162–63
industrialized prefabrication, 40–42, 46–47*b*3.3, 50*nn*15–18
informal sector
   in construction industry, 30–32, 49*n*1
   and use of local materials for construction, 37–39, 49*n*10
information, and community construction projects, 116
information education communication (IEC), 146
infrastructure
   conclusions concerning, 12, 13*nn*11–12
   and distance to school, 6–8, 13 *nn*9–10
   evidence of impact of, 151–55
   and inefficient resource allocations, 10–11
   and overcrowding and multiple shifts, 8–10
   sanitation, 4–5, 13*n*4
   school furniture, 5–6, 13*nn*6–7
   small scale, 83

   temporary structures, 2–4, 13*n*3
   water supply, 4–5, 13*n*4
Intermediate Technology Development Group, 35–36, 49*n*4
international competitive bidding (ICB), 33, 34, 47*b*3.3
   and classic classroom technology in Senegal, 33*t*3.1
   combined with microenterprises, 62–63, 107*nn*6–7
   with community participation, 58–62, 107*nn*3–5
   compared to NCB process, 64–66
   and costs of prefabricated classrooms, 43*t*3.3
   overview, 17*nn*1–2, 55–58
International Development Association (IDA), 26
   and decentralization of contract management to local offices, 88
   financed projects, 62, 107*n*6
   Ghana projects, 35*b*3.2
   and ICB procurement, 58, 107*n*2
   projects by AGETIP, 69, 108*n*13
   and school construction needs, 12*t*1.6, 139–40
International Institute for Education Planning (IIEP), 16, 20
International Labor Organization (ILO), 67

Japan International Cooperation Agency (JICA), 65–66, 103

KfW. *See* Kreditanstalt für Wiederaufbau (KfW)
kickbacks, 130
Kreditanstalt für Wiederaufbau (KfW), 68, 108*nn*12–13

labor, 58, 62
laboratories, 22
large panel system (LPS), 50*n*15
latrines, 4–5, 152
   design to accommodate physically disabled children, 27
   dry-pit latrines, 51–53
   and economies of scale, 17
   examples of latrine technology, 161
LCB. *See* local competitive bidding (LCB)
learning outcomes, 152–53

legal framework
    for decentralization in education, 94, 96t5.10, 168–71
    for establishment of CBOs, 117
LGs. *See* local governments (LGs)
libraries, 22, 27n4
LICUS. *See* low income country under stress (LICUS)
life span of classrooms, 34, 48
local competitive bidding (LCB), 33t3.1, 43t3.3, 62
Local Government Handbook, 120b6.5, 121
local governments (LGs)
    and corruption in school construction, 131b8.1
    and decentralization of school construction, 168–71
    delegation of contract management to, 94, 96–100, 108–9nn30–33
    expenditures as share of GDP and government expenditures, 104–5
    handbooks for, 120b6.5, 121
    implementation schemes of, 173–74
    and maintenance of school buildings, 125–26
    role in CDD school construction projects, 115, 175–76
    and social funds, 87
local materials
    and appropriate technology classrooms, 35–40, 49–50nn4–13
    and ICB procurement, 58
low-cost housing, 39, 50n12
low income country under stress (LICUS), 84–85
LPS. *See* large panel system (LPS)

Madagascar, and prefabricated classrooms, 47b3.3
maintenance, 125–28, 128n1
    costs to close gap in, 141–42
    responsibility for, 122–23
Malawi, 81, 86t5.7, 169–70
Malawi Social Action Fund (MASAF), 81, 86t5.7
Mali, 169
management, training in procurement, 121–22
MASAF. *See* Malawi Social Action Fund (MASAF)
mathematics performance, 27n4

Mauritania, 93b5.2, 94, 164–65, 170
M&E. *See* monitoring and evaluation (M&E)
microenterprises, 62–63, 80, 107nn6–7
Micro-project Program (MPP), 108n23
Millennium Development Goals (MDGs), 12, 25, 135–36, 139
ministries of education (MoEs), 105
    decentralization of contract management to local offices of, 88–92
    and delegation of construction programs to AGETIPs, 68–73
    delegation of contract management directly to communities, 92–94, 95t5.9, 108nn26–28
    delegation of school construction to NGOs, 79b5.1
    and financing school construction, 139–42, 149nn1–2
    knowledge of water and sanitation technologies, 54
    local staff handbook, 121b6.5
    management of ICB with microenterprises, 62, 107n7
    and NCB procedure costs, 61, 107n4
    norms established by, 113, 114b6.1
    and procurement through ICB, 55–63
    role in CDD school construction projects, 113–15, 116, 175–76
    and social funds, 87–88
    stock-taking exercise, 142–44, 145t10.4, 149n1
    and use of informal sector for school construction, 31–32b3.1
ministries of public works, 55–63, 107n6
modern construction model, 45, 47–48, 57
MoEs. *See* ministries of education (MoEs)
monitoring and evaluation (M&E), 116, 146–47
Monterrey Consensus, 136
Mozambique, 170
MPP. *See* Micro-project Program (MPP)
multigrade classes and learning, 17–19, 20
multiple shifts in schools, 8–10
multisector projects, 80, 108n21

national competitive bidding (NCB), 58, 59
    and centralized management with procurement by, 63–66, 107n8
    and classroom construction, 70–72, 108nn14–15

national competitive bidding (*continued*)
    and costs of classrooms in Senegal, 33*t*3.1
    and prefabricated classrooms, 43*t*3.3, 47*b*3.3
National Procurement Code, 118
National Rural Infrastructure Project (NRIP), 108*n*31
NCB. *See* national competitive bidding (NCB)
networks, 67, 107*n*9
NGOs. *See* non-governmental organizations (NGOs)
Niger, 62–63, 170
Nigeria, 170
non-governmental organizations (NGOs), 70
    delegation of contract management to, 73–79, 108*nn*18–20
    examples of, 166–67
    in Guinea school construction program, 78–79
    and implementation schemes for school construction projects, 166–67
    Intermediate Technology Development Group, 35–36, 49*n*4
norms
    established by MoEs, 113, 114*b*6.1
    for school location planning, 15–16
    toolkits to harmonize norms and implementation schemes, 177–78
Northern Uganda Social Action Fund (NUSAF), 81, 86*t*5.7
NRIP. *See* National Rural Infrastructure Project (NRIP)
NUSAF. *See* Northern Uganda Social Action Fund (NUSAF)

OECD. *See* Organisation for Economic Co-operation and Development (OECD) countries
office space, 21–24
Official Development Assistance, 73
oil-free technologies, 35–36
O&M. *See* operations and maintenance (O&M) budget
one-classroom schools, 17–19, 27*n*2
OPEC. *See* Organization of Petroleum Exporting Countries (OPEC)
operations and maintenance (O&M) budget, 125–26, 127*b*7.1, 128*n*1

Organisation for Economic Co-operation and Development (OECD) countries, 27*n*4, 68, 136
Organization of Petroleum Exporting Countries (OPEC), 58, 88–90, 107*n*2
overcrowding in schools, 8–10

Pakistan, 46*b*3.3, 126, 127*b*7.1
Paris Declaration on Alignment and Harmonization, 136
PCUs. *See* Project Coordination Units (PCUs)
PEDP. *See* Primary Education Development Project (PEDP)
The Philippines, prefabricated classrooms, 46–47*b*3.3
physical environment, as learning aid, 22*b*2.1
physically disabled children
    accessibility to schools for, 15–16, 26–27
    and classic classroom model, 50*n*19
    and distance to schools, 8
    handicap-friendly latrines, 52
    impact of school infrastructure on, 151
PISA. *See* Program for International Student Assessment (PISA)
PIUs. *See* Project Implementation Units (PIUs)
plant materials, 2–3
PMCs. *See* Project Management Committees (PMCs)
PNDSE. *See* Programme National de Développement du Secteur Education (PNDSE)
population, and school construction, 16–19, 27*n*1, 102–3
potable water supply, 3–5
poverty alleviation, link to social funds, 83
Poverty Reduction Support Credits, 80
prefabrication, 40–42, 46–47*b*3.3, 50*nn*15–18, 162–63
prices
    and ICB procedures, 56
    price-fixing, 133–34*n*1
Primary Education Development Project (PEDP), 49*n*11, 127*b*7.1
primary gross enrollment ratio, 10

private sector
  and construction of public infrastructure, 67
  and role of CDD approach in school construction, 175–76
  and school construction, 11
procurement
  centralized management of through ICB, 55–63, 107nn1–5
  centralized management with procurement by NCB, 63–66, 107n8
  and classic classroom construction, 32, 33t3.1, 43t3.3
  and corruption in school construction, 130–33
  and costs of classroom technology in Senegal, 32, 33t3.1
  and LCB, 33t3.1, 43t3.3, 62
  and management arrangements, 101
  procedures for, 117–19
  training in, 121–22, 123nn5–7
  See also international competitive bidding (ICB); national competitive bidding (NCB)
Program for International Student Assessment (PISA), 27n4
Programme National de Développement du Secteur Education (PNDSE), 50n19
Project Coordination Units (PCUs), 62
Project Implementation Units (PIUs), 34, 135
Project Management Committees (PMCs), 117
Prouvé, Jean, 50n18
public funds, management of, 117
public sector, performance of, 68
public works, 68, 107n11
purpose-built facilities, 21–24

quality of facilities, 16
  See also *school quality norms*

rainwater tanks, 53
research
  impact of school infrastructure, 151–53
  knowledge gaps in, 148
  randomized trials, 155
retention
  impact of school infrastructure on, 151–52
  link to distance to school, 7
roofing, 2–3, 4, 13n3
rural areas
  access to schools, 11
  and CMAs, 72
  and community participation in policies, 61, 107n5
  and delegation of contract management to local governments, 96, 108n31
  and social fund agencies, 80
  and transportation of prefabricated buildings, 44, 46–47b3.3

sanitation, 4–5, 13n4
  impact on enrollment, 152
  technology for, 51–53
satellite school model, 7, 13n9
school buildings. *See* classrooms and buildings
school location planning
  conclusions concerning, 25–26
  and distance norms, 16–19, 27n1
  inefficiencies of centralized planning of, 24–25
  overview, 15–16
school mapping, 15
school quality norms, 16
  and auxiliary purpose-built facilities, 21–24
  and classroom size, 20–21, 27nn3–4
  overview, 19–20
school shelter model, 32, 34–35, 49nn2–3
Schumacher, Ernst, 35–36, 49n4
Sears and Roebuck, 40
sector strategies, 26
sectorwide approaches (SWAps), 136–38
security requirements, 21, 27n3
Senegal, 165, 170
  Social Fund Community Handbook, 121, 122f6.4, 179
  unit costs of classic classroom technology, 32, 33t3.1
Senegal Social Fund, 121, 132–33b8.2, 179
septic tank systems, 51
shell, 34, 49n2
Single Teacher Schools (STC), 27n2
skilled construction workers, and prefabricated classrooms, 45
small- and medium-size enterprises (SMEs), 80–81, 163
small construction enterprises, 40–41, 50n16

SMEs. *See* small-and medium-size enterprises (SMEs)
social funds, 80–88, 108nn21–24
  Angola, 81
  and corruption in school construction, 132–33b8.2
  Senegal, 121, 132–33b8.2, 179
  Zambia, 66, 81–82, 86t5.7, 171
Social Funds in Angola (FAS), 81
social perspectives of school shelter, 34
social protection sector, 80
sole-source procurement, 130
special needs children, 26–27
  See also physically disabled children
stakeholders
  capacity building for community-based work approach, 119–23, 123nn5–7
  in CDD projects, 112–16, 123n1, 175–76
STC. *See* Single Teacher Schools (STC)
stock-taking exercise, 142–44, 145t10.4, 149n1
storage space, 21–24
students to classroom ratios, 8–10, 13n12
students to teacher ratios, 9–10, 20
subcontracting, 56–57
subsidiarity principle, 114, 123n1
SWAPS. *See* sectorwide approaches (SWAPs)

Tanzania, 170
targeting mechanisms, 80
teachers
  absenteeism, 5, 152
  impact of infrastructure on motivation of, 152
  student to teacher ratio, 9–10, 20
  teachers to classrooms ratio, 8–10
  unit cost of housing for, 24
technical assistance, 58
technical audits, 146–47
technical specialists, 99, 109n33
technologies
  construction. *See* construction technology
  oil-free, 36
  use in United States home construction, 41
  for water and sanitation, 51–54
temporary structures, 2–4, 13n3

theft, of school furniture, 5–6
training
  development of, 144, 146
  to mitigate corruption, 133, 134n2
  in project management and procurement, 121–22, 123nn5–7
transparency, 129–30, 131b8.1, 132b8.2, 146
Transparency International, 129–30
transportation
  and delivery of inputs, 58–59
  and prefabricated classrooms, 44, 46–47b3.3
"Tropical House", 50n18
two-classroom schools, 17–19

Uganda, 93, 108n26, 112, 170–71, 172
UNICEF. *See* United Nations Children's Fund (UNICEF)
unit costs. *See* costs
United Nations, "Another Development", 36, 49n5
United Nations Children's Fund (UNICEF), 5, 7
United Nations Educational, Security, and Cultural Organization (UNESCO), 26, 36
United States, technologies used in home construction, 41
unit space allocations, 20
urban areas
  access to schools, 11
  and community participation in policies, 61, 107n5
  delegation of construction management to CMAs, 96, 109n32

vandalism, to school furniture, 5–6
Van der Rohe, Mies, 40
VCSP. *See* Village Community Support Project (VCSP)
Ventilated Improved Pit (VIP) latrine, 51
Village Community Support Project (VCSP), 79b5.1
Village Development Councils, 168
village populations, and school size, 18–19
VIP. *See* Ventilated Improved Pit (VIP) latrine

wastewater treatment systems, 51
water supply, 4–5, 13n4
   and economies of scale, 17
   impact on enrollment, 152
   technology for, 53–54
water wells, 53
World Bank, 68, 73
   and CMAs, 67
   and distance norms, 16
   and earth-brick construction, 36, 49n7
   and NGOs, 73–74
   as promoter of social funds, 80, 108n22
   ratings of school-delivery projects financed by, 90
   student-teacher ratio, 20
World Bank Institute, 121, 123n5

Zambia, 171
Zambia Social Investment Fund (ZAMSIF), 66, 81–82, 86t5.7, 171

ECO-AUDIT
Environmental Benefits Statement

The World Bank is committed to preserving endangered forests and natural resources. *School Construction Strategies for Universal Primary Education in Africa: Should Communities Be Empowered to Build Their Schools?* is printed on 60# Rolland Opaque, a recycled paper made with 30 percent post-consumer waste. The Office of the Publisher follows the recommended standards for paper usage set by the Green Press Initiative, a nonprofit program supporting publishers in using fiber that is not sourced from endangered forests. For more information, visit www.greenpressinitiative.org.

Saved:
- **7** trees
- **3 million** BTUs of total energy
- **51** pounds of net greenhouse gases
- **3,243** gallons of waste water
- **110** pounds of solid waste

www.ingramcontent.com/pod-product-compliance
Lightning Source LLC
Chambersburg PA
CBHW081218170426
43198CB00017B/2653